URBAN DESIGN: A TYPOLOGY OF PROCEDURES AND PRODUCTS

Illustrated with over 50 Case Studies

Paternoster Square, London in 2004

Urban Design:
A Typology of
Procedures and
Products

Illustrated with over 50 Case Studies

Jon Lang

The Master in Urban Development and Design Program
University of New South Wales
Sydney, Australia

AMSTERDAM • BOSTON • HEIDELBERG • LONDON • NEW YORK • OXFORD
PARIS • SAN DIEGO • SAN FRANCISCO • SINGAPORE • SYDNEY • TOKYO
Architectural Press is an imprint of Elsevier

ELSEVIER

Architectural
Press

Architectural Press is an imprint of Elsevier
The Boulevard, Langford Lane, Kidlington, Oxford, OX5 1GB
30 Corporate Drive, Suite 400, Burlington, MA 01803, USA

First edition 2005
Reprinted 2006, 2007, 2008

Notice
No responsibility is assumed by the publisher for any injury and/or damage to persons
or property as a matter of products liability, negligence or otherwise, or from any use
or operation of any methods, products, instructions or ideas contained in the material
herein. Because of rapid advances in the medical sciences, in particular, independent
verification of diagnoses and drug dosages should be made

British Library Cataloguing in Publication Data
A catalogue record for this book is available from the British Library

Library of Congress Cataloging-in-Publication Data
A catalog record for this book is available from the Library of Congress

ISBN: 978-0-7506-6628-5

For information on all Architectural Press publications
visit our website at www.elsevierdirect.com

Printed and bound in *China*

08 09 10   10 9 8 7 6 5 4

Working together to grow
libraries in developing countries

www.elsevier.com | www.bookaid.org | www.sabre.org

ELSEVIER   BOOK AID
International   Sabre Foundation

Contents

Preface

The term 'urban design' may have been coined in the mid-1950s but 20 years later it was still largely unused outside a small circle of people concerned with the four-dimensional development of precincts of cities. Now it is used for almost anything concerned with human settlements. This change has occurred for two reasons. The first is the importance of urban design's spheres of interest in providing opportunities for the development of, if not for determining, the quality of life of people and, indeed, of the planet. The second is that mainstream architects and city planners have come to understand that it was foolhardy to distance themselves, intellectually and professionally, from urban design activities however demanding they may be. The distancing was a response to the criticism that architectural ideologies and the resultant multi-building architectural schemes of the 1950s and 1960s had received. Those works were based on the paradigms of environmental quality that were inherited from the Modernists. Luckily, a relatively small group of, primarily, architects scattered around the world learnt from the criticism and took the emerging field of urban design forward to the point where it can be seriously discussed as a potential discipline in its own right.

The writing of this book has been motivated by a need: (1) to provide a typology of procedures and products that makes some sense of what various people (and fields) are talking about when they refer to urban design; (2) to present professionals and students with a number of case studies that illustrate the range of interpretations of urban design and (3) to provide an incipient set of such studies that can be used as evidence in arguments about how to proceed in specific circumstances. Urban designing, like any creative activity, is an argumentative process. As the United States Supreme Court decreed during the 1990s, arguments need to be based on evidence, not just opinions or claims of professional expertise. Case studies constitute one source of evidence.

Acknowledgements

It is clear from the most cursory glance at this book that it has drawn heavily on the work of others. Much of the material on the case studies has come from secondary sources. All those of significance have been referenced in the text and are listed in the References and further reading. These sources have often been supplemented by interviews of the people involved – designers, property developers, sponsoring agencies, and residents and users – and by site analyses. Many people have thus been involved in completing this work. I thank them all for without their assistance my contemplating this work, let alone bringing it to fruition would have been impossible.

Assembling the data and illustrations for a book of this type is costly. The research has been supported financially over the years, whether they know it or not, by grants from the Grosser Family Fund, the American Institute of Indian Studies, the Australian Research Council and from the Faculty of the Built Environment at the University of New South Wales. Their support made site visits possible. Without it the production of this work would have been impossible.

The Text

I am particularly in debt to a number of people who read this work in manuscript form at various stages in its development. They are Alexander Cuthbert, Arza Churchman, Bruce Judd, George Rolfe, Arlene Segal, Ahmad Soemardi and Alix Verge. The extremely helpful comments of anonymous reviewers resulted in a major reorientation to the argument presented. In addition, special mention must be made of all the critics, stakeholders and authors with whom I have discussed the cases included in this book or who have reviewed specific case studies. The list of people is lengthy. It includes Amilio Ambaz, Alan Balfour, Jonathan Barnett, David Chesterman, George Claflen, Abner Colmenares, Ian Connolly, Vicente del Rio, Balkrishna Doshi, David Gordon, Gary Hack, Sir Peter Hall, Heng Chy Kiang, Jesus Roman Herrera, Mark Hinshaw, Arun Jain, Kathy Kolnick, Liu Thai Ker, Réne Masson, William Morrison, Waikeen Ng, Laurie Olin, Margaret Petrykowski, Boon Powell, Jim Rez, Susan Shick, Michael Sorkin, Cassio Taniguchi, Bernard Tschumi, Alfonso Vegara, Alix Verge, Elise Vider, Mike Watkins, James Weirick and Tingwei Zhang. They have helped me to enrich the text and to get the story straight.

Tracking down sources of material and illustrations has been a time-consuming affair in which I have been assisted by colleagues and students at a number of educational institutions: the University of Pennsylvania in Philadelphia, the University of New South Wales in Sydney, Sinan Mimarlik Universitesi in

Istanbul and CEPT, the Centre for Environmental Planning and Technology in Ahmedabad. The individuals who have assisted me include El-Hassan Amr, Oleksandra Babych, Clare Billingham, Kevin Brake, Giancarlo Cerutti di Ludovico, Nick Chapin, Carol Chan, Tao Cheehai, Cheng Tan Fui, Chiu Kuo-Wei, Elizabeth Cox, Janaka Dharmasena, Rich Fowler, Fu Yuan Yuan, Ahmad Kamal Abdul Ghani, Hu Min, Hu Xin, Lee Yun Tae, Lesley Thomas Jacob, Wilderich Kalthoff, Keith Koh, Kwon Kwi Suk, Lim Tracee Way Le, Jian Li, Handy Limandibrata, Liu Yu-Ning, Johnson Tan Boon Loke, Nadira Yapa Mendis, John Milkan, Jagdeep Oberoi, Shudong Pang, Andrew Napier, Ni Ming-Te, Yudi Prastowo, Sarah Rock, Ewan Saunders, Monik Setyaningsih, Malvin Soh, Andrew Tam, Tran Thai Nguyen, Wang Bo, Wang Chao, Kathryn Werner, Michael White, Stephen White, Susanti Widiastuti, Dennis Wong, Wong Po Yin, Ringo Kee Fu Wong, Yan Gu, Yang Ke, Yang Lee, Yee Ling Lai, Howard Yu, Yuan Zhe, Yun Ni, Yin Yin, Nor Hamiza Zakaria and Zi Yu-fen.

Illustrations

There are many illustrations in this book. With a number of exceptions the photographs, diagrams and drawings used are by me or I hold their copyright. The copyright has lapsed for some of the others while yet others are in the public domain. The source of each illustration for which I do not hold the copyright and/or which I have used due to the courtesy of others is noted with the item. Giancarlo Cerutti di Ludovico, George Claflen, Vicente del Rio, Rohan Dickson, Ruth Durack, Robert Freestone, Mark Francis, Peter Kohane, Kathy Kolnick, Susannah Lang, William Morrison, Deepti Nijhawan, Laurie Olin, Tata Soemardi, Jennifer Taylor, Bernard Tschumi, the Universität Bielefeld, Alix Verge and Herti Verge all provided me with photographs. Oleksandra Babych, Susanti Widiastuti, Thanong Poonteerakul, Lee Yuntai, Munir Vahanvati, Alix Verge, Wang Chao, Yin Yin and Zhe Xian prepared drawings for me from a variety of sources. These photographs and drawings have enriched my whole work so I owe a great debt to the generosity of many people.

A final acknowledgement

It has been difficult to track down some of the sources of information included in this book. A number of the photographs that form part of my collection were given to me by students and colleagues over the past 20 years. I no longer have a record of their provenance. A number of the drawings prepared for this text are based on more than one source and who holds the original copyright is unclear. Every effort has, however, been made to contact and credit the copyright holders of all this material. In a number of cases it has been in vain. I thus apologize for any copyright infringements that might have inadvertently occurred. If copyright proprietorship can be established for any of the work not specifically or erroneously attributed please contact me at the Faculty of the Built Environment, University of New South Wales, Sydney, Australia 2052 or at jonl@unsw.edu.au.

Jon Lang
Sydney
February 2005

A good city is not the result of individual,
independent, selfish decisions
(Enrique Peñalosa, Mayor of Bogotá)

Man tract und G-d lacht
[People plan and God laughs]
(Yiddish proverb)

For three Verges
Herti
Alix
Madeline

The Grand Arche at La Défense, Hauts-de-Seine in 2004

Introduction: the argument

Of all the design fields, urban design has the greatest impact on the nature of cities and city life. However logical the land-use pattern prescribed by city planners, the beauty and utility of its buildings and the nature of the landscape, it is the overall three-dimensional combination of forms and spaces as seen in time and over time that gives a city its character. Cities evolve at the hands of a myriad designers consciously or subconsciously seeking to fulfil their own interests. Urban design involves coordinated and self-conscious actions in designing new cities and other human settlements or redesigning existing ones and/or their precincts in response to the needs of their inhabitants. Above all it represents acts of will in creating positive changes to the world, physical and social. It needs to be done well. To be done well urban design needs to have a sound knowledge base. That base can probably be best coordinated in the form of an abstract descriptive and explanatory theory of urban form and the forces that shape it but designers generally do not care to derive solutions from such a knowledge base. They rely heavily on precedents. We can certainly learn much from what we have done in the past, from case studies of completed developments.

Urban design is a confusing term. If the goal of this book is to clarify its meaning in terms of the products it creates and the processes used in creating them, then it needs to start by describing why such a clarification is necessary. To some design professionals there may seem to be no need to do this. Urban design can mean anything one wants it to mean. It is, however, difficult for a field to make progress if it fails to be conceptually clear about its nature, purposes and methods. The book's goal is not, however, only to give some clarity to the meaning of urban design but also to demonstrate the variety of types of urban design efforts that have taken place during the past 50 years. It is now possible, given all the experience we have had, to create a preliminary typology of urban design activities that provides some structure to the domain of the field.

This typology is developed from: (1) theories in the disciplines of architecture, landscape architecture and planning and (2) an analysis of a series of what have been deemed to be urban design projects. The typology is then used to classify a number of case studies that illustrate specific points in specific cultural and political contexts. The classification system may not be as sharp as purists might like but the borderlines amongst urban design processes are often blurred and so difficult to draw with precision. If this is so why should we bother?

An Observation

In his essay, 'Politics and the English Language,' written in 1946, George Orwell observed that words such as democracy, socialism, freedom, patriotic, realistic and justice have several different meanings that 'cannot be reconciled with each other'. In the case of democracy, he noted, 'not only is there no agreed on definition, but the attempt to make one is resisted from all sides'. The consequence is that 'the defenders of every kind of régime claim it is a democracy' (Orwell, 1961). The art world also finds high utility in the ambiguity of words.

Words such as 'romantic, plastic, values, human, dead, sentimental, natural, vitality', Orwell claimed, are meaningless. Moreover, those who use them do not expect them to have a meaning. Consequently, critics can discuss a topic without knowing what each other is talking about and can agree or, if they prefer, disagree with each other. Orwell could have made much the same remarks about the field of architecture. The terms human scale, organic, dynamic and context are equally loosely used by architects. It is advantageous in all three worlds (politics, art and architecture) for the words to be ambiguous or multivalent and thus largely meaningless. It allows the discourse to flow freely, albeit without clarity.

The same comment can be made about the use of the rubric 'urban design' today. Certainly the majority of the design professionals and others involved in what they call urban design avoid having to define the term. The advantage is that each can claim to have expertise as an urban designer and, if Orwell is correct, talk about it with others without having a common understanding. This confusion is both unnecessary and unhelpful if architects, landscape architects and city planners are to make a positive contribution to the development of cities and other human settlements. We really need to know what we are talking about when we use the term. Are we, however, capable of clarifying what we mean?

An analysis of the building projects completed during the past five decades that have been regarded as 'urban design' presents us with an opportunity to understand what the domain of urban design has become. A set of systematic case studies focusing on these projects as products and on how they were generated makes it possible to develop a typology, a system of classification of urban design projects, that adds clarity to discussions on urban design. A clear typology also enables design professionals to understand how different approaches to urban design have created the results they have in different socio-political situations. Before creating a typology, however, it is necessary to understand what urban design might mean at a general level. Then the specifics can be considered.

A Preliminary Note on Urban Design

It is 50 years since the term, 'urban design', was first used and probably three decades since it came into widespread usage. It is now difficult, if not impossible, to identify the actual sources of the term. A conference on urban design was held at Harvard University in 1956 under the leadership of José Luis Sert and the first education programmes in urban design were initiated before the end of the decade at Harvard University and the University of Pennsylvania. These programmes had antecedents in the civic design programmes that had worldwide impacts such as those at the University of Liverpool and the École des Beaux-Arts in Paris.

Urban design, as we know it today, has developed in response to the limitations of the philosophies and design paradigms, rationalist and empiricist, of the modern movement in architecture and city planning (see Chapter 1). Somewhat ironically, it developed in response to the very types of design paradigms – generic design approaches that are regarded as exemplars of good practice – that Sert advocated. The types of criticism received by architects involved in the Garden Cities movement and those using the Rationalist approaches to urban design of Continental Europe (as applied throughout the world) drove many city planners away from a concern with the physical character of cities and many architects away from dealing with problems with a social nature. Those architects who maintained their interest in social concerns and four-dimensional physical design were inspired to do better by the criticism of Jane Jacobs (1961), in particular, but also the reflections of architects such as Brent Brolin (1976) and Peter Blake (1977).

There were three points to the criticism of the way urban design was carried out under the aegis of the Modernists. They were: (1) that the models of people, human behaviour and the way people experience the environment used by designers were simplistic; (2) that the person–environment relationship was poorly understood and, as a consequence, (3) the paradigms and theory on which many large-scale urban development projects were based were inadequate for their purpose. Few critics would claim that we have succeeded in fully responding to the criticism but there have been many very well-received urban design projects around the world. Much can be learnt from them. Much can also be learnt from those that have been regarded as failures. Both types are included in this book.

There are many definitions of urban design. Going back 50 years to the very origins of the term 'urban design' serves us well. In 1955, Clarence Stein said urban design 'is the art of relating STRUCTURES to one another and to their NATURAL SETTING to serve CONTEMPORARY LIVING' (Stein, 1955). Implicit in this statement is a concern in meeting public interest needs in the design of the public realm of human settlements. The statement is also so general that few will dispute it. A range of work that has attempted to follow Clarence Stein's dictum is included in this book. The purpose is to understand the resources, intellectual and financial upon which specific projects have drawn. To adequately achieve this end some sort of classification system is, however, needed if other than a haphazard set of observations is to be made.

An Evolving Typology

Typology, when it does not refer to the study of printing fonts, refers to the classification or categorization of specimens. 'We think, conceive, represent, and talk of places in and through categories, and we fabricate, occupy, and regulate places in categories as well' (Schneekloth and Franck, 1994). There is a long history to the classification of projects by architects and other design professionals usually in terms of use – building types, for instance, but also in terms of geometrical types, and structural and constructional systems (Pevsner, 1976). The classification of examples enables designers to refer to processes and products that might be of use in informing them about the situation that they face and the possible ways of dealing with it.

The argument presented in this book, particularly in Chapter 3, is that in order to understand the domain of urban design it is useful to categorize urban design projects using a three-dimensional matrix of types – in terms of: (1) the design and implementation procedure, (2) the product type and (3) the major paradigm that structures the process and gives form to the product. Implicit in the paradigm is the focus of design concern (i.e. the functions of the product considered to be more important). There are many more dimensions that one could add to the typology but there needs to be a balance between striving to achieve exhaustive completeness and the need to be able to use the typology. For the moment a three-dimensional model will have to suffice (see Figure 3.8).

This three-dimensional classification system enables the basic characteristics of any individual project to be identified and thus the important distinctions amongst project types to be understood. For design professionals this categorization provides the basis for asking questions about how best they might proceed in any given situation. The danger is that the similarities between the situation in a case and the situation that a designer faces may be seen to be stronger than they are. A design is then imposed on a situation for which it is inappropriate (see Brolin, 1976 and Marmot, 1982 for examples). The problem being addressed in each case and the success or failure of the patterns used to solve it have to be clear.

Case Studies: Successes and Failures

Case studies represent the accumulated history of many fields of human endeavour. The design fields use them extensively although what is meant by 'case study' varies. When designing we rely heavily on the knowledge developed through individual cases being cumulatively converted into prescriptive theories or paradigms. The design fields are not alone in acting this way. Law and medicine rely heavily on case histories in both practice and education.

If Orwell had been writing today not only could he have included urban design in his set of dubious terms, but also case studies. What we designers call 'case studies' tends to be descriptive statements of the geometric qualities of specific designs. The way the schemes were brought into existence (if they have been), the dynamics of the political forces that shaped them, their cost, and modes of financing, even the way they function, all fall outside the realm of concern of such studies. If done thoroughly, however, case studies can provide empirical evidence of the processes and methods used to achieve specific design ends.

Case studies take a variety of narrative forms. The form chosen here is descriptive and analytical. The purpose is to demonstrate the nature of urban design and urban designing to both professionals and lay people, particularly politicians. The form should also be useful in the education of budding designers. The objective is thus to provide professionals with an information base that they can use in the creation of the appropriate design and implementation process for tackling a given urban design problem, and students and other interested people an understanding of the scope of urban design.

Good case studies present comprehensive histories of projects from their inception to their conclusion. They distinguish between the pertinent and the peripheral, identify the problems being addressed in context, the constraints acting on the development of solutions, the solution and how it evolved, and the strategies and implementation devices used to reach it. They can also identify the successes and failures of design projects in place.

What is perceived to be a success or a failure depends on a perspective. Many of the schemes included in this volume are highly regarded because of their financial successes. Financial benefits and costs can be measured although the arguments as to who has benefited and who has not persist. Yet a number of these apparently financially successful projects have been challenged in terms of the quality of life they provide specific segments of the population that inhabit or use them. The multi-dimensionality of the functions of the built environment means that every project that is studied here is successful in somebody's eyes and a failure in somebody else's.

Most case studies in urban design consider a designed product from the actor's (the creator's) point of view. Case studies courses offered in universities consist of designers explaining what they did and, ideally, why. In doing so they tend to miss describing the dynamics of the design/decision-making process. They focus on the form, the architecture. The emphasis in developing case studies needs to be placed on drawing from the observations, secondary though they may be, of those outside the process looking critically in on them. The designers' voices need to be heard but placed into context. There have been a number of case studies of urban design work that do this.

Martin Millspaugh (1964) wrote a critical study on Charles Center, Baltimore, Leonard Ruchleman (1977) studied the dynamic political and design processes that brought about the building of the late World Trade Center in New York, Alan Balfour (1978) described the various machinations involved in building the Rockefeller Center, and David Gordon (1997) has written on the history of the ups and downs in the development of Battery Park City. There are also extensive statements on La Défense and on Canary Wharf, already volumes on the barely initiated World Trade Center site development. Scattered references to many aspects of the urban development and design processes appear in the architectural and planning literature. This book draws, unashamedly, on existing commentaries. An attempt has, however, been made to triangulate information by studying diverse, often contradictory, data sources, conducting interviews and by carrying out field observations.

The Selection of the Case Studies

The case studies included here are typical examples of different approaches to, and concerns of, urban design. They could have been drawn from one major city that has been self-consciously interested in the quality of its built form over the past 50 years or even those whose citizens have been less interested in or have not known how to deal effectively with physical design issues. The projects instead are a selected sample of what has been happening around the world.

With two exceptions, Rockefeller Center in New York and Riverwalk in San Antonio, the sample has been chosen from those projects carried out since the term 'urban design' came into use in the 1950s. They are not necessarily the best known, the most successful or the most notorious projects. They have been chosen to illuminate particular points in order to enhance our understanding. As urban designs often take a considerable period to evolve from initial idea to built form, a number of the cases covered have their origins in the 1960s, 1970s and 1980s. Others, however, were initiated much more recently and have moved ahead rapidly. They were begun and completed during the late 1990s and early 2000s.

Completed Projects

Many of what are called case studies deal with projects that have never been built but are architecturally interesting. These schemes sit in reports on the shelves, some very dusty, of redevelopment authorities and architectural offices around the world. Other schemes do deal with significant issues – sustainability, contextuality and scale – but are only at the design stage. All the schemes receiving *Architectural Record* Urban Design Awards in 2004 – the Chicago Central Area plan, the latest of many plans for Mission Bay in San Francisco, the Urban River Vision for Worcester, Massachusetts, the Coyote Valley plan in California, and the Recreation Corridor plan for St Louis – are projects that exist only on paper (Urban Design, 2004). Interesting and well crafted though they may be, when and how they are implemented, if they are, and the final form they take remains to be seen.

The cases presented here focus on the process used to complete schemes as much as their final forms and how they function. Thus, all but four have been brought to fruition although many (e.g. Lujiazui in Shanghai) are only partially complete and others have undergone radical changes since their official completion date. The schemes still largely on the drawing board (i.e. in 2004) are the World Trade Center redevelopment in New York, the Shanghai Waterfront scheme, the use of new schools as catalysts for development in Chattanooga and the Shenzhen Citizens Centre. The comments on them are referred to as 'notes' rather than 'case studies'. They have been included because they are of particular interest in the political climate of today. The Heritage Walk in Ahmedabad has also been included as a note because it does not involve much physical design. Arcosanti is still far from completion so its study is also referred to as a note.

The International Character of the Case Studies

The studies have been drawn from across the world. In an era of global practice it is important to understand the similarities and differences in the range of work being done in a variety of locations. The form that urban design products take is very much shaped by the aspirations of the social and political context in which they take place. It is fine to examine the form of products but if one does not understand the values that brought them about one learns little from them.

There is some emphasis in this book on schemes in the United States, the United Kingdom and other countries whose legal systems have antecedents in English common law rather than the Napoleonic Code. The reason is that if one can understand urban design processes in the societies where individual rights, particularly individual property rights, are held to be paramount and where the role of precedents is important in establishing legal rights then one has the background for asking questions about the nature of urban design in the political and legal context of other societies. There are, however, also examples drawn from countries whose constitutions, legal systems, and the rights of individuals and communities within them are unknown to me. Cases that fall into this category have been covered because they illustrate a specific procedure that is common to all urban design.

Developing the Argument

The book is divided into four parts. The first part, 'The nature of urban design and urban designing', is concerned with defining the nature of urban design as a professional activity. The argument is that urban design deals with enhancing the qualities of the public realm of cities and other urban places. In so doing, it deals with what actually constitutes the public realm and with the role of conflicting public and private interests in shaping it.

It is more important to think of differences amongst urban design projects not in the usual way in terms of the nature of products (new towns, urban renewal, squares, etc.), but in terms of the differences amongst four ways of carrying out a project. In particular, a distinction, as explained in Chapters 2 and 3, is drawn amongst 'total urban design' and 'all-of-a-piece urban design', 'piece-by-piece urban design' and 'plug-in urban design'. The typology developed in the first part of the book is based on these differences.

The second part of the book, 'The traditional design professions: their products and urban design', argues that the design fields tend to look at urban design in terms of product types particular to each. City, or town, planning tends to look at urban design as the distribution of land uses in relationship to transportation systems although this view varies from country to country. In some countries urban design is city planning and to some people within all countries city planning is synonymous with urban design. Landscape architecture tends to look at urban design as the design of the horizontal plane between buildings: streets, parks and squares. Architecture, in contrast, tends to consider urban design to be the design of buildings in context and/or the design of building complexes. The argument in this book is that urban design while recognizing these views encompasses much more.

The heart of urban design work is described in the third part of the book titled, unimaginatively, 'The core of urban design work: procedures and products'. The four chapters outlining the range of types act as a defence, or a demonstration, of the typology proposed here. The goal is not only to show how the typology frames the field of urban design but also to illustrate the examples of urban design work that can be used as precedents (or should not be used as precedents) for urban design projects of specific types in the future. Some of the examples have already served as precedents for later urban design projects.

The final part of the book, 'The future of urban design' is, perhaps, the most important. It addresses a series of questions: 'What can we learn from the case studies?' 'What are the issues being addressed today in urban design and what are they are likely to be in the future?' 'And where do we go from here?' and 'Is urban design a field of professional endeavour or is it a discipline and profession in its own right?' The answer to this last question depends on the willingness of the traditional design professions to engage in serious discussions about the future of cities based on a knowledge of how built forms function rather than a set of beliefs about what makes a good place drawn from their own professional interests or dreams. The fields need to have a sound empirical foundation on which to base their decisions. Case studies can provide an important part of that base.

The Barbican, London in 2004

THE NATURE OF URBAN DESIGN AND URBAN DESIGNING

PART 1

Today the term 'urban design' is used to describe almost any design that takes place in any city setting. 'It seems that every person and their dog is an urban designer; it's sexy and it's chic' (Tennant, 2004). Legally any person can call himself or herself an urban designer. Many people in the design fields without experience or formal training or any observable interest in dealing with urban design concerns automatically tag the title on to their basic qualification in order to better market their services. Designers are, after all, generally small business operators.

Many architects believe anybody who can design a building well is capable of designing a good city. Many architects and fewer, but notable, landscape architects have designed (or rather led the designing of) fine urban environments for people (and, sometimes, other animate species). Sadly, although being well intentioned, they have also created some less than desirable worlds. The design process is indeed similar in all decision-making fields but the problems addressed are very different. The objective of the first part of this book is to identify the different ways in which the design process is carried out in dealing with urban phenomena and the types of products to which the label 'urban design' has been applied. The story presented in this book begins, in 'Chapter 1: The public realm of cities and urban design', with a discussion of the concerns of urban design and the nature of the public realm of cities and societies.

Many fields are concerned with the quality of the public realm of cities and other human settlements. It is an interest shared by city planners and often landscape architects. Architects, working as architects, are in contrast primarily concerned with the design of buildings for specific clients. They become strong advocates for their clients' interests and for their own rights as artists. Urban design, however, is seen as an integrative design field addressing the traditional and overlapping concerns of city planning, landscape architecture, civil engineering (now often called environmental engineering) and architecture. It is concerned with the design of specific products: new towns, new suburbs, new precincts of cities and suburbs, urban renewal, and urban squares and streets. The list is almost endless. Broadly speaking, however, there is a single concern: the design of the public, urban realm at a city and precinct level.

Urban design deals with the creation of the physical public realm of human settlements within the public realm of decision-making. The objective in the opening chapter is thus not only with giving a broad definition to urban design but also with coming to some understanding of the nature of the public realm of the physical fabric of cities and the public realm of decision-making. There are many questions about what actually constitutes the physical public realm. The answers depend on prevailing political attitudes towards community and individual rights. The stand taken here is a broad one and with it in mind the nature of urban designing is described and explained in 'Chapter 2: Urban design processes and procedures'.

The nature of urban design varies considerably based on the process by which its various product types are implemented. Historically, many now much-admired urban design schemes were implemented through the use of autocratic power, political and/or financial. Some still are. Examples of both are included in this book. The principal concern here is, however, with urban design in democratic, capitalist societies. After his experiences with the evolving design of the World Trade Center site development in New York, Daniel Libeskind noted that design in democratic societies is 'complex . . . with many pressures and tensions . . . We are not living in Haussmann's Paris . . . We live in a pluralistic society' (Lubell, 2004). Actually Haussmann found many tensions in the redevelopment of Paris too (see Jordan, 1995).

The objective in this second chapter is to outline the steps involved in design: the analysis, synthesis, and evaluation of potential designs on the drawing board, their implementation and the evaluation of how well they function in place. Function too is an ambiguous term. In any discourse on urban design there is thus also the need to take a stand on what 'function' means. It is defined here to include how the physical forms of cities work symbolically, as an aesthetic ensemble, and as a supporter of desired activity patterns. The physical fabric of cities is also a financial investment and those investing in it expect a financial return on their investments.

A fundamental question in both autocratic and democratic societies is: 'Who actually controls the development of an urban design product whatever it is?' This question leads to a series of others. 'Who defines the problem to be addressed and the opportunities to be seized?' 'Who designs the solutions?' No definitive single answer can be given to these questions. The chapter describes the possibilities. In the past I have argued for a strongly problem-oriented urban design process relying on a knowledge base of abstract descriptive and explanatory theory (see Lang, 1987, 1994). The criticism of this position has been that designers simply do not want to work that way nor will they (see Frascati, 1989). They will rely on precedents and generic solutions.

In the final chapter of this part of the book, 'Chapter 3: An evolving typology of urban design projects', the domain of urban design is mapped. Explicitly stated in the chapter is that it is primarily the processes of implementation and control that should differentiate amongst types of urban design projects. In the typology, the distinction between the four procedural types of urban design identified in the 'Introduction: the argument' – total urban design, all-of-a-piece urban design, piece-by-piece urban design and plug-in urban design – forms the primary dimension of any categorization.

A further distinction can be made amongst urban design projects based on the vocabulary of patterns that forms the basis of their design. The vocabulary, in turn, depends on what is perceived by a set of design theorists, or ideologists, to be the model, or paradigm, of good practice. During the past 50 years we have seen Modernist views on what makes a good city give way to other ideas based on a much broader definition of the functions of the public realm than the Modernists had. Nevertheless, the major paradigms that have shaped urban design schemes over the past 50 years are still with us and are still valid in specific circumstances: the City Beautiful (or Baroque), the Modernist in its rationalist and empiricist forms, and the post-Modernist in its rationalist and empiricist forms. The typology is thus based on the observation that urban design projects can be divided into categories based on the procedure that was used to implement them, the product types they represent and the paradigms within which they were designed.

The case studies included in this book provide the evidence for the typology being a useful way of organizing the examples of work that define the urban design field. The utility of the typology will be demonstrated in Part 3 of this book. Prior to that, however, Part 2 argues that the traditional design disciplines consider urban design in terms of the types of products they, themselves, produce. They do not see urban design as a collaborative venture. Their typologies are product-driven. That approach reveals neither the dynamics of the decision-making process nor the full scope of concern of urban designers.

1

The public realm of cities and urban design

Almost all definitions of urban design state that it has something to do with the public realm (or the public domain or with public space) and the elements that define it. One of the best is:

> Urban design draws together the many strands of place-making, environmental responsibility, social equity and economic viability; for example – into the creation of places of beauty and identity. Urban design is derived from but transcends related matters such as planning and transportation policy, architectural design, development economics, landscape and engineering. It draws these and other strands together. In summary, urban design is about creating a vision for an area and the deploying of the skills and resources to realise that vision (Llewellyn-Davies, 2000: 12).

The last sentence is particularly important. Here is another statement:

> Urban design should be taken to mean the relationship between different buildings; the relationship between buildings and streets, squares, parks and waterways and other spaces which make up the public domain . . . and the patterns of movement and activity which are thereby established; in short, the complex relationships between the elements of built and unbuilt space (DoE, 1997: paragraph 14).

Urban design consists of multi-building projects that vary in size from building complexes to precincts of cities to whole cities. Sometimes urban design includes the design of the buildings themselves, but often it impinges on the architecture of buildings only to the extent that their uses and façades, particularly on the ground floor, define the public domain. But what then is the public domain?

Human organizations consist of public and private components. The distinction is not always clear because there are also semi-public and semi-private behaviours and places. In addition, what is considered to be private and what is considered to be public varies from culture to culture and within cultures over time (Madanipour, 2003). For professionals involved in any of the environmental design fields the public realm is comprised of two parts. The first deals with the public components of the physical environment (artificial and natural) in which behaviour occurs and the second specifies how communal decisions are made by governments and in the marketplace as defined by a country's constitution (or in the case of the United Kingdom by precedent). The first affects perceptions of the elements of urban design and the second, the process of urban designing.

The Physical Public Realm

Does the physical public realm simply consist of all the open spaces outside the private domain of building interiors, secluded courtyards, and gardens? Is it everything that can be perceived (seen, smelled, heard or touched) from places to which everybody has right of access? Does it consist of all those elements that have an impact on the quality of publicly owned open space and/or space to which the public has freedom of access? All answers to these questions are politically charged.

The physical public realm is not necessarily conterminous with publicly owned property. In a society where property rights are sacrosanct and where individuals have the right and freedom to build what they desire, the public realm and public open space – spaces to which the public has right of entry – may refer to the same thing. The definition has, however, often been extended to include all publicly owned property, such as schools and libraries, whose location is determined by the public sector.

In an editorial (27 December 2002), the French newspaper, *Le Monde*, took the position that anything visible *in situ* should be part of the public realm in terms of photography work. The position taken here is that the public realm consists of those places to which everybody has access, although this access may be controlled at times. It consists of both outdoor and indoor spaces. The outdoor spaces include streets, squares and parks, while the indoor may include arcades, and the halls of railway stations and public buildings, and other spaces to which the public has general access such as the interiors of shopping malls.

The problem is that the nature of many 'public' places is ambiguous because although the public has relative freedom of access to them they are under private ownership. As the common domain of cities is increasingly privatized (or rather, the private domain is providing public spaces), this ambiguity is likely to continue. If past history is any guide, attitudes towards what is private and what is public will follow a cyclical pattern in the future. The scope of what is regarded as public will wax and wane. The perceived need to control or not control in the name of the public interest what is designed will follow as political attitudes vary.

The Elements of the Physical Public Realm

Any statement of what constitute the elements of the public realm of built forms is likely to evolve over time. It will depend on a political stance and help to define that stance. In the 1930s, Le Corbusier wrote that the basic elements of urban design are: 'the sun, sky, trees, steel, cement, in that order of importance'

Figure 1.1 Sixteenth Street, Denver in 1993.

(Le Corbusier, 1934). Certainly the sun and sky are of importance everywhere and have been commodities with which to bargain in recent urban design work. Nevertheless, Le Corbusier's list is not a particularly helpful one in thinking about the nature of the public realm.

A fruitful way of looking at the public realm is to consider it as a set of behaviour settings – a term coined by ecological psychologists in the 1960s (see Lang, 1987). A behaviour setting consists of a standing (or recurring) behaviour pattern, a milieu (pattern of built form) and a time period. The milieu must have the *affordances* for the behaviour to occur, but because the affordances are there does not mean that a specific behaviour will take place there. What actually occurs depends on the predispositions, motivations, knowledge and competencies of the people involved. Thus the same pattern of built form may afford different patterns of behaviour for different people at different times of the day, week or year. Some of the patterns may be occurring frequently on a daily basis or even throughout the day or year, while others may occur only on special occasions (e.g. the celebration of national days).

The milieu consists of the floor of the ground, the surfaces of buildings and other physical elements, and the objects that both bound it and structure it internally. The variables are diverse and their attributes even more so. Of particular importance in urban design are such concerns as the sequential experiencing of the environment as one moves through it, the ground floor activities, or lack of them, that are housed in the milieu, and the attributes of the enclosing elements of spaces. In the urban scenes shown in Figures 1.1 and 1.2, the physical public realm consists of the elements of the artificial environment around a person. In

Figure 1.2   Orchard Road, Singapore in 2003.

the former it consists of the square, the trees, the façades of buildings, the ground floor uses, and the entrances onto the open spaces. On a more typical street (Figure 1.2) the elements are essentially the same but take on a different form. If, however, urban design is concerned with the whole nature of human experience it has to address the nature of the activities and the people who engage in them as well. It is the set of behaviour settings and how the milieu affords activities and simultaneously acts as an aesthetic display that is important.

In 1748 Giambattista Nolli drew a figure–ground plan of Rome (see Figure 1.3). It shows the public space of the city at the ground level during the time of Pope Benedict XIV. Much interior space (principally of churches) and courtyards was accessible to the public. It also illustrates the amount of open space that existed in cities of that time. Much of it is not discernible from the streets.

As important as the figure–ground relationship is the nature of the façades that form these spaces. What are they made of and how are they fenestrated? What are the uses that face onto the open space? How frequent are entrances along the streets and squares? What is the nature of the pavement, or sidewalk? How tall are the buildings that enclose the spaces? How are the spaces illuminated? What are they like at night? What are the activity patterns that take place in the spaces? Who are the people engaged in them? These are the variables that distinguish one place from another – one city from another, and one precinct, or neighbour-hood, in a city from another. The bird's eye perspective of the Banking District of Mumbai and the cut away ground floor plan tell much about the nature of the public realm (see Figure 1.4). They tell little about the life of the place, although

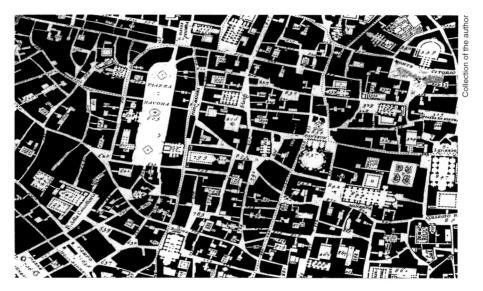

Collection of the author

Figure 1.3   The Nolli Map of Rome, 1748.

it is possible to speculate on what it is. The functions afforded by the pattern are very different from that provided by Double Bay in Sydney (see Figure 1.5).

The Functions of the Physical Public Realm

Conceptually, the functions afforded by the built environment have not changed over the millennia. What has changed is what its users, policy-makers and designers consider important. Designers seldom consciously include more than a limited set of the potential functions that the built environment can serve in their analyses and designs. The world is too complex for every function of built form to be considered simultaneously. The same patterns of the physical public realm, either as surroundings or as objects, will, almost certainly, serve different functions for different people. One of the major functions of the components of the built environment is as a financial investment. All designers know this but it is seldom clearly articulated as a function of buildings in architectural theory. Architectural critics seldom write about it.

Many urban development decisions are made on fiscal grounds. For banks and other lending institutions, and for their owners, buildings represent an investment on which they hope to make a profit. The public realm, in this case, is only important to the extent that it affects investment decisions. Property developers may, however, voluntarily or under public coercion use their own funds to improve those aspects of the public realm that their developments affect or that affect their developments. Public agencies may use tax income to improve the public realm created by buildings in order to increase the value of properties and increase the inflow of tax revenues. These revenues are then used to support other governmental activities. For architects, landscape architects and sculptors

Drawing by Yudi Prastowo

(a)

Drawing by Oleksandra Babych

(b)

Figure 1.4 Horniman Circle, Mumbai in 2003. (a) Bird's eye view and (b) cut-away ground floor plan.

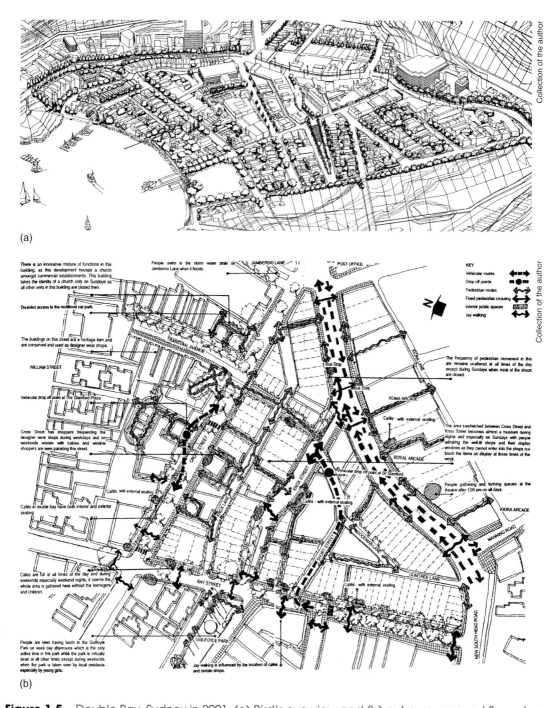

(a)

(b)

Figure 1.5 Double Bay, Sydney in 2001. (a) Bird's eye view and (b) cut-away ground floor plan.

their professional work is not only a means of income but also an advertisement of their tastes and skills that, they hope, will yield additional income in the future.

In summary, there are three basic amenities that the milieu can provide. It can afford activities, provide shelter, and act as a display that communicates meanings. The design concerns thus range from '(1) instrumental aspects which are the most manifest through, (2) how activities are carried out, (3) how they are associated into systems, to (4) their meanings, their most latent aspect' (Rapoport, 1997). These functions can best be understood within a model of human needs. There is nothing new in this statement. It was central to the thinking of the Modernists. Our models are, however, much richer than those they had.

Human Purposes and the Functions of the Public Realm

There are a number of models of human needs. None is perfect but that developed by Abraham Maslow is held in the highest esteem because it seems to explain the most (Maslow, 1987). Maslow suggested that there is a hierarchy of human needs from the most basic (survival) to the most abstract (aesthetic). These needs trigger motivations to behave in one way or another and inspire people (and communities) to own valued objects and to be in settings that display specific characteristics. These motivations may result from inner drives but they are culturally shaped and often define a culture. This observation is one reason that urban design patterns developed within one culture are not necessarily transferable to others with success.

A model relating Maslow's hierarchy of human needs to the functions of built form is presented in Figure 1.6. The model specifies that both needs and the mechanisms to fulfil them have to be perceived within a social order. In urban design, the polar extremes of social order are represented by autocratic and democratic societies. In the former, decisions are centralized in the hands of an individual or a coterie of people; in the latter it is more diverse and, ultimately subjected to the opinions of the population concerned.

The diagram shows that the mechanisms (or patterns of built form) for achieving many needs are interrelated. The most basic needs, according to Maslow, are physiological. The fundamental need is for survival, which means that the environment has to afford us shelter. It must also protect us from life-threatening events. Some of these events, such as earthquakes, are natural phenomena, but we humans have created others. The perception of the potential occurrences of such events very much shapes what we demand of the built environment.

Once basic physiological needs are at least partially met, people are motivated to seek a sense of safety and security. Physiologically, safety and security needs are highly related to the need for survival. How best to segregate pedestrian and moving vehicles is a recurrent issue in urban design. Dealing with crime and now terrorism has become a constraint on what we can do to celebrate cities. Providing for people's psychological sense of security involves them having appropriate levels of privacy and their being in control over their social environments. People

13

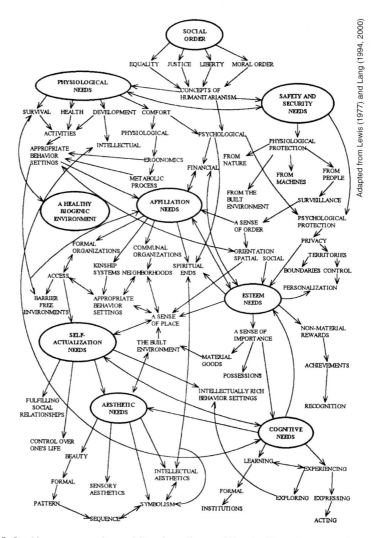

Adapted from Lewis (1977) and Lang (1994, 2000)

Figure 1.6 Human needs and the functions of the built environment.

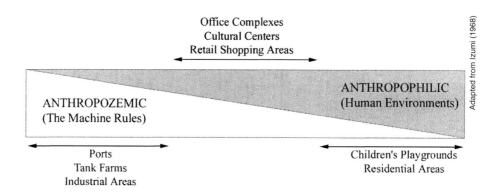

Adapted from Izumi (1968)

Figure 1.7 Anthropozemic and anthropophilic environments.

have an expectation of privacy for every activity pattern in which they engage as individuals or groups. Many of these expectations are subtle and depend on the personalities of the people involved.

The diagram also shows that the socio-physical mechanisms used by people to attain a feeling of self-worth are closely related to the achievement of safety and security. The built environment is very much an indicator of people's social status. It acts as a symbol of who we are. One of the debates in current urban design is whether to create images that refer to specific locales or to create international images favoured by the institutions of the global economy. (Compare for instance the designs of Battery Park City, Canary Wharf, Lujiazui and Paternoster Square as described in Chapter 8). For many people the layout of the built environment being in accordance with spiritual beliefs also meets these needs. It is important to recognize that the built environment, public and private, is a symbol of who we are and/or who we aspire to be.

The highest level in Maslow's hierarchy of basic needs is that for self-actualization – to be what one can be. The design implications for this level of need are unclear. Cognitive and aesthetic needs, however, have more understandable implications. They are manifest throughout our lives. We need to be able to learn to survive as well as to make advances in life so learning is present in achieving all our basic needs. Aesthetic needs not only have to do with the symbolic meanings of the environment as they refer to status and aspirations but also, for some people, to the understanding of designers' logics. For instance, understanding the nature of deconstruction philosophy and seeing it applied in the creation of architectural and landscape forms (as in the design of the Parc de la Villette; see Chapter 5) is meaningful to some observers. For most people, however, it is what they perceive and not the logic behind its creation that is important.

It is not only we humans that have needs but also the biological world of other animate species as well as, implicitly, the inanimate. Vegetation and animals serve many purposes in defining a healthy world but machines often rule. Kyoto Izumi, a Canadian architect, drew a diagram that distinguishes between those settings where questions of meeting human motivations are paramount (anthropophilic environments) and those in which the needs of machines are most important (anthropozemic environments) (see Figure 1.7; Izumi, 1968). Machines, it must be remembered, serve human lives. This book is primarily concerned with anthropophilic environments in Izumi's terms. Tank farms could certainly be regarded as an urban design product type but their design really falls into the domains of engineering and ergonomics.

Multiplier and Side Effects: The Catalytic Function of Urban Design Decisions

Multiplier effects generally refer to the positive impacts of particular investment decisions and patterns of the built environment on their surroundings; side effects generally refer to the negative. The urban design concern is with the catalytic effect both have on future developments. Do they start trends in investment policies or not? Do they establish new aesthetic attitudes? Many of the case studies presented in this book show how specific buildings (e.g. the Guggenheim Museum in Bilbao) and building complexes (e.g. Pioneer Place) have been successful in this sense (see Chapter 6).

A prime function of many urban designs is to enhance the quality of the urban environment by changing investment patterns. Unfortunately some urban design paradigms have been inappropriately applied and have had unanticipated negative impacts. The 'de-malling' of many streets that had been converted to pedestrian ways is an example (e.g. Oak Park, Illinois; see Chapter 5). Of great public concern nowadays is the impact of the built environment on the natural environment but it has yet to be reflected in urban design on any large scale. Although there have been some preliminary explorations, the paradigms for designers to follow have yet to be clearly articulated.

Buildings and other hard surfaces change the patterns of winds and breezes flowing through the environment, the processes by which water tables are created, and heat is reflected and absorbed. They, in particular, create heat-islands changing local climatic patterns. We are only just beginning to be conscious of these matters in urban design and in most localities the political will to deal with them has yet to emerge. In addition, our science is still poor on many dimensions. For instance, our knowledge of how winds move through cities flushing out pollutants is in its infancy. We are much better off in dealing with issues of energy consumption.

The Cultural Dimension

'All people have the same needs' Le Corbusier observed. Assuming that the models for designing the built environment can be reduced to a number of universal paradigms has proven to be a costly error. The ordering of needs, as Maslow perceived them, may be universal but the ways we strive to meet them show considerable variability. The activity patterns, from those of everyday life to the most obscure ceremonies, depend on our stage in life cycle, our gender, and our social roles, within specific cultural contexts. What we are accustomed to do and the environments we are accustomed to inhabit very much shape what we seek in the future. We are habituated to what we know. Departures from the norm, particularly major departures, can be highly stressful. Yet history is replete with examples of attempts, sometimes successful, sometimes not, to change the face of society through radical architectural and urban changes.

It is not only the activity patterns that vary from culture to culture, but also concepts of privacy and territoriality and attitudes towards public displays of status and wealth. In some societies there is considerable social dislocation and high crime rates and in others much less. Patterns of the environment, the materials of what they are made, their colouring and the whole manner in which they are illuminated carry meaning based on learnt associations. In some societies, the coding of status through design is readily observable and in others it is highly subtle.

Possibly the most important culturally based variable for urban design is the attitude towards individualism and cooperation. Much-admired urban places such as Piazza San Marco in Venice were built piece-by-piece over the centuries with each new developer and architect being conscious of fitting in with what had already been built. They had, what architectural historian Peter Kohane calls, a 'sense of decorum'. The same attitudes were a hallmark of traditional Islamic societies where a host of unwritten laws drawn from the Koran governed the design of individual components of the environment, ensuring an integrated whole. Such attitudes do persist but they are not a significant characteristic of the societies in which the case studies included in this book exist. The reason urban design has emerged as a field of professional endeavour has been in order to seek cooperative procedures that will enhance the quality of specific areas of cities.

Cultures evolve; they are not static. In an era of globalization, not only of the economy but also of information, various patterns of the public realm are perceived by officials as symbolically desirable because of what the international media promote as desirable. The desire for universal images in the public realm of cities often means that the requirements of many local activity patterns are overridden in the search for international symbolic patterns that enhance people's self-image. Many professionals receive their education, particularly at the advanced level, in societies other than their own and they bring home the patterns appropriate to their host societies as part of their intellectual equipment. They take time to readapt to facing their own societies' needs. Some never do!

The Public Realm of Decision-making

The obligations that members of a society have to each other establish the respective roles of governments and individuals in the conduct of their lives. The debate over what is private and what is public, and what the rights of individual are versus the rights of the community (however one defines the term) is central to urban design. The debate is over the rights of individual property owners to build what they want versus the rights of their neighbours and the broader society to impose restrictions on those rights in the name of the public interest.

The Scope of Concern of Public Sector Decision-making

Perceptions of what should be public concerns and what private vary over time. The twentieth century saw the flow and ebb of the welfare state. The late 1980s saw the beginning of the second capitalist revolution and a greater emphasis being placed on the individual and individual rights than earlier in the twentieth century. The belief is that personal freedom of action benefits everybody. In many ways the translation of this ideology into action has been highly successful especially at the global marketplace level of finance. The processes of change have, however, been a painful experience for many people and laissez faire approaches to urban development have had many opportunity costs associated with them.

'To what extent should the public sector decision-makers intervene in the property development process?' 'Should it be only to control development to ensure public health and safety?' or 'Should it be to promote public amenities?' In other words, should the public sector be concerned with the use of sticks or carrots or both in shaping the nature of human settlements, and their components? 'How far can the public sector support, through legislation or subsidies, private profit making investment actions that are perceived to be in the public interest?' In the United States, recent court cases (e.g. *Southwestern Illinois Development Authority versus National City Environmental*, 2002) have limited the power of governments to use the power of eminent domain to acquire land to be sold on for private uses even though the public amenity of any ensuing development might have highly beneficial consequences.

The case studies included in this book show a wide variety of roles of the government in property development. In some cases the development has been part of a national policy to redistribute a population. These policies have been implemented through the acquisition of land, the creation of a development programme, the hiring of a designer or set of designers, and the implementing of a design for whole cities. In other cases the whole development process has been entirely privately funded and subject only to standard zoning controls. Many urban development projects have involved the public and private sectors of an economy in a partnership that has set the requirements for a scheme, organized the process of its development and its funding, and then implemented it (Frieden and Sagalyn, 1991; Garvin, 1995).

The scope of the public's concern about the cities they inhabit (as represented in a government's rights to make decisions on everybody's behalf) has varied over time. Recently, for instance, it has been seen as the government's role to be concerned about the health of the planet Earth. Inevitably this concern raises questions about the shape of cities, policies for reducing pollution and the heat-island effect of large-scale developments and the use of breezes to flush cities. Dealing with such issues all requires communal action. So do the broad questions about the liveability of cities.

As the twentieth century progressed governments intervened more and more in the ways cities are developed. Municipal authorities have, for instance, been determining land-use policies, where and how the infrastructure necessary for development should be provided, and they have been ensuring that what is built is safe and healthy. They have also intervened in determining the aesthetic nature of the environment, from the ambient quality of streets and public spaces to the appearance of buildings. In using their power to do so, they have had, in the United States at least, to demonstrate that the goals they establish are in the public interest and that the mechanisms they use to achieve those goals are constitutional and are based on evidence that they work (see *Daubert versus Merrell Dow*, No. 92-102, 1993; and *Dolan versus the City of Taggert*, 1994; Stamps, 1994). In an even more recent hearing (the United States Supreme Court decision in the case of *City of*

Los Angeles versus Alameda Book, 2002) it was stated that a municipality 'cannot get away with shoddy data or reasoning.' These legal decisions are not universally applicable but the implied suggestion is that designers should seek evidence before claiming what the outcomes of design decisions will be. Knowing the outcomes of previous urban design efforts is one source of supportive evidence.

The Quasi-public Role of Property Developers

The entrepreneurs creating large-scale property developments often play a quasi-public role in the development of cities. This observation is particularly true of the 1980s and even more so of the 1990s. Public institutions now rely heavily on private sector investments in developing the public realm. Simultaneously there is demand for regulation on what these private sectors entrepreneurs seek to achieve and how they seek to achieve it.

It is the private sector that sees opportunities for investing profitably in new buildings or building complexes. They, like the banks who sponsor their works, want what they do to be a financial success. To be a financial success there must be some public demand for the products they are creating. At the same time, developers often have to be cajoled into building items that are perceived to be in the public interest but are not as profitable as other types of development. It requires public sector incentives to make the private sector take on such less-profitable ventures (see Chapter 9).

Property developers generally look at the city in terms of the opportunities for creating what they are used to building. For instance, a developer of office buildings will look for opportunities for building office buildings; one interested in parking garages will look for opportunities for building parking garages. Few ask the question 'What is the best use of this site?' or 'How will the way I do this building improve the cityscape and the amenity for pedestrians?' The conservative political view is that this process of individuals 'doing their own thing' benefits us all and should only be interfered with on health and safety grounds.

Developers' attitudes vary considerably and they do not represent a common block of thought. Some are vitally interested in the common good; others are not. They do, however, have one thing in common. They have to make a profit on their investments. They are not necessarily opposed to governmental controls over their work provided the controls make sense and do not inhibit their work arbitrarily. Developers have a history of supporting design guidelines if the improvements the guidelines lead to ensure that their own investments are successful. Most developers, nevertheless, like architects, have powerful egos – they want to do things their own way.

A major debate nowadays in thinking about urban design is over how comprehensive a set of concerns it should encompass. What should be subject to public control and what should be left to the prerogative of the individual? The case studies included in this book vary considerably in their answers to this question. Much depends on the context of a project and the goals that it is supposed to fulfil.

The Objectives of Urban Design

A number of generic objectives can be identified in the writings on urban design. The built environment should be efficient in the way it handles the variables described in Figure 1.6. It should be designed to encourage economic growth. It should provide a sense of historic continuity to enhance people's self-images. It should help sustain the moral and social order of a society and should be designed with a sense of justice for all to the extent that these are physical design concerns (see Harvey, 2003).

The broad goal of urban design is to provide opportunities, behavioural and aesthetic, for all the citizens of and visitors to a city or one of its precincts. These opportunities have to be accessible. What, however, should the opportunities be and how does one deal with accessibility? Who decides? The marketplace? The public policy question is 'How far should the public sector intervene in the marketplace in providing opportunities for what range of people?' and then 'How accessible should the opportunities be?' 'For whom?' 'People in wheelchairs?'

Secondarily, if one accepts Maslow's model, there is a need for people to feel comfortable in engaging in the activities they desire and that are regarded by society as acceptable. Comfort has both physiological and psychological dimensions. The concern is with the nature of the microclimate and with the provision of feelings of safety and security as people go about their lives. Safety and security are related to feelings of control over one's privacy levels and over the behaviour of others towards one. How much privacy are we prepared to give up in order to feel safe because we are under public surveillance? Safety concerns are also related to the segregation of pedestrians from vehicular traffic flows and the construction quality of the environment around us.

One design concern is to enhance the ambience of *links* (streets, arcades and sidewalks) and *places* (squares, parks and roofs). The ambience of places and links is related to the provision of a sense of security as well as to feelings of self-worth and being part of a worthwhile society. Ambience is also related to the aesthetic qualities of a place, its layout and illumination, the activities that are taking place there, and to the people engaged in them.

The artificial world does not exist in a vacuum. It exists in terrestrial niches formed by the climate, geology, and flora and fauna of a place. One of the objectives of urban design is certainly to ensure that this niche is not destroyed. The concern is, or should be, with improving its quality so that it functions better as a self-sustaining system that, in return, enriches human experiences.

The Issues

The basic urban design question is always 'What makes a good city?' The question is asked at both a global and at a detailed level. 'Who should decide?' 'Once decisions are made, who should be responsible for implementing them?' 'Is a good city the product of a whole set of individual decisions largely uncoordinated, or does one attempt to coordinate them?' 'What are the opportunity costs for working one way or another?'

Secondly, 'How far should the controlling authority (public or private) go in defining the specification of ends and means?' The corollary is 'What are the limits, if any, to the rights of individual developers and their architects to build what they want, where they want, and how they want?' 'What is in the public interest?' 'What is the public interest?' It has been notoriously difficult to define. It is represented in democracies by the stands that politicians take but they are hardly disinterested parties. Presumably, the goal is to design for the welfare of all concerned but, at best, any design product should represent the interests of particular parties without harming the interests of others. What is in the public interest will always be a bone of contention.

Thirdly, although in an age of fiscal pragmatism one might argue that it is the primary issue, is the concern for return on capital invested. In capitalist societies, property developers (private or public) take the lead or have to be coerced into building the city piece-by-piece. One of the objectives of urban design is indeed to ensure fiscal responsibility. Another is to develop carrots and sticks through incentives and penalties for developing cities in particular ways: to create specific facilities in specific locations.

Fourthly, how is development to be phased? 'Where does one begin?' 'How disrupted will the lives of those who inhabit the first phase be as the project moves into another phase of construction?' 'Whose responsibility is it to ensure that those people's lives are disrupted as little as possible?'

The goal of this book is to show through case studies how architects, landscape architects and city planners have addressed these issues in urban design projects of various types. Having done so it will be possible at the end of the book (in Chapter 11) to return to this discussion and ask the questions: 'What concerns have really been addressed in the urban designs of the past 50 years as represented in this book?' and then 'What will the issues be in the future?' Many of them will continue to be the ones that we have addressed in the past and are addressing now. Some will be a surprise.

The Design Professions and Urban Design

All three of the major environmental design fields use the term 'urban design' to describe aspects of their own work. Civil engineering has yet to do so even though infrastructure design is a key element in urban design. To many people urban design and urban planning are the same thing but the products they produce are very different (see Chapter 4). Often, however, urban planning is concerned primarily with the distribution of land uses in relationship to transportation networks. It has focused on economic development regardless of the physical design consequences. Yet, at its best city planning does consider the third and fourth dimension of cities rather than allowing them to be by-products of other decisions. Urban design as a separate design activity arose largely because city planning neglected the built environment in its deliberations of urban futures.

The quality of the urban landscape is a major contributor to perceptions of the qualities of cities. A city's physical character is defined by the nature of its streets, squares and other open spaces in terms of how they are shaped by enclosing elements (Goldfinger, 1942). The biological health of cities depends on the interactions between the natural and the artificial. Few landscape architects since the era of Olmsted have, however, engaged themselves in urban design. They have tended to shy away from dealing with more than designing open spaces. They have been concerned only with select types of products (see Chapter 5).

Architects, as architects, too have looked at urban design in terms of specific types of products: buildings as objects rather than as space makers (see Chapter 6). The leadership in developing urban design as a professional field has, nevertheless, come from architects with broader concerns. They have been interested in the design of complexes of buildings, and what cities and neighbourhoods might be like. Some of their ideas and conceptual schemes have been based on rationalist thought and others on empirical observations about cities. Still other architects have, however, been highly pragmatic. They have been concerned only with how to get projects initiated and carried through. Some of the projects reviewed here may have been whimsical ego-trips but most, I would argue, have been based on a sense of idealism.

Part of the difficulty in defining the scope of urban design today is that each of the professions wants to claim it as its own. Architectural societies give urban design awards to single buildings, landscape architects to squares, and city planners to a wide variety of items. Urban design, however, involves all these matters, not individually but in concert. It is a collaborative effort between public and private sectors, between professions, and between practitioners and researchers. It deals with the four-dimensional inhabited world.

Commentary

Urban design covers a multitude of professional activities. It does involve *design*. Defining the context, political and physical, of urban design work with precision is difficult. The model of the purposes served by the public realm and the built environment in general as shown in Figure 1.6 provides a framework for considering what variables have been of importance in the different cases to be covered in this book. The more multipurpose the public realms in the case studies covered here are supposed to be and the more varied their contexts, the more complex the issues and the process of decision-making. Many more actors are involved. The more open and diverse a society, the more intricate and involved are the debates over ends and means and the more diverse the opinions about the results achieved. Collaborative work dealing with planning, landscape architecture and architectural concerns as well as those of various types of engineering in a politically volatile context is difficult and, often, highly stressful.

The goal of this chapter has been to set the scene for the discussion of the various types of urban development work that have been subsumed under the rubric of *urban design* by somebody or other. The objective of the next chapter is to present a framework for considering urban design procedural types and the understanding of the mechanisms available for shaping design ends and means. Its goal, in turn, is to provide a typology for understanding the range of urban design work that has been conducted over the past 50 years and is being conducted today – the subject matter of Chapter 3.

2 Urban design processes and procedures

Around the world many urban design schemes have been brought from the glimmer of an idea in somebody's head to being a completed part of a city. Many proposals remain unimplemented. Some were simply explorations of possibilities. Many were, in contrast, concrete proposals for specific projects. Some were designed with implementation processes that proved to be unfeasible. Some were the victims of political vagaries. Others simply disregarded the rights of individual landowners and/or the implied sources of funding were unavailable. Many were not implemented because property developers could not be induced to participate in building the scheme's components.

Many developers, public and private, hold competitions for design projects. A noticeable proportion of the case studies presented in this book were initiated through competitions. In its short history the World Trade Center site has been the subject of a number. There are many more examples. The People's Committee of Ho Chi Minh City, for instance, held an international design competition in 2003 for the design of a new central business district for the city. The entries had to consider the phasing of development but not how it was to be financed. They presented the officials of the city with a lode of ideas to mine. In such competitions winning entries often have to undergo substantial changes to make it financially possible to implement them.

Many architects and landscape architects regard issues of the financial feasibility of the urban design schemes they propose to lie outside their concerns. This attitude is surprising because the budget available is a central factor in the design of buildings and landscapes. Often, however, the issue of financing and how to get property developers to build what is desired only becomes an issue when a design proposal has been prepared. A proposal gives stakeholders something that they can understand. In almost every case the design is likely to change due to fiscal limitations. An urban designer with any stamina soon becomes embroiled in the issues of financing and the design of carrots and sticks to shape designs in particular directions. In autocratic societies implementing grandiose schemes is easy provided one is working for the dictator!

Urban Design in Autocratic and Democratic Societies

The major difference between urban designing in autocratic states and in democratic is that centralized powers of decision-making in autocratic societies are not subject to any control from the citizenry or their representatives. As a result they tend to be large scale and located where the whim of the dictator decrees. In urban renewal, projects are ruthlessly driven through existing built-up areas (e.g. the redevelopment of Bucharest under Ceausescu; see Chapter 7). Baron Georges-Eugène Haussmann in the Paris of Napoleon III set the example for modern times in 1853. In the first half of the twentieth century Hitler, Stalin and Mussolini all had grandiose projects on the drawing board. The latter two dictators saw parts of their urban design ambitions in place. Mussolini's Via della Conciliazione, lined with new buildings and 28 obelisks, gives a commanding view of St Peter's (see Figure 2.1). Such projects have been difficult to put in place in democratic countries because of the amount of demolition of the existing city required to build them. The City Beautiful scheme for Philadelphia saw only one component, the Benjamin Franklin Parkway, built. It had to be cut through a number of neighbourhoods (Brownlee, 1989).

During the middle third of the twentieth century in both totalitarian and democratic countries many urban design schemes were housing estates (e.g. the public housing schemes in the United Kingdom, the United States and continental Europe and, more spectacularly, the mass developments across the former Soviet Union, and in many Asian countries). Their sizes have varied enormously. Few new towns, other than company towns, in democratic countries have turned out

Figure 2.1   The Via della Conciliazione, Rome in 1961.

to be autocratically developed. They tend to be a collage of work by different designers. In socialist countries with centralized political and administrative power much was achieved in quantity if not quality.

Major references

Benevolo, Leonardo (1980). *The History of the City* [translated by Geoffrey Culverwell]. Cambridge, MA: MIT Press.

Cavalcanti, Maria de Betânia Ochôa (1992). Totalitarian states and their influence on city form. *Journal of Architectural and Planning Research* **9**: 275–86.

Mazumdar, Sanjoy (2000). Autocratic control and urban design: the case of Tehran, Iran. *Journal of Urban Design* **5** (3): 317–38.

The Urban Designing Process

There have been a number of efforts to model the process and procedures of urban designing. Most generic models suggest a rational step-by-step procedure that moves from perceptions of a problem to post-implementation evaluation of a completed work as in Figure 2.2. While the models give some structure to our thinking and to our design of the decision-making process appropriate to a job at hand, urban design does not take place in the neat sequential manner that the models suggest. It is a highly argumentative process of conjecturing – putting out ideas – and testing them in an iterative fashion.

The participants in the development of any urban design project will be arguing with each other and with themselves as they speculate about what the issues are and how best to deal with them. Urban designing is an argumentative process

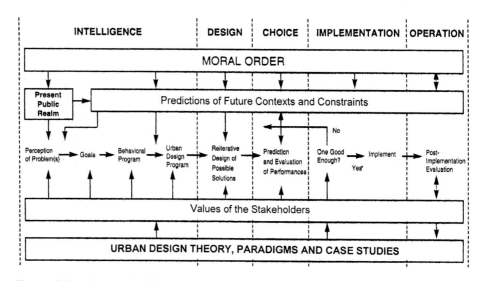

Figure 2.2 A model of the rational design process.

in which participants in it learn as they go along. They learn about goals and means as perceived by different stakeholders, they learn from the evidence that each provides for its views. They take stands on what they believe the public realm should be to be in the public interest. They argue about the variables that should be taken into consideration and what good design entails. Conjectures are tested by individuals using their own logics based on their predictions of the consequences of different design actions.

It is easy to be cynical about who wins the arguments (i.e. those holding the purse strings) but good information based on empirical knowledge is a powerful tool that designers can employ. So are their reputations (except when facing cross-examination in court). In his design for the DG Bank building on Pariser Platz in Berlin, Frank Gehry showed that reputations allow for concessions that less-renowned architects might not get (see Chapter 8).

The rational model of design suggests that the urban designing process begins with the perception of an opportunity worth exploiting or a problem worth over-coming. According to the model a designer should start with an open mind. We all, however, have heads full of generic solutions, examples and anecdotal know-ledge that guide us. It is likely that all designers begin designing with some vague image of a possible solution in mind. This design gets shaped though a series of approximations as designing progresses and new information becomes available. Most, if not all, of the case studies included in this book have antecedents or a mix-ture of antecedents. How much should designers rely on precedents? (see Rowe, 1983). Case studies and sound generic solutions are certainly helpful both in understanding the problems that require attention in specific situations and in creating solutions. The world is, however, changing. Inventing new generic solu-tions is thus a worthwhile task. Whose responsibility is it to do so? In the past they have been the products of visionaries and practitioners, professionals and lay-people, social scientists and artists. Future models need to be culture and climate specific. Much can be learnt from the generic qualities of case studies.

There are great similarities amongst the decision-making processes used in all the case studies included in this book. All urban designing involves the basic steps of deciding to engage in a situation, developing a brief and building programme, finding the finances, and seeing that programme through to completion. What differs is how the overall process is handled and the way each step is carried out. Who controls? Who does what?

There are four generic types of urban design work that vary in the procedure that is followed and/or the degree of control that a designer, as an individual or as a team, has over the creation of a product. They are as follows:

1 Total urban design, where the urban designer is part of the development team that carries a scheme through from inception to completion.
2 All-of-a-piece urban design, where the urban design team devises a master plan and sets the parameters within which a number of developers work on components of the overall project.

3 Piece-by-piece urban design, in which general policies and procedures are applied to a precinct of a city in order to steer development in specific directions.

4 Plug-in urban design, where the design goal is to create the infrastructure so that subsequent developments can 'plug in' to it or, alternatively, a new element of infrastructure is plugged into the existing urban fabric to enhance a location's amenity level as a catalyst for development.

The borderline between categories is fuzzy. The first two types, total and all-of-a-piece urban design have historically been the core of urban design work but all four are considered as such in this book because they focus on the four-dimensional built environment and require the collaborative actions of all the design disciplines.

Total Urban Design

Total urban design is really a combination of large (in geographical area or number of buildings) architecture and landscape architecture. It involves the design of both the public realm and the buildings that frame it. A team of people working as an individual unit holds total development and design control. The infrastructure and buildings are designed as a unit by the team. Much of the detail of the design is then completed by transportation engineers, architects and landscape architects who form part of the team. The debate about ends and means takes place within the team. In many people's minds, total urban design is seen as the norm of urban design practice. It seldom is.

There have been some major urban design projects around the world that sit comfortably in this category of total urban design. They vary in scale from new cities to precincts of cities to the design of plazas and other urban open spaces. Brasília, as described in Chapter 7, is perhaps, the best known of such city designs (see Figure 2.3). Many of the new towns built in the Soviet Union between 1950 and 1980 are similar in character and the myriad of company towns around the world are other examples of total urban design. Company towns are all 'administered communities' at the outset although they may evolve into ones in which controls are in the hands of the inhabitants themselves rather than being dictated by a single authority – the company (Gottschalk, 1975). Administered communities are totalitarian in nature even when located in the most democratic of countries.

Most total urban designs deal with precincts of cities rather than cities as a whole. Two of the best known are the capital complex (see Chapter 7) and the city centre superblock in Chandigarh (see Figure 2.4). Le Corbusier was given a free hand in their design. Over the past 50 years there have been many precincts of cities that have been designed and developed by one organization but the developments are seldom more than three or four traditional city blocks in size. In contrast, there are many large developer-initiated suburban estates around the world that are total urban designs. In many countries with socialist governments they were developed, designed and built by Public Works Departments or their

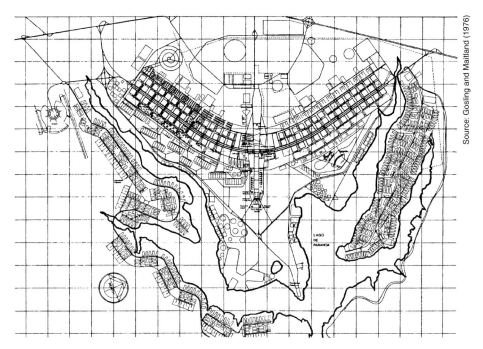

Source: Gosling and Maitland (1976)

Figure 2.3   The plan of Brasília.

Figure 2.4   The City Centre, Chandigarh in 1996.

equivalents but in capitalist countries they have also been privately developed. Some total developments have been vast in size, covering many square kilometres. Often they have ended up being visually and behaviourally boring!

Caution is needed in thinking of total urban designs as really *totally* under the control of a single auspice. Within the market economy of democratic societies the development team seldom has a completely free hand to do as they wish. Almost all projects are embedded within geographical areas whose population imposes some control over what can take place, either through having elected representatives to act on their behalf or by direct community action. In addition, the project has to be carried out within the laws of a country. There are, however, many examples of the laws being relaxed for political reasons. Raleigh Park in Sydney is an example (see Chapter 7).

In totalitarian societies the situation is different. In redeveloping Bucharest during the 1970s, President Nicole Ceausescu did what he wanted to do (see Chapter 7). After his demise market forces have ruled. A totalitarian ruler was also responsible for the development of Yamoussoukro, the new capital of the Ivory Coast. The future of that city is open to question. By all reports it stands empty, unused and unloved. Perhaps, in the future it will come to life.

All-of-a-piece Urban Design

Many urban redevelopment projects and suburban developments are so large in size that single developers and their backers are incapable of financing them single-handedly. In other cases land holding patterns are so fragmented that having a single developer tackling all the sites in a coordinated manner is legally or administratively impossible. In these cases, a consulting team develops one illustrative three-dimensional design (or master plan or concept plan) of the whole development. The pieces of the scheme are then parcelled out to different developers and their design professionals to finance and design. The scheme illustrated in Figure 2.5 has potentially over 30 sub-developments within it. Difficulties in financing so many projects often mean that the construction period can extend

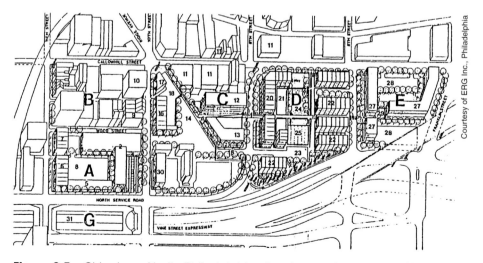

Figure 2.5 Chinatown North, Philadelphia: development proposal, 1990.

into three or four decades. Devised in 1989, by the year 2000 only the projects designated as 20 and 22 of the example had been built. In such projects the major developer, public or private, may build the overall infrastructure, or alternatively all the sub-developers may have to provide those components that relate to their own schemes or contribute to the cost of having them built.

Once the conceptual design devised by the master planner is accepted, a pro-gramme and set of guidelines is developed for each block that is to be built by a sub-developer (see Figure 8.1 for the example of the Dallas Arts District). Some design review and overall development and construction management procedures then have to be created to administer the whole development along with the process for managing the project when it has been completed. In some cases a single review committee presides over all the developments in a city; in other cases the review committee is appointed to oversee a single project. The problems in implemen-tation, either in financing projects or in meeting the goals of a project as assessed by its clients or a review board, often lead to the redesign of the master plan. The end result may be vastly different from that originally envisaged (e.g. see Battery Park City, or Charles Center, or Potsdamer Platz; all described in Chapter 8).

The all-of-a-piece design process follows a set of steps approximating that shown in Figure 2.6. A prime developer, public or private, initiates the project through the acquisition of land and then decides on what to build (or vice versa) given either a local market demand and/or some assumption as to what is in the public interest. Some private developers may forgo profit to pursue public inter-est goals but, in general, it is a public agency that sets the public interest agenda for a project. It is the property developer, public or private, who hires the urban designer, an individual or a team, to produce a conceptual design and to develop the design brief. In democratic societies this process benefits from and is buffeted by a whole set of public and private interests.

To ensure that the intention of the master plan is not lost, each sub-development has to be built in accordance with a set of guidelines. Sometimes these guidelines

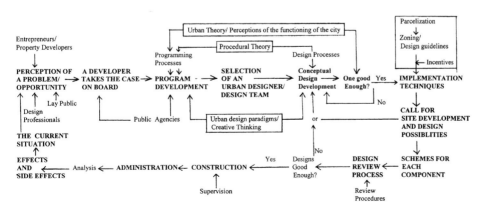

Figure 2.6 The major steps in an all-of-a-piece urban design.

Photograph by Susannah Lang

Figure 2.7 Battery Park City, New York as seen from South Cove in 2003.

are generic to the whole development and sometimes they are applied to each site to be developed. One of the best-known examples of an all-of-a-piece urban design scheme is Battery Park City in Lower Manhattan, New York (see Figure 2.7). Dating back to the early 1960s the project was all but completed in 2004. A number of illustrative site designs for the project were developed under different political and economic conditions over a period of almost 30 years. Finally, what is generally, but by no means universally, regarded as a fine urban precinct has resulted from the work of several developers and their architects. What is important is that the guidelines are adopted legally as public policy. In New York's World Trade Center site development proposal they do not seem to have been (see Chapter 8).

Piece-by-piece Urban Design

All cities have a design. It is created by thousands of individual design decisions within a framework of capital investment decisions and within a legal code. If total urban designs tend to be comprised of large-scale architecture projects, piece-by-piece urban design tends to be city planning. While piece-by-piece urban design is precinct, or neighbourhood, based, it is in contrast to all-of-a-piece design not site-by-site, building-by-building, based. The process involves first setting the objectives for an area and then the development/design policies for achieving them. The creation of the objectives is a highly political act ideally, but often only reputedly, based on perceptions of the public interest. Once the objectives are accepted, the next step is to design incentives and controls, carrots and sticks, to achieve them.

Possibly the best-known examples of piece-by-piece urban design are those from New York in the 1960s and 1970s (Barnett, 1974, 2003). Developers were given incentives in specific areas to build specific facilities (see Chapter 9). In the Theater District, the objective was to include new theatres around Broadway at a time when the existence of theatres was imperilled by opportunities for developers to erect more lucrative types of buildings. They were allowed to build more than the total floor area permitted by existing zoning ordinances in order to obtain the perceived public good of more theatres. Many cities have applied similar procedures to obtain a wide variety of building and/or facility types from crèches to housing for people on low incomes in precincts where property developers see no financial reward in building them.

Plug-in Urban Design

Plug-in urban design refers to the design and implementation of an infrastructure project in order to obtain some catalytic reaction. There are two types of plug-in urban design projects. The first type involves the provision of the infrastructure of, usually, a precinct of a city or suburb, and the selling of sites into which individual developers can plug buildings. The second type involves plugging the infrastructure into an existing urban fabric to enhance its amenity value.

Sometimes the process of building the infrastructure and then the fabric of a city or suburb is heavily controlled. Building uses are specified and design guidelines are created for each developer to follow. In this case, the process is really a variant of all-of-a-piece urban design. In other cases those property developers plugging their projects into the provided infrastructure are free to respond to the marketplace, as they will. The assumption in this case is that the market knows best what is in demand and thus appropriate to build.

The second type of plug-in urban design refers to the situation where elements of infrastructure are plugged into an existing city in the hope of spurring new developments or providing some public amenity. The elements of infrastructure may be links, places or buildings providing for special uses that will, it is hoped, have a catalytic effect on surrounding property development (Attoe and Logan, 1989). The skyway system in Minneapolis began in this way but, as is described in Chapter 10, it has become an integral part of almost any development in that city's centre.

Financing

All urban designs are affected by the financing available. Somebody has to pay the bill. There are two major aspects to financing projects: (1) their capital costs and (2) the cost of operating them once they have been built. The second is often forgotten in the haste to get buildings erected or public spaces created. The fundamental questions are: 'Where does the money come from?' and 'Who pays for what?' Then the question is: 'What is the cost of the money?' Interest rates affect many design decisions.

The viability of any proposal depends on the availability of capital funds. There are two sources of financing – public sector through tax revenues and the private sector through the money available to be loaned at interest. In socialist countries the funds have come primarily from the government. In capitalist the funding of projects has sometimes come from taxation income and sometimes from borrowed money but usually a mixture of the two. Each group involved in developing a project negotiates based on its perceptions of the equity necessary to be raised and the financial guarantees it obtains. In totalitarian societies the centralization of power makes funding easier.

It has generally been easier for governments to raise money because their credit is based on their ability to raise revenues from future taxes. Many cities, however, have precarious economies. Private developers have to raise funds on a project-by-project basis and seek loans with the lowest interest rates, the least amount of equity required and, ideally from their viewpoint, with government subsidies. Such subsidies take many forms: paying for the infrastructure development, mortgage guarantees, the leasing of parts of a project, or structuring a pooled commercial paper programme. Conversely, the private sector can subsidize government investments by building parts of the infrastructure.

The sums needed for major urban design schemes are considerable and much investment has to be made before any financial return is seen. These upfront expenses are for the purchasing of land, planning the development, developing the infrastructure, mapping out sites for development, writing building design guidelines, negotiating the sale of land, and reviewing individual development proposals. The phasing of developments is thus crucial because premature development of infrastructure can be costly. On the other hand, if it is delayed a developer incurs real costs and the community foregoes potential tax revenues. Large projects have come to a halt during periods of fiscal difficulty. Only changes in economic conditions and/or new injections of public funding or a change in the programme or the design controls have started construction moving again. The case studies here are replete with examples.

Public investment in infrastructure has served as a catalyst for many important developments. The failure of such expected investments to eventuate has led to financial crises in many projects (e.g. Canary Wharf; see Chapter 8). There are also many schemes where the infrastructure has been built and yet the private sector sees no gain in building the other components of a project (e.g. Penn's Landing, Philadelphia has stood undeveloped with its infrastructure in place for over 20 years now). Today, public sources of financing have dried up in many capitalist countries and the private sector is being required to subsidize the development of the public realm in return for being allowed to build what it wants to build. The incentives for the private sector to take this role are substantially higher in growing economies than in those that are stagnant or declining.

Public and private property developers alike compete or cooperate within an 'invisible web' of existing laws, codes and design guidelines (Lai, 1988). They have to see the rewards that can accrue to them if an urban design proposal is to proceed. Somebody must want the product that is being sold. There has to be a market for it.

The Market

No project in capitalist societies proceeds without some image of it being marketable. It needs to be saleable. The market required to support a project and make it feasible in its developer's eyes is made up of the population seeking real estate and other services and its ability to pay for them. For all the types of urban design schemes that one is considering the question is: 'Is the market large enough to support it?' – as all but two of the studies included in this book have been largely implemented, the answer in all the cases was that in somebody's mind it was. There are some schemes that are based on market research and others based on intuitive feelings and yet others simply on hopes. There are a number of urban design projects around the world, however, that are largely uninhabited because the market was incorrectly identified. Muong Thong Thani in Bangkok is possibly the best known (see Marshall, 2003).

The public and private sectors have different but overlapping images of the marketplace. The former thinks in terms of future tax revenues and the latter in terms of the perceptions of current or future demands. The private sector is concerned about the purchasing power of potential investors and their disposal incomes in deciding on programme mixes. The public sector may intervene in terms of its perceptions of the public interest and, ideally, on behalf of the needs of those people in whom the private sector is uninterested.

The market and its values are not static. Fashions change. All-of-a-piece designs that evolve over long periods of time thus often undergo substantial changes not only in the facilities provided but also in aesthetic qualities in order to be up-to-date. The market is segmented into many parts in terms of the culture, stage of life cycle and socio-economic status of the people who form it. Each urban design project described in this book has been aimed at a particular segment of the market. Each property developer feels comfortable in targeting one sector rather than another. One of the urban design questions is: 'How can developments be shaped so that private developers will provide public interest facilities when the market is incapable of supporting them?'

Controls and Incentives

A number of the legal mechanisms used in city planning shape the built environment. Zoning (often called land-use regulation) is a prime example. Taxation policies are another. Most zoning ordinances demand the segregation of activities on behalf of the public interest in terms of public health and other amenity variables.

Many such ordinances are now being rewritten to encourage the integration of mutually supportive uses. Zoning is also used to establish the height and size of buildings, building uses and parking requirements, the setbacks (or not) required from the street and, often, building materials. It is, however, generally used for establishing land uses at a block-by-block level. Zoning categories generally apply to areas of cities bounded by streets creating what are called 'planners' blocks'. They are not the blocks of life. Urban designers should generally be concerned with what happens on both sides of a street. Streets are the seams of urban life.

The limitation of zoning as a design tool is that it does not deal effectively with the creation of behaviour settings and aesthetic displays. The courts generally frown on spot, site-by-site zoning. Yet the quality of the public realm depends on such details. The use of zoning in conjunction with special districts and incentives can, nevertheless, accomplish much.

Carrots and Sticks in Urban Design

Both incentives and disincentives have been widely used to shape cities and often form part of piece-by-piece urban design packages to structure city precincts in specific directions (see Chapter 9). The incentives involve financial subsidies in some form or other. The sticks involve measures that are financially punitive, directly or indirectly. Many urban design control packages have both punitive and incentive components operating simultaneously in order to get schemes built in accordance with a conceptual design's objectives. What is legal very much depends on the political system in which public actions take place. Control packages, however legal they may be, cannot operate against market forces; they have to operate with them.

Carrots

Many of the carrots encouraging developers to do what they would otherwise be disinclined to do involve the use of zoning codes. Land-use plans and zoning codes have traditionally been employed to avoid the negative impacts of development. The questions then asked in situations like that in New York already mentioned were: 'Can these tools be used to shape cities to achieve desired ends?' and 'Can incentives be developed to encourage development to take a particular direction and provide particular facilities that are desirable and in the public interest but not as profitable for developers as building for other uses?'

A number of possible incentives are available for shaping and supporting urban design objectives. Government subsidies have already been mentioned. There are other types of carrots. Floor space incentives usually allow a developer to make a greater profit by building a taller or bulkier building than a zoning ordinance allows in return for including some non-profit making or not-so-profitable amenity in a proposed development. Such a design incentive involves a trade-off between having a desired facility and pedestrians (and vegetation) having less exposure to the sky at ground level.

The transfer of development rights from one site to another has been another tool that has been used to protect specific buildings and districts deemed worthy of maintaining in their present character yet being located where a property developer has the legal right to develop in a different manner. The incentive is to provide the developer with above legal rights in another location while buying out development rights in the original location at less than market value.

All incentives boil down to assisting property developers with financing in some form or another. Lowering taxes is one. Another used to meet urban design ends is through tax increment financing. It is not a legal technique in most countries. In the United States, however, it is available in a number of states. In California it was made possible by a 1962 amendment to the state's constitution. The amendment allows property developers working in a precinct of a municipality that has a plan supported by its citizens, to benefit directly from the increment in property taxes that accrue due to the improvements made by them within that area. This increase in tax revenue is ploughed back into further improving and/or maintaining the area well. The coordinating frame – the development plan and controls – for the continued development of the area can then be publicly funded (see the description of Glendale in Chapter 8).

Sticks

There are a number of specific disincentives that urban designers can use for shaping development. Their use is often problematic unless supported by evidence that can persuade the courts and/or administrative tribunals that they are justified. One of the major disincentives to carrying out a project is the financial cost of doing so in comparison to the financial return to be received. Such sticks may take the form of increased taxes, slowing down the approval process for projects not regarded as complying with design guidelines, for instance, and the direct payments of fees.

Many city centres are crowded with drivers in automobiles. The standard response is to create wider roads, more one-way streets and more parking facilities and/or to improve mass transit systems. An alternative that involves no physical design, but rather requires the direct payment of fees is in place in Singapore and in London. It is to charge people for driving into the central business district. In the City of London, the traffic moved at 16 kilometres per hour (10 miles per hour). In early 2003, a road levy of £5.00 was imposed in an effort to persuade people to use the metropolitan area's bus services and antiquated underground system. The goal was to reduce journey times within the City by 20% to 30%. Reports are that it has been at least partially successful.

A different tactic was used in Bellevue near Seattle to encourage workers in the central area of the city to use the bus system (see Chapter 9). It was to make parking more difficult. The number of parking spaces required per 1000 square feet

Figure 2.8   MetroCenter, Bethesda, Maryland in 1993.

of new development in the area was reduced thus raising parking costs. At the same time bus services were improved. The increase in ridership has been noticeable but some organizations have chosen not to locate in Bellevue because of parking costs. The trade-off has been thought to be worthwhile by both citizens and officials of the city.

Another example, often challenged in court, is the use of moratoria. Moratoria to halt development for a period can be used to:

1 create a pause while a coordinating plan is developed;
2 halt development when the consequences of development will be negative;
3 divert growth from one area to another (when there is a demand for growth).

The application of moratoria can have a direct impact on urban design, particularly in the development of a building programme and the implementation of projects. In Bethesda, Maryland a series of moratoria were used to shift potential development in outlying areas into its downtown core where a station on Washington's Metro system had been built. The MetroCenter project (see Figure 2.8), a large-scale transportation/building/urban design scheme, was helped considerably by two moratoria on building outside the city centre. The legal basis depended on the prediction that dispersed development would swamp the road system of the suburb with traffic beyond its capacity to cope. The moratoria encouraged further development in its downtown creating a strong downtown core associated with the Metro stop. The quality of the development was ensured by the use of design guidelines and the use of a strong design review process.

A moratorium needs hard data on a development's potential negative effects to validate it. Nassau County, New York successfully imposed a moratorium on growth until the problem of the increased salination of its groundwater supply could be solved. A moratorium on commercial development over 10,000 square feet in size in Walnut Creek, California until the traffic congestion problems could be remedied was, however, struck down in the courts because it was inconsistent with the master plan (*Lesher Communications, Inc. versus City of Walnut Creek, Contra Costa Supreme Court, 1986*). The use of moratoria in the United States received a boost in 2002 when the United States Supreme Court supported their use without having to compensate those whose development proposals were delayed (*Tahoe-Sierra Preservation Council, Inc. versus Tahoe Regional Planning Agency, 23 April 2002*) (Lucero and Soule, 2002).

Design Review

To some observers, the truly creative activity in the design process lies neither in the design of the programme nor that of the building or complex but rather in the evaluation of possible schemes. Recognizing and selecting good designs, especially departures from the norm is a highly risky business and there are many examples of award-winning schemes that have turned out to be failures in terms of people's lives. The evaluation of designs involves:

1 predicting the future context in which the scheme will function aesthetically and behaviourally;
2 predicting how the scheme will work in that future;
3 evaluating its performance against other possible schemes.

The future is, however, unknown although we can make reasonable predictions based upon sound information about trends in society. Should, however, one 'play safe' or 'go for broke'?

In some places the process of design review is carried out purely subjectively and in others an open-to-view system of scoring is used. In the latter case the goals are weighted, recognizing that some goals are more important than others. Each aspect of design is evaluated numerically based on experts' opinions in terms of the stated goals for a development site. The process may be highly transparent but it has received considerable criticism because of the subjectivity of the evaluation on each of the dimensions of a design. The openness does, however, present a developer with an understanding of the logic of the review process and what is purported to be in the public interest and what is not.

The Battery Park City Planning Authority received 27 proposals from property developers for the building of Rector Place in Battery Park City, New York (see Chapter 8). The question was: 'How should each possibility be evaluated?' Some variables such as financial return to the city in terms of tax revenue can be assessed with reasonable accuracy. Other dimensions of design such as 'fitness to

Numerical ranking	Name of project	A. Residential provision of dwellings	B. Pedestrian 1. links out from Metro	B. Pedestrian 2. pathways on private land	B. Pedestrian 3. places for public activity	B. Pedestrian 4. streetscape materials	B. Pedestrian 5. magnet uses	B. Pedestrian 6. encourage walking	B. Pedestrian 7. other enhancement	C. Effectiveness 1. building massing	C. Effectiveness 2. efficient interior	C. Effectiveness 3. orientation	C. Effectiveness 4. environmental quality	C. Effectiveness 5. other enhancement	D. Management provision of organization	Total score	Difference
1.	Chevy Chase Garden Plaza	8	7	1	1	2	6	2	4	1	2	2	1	2	3	42	12
2.	Artery Organization Headquarters Building	9	7	7	4	1	4	4	6	2	1	1	2	1	5	54	4
3.	7475 Wisconsin Avenue	9	1	2	5	6	1	1	5	4	4	4	5	5	6	58	10
4.	Gateway Building	9	8	7	3	3	2	3	8	3	3	3	4	8	4	68	11
5.	4600 East-West Highway	9	2	7	7	7	3	6	9	5	5	8	7	3	1	79	4
6.	Community Motors	6	5	5	7	4	6	7	9	6	7	5	3	6	7	83	3
7.	Franklin C. Salisbury Building	9	4	3	2	5	8	5	9	7	6	6	6	9	7	86	14
8.	Air Rights Hotel	5	3	6	6	8	5	7	9	8	9	9	9	9	7	100	4
9.	Woodmont Air Rights	9	6	4	6	8	7	7	9	9	8	7	8	9	7	104	
	Totals	73	43	42	41	44	42	42	68	45	45	45	45	52	47	674	

Courtesy of the Maryland-National Capital Parks and Planning Commission, Department of Parks and Planning

Figure 2.9 Potential projects evaluation scorecard, Bethesda, Maryland.

context' or 'urbane character' are not. They can, however, be defined operationally in a set of design guidelines as they were for Rector Place. Whether one agrees with the definition explicated in the guidelines or not, a building design can be objectively assessed by a review panel against the guidelines' demands. When the criteria are less sharply defined a scorecard such as that used in Bethesda, Maryland for projects forming part of the MetroCenter complex at least displays the design reviewers' thinking (see Figure 2.9).

In many planning jurisdictions around the world design policies and controls are poorly articulated or miss important issues. As a result, the review of development proposals and of designs is opaque. The clearer the design policies and guidelines, the more logically the choice of the best scheme can be made from amongst the possibilities available. The guidelines need to be based on evidence that they meet required ends in order to withstand challenges in the courts (Stamps, 1994).

The power that design review boards have in enforcing design guidelines and other design controls varies. At one extreme they have absolute veto power; at the other end they can merely make suggestions. In jurisdictions where there is a demand for development the coercive powers of design review boards are potentially more substantial than in places crying out for anybody to develop anything. In capitalist societies where the developer is a private company contracting out work to other property developers or selling off land to be developed by others, the power of the company's review panel may well be absolute. In the new town of Las Colinas outside Dallas in Texas, for example, the Las Colinas Association is a quasi-governmental group responsible for overseeing the quality of all the work done in the new town. It had a veto power over proposals as did the panel supervising the development of the Denver Technological Center (see Chapter 8).

Commentary

All urban designs are ultimately shaped not only by design ideas but also by public and private sector marketing decisions and sources of financing. The change in nature of urban design products since the beginning of the 1990s is due not only to changes in urban design ideologies but also to the change in capital markets. Finances for investments are being moved around internationally. Much development in the United States is financed by British and Canadian sources. Asian institutions have invested heavily in Australia, Canada and the United States. Much of the recent development in Vietnam (e.g. South Saigon) has come from Taiwan. Reliance on local sources still exists but financiers look for investment opportunities internationally and architects work internationally. Neither architects nor investment sources have shown much interest in local sensitivities (Abel, 2000; Olds, 2001). This attitude explains why so many projects (e.g. Lujiazui, Shanghai; see Chapter 8) are now financially pragmatic designs that are architecturally global in nature.

The range of mechanisms available to public officials and urban designers aiming to shape the behaviour settings and aesthetic qualities that they aim to create in specific schemes are generally universal but subject to local legal codes and precedents. The willingness of public agencies charged with protecting the public interest to do so varies from place to place too, as does the level of corruption and the willingness of government bodies and the courts to enforce laws and design guidelines. The case studies presented in this book range from those in totalitarian societies to laissez faire ones. Each needs to be seen within its political and social context.

3

An evolving typology of urban design projects

Urban designing involves the self-conscious intervention, great or small, into the marketplace for development and architectural services and the legal processes that shape the public realm of cities. The term public realm is understood here, as outlined in Chapter 1, in its broadest sense to include not only those elements of the built environment that are publicly owned and serve the public but also those elements, physical and social, that define public space and impinge on it visually and behaviourally. The question is: 'Can the cumulative experience represented in a set of case studies be organized into a framework that aids professionals to deal with the situations they confront?'

Types and Typology

A type, as understood here, is a construct of a product or a process that serves as a generic model of a way of thinking. There are many books in architecture on building types: schools, hospitals and houses. Design professional use them because they bring attention to the commonality of form requirements resulting from the purposes a building serves primarily in housing human activities, efficiently and in comfort. The concept of type has also, but less often, been applied to the aesthetic qualities of buildings.

Architects also design types to be emulated in solving categories of problems. Historically, the Unité d'Habitation was developed by Le Corbusier to be a type to be reproduced across the world (see Chapter 6). More recently, the pedestrian pocket has been promoted as a way to deal with problems of transportation and quality of life issues in residential area design (see Calthorpe, 1993). Contemporaneously the New Urbanist paradigm proposes an approach to design to be emulated (*Staff of New Urban News*, 2001). In all-of-a-piece design the buildings required to meet the specifications of a master plan are often identified by type (use, mass, aesthetic character). Here a type is concerned with the communality between cases, or examples, of urban designs. There are many ways of looking at types of urban design. The goal here is to make some sense of them by placing them in categories – by developing a typology of projects.

The word 'typology' is ambiguous. In its purest sense it refers to the study and theory of types and of classification systems. Here typology refers to a classification system. A good one is simple but powerful. It must be easy to use and cover all the types of concern with clarity. It has the least number of variables that can explain phenomena. It must enable a person to understand the constancies that lie behind specific examples.

Categorization helps us to organize our thoughts. One simple way is to distinguish among the various product types generally subsumed under the rubric 'urban design' and, more importantly, procedural types. The former deals with the products of urban design work and the latter the processes by which they are implemented. It is the latter, as argued in Chapter 2, that really gets to the heart of urban designers' activities.

In a diverse field it is inevitable that types of activity overlap and are not necessarily easy to categorize. Is a building such as the Unité d'Habitation, a vertical neighbourhood, a work of urban design or a work of architecture? Or both? It was part of a broader plan for the city of the future (Le Corbusier, 1953). The investment in individual buildings so that they act as catalysts for urban development is both a policy issue and a concern for buildings as urban design. As a result, the idea of buildings as catalysts for urban development appears in two chapters in this book: under the rubric of 'The Products of Architecture and the Nature of Urban Design' (see Chapter 6) and 'Plug-in Urban Design' (see Chapter 10). The ambiguities in any categorization can be disturbing but have to be tolerated. As the field of urban design develops so no doubt will the precision of the categorization of its types.

The Utility and Problems of Typologies

The design fields rely heavily on types in thinking about designing building programs, or briefs, and buildings themselves (Symes, 1994; Francis, 2001). All professional offices have books describing building, street, or open space configurations pertaining to classes of activities. Any classification system that can help recall information and/or bring attention to key variables that have to be addressed by a designer in a particular situation is helpful. How good is the typology developed here?

Fifty-odd case studies have been classified in this book. The typology presented has enabled them to be classified firstly according to the process by which they were generated and built, secondly, according to the type of product they are and thirdly, according to the urban design paradigm within which they were designed. By using the typology presented here a person can begin to understand the process, the product and design ideology within which a particular design was created.

The potential problem in using any typology is that it focuses on classifying the similarities between examples and not their differences. In practice it is easy to see the situation one is facing as being a particular type because of some superficial similarities and then to use the procedures common to that category in trying to solve current problems (Schneekloth and Franck, 1994). There are a number of examples in this book where urban design paradigms have been used out of the contexts in which they were developed. This problem can be avoided if the cases are presented clearly focusing on their essences rather than their superficialities.

Urban Design Procedural Types and Product Types

I stated earlier that there are four major procedural types of urban design. They were:

1 total urban design where one team is in control of the whole project;
2 all-of-a-piece urban design where one team creates a master, or conceptual, plan and writes guidelines for the development of individual sites within that plan by different entrepreneurs and their architects;
3 piece-by-piece urban design where proposals to get specific activities into an area are controlled by zoning codes and incentives and penalties;
4 plug-in urban design in which infrastructure elements are used as catalysts for development.

Design professionals, however, most frequently think of urban design in terms of product types and much of the literature deals with urban design in that way.

Urban design product types can be categorized in many ways. It is impossible to devise a fine-toothed categorization system that is exhaustive and in which the types do not overlap. The typology used here is simple. Urban design product types can be:

1 new towns;
2 urban precincts of which there are many types, new and renewed;
3 elements of infrastructure;
4 possibly individual items within the city that add lustre to it: clock towers, monuments, works of art and curiosity objects.

The focus of attention in this book is on the first three types but each has many subcategories. They all encompass planning, landscape architecture, and architectural work in a unique manner that adds up to being urban design.

New Towns

A 'new town', to purists, is a settlement that is self-consciously built from scratch, usually on previously unbuilt-on land. To be a new town it has to provide all the amenities of life including employment opportunities. There is no census of new towns designed and built during the second half of the twentieth century but the number is in the thousands. They range in size and importance from small company towns to the capitals of countries. Almost all have been either total or all-of-a-piece urban designs.

A number of countries have had the creation of new towns as part of their political agenda. The policies have resulted in fiat towns, some large enough to be thought of as cities. Between 1950 and 1990, the Soviet Union employed new settlements to extend central control over its constituent republics. The reasons elsewhere have been economic or social. During the latter half of the twentieth century, over 20 new towns were built in the United Kingdom in order to keep London's population down to a manageable size and to encourage industry to locate outside the southeast corner of the country. Runcorn is an example (see Chapter 4).

In Europe the new towns tend to have been the products of government policy. In North America, in contrast, private companies have built the genuine new towns (rather than simply large suburbs) not the public sector. Columbia in Maryland and Reston, Virginia are probably the best-known examples. Begun in the 1960s, Columbia has a population of 100,000 and employment opportunities approximating the number of workers in the city although many people commute into Columbia to work and many residents in the city commute out. There are few such new towns in the United States because the land acquisition and infrastructure costs are high and the developing company must be capable of considerable investment prior to any return on capital being received. New towns do, however, continue to be built in the country. Las Colinas in Texas has been under construction for almost 20 years now (see Figure 3.1a to see the imagery sought). Elsewhere too they are being built, especially satellite cities. Shongshang Lake in southern China, for instance, is barely underway (see Figure 3.1b).

Many new towns are company towns. Some have a mining or other resource base and others have been manufacturing cities or military settlements. Some of the non-military examples are the products of government policy, particularly in socialist countries, but others have been built by private industrial organizations to suit their own purposes. The towns vary considerably in size and longevity. They have been as small as 500 people while others have over a hundred thousand inhabitants.

The designs of the new towns fall into a number of categories depending on the paradigms prevalent at the time of their creation. The new towns in the Anglo-American world have generally followed Garden City principles while those in Continental Europe and East Asia have followed Rationalist principles. Evenwithin the prevailing paradigm there have been differences in designs. British new town designs, all loosely garden cities, fall into four eras depending on contemporary perceptions of the problems to be solved and the patterns required to solve them. Las Colinas is being designed with the automobile in mind. In addition, individual designers strive to stamp their own identity on the designs.

Precincts

Most urban designs do not deal with new towns but with precincts – smaller areas of cities and new, predominantly residential, areas on the edge of cities. They may

(a)

(b)

Collection of the author

Figure 3.1 New town design. (a) Central Las Colinas proposal, 1986 and (b) Sonshang Lake, Guangdong proposal, 2004.

be designed *de novo* or be the subject of renewal. The precincts in cities may be for commercial, residential, or for entertainment uses, but many are now mixed types. Some have been built as total designs; others have been all-of-a-piece designs.

There are a number of new precincts of cities that have been called 'new towns'. The use of this term can be a little misleading. The new towns of the city-state of Singapore, although they contain many of the amenities of a city and are also employment centres, have little industry and the heart of Singapore remains the cultural centre of the city. These new towns are, given the terms used in this

Figure 3.2 Roosevelt Island, New York in 1993.

book, major precincts of the larger Singapore metropolitan area. There are other similar examples.

During the 1970s the term 'new-town-in-town' was used to describe large mixed-use urban design projects on cleared brown-field sites. In New York City, for instance, Roosevelt Island (see Figure 3.2), formerly Welfare Island, and Battery Park City were referred to as such. Welfare Island, the home to a number of aging hospitals and other obsolete institutions has been transformed into a residential precinct with the retail and other institutional facilities required to support it. Surrounded by water, it is indeed a clear entity. So is Battery Park City with the Hudson on one side and the West Side Highway on the other. Neither was considered to be a self-contained entity.

Much urban design in cities consists of relatively small enclaves of like use buildings. They may be commercial or institutional types. Penn Center in Philadelphia, a relatively small enclave of commercial buildings related to a railway station and the new CBD for Beijing, are examples of commercial precincts (see Figure 3.3a). Lincoln Center in New York is an example of a cultural complex (see Figure 7.7). One of the great urban debates is over whether such facilities should indeed be agglomerated into a single unit or distributed throughout the city. This question was also raised about the decision to assemble so many of the facilities that were required for the highly successful 2000 Olympic Games in Sydney, Australia into a single precinct (see Figure 3.3b).

Campuses are a special type of precinct – a unified set of buildings set in a predominantly park-like environment and separated by distance (by the use of a park or roadway) or fences from the remainder of the city or countryside. The university campus is typical. While some universities are merged into the surrounding city: the Sorbonne, Stellenbosch and the University of the District of Columbia, many others, especially recent ones, are separate entities. The same urban design idea appears in the layout of office and business parks. The Denver Technological Center on the periphery of that city clearly falls into this category and it is, in many ways, the city's new downtown (see Chapter 8).

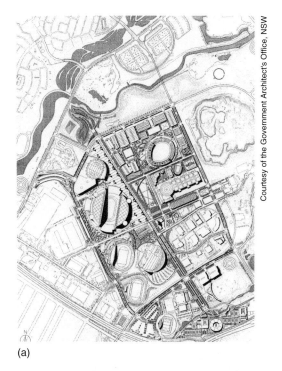

Courtesy of the Government Architect's Office, NSW

(a)

(b)

Figure 3.3 Precinct design. (a) The plan of the 2000 Olympic games site, Sydney and (b) a model of the proposed CBD for Beijing, 2004.

In cities throughout the world the considerable expansion has taken place at the periphery. While the population of the metropolitan Philadelphia continues to grow, the population of the core city itself declined from over two million in 1950 to a little over a million in 2000. The major growth has been suburban. Vast tracts of housing and accompanying commercial and retail facilities have been built in the suburbs. In countries, such as India, the major developers of such urban designs have been the Public Works Departments of the Central and State governments. In the United States, it has been the private developer who has been responsible for almost all the development although much has been made possible by the federally funded highway system and other federal government subsidies. At best these suburbs have been thoughtfully designed in terms of providing the amenities to enable all segments of the population to lead full lives. At worst, they are simply dormitories.

The new suburbs have generally been built along one of two different lines of thought: the Bauhaus/Le Corbusian model or the Garden City model. The outskirts of many cities in Europe (such as Paris and Madrid) and Latin American cities (such as Caracas; see Figure 3.4) have major developments of tower or slab blocks of housing set in park-like areas on their peripheries. They have been influenced by Le Corbusier. Most of the suburban development in countries such as the United States and Australia have followed the Garden City ideal and still do. More recently the New Urbanist ideology, a Neo-Traditionalist approach to urban design, has had a wide degree of support.

Many precincts do not have clear edges but have strong cores such as a square or a street. The design of streets and squares is generally the purview of landscape architecture but it can be urban design. It is landscape architecture if only the open space is designed; it is urban design if the enclosing elements are included in the design. In the latter case they form a precinct.

Urban renewal

Urban renewal, as its name suggests, refers to the process of rebuilding areas of cities that have become obsolete and abandoned, or are in a state of considerable decay. Unless cities become economically static urban renewal projects will continue to be undertaken. Over the last half of the twentieth century much has been learnt about how best they can be conducted. The field of urban design as a professional endeavour has grown with the experience of building total or all-of-a-piece urban renewal projects.

Sometimes, urban renewal has involved slum clearance and the total rebuilding of environments but more usually now it has involved selective demolition and the integration of the old and the new in their design (e.g. Charles Center, Baltimore; see Chapter 5). Often the urban renewal occurs in a laissez faire manner without any overall cooperative intention. It would not be regarded as urban design here (although some projects might be regarded as piece-by-piece urban design). Some urban design projects have involved the retooling of existing areas by upgrading their physical infrastructure and the provision of new uses for existing buildings

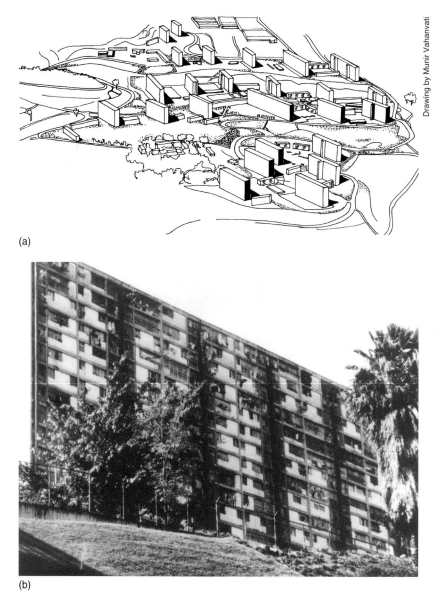

Drawing by Munir Vahanvati

(a)

(b)

Figure 3.4 The 23 de enero (originally 2 de deciembre) housing development, Caracas in 1998. (a) Massing diagram and (b) a view of one housing block.

(e.g. Ghirardelli Square, San Francisco and Clarke Quay, Singapore, both described later in this book). Others have retained the original mix.

After the devastation of World War II in Europe, vast segments of cities were rebuilt sometimes replicating the past (e.g. Warsaw), but more frequently they were modernized. Cities such as Coventry and Rotterdam acquired new hearts. In European and the North American cities, major slum clearance and new housing estate projects have been carried out. They have had mixed results because the highly physically deteriorated world they replaced was often socially viable. The new products were unable to provide an environment for the re-creation of that social stability. Many of them have been demolished and rebuilt too. In some cases, such as the Paternoster Square precinct north of St Paul's cathedral in London, areas were rebuilt only to be later demolished and rebuilt anew (see Chapter 8).

A new type of urban renewal project began to appear during the last two decades of the twentieth century. As the demographic characteristics of suburban areas changed so the demand for new facilities in their shopping centres occurred. What have appeared are new suburban downtowns rather like the traditional cores of cities. Sometimes this process has been abetted by the building of a new rail link (e.g. Bethesda, Maryland; see Figure 2.8). At other times it has happened because the suburbs have strategic locations on major traffic routes between major cities (Garreau, 1991). What has generally occurred has been that two- or three-storey high precincts have been replaced by high-rise commercial and residential developments. This process has often taken place willy-nilly but there are many examples where the redevelopment has involved a concerted urban design effort (e.g. Glendale, see Chapter 8 and Bellevue, Washington, see Chapter 9).

Infrastructure Design

The nature of the infrastructure is what visually distinguishes one city from another as much as the nature of its architecture. There are various ways of considering the infrastructure of cities but the most inclusive manner covers everything that is part of the public domain whether privately or publicly owned. In this view the streets and other transport facilities, the schools and public institutions, such as libraries and museums, can all be part of the infrastructure of cities.

Many of the issues involved in the design of infrastructure fall outside the scope of urban design *per se*, falling into one or other of the realms of city planning and civil engineering. The consequences of such decisions for the design of precincts of cities are, however, substantial because of the multiplier and side effects they create. The public concern in designing infrastructure components is not only with the services they supply but also with their catalytic effect. Clearly the location and design of roads and streets had a major effect on the twentieth century city. It will in the twenty-first too. For instance, highway development has made edge cities possible and the building of rail links and new train stations has spurred major developments around them in many cities. Bethesda in Maryland has already been cited. In London the hope has been that the new Jubilee Line of the underground system will do the same thing (Wordsearch *et al.*, 2001). Sometimes land development and station location have followed a coordinated plan before construction begins, as in Singapore (see Chapter 10).

Source: Turner (1984)

Figure 3.5   The University of Illinois, Chicago campus in 1970.

Often, however, it has been left to the marketplace to dictate the results after the infrastructure has been built.

There are a number of issues involved in infrastructure design that have been of direct concern in urban design. One has been the separation of pedestrian and vehicular traffic in order to provide a more congenial and safer environment. The separation can take place in horizontal or in vertical space. The former approach has been standard, with separate sidewalks being provided for pedestrians, but there have been many examples of vertical segregation too. In many places throughout the world some vehicular streets have been closed off to traffic and turned into pedestrian malls. The goal has been to attract people to use the facilities that line them. Sometimes such malls have proven to be highly successful, and at other times not (see the case of Oak Park, Illinois, in Chapter 5). These schemes have been predominantly landscape architecture projects. They continue to be built.

The separation of pedestrians and vehicular traffic vertically has been carried out in many places, again with varying degrees of success. These systems take various forms. One form is with vehicular traffic kept at ground level and pedestrian plazas and walkways built above them (e.g. La Défense, Paris; see Chapter 8), and the University of Illinois, Circle Campus, Chicago; see Figure 3.5). Another such type provides pedestrian bridges linking interior quasi-public spaces of buildings in an extended skyway pedestrian system (e.g. Minneapolis, Minnesota; see Chapter 10). Another form has pedestrians moving below vehicles. Many cities have underground networks of passages enabling pedestrians to cross from block to block without interference. They continue to be built too. They can be bright and vibrant places but often they are gloomy.

Photograph by Susannah Lang

Figure 3.6 Pedestrian ways as objects in space, Battery Park City, New York in 2003.

Miscellaneous: Individual Objects in Urban Space

There are two types of objects apart from buildings that get awards for urban design. The first is comprised of works of art, usually sculptures but also murals that are often introduced to give some focus and interest to a dull space or to enliven a blank wall, or as an element of civic or corporate boosterism. The second category is primarily comprised of individual elements of the city, such as monuments, fountains, clock towers and street furniture. The design of such objects falls outside the scope of this book although when included as part of a larger scheme they are discussed in passing.

Monuments are of particular importance. They have a special significance as preservers of collective memories and as symbols of the identity and the self-worth of nations or smaller groups of people. They can sometimes be the foci of the collective life of a people. Clock towers, obelisks and fountains are used as visual focal points in many urban design schemes, particularly those imbued with City Beautiful, or Baroque, overtones (Robinette, 1976). They act as landmarks and reinforce the nodes of urban life (Figure 3.6).

Urban Design Paradigms

Another way of classifying urban design is by the major paradigm used as the basis for design. Paradigms are models regarded as exemplars of good practice. Much architectural history involves identifying the paradigms of the major movements in architecture and the patterns they promoted in response to what their proponents perceived to be contemporary problems. In urban design the twentieth century began with the City Beautiful, a Baroque approach to the geometry of cities, as the predominant paradigm (see Figure 3.7a). Almost all the entries in the competition for the design of Canberra (1911) were City Beautiful schemes. Contemporaneously the Empiricist (the realist) and Rationalist (the idealist) branches of the modern movement developed. The Garden City (see Figure 3.7b) and the neighbourhood unit (see Figure 6.10) exemplify the former; Tony Garnier's Cité Industrielle (*c.* 1910) and the generic urban design models of Le Corbusier (see Figure 3.7c) and the Bauhaus (see Figure 7.18) exemplify the latter. Throughout the twentieth century there were tensions between the two lines of thought that still persist (Buder, 1990; Ellin, 1999). There has also been the urban design of commercial pragmatism (see Figure 3.7e) and explorations with radical geometries (mainly implemented at the building scale: see Figure 3.7f).

The Empiricists tend to rely on precedents and the observation of what works and does not work as the basis for design thinking. There are many pasts that one can look at so there are divergent lines of thinking about the future amongst Empiricists. The small country town was one past; the medieval city was another. Similarly there are divergent lines of thinking about the future amongst Rationalists. Rationalists break away from past ideas (or, at least they claim to do so). Their models are based on various assumptions about imagined future ways of life. Simplistically, the urban design paradigms of the former school of thought are exemplified by organic plans and the latter by rectilinear geometries. The former face streets and the latter turn their backs to the street (see Ellin, 1999, for a fuller analysis of current directions in urban design).

All these paradigms held sway to a greater and lesser extent during the second half of the twentieth century giving way, partially at least, to post-Modernist ideas as the result of the severe criticism that Modernist design ideologies received in the 1960s and 1970s. These ideas are represented in the work of both the Neo-Rationalists and the Neo-Empiricists (see Broadbent, 1990; Lang, 1994; Ellin, 1999). The latter is best represented by the Neo-Traditional approaches to urban design that evolved into the New Urbanist (Katz, 1994) and Smart Growth models. Understanding these paradigms is important because they illustrate what many urban designers considered and consider the contemporary problems of their societies to be.

Each paradigm represents a worldview. Each represents a perception of the best way to go about addressing the urban problems of the world in the public interest. None address the question of how one goes about identifying problems and their potential solutions; they deal with products not procedures. The development of each paradigm, nevertheless, involves considerable creative thought. The difficulty is that each tends to become frozen into a formula of patterns that are applied without much thought because they are perceived to represent the 'best practice' and being 'up-to-date' – modern.

Figure 3.7 A sample of twentieth century design paradigms. (a) The City Beautiful, (b) the Garden City, (c) the Rationalist City, (d) the Neo-Traditional City, (e) the city of commercial pragmatism and (f) a model for the deconstructed city?

A Typology of Urban Design Projects

Each project described in this book can be categorized by procedural type, project type and the major paradigm employed, and thus the foci of concern it represents (Figure 3.8). The capital complex in Chandigarh (see Chapter 7), for instance, is a total urban design, a precinct design, with its major focus being on the symbolic function of urban design as a display (what some critics call 'urban design as theatre') and carried out within a Rationalist mode of thought. Battery Park City, in contrast, is an all-of-a-piece precinct design carried out within a Neo-Empiricist intellectual framework.

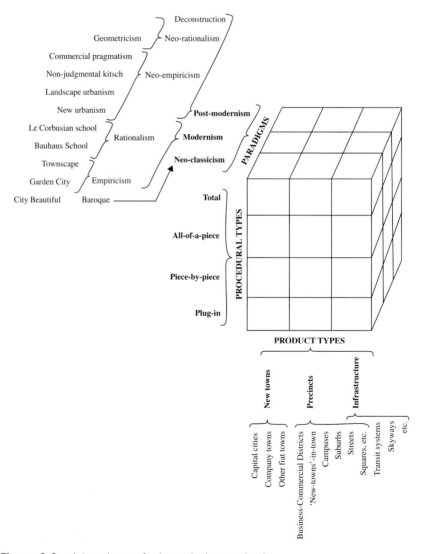

Figure 3.8   A typology of urban design projects.

Commentary

In discussing the nature of urban design, the literature has focused much more heavily on product types and design paradigms than on procedural types. There are many books on new towns and new urban places. They focus on the architecture of places and neither on the processes of bringing them into existence nor on what dimensions they are successes or failures. The reason is that design is largely a mimetic process in which known, or generic, types are adapted to particular situations. In this book, I have classified projects primarily by procedural type and then by product types but have attempted to point out their focus of attention and the intellectual paradigms within which they fall.

An understanding of types is the basis for problem solving in all the design fields. For architecture it is building types (e.g. for housing types, see Building Types Study 832, 2004), for landscape architecture open space types (e.g. Plazas; see Krier, 1990) and for planning it is probably city types (e.g. global cities; Simmonds and Hack, 2000). How types will be used, professionally and in education, shapes their nature. No single typology is correct. Each has advantages and poses potential constraints on whoever uses it. The one presented here should be regarded as a first, but significant, step in developing a typology of urban design projects. Its utility will depend on how others can or cannot use it. The basic categorization is, however, sound although the labels given will sound strange to many ears. No doubt the typology will evolve as the field of urban design and the range of projects that are subsumed under that title evolve.

Kresege, College, Santa Cruz, California in 1993

THE TRADITIONAL DESIGN PROFESSIONS, THEIR PRODUCTS AND URBAN DESIGN

PART 2

One of the reasons for there being so much confusion over the nature of urban design is that each of the traditional design professions regards the products of its own domain as urban design if they are located in cities. In addition, architects assume many urban problems can be treated as architecture, landscape architects as landscape architecture and city planners as city planning. They look at urban design through the norms of their professional products. The position taken here is that most of such professional work in urban environments is on the periphery of urban design *per se*. By stating that it is on the periphery does not mean that it is unimportant in enhancing the quality of human settlements, but that it really is part of the core work of the three professions: city planning (see Chapter 4), landscape architecture (see Chapter 5) or architecture (see Chapter 6).

The labours of these three major environmental design fields (civil engineering could easily be added to the list) involve collaborative work. City planning involves the collaboration of sociologists, economists and lawyers as well as planners in designing urban policies and programmes. Architecture involves a variety of engineers and specialists in the design of any building and landscape architecture the assistance of engineers and horticulturalists. Urban design is the field that involves all three design fields but except for some total urban designs not at the level of detail that they address. Urban design products are different and so is the process by which they are developed.

The nature of the city-planning endeavour varies considerably across the world. In a number of countries in Europe and Asia, it is very much urban design oriented. It deals not only with broad urban policies but also with precinct plans and specifications for the buildings within them. More generally in the English-speaking world, however, city-planning deals with broad policy concerns that may or may not have an impact, predicted or not, on the physical quality of cities. Much of the attention in recent years has been focused on social and economic change with policies and programmes as the products of this type of planning. Physical planning, other than in dealing with the desired distribution of land uses, has been very much neglected. The product of such city-planning work is the land-use master plan with zoning codes as the mechanism for achieving its ends. The social and economic policies developed by municipal governments do impinge on urban design, but whether city planning and urban designing are conterminous or whether urban design is simply a sub-field of city planning or vice versa is open to considerable debate. Some product types may well be both city planning and urban design. Many new towns fall into this category.

Both landscape architecture and architecture are concerned with the detailed design and implementation of specific products at one time. Given this observation it could be argued that what has been identified as total urban design is often simply large-scale architecture. The logic for including some such work in the mainstream of urban design in Part 3: 'The Core of Urban Design Work: Procedures and Products' is that its comprehensive treatment brings together all the design fields into focusing on single three-dimensional, multi-building design endeavours. Neither landscape architectural nor architectural work, *per se*, does that.

The qualities of streets, squares and other urban places and the links between them, as behaviour settings and as aesthetic displays, are amongst the core concerns of urban design. The distinction between landscape architecture and the core of urban design work described in 'Part 3' depends on whether the enclosing elements form part of the design or whether it is simply the ground surface between buildings that is of concern. The first is urban design; the latter falls into the realm of landscape architecture. Many landscape architects will dispute this position saying that any design in cities is urban design. In this way, landscape architecture differentiates itself from horticulture and garden design. If landscape architecture broadens its concerns to embrace the three-dimensional world of buildings it is well placed to claim urban design as its very own.

Architectural societies around the world give urban design awards to the products of everyday architectural work – individual buildings. Certainly, all buildings affect their surroundings but many architects pay little heed to how their work affects the public realm. Either they know not how to do so or the social context in which they are working prevents them from doing so. Most buildings represent private rather than public interests. Architects' prime obligations are to their clients – those who pay them – and to their own need to market themselves in order to stay in practice. It is only through the application of controls and design guidelines that they are compelled to deal with public interest concerns. Single building design is not urban design except, perhaps, when a building has been located as a catalyst to encourage development around it as part of a public policy. Designing a complex of buildings may well be urban design.

The three chapters that comprise this part of the book cover the work of the traditional design professions and the products that are associated with them. The products described in the case studies used to illustrate the work of what these three professions regard as urban design are only really urban design if they deal: (1) with the three-dimensional world and (2) their impact on their context, and not simply the consequences of the context for the design. The conclusion ultimately is that the product-oriented view of urban design is an important but limited one, if the desire is to really understand the nature of the field and its complexities.

The products of city planning and the nature of urban design

Urban design is often considered to simply be city planning. Is it? To many architects any scheme containing more than one building is city planning. Thus to them most of what is described as the core of urban design in Part 3 of this book is city planning. To other observers, city planning is land-use planning and to yet others it involves the formulation of economic and social policies. All city plans deal, explicitly or implicitly, with urban design in one form or another. This statement does not mean that city planning is focused on urban design, but that many planning policies that are not seen to have design implications do shape the architectural and urban landscape of cities and rural areas alike (Craighead, 1991).

City, or town, planning is seen differently in much of Europe, Latin America and Asia than in the English-speaking world. In addition, the concerns of the field have not been stable. In the United States, for instance, emphases have varied from city to city and have changed over time. For much of the period covered in this book, the focus of attention has been on social and economic planning. In continental Europe, planning and architecture are generally more closely allied in a single field that focuses heavily on the physical qualities of cities. As a result city planning is often urban designing.

A number of city-planning leaders such as Edmund Bacon, once head of the City Planning Commission in Philadelphia, were very much concerned with urban design in the 1960s and 1970s (see Bacon, 1974). The economic state of American cities in that era and the following decade was, however, so precarious that urban design concerns were often thrust aside. Planners began to regard the built environment as only marginally important in establishing the quality of life of people. The lesson of having done so has been learnt from those cities that strove for development at any cost as well as those that successfully maintained an interest in urban design. The latter have tended to do well.

The quality of the built city and its behaviour settings has proven to be economically important. From the early 1990s onwards many planning agencies have established sections on urban design and have been employing professionals knowledgeable either through education or practice about urban design. In many places this heightened awareness of the importance of the cityscape represents a dramatic turn around in the perceptions of what makes a good city amongst mainstream city planners. It also represents an effort by the planning profession to recapture an area of concern that they turned their backs on.

Traditional Planning Product Types: Comprehensive Plans

Most city-planning deals with existing cities. If its purpose is to shape the future of a city, the products will be in the form of written policies. These policies have to be accepted as binding by some legislative body – at the city level it is the municipal council – if they are to lead to any action. The task of creating specific programmes then has to be assigned to specific agencies and a budget has to be established to fund the programmes. If the goal of planning is to create a land-use pattern for the future city, the product will be in the form of a two-dimensional master plan coloured according to a code designating the type of activities (industrial, commercial, residential, etc.) that a block of land should house. Almost always the streets have been regarded as borders between land uses not as seams linking their two sides into a unified precinct. To implement such plans, zoning codes are developed, and the site coverage and, in the United States, the Floor Area Ratio (FAR) (the ratio of total usable floor area to the site known as Floor Space Ratio (FSR) elsewhere) are specified. The zoning code will assign permissible land uses but may also specify the allowable height of buildings and the number of parking places required. The goal has been to avoid conflicts between the activities that take place in each area of a city. The design implications of these ordinances on what the resulting built environments will offer are seldom fully considered. One of the reasons for the development of urban design as a specialized professional activity is that environmental quality has been poorly considered in city planning.

Urban design and city planning overlap when city planning involves the actual physical design of cities or their precincts. It overlaps when these plans deal with visions for the three-dimensional city and with methods to achieve that vision. Thus the design of Brasília (see the case study in Chapter 7) or Seaside (see Chapter 8) can be seen as both city planning and urban design. The prime product of city planning has, however, been the comprehensive plan. It is clearly a city-planning product.

The Design Dimension of Comprehensive Planning for Existing Cities

Comprehensive planning attempts to deal simultaneously with economic, social, and physical development and design policies. Sometimes the quality of the built environment is a concern but at other times, particularly in eras or localities of slow economic growth, it is peripheral. What becomes important then is development at any cost, provided it brings in jobs and/or increases in the tax base of the cash-strapped municipality. In such circumstances even the most basic of environmental concerns – pollution, traffic problems and the degradation of the natural world – are shelved in the name of progress. Design quality is seen as a minor issue; it is perceived to be concerned only with urban cosmetics and not with life – not with behaviour settings.

Physical planning has very much focused on the distribution of land uses and transportation concerns (ideally in an interrelated manner) and, until recently, certainly with the segregation of activities so that polluting and annoying uses are kept out of residential areas. Much planning legislation began with concerns for public health and safety by insisting that buildings and neighbourhoods be designed to provide at least a minimum standard of public open space and sunlight and ventilation to habitable rooms. These concerns together with efficiency in transportation and the elimination of air and water pollution remain important in city planning and in urban design, but they are not the only matters that require attention in making good cities.

Urban design concerns within city planning reflect the state of public policies towards planned intervention in the development process. At times there are calls for more control over what is being built and how it is built and at others there are calls for less control and greater freedom for private actions. Economic conservatives see design controls as a deterrent to economic growth while socialist politicians see design quality as an elitist concern. Interestingly enough many large-scale property developers recognize both the financial benefits derived from rich, high-quality design and that purchasers are making increasingly discerning choices. Sometimes developers form their own private regulations to control the quality of the public realm created by sub-developers. They take on the quasi-public role described in Chapter 1.

In many places the public is demanding a greater role in deciding the future directions in which their cities should go. The diversity of its views has led to many architects, in particular, taking the position that all design concerns are arbitrary and subjective and that their personal beliefs are as good as those of anybody else. The development of the theoretical body of knowledge about the interaction of people and the environment has, however, led to the recognition that serious questions about goals and means can be discussed intelligently within public forums.

City Planning Public Realm Policies and Urban Design

It is the public realm policies within city planning that are often closely related to the urban design endeavour. Most such policies do not deal directly with the geometrical qualities of built form but they, nevertheless, have a direct impact on the form, liveliness or quietness, and general ambience of the places and links of a city. They deal with such matters as eliminating antisocial behaviour and providing a high-amenity level for the inhabitants and users of public spaces. These general policies may be urban-wide or targeted at specific precincts of cities. The urban design guidelines for the central area of Glendale in California, for instance, form the public realm policies for the downtown area of the city (see Chapter 8). Much can be learnt about the interrelationships of city planning and urban design from such examples.

Public realm policies deal almost universally with accessibility, the servicing of buildings and the ways traffic is to be handled. Strong lobbying has led to the almost universal development of policies specifying accessibility for people in wheelchairs to places open to the general public. As the public's fear of crime increases so are public policies being more specific in formulating design principles that deal with the natural surveillance, territorial control and the lighting of public spaces. These concerns are related to the accessibility and safety needs of people shown in Figure 1.6. The more general concerns of urban design are, however, poorly considered. 'Broader considerations of the network of public streets and public spaces, the permeability of blocks and . . . questions of the quality of the public realm are largely neglected' in city planning in Britain (Punter and Carmona, 1997: 169). Design issues come to the forefront only when citizens and planners are discussing the physical and symbolic character of an existing place and the desire to retain it.

Questions of the character of places are seldom addressed with any specificity. When they are, the formulation is poor. For example, at a community meeting the inhabitants of a town decided it wanted to retain its 'rural character'. What was meant by this objective was not articulated with precision verbally or in drawings. The town planning board developed a land-use regulation for two zones in the locale: one a rural/agricultural zone and the other a commercial zone. The former was aimed at retaining the rural character of the area by specifying 1-acre (0.40-hectare) lots. Where an extensive amount of road frontage was required, the lots were to be 3 acres (1.21 hectares) in size. In the commercial zone the lot size was to be at least 1 acre. The goal was to have houses scattered in a dotted pattern around the countryside. Instead what was achieved were the sites with short street frontages and thus buildings lining the roads. The rural character that citizens sought was lost (Craighead, 1991). Many planning policies conceal such hidden urban design processes.

One of the major areas in which hidden urban design occurs is in the design of roads. The prime criterion may be designing for public safety and accessibility. The definition of safety is, however, often established only by the size of the equipment – ambulances and fire engines – that have to be able to manoeuvre through a street. Such space requirements are often grossly overstated. Accessibility is also narrowly defined in terms of the speed of traffic flow. Streets have other functions and if simple criteria alone are selected as the basis for their design, their amenity level for pedestrians and their overall character may well be lost. Street width becomes the sole design specification. Visualizing dimensions and their consequences is not easy for lay-people on planning boards.

Many of the design ideas developed by well meaning architects during the first half of the twentieth century have been found to be counter-productive when translated into zoning regulations. The idea that sunlight should penetrate all habitable rooms in housing area design is a sound one but when applied as the sole criterion in the design of residential precincts of high-rise apartments it creates dull boring environments with few opportunities for exploratory behaviour by children (e.g. see Figures 7.1 and 11.3). At least the space between buildings needs to be well considered and a greater range of behavioural opportunities provided.

A recent review of the impact of land-use regulations in Houston, Texas shows their unintended impact on the quality of urban places (Lewyn, 2003). Decrees about lot size for single-family homes, parking requirements (1.33 cars per bedroom in apartment buildings) street widths and block sizes (600 feet/185 metres between intersections) makes life hard for pedestrians and encourages driving for even the most local of necessities. The density of development that results from such codes makes all kinds of housing developments and public transit financially unfeasible. At the same time the codes have not alleviated the problems of traffic congestion that they were legislated to address. What is needed in developing item-by-item planning and building regulations is to fully understand their three-dimensional implications and how they work as a system of controls.

Current zoning regulations throughout the world make it impossible to build new precincts that have the characteristics of the well-loved areas of existing cities. They would make the design of today's Paris, London, Boston and San Diego impossible. The codes were designed to avoid obnoxious facilities such as smoke-belching factories being located in residential areas and not much more. The world has changed and much needs to be rethought.

Urban Design as Part of Comprehensive Planning

Urban development is an endless process. Edmund Bacon portrayed it as in Figure 4.1 (Bacon, 1969). Urban design is very much part of the development

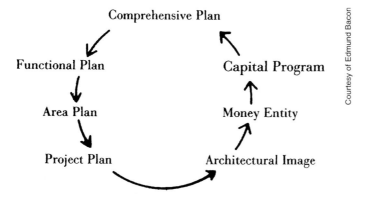

Figure 4.1 Urban design (project planning and architectural imagery) as part of the development process.

process as he considered it. He thought of area plans and, particularly, project plans being urban design because they show the three-dimensional character that is sought for precincts of cities. The problem with these area plans is that they failed to deal with the implementation process beyond the formation of zoning codes. They did not consider the plans to be representing end states to be actively pursued and built.

The diagram does not show that the urban development process, explicitly or implicitly, involves social and economic designs for a city. Nor does it show the battle amongst different interest groups for the attention of planners – the tugs between physical design, social design and economic design concerns. What it does show is that urban design concerns should be derived from and then fed back into any comprehensive plan for a city's future. Most comprehensive planning fails to do so. Singapore is one place where that is different.

The statutory comprehensive plan for Singapore is based on a two-dimensional concept plan (originally developed in 1971 but updated in 1991 and again in 2001; see Figure 10.12). The plan envisioned a series of new towns strung along transportation routes binding the city-state into a single entity. For planning purposes the city-state is divided into 50 planning precincts, each with its set of design objectives, specifications for building uses and with design guidelines for each new development. Until recently, all these decisions were made by either the Urban Redevelopment Authority (for central Singapore) or the Housing Development Board (for the new towns) in accordance with the specifications of the statutory authorities. Now the market is allowed to play a greater role. No other city with a democratically elected government has had such clearly delineated lines of authority and such centralized control in setting design directions. In Singapore urban design occurs within an overall city-planning framework or, perhaps more accurately, city planning occurs within an urban design framework!

Singapore is a case where highly educated politicians, in particular the country's leadership ever since independence, have been concerned with the quality of the physical environment. Their concern has been with both its efficiency and aesthetics. The leadership has recognized that the economic benefits of a positive working and living environment with a modern image are vast. It came belatedly to understand that the preservation and rehabilitation of the city's history through its physical fabric has important economic (in terms of tourism) and social benefits (in terms of identity) for Singaporeans. Many outsiders see the controls imposed to achieve the state's objectives to have been too harsh but nowhere in the world has a city upgraded itself as much in as short a time period.

A very different approach was used in Curitiba, Brazil (see Chapter 10). There the comprehensive plan was translated into a number of infrastructure development strategies. The goal was to have development projects plugged into the new infrastructure of transportation links and other facilities, such as community centres. The infrastructure design involved urban, engineering and architectural components.

Major references

Hopenfeld, Morton (1961). The role of design in city planning. *American Institute of Architects Journal* **35** (5): 4–44.

Lewyn, Michael (2003). Zoning without zoning. *http://www.planetizen.com/oped/item. php?id=112.*

Punter, John and Matthew Carmona (1997). Public realm policies. In *The Design Dimension of City Planning: Theory, Content, and Best Practice for Design Policies.* London: E & FN Spon, 169–77.

Wasserman, Jim (2004). Growth experts push new zoning to spark aesthetic renaissance. *San Diego Union Tribune.* 22, February. *http://www/signonsandiego.com/news/state/ 20040222-1144-ca-reinventinggrowth.html*

New Town Planning and Urban Design

In the design of new towns, the comprehensive planning objectives are presented in the form of a master plan. The master plan presents a vision of what the city hopes to be at some future date. Often this master plan is a statement allocating land uses to areas based on some image of a transportation network. At other, but less frequent, times it is a three-dimensional representation of the future state of a city as was the case for Runcorn, the case study included here.

Runcorn has been chosen because it was celebrated for its architectural experiments and also because the distinction between planning and urban design is totally blurred in its development. Runcorn consists of a number of clear urban design projects within an overall master plan that was developed in three-dimensional form. Its overall organization follows a standard model. The first generation of twentieth century British new towns as well as places such as Columbia, Maryland (see Figure 4.2) all follow it. It is a normative model still widely used. A city is divided into a hierarchy of precincts. Runcorn's design was also so based on a clear transportation network that it could almost be regarded as a plug-in urban design.

The planning and designing procedures in Runcorn were similar in character to much current work in continental Europe. Planning and designing are wrapped up into a single design effort. In the development of Zuidas, the new central business district for Amsterdam, planning and urban design have gone hand-in hand. Its designers refer to their work as city planning rather than urban design showing that the distinction between the two is often not made even though much in Zuidas is architecturally specific. The same was true during the second half of the twentieth century in the communist countries of Eastern Europe. In the former Soviet Union a number of *fiat* cities with populations as large as one million people were developed across northern and central Asia in the same manner.

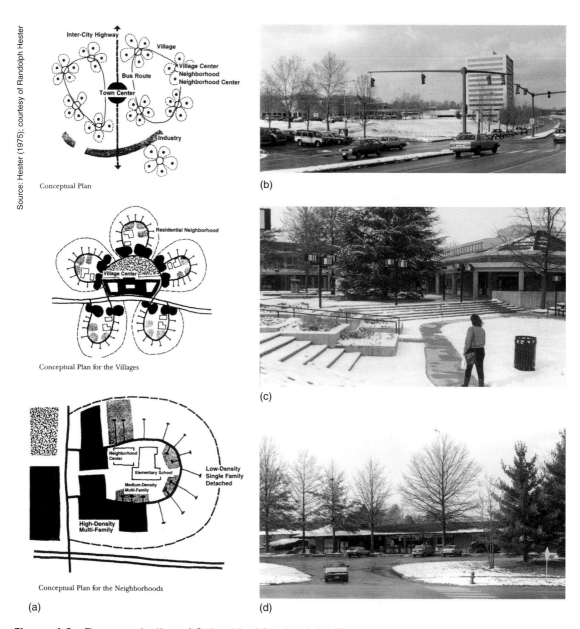

Source: Hester (1975); courtesy of Randolph Hester

Conceptual Plan

Conceptual Plan for the Villages

Conceptual Plan for the Neighborhoods

(a)

(b)

(c)

(d)

Figure 4.2 The organization of Columbia, Maryland. (a) The conceptual layout of the city, (b) a view of the city centre in 1993, (c) a village centre and (d) a neighbourhood centre.

CASE STUDY

Runcorn, England, UK: city planning as architecture as urban design (1965+)

Runcorn is a satellite town of Liverpool located on the south bank of the Mersey River. It was designed to house a population of 90,000 people on a site of 7250 acres (about 2800 hectares). The goal was to provide new employment opportunities and good housing for the people of Merseyside. The development was heavily subsidized by the central government in London through the Runcorn Development Corporation and designed by the corporation in conjunction with Arthur Ling Associates.

Ease of accessibility and providing for high mobility were major criteria in designing Runcorn. The goal was to establish a balance between the use of private vehicles and public transport. The importance of the infrastructure can be seen in the conceptual diagram and model of the layout of the town (see Figures 4.3a and b). An expressway encompasses the town. Feeder streets off it give access to the Runcorn's various precincts. The local mass transportation system was based on having single-decker buses operating on a dedicated track. The objective was to have a rapid public transit system and to have easy access to it (i.e. to have the majority of the population living within 500 yards of stops).

A figure eight plan was deemed to be the most efficient high-speed road system. It would link residential areas to both what was proposed to be the town centre – an enclosed shopping mall – and the industrial areas on the outside. The proposed centre – now the Halton Lea Shopping Centre – would also be reached by cars off the expressway and be encompassed by a road giving access to car parks that surround it. Such concerns are as much urban design issues as planning ones. What is now called the Town Centre is not the shopping centre as designated in the original plan but rather the core of the old Runcorn village (see Figure 4.4a). People's hearts designated it as such.

The Halton Lea Shopping Centre is a total precinct design (see Figures 4.4b and c); it is a megastructure. David Gosling and Keith Smith were the principal architects. It is a proud architectural statement representing the abandonment of the past idea of a town centre as an accretion of buildings (as in the core of the village of Runcorn) and of all-of-a-piece precinct design as the modus operandi of urban design. Coordinated urban design using controls, incentives and guidelines were replaced by architectural design on a grand scale as an embracing of the future.

The actual functioning of centres of this type (e.g. the similar one at the last of the British new towns, Milton Keynes) has led to the abandoning of such designs as a prototype for town centres (Francis, 1991). The limitations of such 'functional' designs have given rise, sensibly or not, to the Neo-Traditional movement in urban design. The standard suburban shopping mall in Columbia, Maryland operates more successfully as a centre than that at Runcorn being tied into an automobile-based transportation society well understood by property developer James Rouse.

In Runcorn the line of thinking applied to the shopping centre as the heart of the town

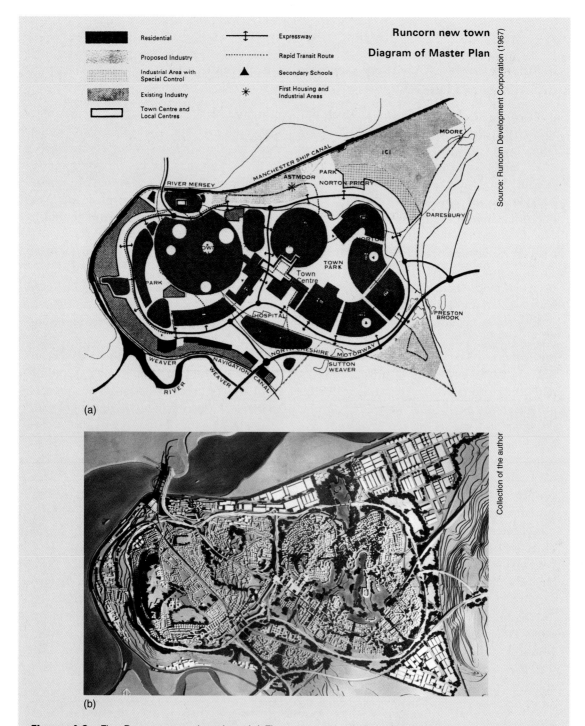

Figure 4.3 The Runcorn master plan. (a) The conceptual diagram for the town's layout and (b) the model of the proposed Runcorn.

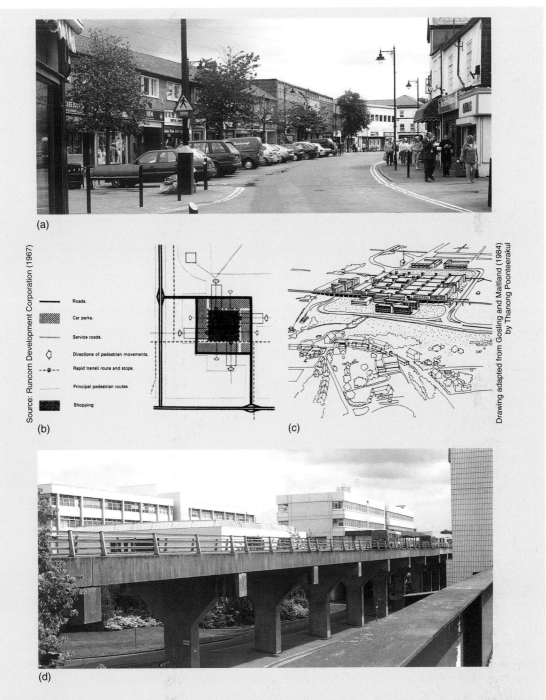

Figure 4.4 The Town Centre and the shopping centre, Runcorn. (a) The Town Centre in 2004, (b) a conceptual diagram of the proposed Town Centre (now Halton Lee Shopping Centre), (c) the Halton Lee Shopping Centre (first stage) and (d) Halton Lea Shopping Centre in 2004.

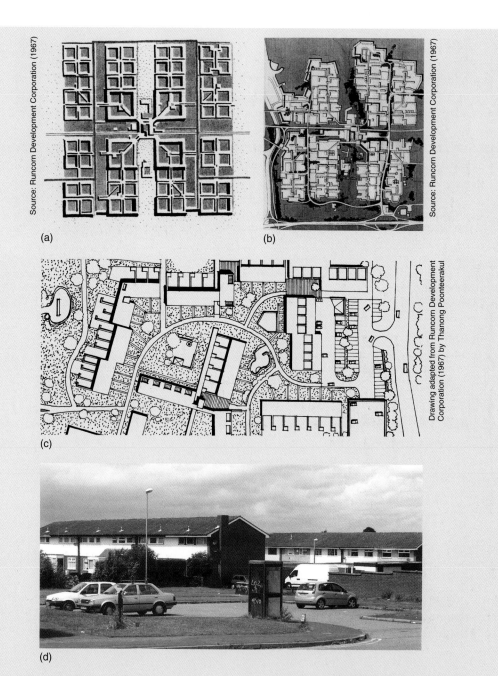

Figure 4.5 Residential area design, Runcorn. (a) A conceptual diagram of the community structure, (b) a sketch plan of a community layout adapted to the topography, (c) a conceptual diagram of the dwelling–parking relationship at the cluster level and (d) a view of a residential cluster in 2004.

was also applied to the transportation structure – pedestrian and vehicular – at the 'community' level. Each community has its own centre that provides everyday social and shopping needs. The infrastructure was designed with this end in mind and the residential areas were then plugged into the system. The community centres, like the bus stops, lie within 500 yards (5-minute walk) of all residents. The vehicular routes act as seams for residential areas and a network of pedestrian paths links the various components of a community together.

The communities have about 8000 people in them subdivided into four neighbourhoods (see Figure 4.5a). The neighbourhoods are further subdivided into clusters of 100 to 200 people who form the local social unit. The distance of the walk to primary school, the picking up points on the transit system and the nature of the service areas of different facilities determined the sizes of the various residential areas not any social statement on the nature of 'community'. The provision of electricity and a reticulated water system can be provided within almost any framework, but sewer lines and drainage systems need to take the natural topography into consideration (see Figure 4.5b). These latter two elements of infrastructure and the greenway system further structure the town. The open areas consist of an outer green belt and fingers following lower land areas in towards the centre of the town and the centre of the communities.

Clustering the dwelling units around pedestrian quasi cul-de-sacs afford the development of a social network. The parking of cars is clustered in landscaped parking areas. From there people walk to their dwellings all of which are located within 50 yards of the parking lots (see Figure 4.5c and d). The goal was to provide opportunities for the types of activities that would foster social interactions between neighbours, particularly children, by encouraging casual contacts that would lead to neighbouring.

The layout of Runcorn's infrastructure has many generic qualities. The hierarchical nature of the town is similar to that of many other new towns around the world. The designs of Brasília and the Gujarat State Fertilizer Corporation (GSFC) Township in Vadodara were based on a similar idea (see Chapter 7). The search for efficient layouts is also clear in the design of Aranya Township (see Chapter 10). The detailed design of their infrastructure systems, the nature of their streets and the relationship of buildings to open space distinguish them from each other.

Major references

Runcorn Development Corporation (1967). *Runcorn New Town*. Nottingham: Midlands Engraving Co. Ltd.

Gosling, David and Barry Maitland (1984). *Concepts of Urban Design*. London: Academy Editions, 91–4.

Thomas, Ray and Peter Cresswell (1973). *The New Town Idea*. Milton Keynes: The Open University.

Commentary: Is Planning just Urban Design? Is Urban Design just Planning?

The overlap between mainstream urban planning and urban design concerns is clearly substantial, particularly in precinct planning and design. It is easy, but misleading, to see the process of planning as a unidirectional one in which city-planning decisions are translated into urban design decisions that are then translated into building and landscape designs. The flow of decision-making should go the other way as well.

Important decisions at the detailed level have ramifications for larger-scale decisions. Thus the whole process of city planning can be seen as moving from the precinct level to the city level, and then to the regional level. As decisions and their effects are so interwoven at each scale, it is possible to see urban design as a sub-specialization within planning, where planning meets architecture and landscape architecture. On the other hand it is possible to see urban design as the mediator between planning and architecture and neither one nor the other, although it encompasses both. Perhaps planning is a sub-area of urban design! In this view once decisions are made at the precinct level the problems of interrelationships amongst precincts can be addressed.

The design of linkages is particularly part of the overall planning and physical development strategy of a city. It is the armature on which the whole fabric of a city hangs. It is the shaping force of new town design; it feeds into urban design at the precinct level. Thus urban design is part of and contributes to city planning. City planning itself is seldom urban design, although in the design of places such as Brasília, city planning and urban design are indistinguishable. Perhaps the same can be said of Runcorn.

There are two types of products of city-planning work that can be urban design: master plans and precincts plans. Precinct plans can be divided into large number of types; city centre designs and neighbourhood designs in particular. There are other examples of precinct plans as well; for example, industrial precincts and urban renewal districts. To be urban design all need to deal with the three-dimensional qualities of the city and with the processes required to meet specific objectives in accordance with the vision of the future that they represent.

The products of landscape architecture and the nature of urban design

5

All, without exception, total and all-of-a-piece urban designs include elements of landscape architecture. Many plug-in urban designs are landscape design projects and vice versa. The historical trails, squares and parks described here are all plugged into existing city frameworks to act as catalysts for development or, at least, to halt decay. What then differentiates the products of landscape architecture from those of urban design?

The landscape quality of open spaces is crucial to the experiencing of cities and perceptions of their quality. The streets, squares and parks of cities, such as London form part of their international image. It is difficult to consider Paris without its boulevards, or Singapore without the walkways along its riverfront or St. Louis without Gateway Plaza (see Figure 5.1). The character of all these places is, however, defined not only by the landscape but also by the buildings that face them and the activities they generate. It is this consideration of the three-dimensional world as experienced in time that is central to urban design work. Much landscape architecture in the city is, however, concerned only with the space between buildings. It is concerned primarily with the horizontal surface.

The Products of Landscape Architecture: Malls, Squares, Streets and Parks

The design of streets, squares, parks and other public spaces is often referred to as urban design by landscape architects. A number of the Bruner Awards for urban design, which have an intellectual basis in the broad thinking about the functions of built form represented in Figure 1.6, have gone to such designs. Many, if not most, of such spaces are actually designed by architects rather than landscape architects perhaps because of their 'hard' rather than their 'green' character. Sometimes they are the result of collaborative work between architects and landscape architects (e.g. Pershing Square in Los Angeles). Historically, the buildings that frame many of the best-loved plazas in Europe have been built up piece-by-piece over a long period of time. Sometimes each piece has been subjected to design controls but at other times the architects involved have designed with a sense of decorum – with a sense of concern for the context in which they are designing. Piazza San Marco in Venice is probably the best-known example (see Figure 5.2).

Courtesy of Development Strategies, St. Louis

Figure 5.1 Gateway Plaza, St Louis.

Collection of the author

Figure 5.2 Piazza San Marco, Venice.

Figure 5.3 Stairway to Bunker Hill, Los Angeles.

Some designs of walkways, staircases, experiential trails, plazas, street beautifications and parks sit more easily under the rubric of urban design than others. The design of an open space is, however, really simply landscape architecture unless designed as a unit with surrounding buildings (as in Pariser Platz, Berlin; see Chapter 8). Such designs occur more frequently in the creation of new towns and *de novo* precinct designs (e.g. Paternoster Square; also in Chapter 8) than when redesigning open spaces in existing cities (Figure 5.3).

More and more city administrations recognize the importance of open-space design in creating positive images of their cities. For example, this attitude is clear in Canary Wharf (see Chapter 8). Portland, Oregon, with its variety of squares in its downtown and attention to streetscape has been particularly successful in creating a positive image of its central area. Lively squares, stairways (often as pieces of sculpture), and well-paved sidewalks add a sense of dignity to urban life and provide places at which to pause. We have learnt much about their design from examining those that are regarded as lovely, and are well used (see, for example Broto, 2000; Billingham and Cole, 2002; Gehl and Gemzøe, 2003). We need to learn as much from those that are deserted, and those that have decayed rapidly (e.g. Plaza d'Italia in New Orleans, 1975–8, a sculpture; see Figure 5.4). In these cases it is often not the design itself that was the problem but the surroundings. The context was either not considered in terms of what it offered a new design or else the predicted catalytic value of the new landscape did not materialize.

Deeply embedded in both architectural and landscape architectural thinking is that open spaces in cities are always a good idea, anywhere and everywhere. One of the lessons of the twentieth century is that in terms of urban life this belief

(a)

(b)

Photograph by Ruth Durack

Figure 5.4 Two urban squares. (a) The Ira C. Keller Fountain, Portland, Oregon and (b) Plaza d'Italia, New Orleans in pristine state.

needs to be tempered (see J. Jacobs, 1961). In the Anglo-American world there is also the belief that trees and plants are automatically desirable elements of the cityscape. Often they are, but the world is replete with examples of much-loved treeless squares, such as the Piazza San Marco, and streets. Cities are replete with forlorn, tired, unloved parks that do not even serve as 'lungs' for the city. In arid climes they can be detrimental.

The intellectual level at which landscape architects are best placed to make a contribution to urban design is not only at the detailed design level but at the citywide scale (Bunster-Ossa, 2001). Landscape architects' concern should extend to include the health of the biogenic environment of cities and its side effects on the functioning of the planet, Earth. While there have been ardent proponents of 'designing cities with nature in mind' (e.g. Spirn, 1984), few landscape architects have become deeply involved in urban design.

Major references

Billingham, John and Richard Cole (2002). *The Good Place Guide: Urban Design in Britain and Ireland*. London: T. Batsford.

Broto, Carles (2000). *New Urban Design*. Barcelona: Arian Mostaedi.

Gehl, Jan and Lars Gemzøe (2003). *New City Space* [translated by Karen Steenhard]. Copenhagen: Danish Architectural Press.

Jacobs, Jane (1961). The peculiar nature of cities. In *The Death and Life of Great American Cities*. New York: Random House, 29–140.

Spirn, Ann Whiston (1984). *The Granite Garden: Urban Nature and Human Design*. New York: Basic Books.

Pedestrian Malls, Walkways and Experiential Trails

Links, as part of urban design projects, can take many forms depending on the mode of transport being used. At one level of speed of movement it involves the use of vehicles. At another, walkways, stairways and arcades have been designed to enhance the experience of pedestrians. Sometimes the purpose is simply to provide shelter and comfort, but at other times it is to enhance the sequential experiencing of cities as one walks their streets.

One of the prejudices of many design professionals is that cars are bad and need to be kept out of the way. What needs to be recognized is that automobile usage is very much part of many lives and the generator of activity. Often cars and pedestrians really need to be segregated. The standard manner is to provide streets with pavements/sidewalks. Pedestrianizing streets and forming super-blocks is another way. Yet another way of separating pedestrian and vehicular traffic has been vertically. Skywalks and subterranean passageways have been designed to ease the flow of people. However, their designs have not been considered to be the purview of landscape architects.

In many cities around the world, key streets have been closed to vehicular traffic and converted into pedestrian malls. Some, such as the Strøgret in the narrow winding streets of Copenhagen are internationally famous (see Figure 5.5). Such conversions continue to be built (e.g. Nanjing Road, Shanghai, 1999). The goal

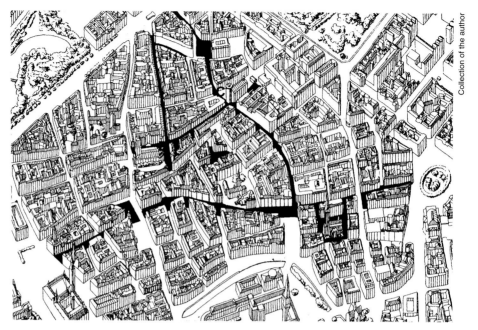

Collection of the author

Figure 5.5 Strøget, Copenhagen.

has been to make life more pleasant for pedestrians and so to enhance their shopping experience and thus boost the economic status of the shops. In some places, usually where the street is narrow and there are clear destinations at both ends, these conversions have been highly successful. At other times they have failed and many have been converted back to use by vehicular traffic. In these cases, they have been accused, sometimes unfairly, of having speeded up the process of retail decay.

Experiential trails highlight places and link them together based on some theme. These themes are usually historical but could be based on odours and touches for the blind or some set of activities or simply a set of aesthetic experiences. One of the goals of these trails has been to enhance the image of areas and/or the self-image of subgroups of people by bringing attention to socio-historic places whose importance might otherwise not be recognized. Places along the routes have had their images enhanced primarily through landscape design and building renovation. Some of the trails simply link places where events took place without much additional detail (e.g. the Haymarket Massacre trail in Chicago), while others have plaques and photographs and have received considerable recent landscape architectural attention to raise their ambient qualities. This step may include special paving and street furniture (lamp poles, seating and rubbish bins), murals and planting.

There are many such trails. Almost every large city and many smaller cities have them. Many cities have architectural trails showcasing their architectural histories. To many people the design of these trails is urban design work; to others it is landscape architecture or even social planning. Much depends on the extent to which the trail integrates buildings and the space between them, and to what extent it is simply a path through a city's streets. Boston's Freedom Trail has had much attention to its design over the years; Ahmedabad's almost none.

Major references

Brambilla, Roberto and Gianni Longo (1977). *For Pedestrians Only: Planning and Management of Traffic-Free Zones*. New York: Whitney Library of Design.

Hayden, Dolores (1995). *The Power of Place: Urban Landscapes as Public History*. Cambridge, MA: MIT Press.

Rubenstein, Harvey M. (1992). *Pedestrian Malls, Streetscapes, and Urban Spaces*. New York: John Wiley.

CASE STUDY

Oak Park Center Mall, Oak Park, Illinois, USA: a mall built and demolished (1967, 1989)

City planners, architects and landscape architects promote the 'malling' of streets in many countries, as a mechanism to help marginal retail activity along them thrive. Retailers have collaborated because they were 'clutching at straws' in the hope of their businesses surviving. Sometimes they have been rewarded by the closures, sometimes not. Lake Street between Harlem Avenue and Forest Avenue in Oak Park, Illinois was closed to traffic and pedestrianized in the early 1970s. It has now been reopened to vehicular traffic.

In the mid-1960s Oak Park city planners followed a well-developed generic urban design solution of the era with the goal of renewing interest in Oak Park's downtown. The street became the Oak Park Center Mall. Joe Karr and Associates of Chicago were the landscape architects. Street furniture was installed and 10-year-old oak trees were planted to create an attractive pedestrian-friendly retail area at a cost of $1.5 million (see Figure 5.6a and b). Trees dominated the design as can still be seen on the one segment of the malled area, Marian Street, that remains. The design of the mall was much admired but by the late 1980s the total retail sales on the strip had declined and a number of stores had closed.

Retail sales along the mall peaked at $50 million in 1972 but declined to $26.5 million in 1987. The mall was blamed. Fairly? The major anchor stores – the Wiebolt, Lytton, Montgomery Ward and Marshall Field had left. The first three had planned to leave before the mall was built and the last mentioned had vehicular access so the mall could not be blamed for their demise. In 1988, Projects for Public Spaces (PPS)

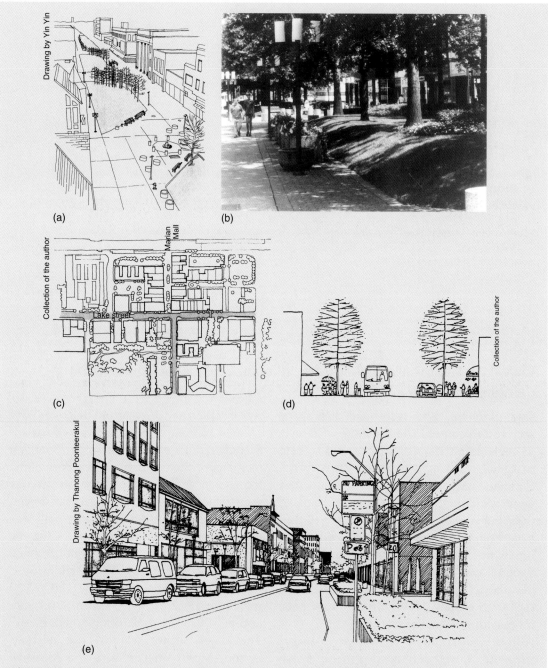

Figure 5.6 Oak Park Center Mall. (a) A sketch of Lake Street pedestrianized, (b) a view of the Mall in 1988, (c) the master plan for returning Lake Street to vehicular traffic, (d) a cross-section of Lake Street as proposed in the master plan and (e) Lake Street in 2004.

worked with the Oak Park Mall Commission, property developers, and city officials to determine the mall's successes and lack of them. It conducted surveys and used time-lapse photography to ascertain the frequency and intensity of pedestrian activity on the mall. The results were presented in a series of public meetings and consequently a set of design and management decisions were made.

The city-planning commission decided, over considerable local opposition and that of critics, to re-open the street to vehicular traffic. Opposition to the idea arose because people liked to stroll down the mall. It was a pleasant place. Henry Arnold (1993) said it would have become an exemplar of urban design if it had been allowed to develop for another 10 years and shops to adapt to the changes in the surrounding neighbourhood. In addition, the idea of spending $2.76 million on returning the street to what it was before the conversion when the original bonds were only due to be retired in 1992 was anathema to many people. PPS prepared a design and integrated the reopened street with a retail management plan and a public space plan. The master plan was prepared by the Lakota Group with S. B. Friedman and Company, DLK Architecture and Metro Transportation on the team (see Figure 5.6c and d).

The destruction of the mall and the reconstruction of Lake Street took place in 1989. Considerable attention was paid to the landscape design of the sidewalks and to the planting in order to retain the admired atmosphere that the pedestrian mall had possessed. In 1990, there was a decline in vacancy rates to 19% and much interest in other retail properties by potential new tenants. Pleasant enough, Lake Street is now simply another suburban shopping street (see Figure 5.6e).

What city planners have learnt is that a landscape architectural project by itself will not improve business in such situations however well it is executed. It is not a lesson that has been universally taken to heart (Fitzgerald, 2004). The pedestrianization of streets is still an idea that appeals. To be successful such road closures have to be in highly strategic, well-functioning locations. Lake Street is successful now because two unobtrusive parking structures were built to enhance access and the mix of types of stores has responded to marketplace demands. It serves the affluent shoppers that the gentrification of Oak Park has brought into the area but on a considerably smaller scale than in its heyday.

In the smaller cities in the United States that have strong competition from suburban strip retail development and shopping centres, such 'malling' of main streets does not work. In Europe, there are many examples of highly successful pedestrianized central areas of cities: Gloucester in England, Wageningen and Arnheim in the Netherlands, Grenoble in France and Munich in Germany are amongst them. Pedestrianization is not, however, a panacea for a city's ills. Nor is it strictly urban design. At the policy level it is city planning and at the design level it is landscape architecture.

Major references

Arnold, Henry F. (1993). *Trees in Urban Design* (second edition). New York: Van Nostrand Reinhold, 105–8.

Houston Jr, Lawrence O. (1990). From streets to mall and back again. *Planning* **56** (6): 4–10.

Zotti, Ed (1988). Un-malling a downtown [Oak Park, Illinois]. *Inland Architect* **32** (4): 14, 18.

CASE STUDY

The Freedom Trail, Boston, Massachusetts, USA (1951–8+)

The Freedom Trail through the heart of Boston is a 4-kilometre (2.5-mile) pedestrian route that links 16 sites of historical interest in the city (see Figure 5.7a). They are primarily places of importance in the United State's independence movement but the trail touches on many twentieth century developments. It begins at Boston Common, once a cattle pasture, and leads via important buildings (e.g. the Old State House; the home of the British colonial government prior to independence), the location of important events (e.g. the Boston Massacre site), a site of literary importance (Old Corner Bookstore), burial grounds (e.g. Granary Burial Ground; see Figure 5.7c), the Quincy Market/Faneuil Hall area (an eighteenth century public meeting hall revitalized as part of a shopping district in mid-twentieth century; see Figure 5.7d) to an ending at the Bunker Hill Monument across the Charles River.

The Government of the City of Boston provided the funds and sponsored the trail. Since 1976 (spurred by the bicentennial of the American declaration of independence) the National Park Service has spent more than $50 million on capital improvements of sites along the trail. The project was, however, initiated in 1951 as the result of public pressure led by a journalist, William Schofield of the *Boston Herald-Tribune*. Schofield wrote editorials decrying the lack of recognition of the role of Boston in the history of the United States and agitating for the trail to be created. He received political support from the Mayor of Boston, John Hynes. The development of the trail illustrates the power of simple, workable ideas in fostering a variety of public realm designs.

Schofield lived until 1996 seeing his dream fulfilled.

The Freedom Trail Foundation (FTF) was established in 1958 with the John Hancock Insurance Company a major sponsor. The Boston Chamber of Commerce and the Advertising Club of Boston later joined the group. The Foundation finances maps and guides but volunteers run the whole programme. In 1964, the FTF was incorporated as a non-profit organization committed to the development of the trail and to a variety of activities, such as educational programmes, related to it.

Although the trail has been added to continuously over the years, its development can be said to have taken place in two phases. The first was somewhat casual with a red line painted on the surface of the ground leading from one site to the next. The line was regarded as aesthetically unacceptable. During the second phase more attention was paid to the landscape quality of the trail. The red line was replaced with red paving stones, pedestrian ramps were installed, signage quality was enhanced and bronze medallion location markers were put in place. The trail is regarded as a major success. Over 4 million people walk it each year and the visitors to each point along the trail increased as soon as it was put into place. It is estimated to contribute $400 million to Boston's $9 billion per annum tourism industry.

Walking the trail is an emotional experience for patriotic Americans and many international tourists alike. It has enhanced the knowledge that Boston's citizens have about their own city's history and,

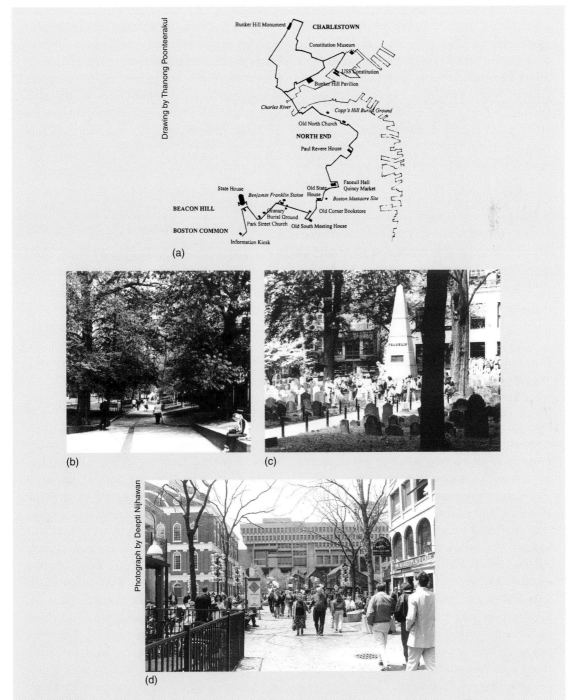

Figure 5.7 The Freedom Trail, Boston. (a) The Freedom Trail route, (b) Boston Common, (c) the Granary Burial Ground and (d) Quincy Market/Faneuil Hall area with Boston City Hall in the background.

particularly, in the historic preservation of significant buildings. The existence of the trail has indirectly raised the city's profile. It might be regarded as a catalyst for the later Quincy Market redevelopment because it showed what could be done when interested parties rally around a cause. In the year 2000, the Freedom Trail was one of 16 such trails in the United States to receive an award as part of the White House's Save Our National Treasures project.

Places change. As the Freedom Trail winds its way through the city's financial district the fear is that the increasing number of skyscrapers being built along the way will overshadow it. The question then arises:

'What is in the public interest – development and/or preservation?' The French government decided to maintain the scale of buildings of the historic core of Paris and displace development to the periphery of the city. The creation of outlying Amsterdam Zuidas as a business district is preserving the historic core of that city. This tactic has not been pursued in Boston.

Major references

Freedom Trail Foundation, The (2002). *www.thefreedomtrail.org*

Kanda, Shun and Masami Kobayashi (1991). *Boston by Design – A City in Development*. Tokyo: Process Architecture.

A Note

The Heritage Walk, Ahmedabad, Gujarat, India

Not all heritage walks link iconic monuments nor are they all in the western world. The concern for cultural history is universal. It appears to be especially strong when people see the world around them changing rapidly. The Heritage Walk in Ahmedabad, the major industrial city of the Indian state of Gujarat, was initiated by the Foundation for Conservation and Research of Urban Traditional Architecture (CRUTA). The city, founded by Ahmed Shah in 1411, is rich in historic buildings and places, but the city administration has been unwilling or unable to effectively preserve or exploit them. The city is not on the major tourist circuit of India and many of those who visit are either interested in seeing the Ashram of Mahatma Gandhi or the Modernist architecture of Le Corbusier and Louis Kahn for which the city is renowned.

CRUTA's goal is to preserve the old, walled city of Ahmedabad sadly often rent by sectarian violence between Hindus and Muslims. The focus of attention in developing the Heritage Walk is not only on the city's major monuments (many Islamic) but also on its *pols*. Pols are tightly knit, self-contained, cul-de-saced, gated neighbourhoods of caste (and occupation) groups (see Figure 5.8c). The walk begins at the Swaminarayan Mandir in Kalupur and ends at the Jamma Masjid (the City's Friday Mosque; see Figure 5.8b). Along the way, it passes through a series of *chowks* (squares), linking a number of pols, mosques and temples. It also includes one of the city's outstanding Modernist buildings – the Calico Shop (1962, a shallow domed building designed by Gautam and Gira Sarabhai who had worked for Frank Lloyd Wright at Taliesen) – and the Fernandez Bridge, an overpass from which the street-life of the city can be seen below.

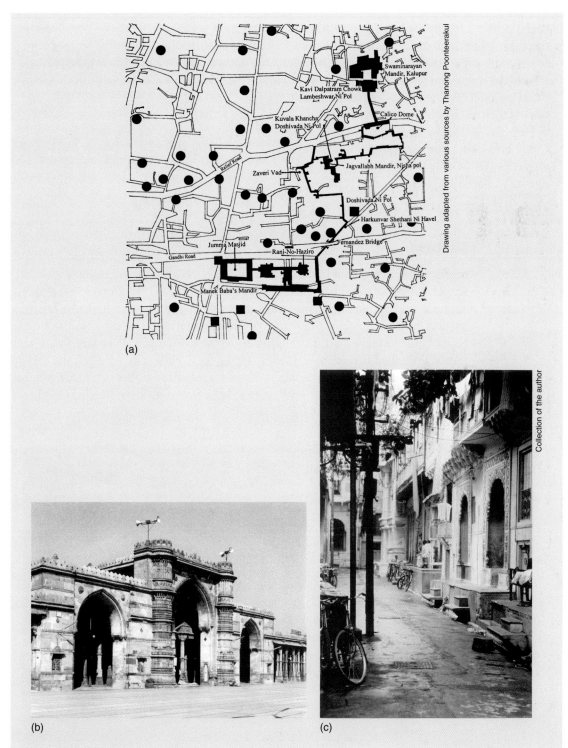

Figure 5.8 The Heritage Walk, Ahmedabad. (a) The route map of the Heritage Walk (dots indicate historical sites/buildings), (b) the Jamma Masjid and (c) a pol.

Little has actually been designed along the way. What has been designed is the idea of the trail not a physical entity. Whether it should be regarded as urban design is a moot point. The identification and publication of the trail has led to a rise in the number of tourists in the area and encouraged CRUTA to catalogue almost 30,000 buildings deemed worthy of preservation in the old city. Perhaps pride in the trail as a community asset can lead to the healing of the deep scars of mob violence in Ahmedabad. Much depends on the leadership role of the middle class in the city.

Major references

Ahmedabad Municipal Corporation (*c.* 2002). *The Heritage Walk of Ahmedabad*. Ahmedabad: Danapith.

Squares

Squares, or plazas, take on an extraordinary range of configurations with a variety of enclosing elements (Krier, 1990; Cerver, 1997). The character of a square depends on the enclosing buildings, their heights and what happens on their ground floors as much as the design of the square itself. The urbane character of Rittenhouse Square in Philadelphia today (see Figure 5.9) is largely as Jane Jacobs described it years ago (Jacobs, 1961). Its liveliness depends on the variety of the building uses around it: clubs (largely incognito), hotels, a church, a music institute and apartment buildings all of at least three stories in height. People are

Collection of the author

Figure 5.9 Rittenhouse Square, Philadelphia in 1985.

coming and going all the time. As a result people use the square at different times of day as a short cut and for relaxation; children wade in the fountains during the summer and clamber on the statues. Dogs are walked and people sit watching the people cutting across the square who, in turn, are watching them. The design of the square by Paul Cret adds to its ambience but, by itself, would have achieved little.

The Lawrence Halprin designed squares in Portland, Oregon add much to the city. Individually they provide attractive destinations and are much used. As a group they might be regarded as part of an urban design effort to give life to the central area of the city. They remain, however, works of landscape architecture and should be celebrated as such. The water garden Philip Johnson and John Burgee designed in Fort Worth, dramatic though it is, has yet to act as a catalyst in the development of its surroundings (see Figure 5.10). It remains an isolated work of art in a forlorn cityscape.

The two examples of squares included in this book are of the types that many landscape architects regard as urban design. The physical frame in both cases was, however, given and not part of the design commission. The first example, Pershing Square, is certainly a highly urban space. It has had a life of being designed and redesigned. It has yet to fulfil a role as a great urban outdoor room. The second of them, the La Place des Terreaux in Lyon, France, is included in Carles Broto's collection of new urban designs (Broto, 2000). Through careful research we have learnt much about what makes lively, well-loved urban spaces (Whyte, 1980; Cooper Marcus and Francis, 1990; Madanipour, 1996, 2003; Carmona *et al.*, 2003). The problem is that the desire to create active places often conflicts with the desire to create a work of art. The two can be reconciled.

Photograph by Alix Verge

Figure 5.10   The Water Garden, Fort Worth in 2003.

Handling cars in cities remains a problem. Many great squares of Italy and other European countries serve as parking lots today, at least during the daytime. The original functions have been lost. Both the squares described here have parking garages below them. The garage is handled well in one case but not in the other.

Major references

Carmona, Matthew, Tim Heath, Taner Oc and Steve Tiesdell (2003). *Public Places, Urban Spaces: The Dimensions of Urban Design*. Oxford: Architectural Press.

Gehl, Jan (1987). *Life Between Buildings: Using Public Space*. New York: Van Nostrand Reinhold.

Krier, Rob (1990). Typological elements of the concept of urban space. In Andreas Papadakis and Harriet Watson, eds., *The New Classicism: Omnibus Volume*. New York: Rizzoli, 213–19.

CASE STUDY

Pershing Square, Los Angeles, California, USA: a revamped urban square (1950–2, 1994)

Pershing Square (named in 1918 in honour of World War I General John Pershing) has a long history dating back to its designation as a formal Spanish plaza in 1866. It has gone through a number of redesigns since then at the hands of a variety of architects, landscape architects and gardeners: Fred Eaton's (in the 1890s), John Parkinson's (1911), Frank Shearer's (1928), Stiles Clements' (1950–1) and in 1994 those of Ricardo Legoretta and Laurie Olin. It is the last mentioned proposal that is of interest here. The history of the square's transformations shows that urban spaces in cities are surprisingly enduring despite the changes in a city's fortunes.

The 1951 building of the underground parking garage led to the square being a patch of grass with trees in planter boxes on its edges. The decision made by the city government to build a car park was predicated on the belief that it would decongest the area and lead to a revival of the city's theatre district. Downtown Los Angeles today is remarkably uncongested by world standards but this state is due to the buildings in the area being largely abandoned above ground floor level – something that is beginning to change. The garage failed to recharge the theatre district and the entrances to the parking garage tended to cut the park off from its surroundings.

By the late 1980s, the square has become a place for the homeless, indigent and drug addicts to 'hang-out' in (see Figure 5.11). It was so despised that the Biltmore Hotel had turned its back on the square by establishing an entrance on its side away from the square. The square was decrepit and the furnishings vandalized. The surroundings, while housing a noticeable number of middle-class people, were populated heavily

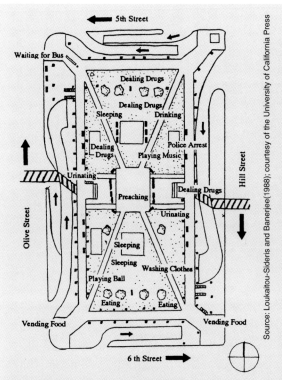

Source: Loukaitou-Sideris and Banerjee (1988); courtesy of the University of California Press

Figure 5.11 A behavioural map of Pershing Square, Los Angeles in 1988.

by inhabitants of single-room occupancy units (SROs). The two groups inhabited two different worlds and the park was no seam. The former inhabited private spaces and the latter public. What then to do with the square? The Pershing Square Management Association commissioned the Jerde Partnership to conduct an evaluation of the park in 1984. This study initiated the process that led to the park we see today.

The redevelopment of the square in 1994 cost $US14.5 million. The Center City Management Association representing property owners and the Community Redevelopment Agency (CRA) of Los Angeles financed it. The goal was to have an open public space of broad appeal. It was to be a place of meeting,

have a positive image and be an oasis for casual leisure activities. Special events and temporary facilities (e.g. an ice rink in winter, a bandstand in the summer) were to be able to be accommodated. The park level, because of the parking garage below, was unfortunately a metre above that of the surrounding streets but the park did have a promising set of enclosing buildings that give the square some character. Most of these buildings date back to the 1920s with the building of the Subway Terminal Building, the Title Guarantee and Trust Building, the Biltmore Hotel and the Philharmonic Auditorium. The Public Library is only a block away. They provided the basis for making a fine square but it has not happened.

The Center City Management Association, other civic associations, the CRA of Los Angeles, the City's Department of Parks and Recreation and the Cultural Affairs Commission organized an international competition for the redesign of the square in 1986. It attracted 242 entries from 17 countries with the winning entry being produced by Sculpture In The Environment (SITE), a New York based architectural firm headed by James Wines and Michelle Stone. It was designed in collaboration with landscape architects EDAW, Inc. with architects Charles Kober Associates and engineers Delton Hampton and Associates. The predicted cost of building their design, a 'metaphorical carpet', was $12.5 million but $20 million was thought to be more realistic by many observers. That price plus the expectation of cost overruns was simply too high to be considered feasible.

The SITE scheme (see Figure 5.12a) was based on a 13′6′ grid (the column spacing of the garage below). The surface of the park was designed to be undulating and

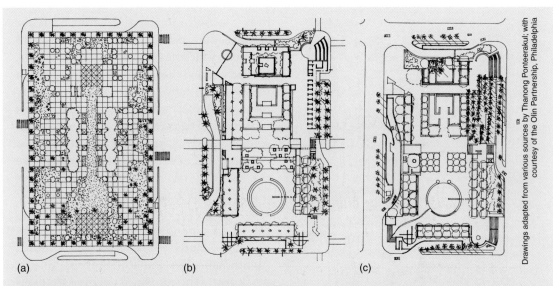

Drawings adapted from various sources by Thanong Ponteerakul; with courtesy of the Olin Partnership, Philadelphia

(a) (b) (c)

Figure 5.12 Three proposals for Pershing Square, Los Angeles. (a) The SITE proposal, (b) the second Legoretta and Olin scheme and (c) the final Legoretta and Olin scheme.

planted with tropical trees in order to create mini-environments that would attract people. The design was, however, an independent object that 'turned the park on its surroundings'. Construction was supposed to begin in 1988 but the surrounding property owners protested. They would have had to make up much of the shortfall between the public funds available ($6 million from the Los Angeles Redevelopment Authority and other contributions from the Department of Recreation and Parks, and the Board of Public Works) and the expected construction cost.

The design that was implemented was a product of the collaboration of architect Ricardo Legoretta, landscape architect Laurie Olin and artist Barbara McCarren (see Figures 5.12b–c and 5.13). Maguire Thomas Partners, the leading property developers in Central Los Angeles, hired them. One of the design goals was to have a park that represented both the Latino and Anglo populations of the city. The design

went through several iterations but the final one the team produced was never fully implemented. Legoretta aspired to create a *zócalo*, the heart of many a Mexican city, but it is difficult see the connection in the design.

An orange grove marks the centre of the park as a reminder of the importance of orange farming in Los Angeles County. At the southern end of the park is a sculpted court with a fountain, pool and a reminder, in the form of a jagged line cutting across the park, of the fault line on which Los Angeles is located. The park also contains a 'Mayan' style amphitheatre, benches in which images of Los Angeles are embedded, works of art and mementoes of the past (e.g. a canon). A Star Walk paving pattern resembles a constellation visible in the winter and the summer sun. Despite these varied components, the park is a still lifeless place. The former inhabitants have been chased away by the police but users to replace them are few and those that are there tend to be similar to the ones who were there before the changes took

Figure 5.13 Pershing Square, Los Angeles in 2004. (a) Pershing Square in context, (b) Pershing Square with the Biltmore Hotel in the background and (c) a view of the square from the northwest corner.

place. Perhaps the idea of a square is out of place in the contemporary social and cultural climate of Southern California. It is more likely that the surrounding uses do not generate the variety of people who would be square users. Only the poor are habitués.

The events in the Square do attract people even though questions have been raised about how the park is managed by the Los Angeles Parks Department. The benches in Pershing Square do provide a place for the homeless to gather. At lunchtime workers from the surrounding buildings take lunch there and the square is a popular place for rallies. It, however, consists of a number of poorly integrated fragments. Time will tell whether the mixture of elements will hold up well. Overcoming the presence of the underground garage has proven to be a continuing concern. Having a plaza above the surroundings ground level presents a difficult design problem. Maybe having too many

panhandlers for the middle class to tolerate cannot be overcome by design although the redesign of Bryant Park by Olin seems to have been successful in revitalizing a previously notorious open space. Perhaps the revitalization of central Los Angeles that is now (in 2004) beginning to take place will make the park a more congenial place without any design changes.

Major references

Boles, Daralice D. (1986). SITE selected for Pershing Square. *Progressive Architecture* 67 (10): 36.

Hinkle, Ricardo (1999). Panning Pershing (the flaws and shortcomings of Pershing Square). *Landscape Architecture* 89 (6): 9.

Loukaitou-Sideris, Anastasia and Tridib Banerjee (1998). *Urban Design Downtown: Poetics and Politics of Form*. Berkeley and Los Angeles: University of California Press, 153–60.

McCarren, Barbara (1999). And in this corner (designing the landscape for the Pershing Square project). *Landscape Architecture* 89 (6): 9+.

CASE STUDY

La Place des Terreaux, Lyon, France: a revamped historical square (1994+)

Improving the quality of the public realm can be a catalyst for urban development and/or redevelopment. During the 1980s the municipality of Lyon, France's third largest city, initiated a series of planning and design initiatives – the Lyon 2010 project. The model was the designs in Barcelona carried out under the direction of Oriel Bohigas. In Lyon a series of public works has been undertaken, many by internationally renowned architects: the Opera House was renovated by Jean Nouvel, the Satolas

Station was designed by Santiago Calatrava and the Cité International by Renzo Piano. The process was driven by politicians Henry Chabert (who was closely aligned with Lyon's mayor) and Jean Pierre Charbonneau.

These works were part of a number of coordinated plans of which the Schema d'Amenagement des Espaces Publics focused on seven spaces in the city. The Place des Terreaux was one of them. The overall budget for the seven spaces was tight – 350 million francs (about $US60 million). The square (named for the city's earlier fortifications) is located in the very heart of Lyon. It has a long history but its present form began to take shape in the seventeenth century. The square has served as a marketplace, a place for public executions, and as an administrative centre. The nature of its enclosing elements and the history embedded in them has given the Place des Terreaux its character.

In 1990 the paved square was directly abutted on three sides by buildings and on the fourth a narrow street separated the adjacent buildings from it. Trams still run along this street adding life to the square. The buildings, largely unchanged, still serve to enclose the square. They themselves are of great historic note: the St. Pierre Abbey (1687 in its present form), the Hotel de Ville de Lyon (Town Hall, 1545–1651), houses that had become banks and other commercial uses, and a museum. Coffeehouses were located on the ground floor of a number of the buildings. On the south side was a fountain designed by Auguste Bartholdi. This sculpture was bought and erected in 1892 under the direction of the then mayor of Lyon. Called the 'Tank of Freedom', it symbolizes the flowing of the Garonne, the river running through Lyon, into the sea.

The automobile parking problem in the tight-knit heart of Lyon became acute in the 1990s so a decision was made to plug in a parking garage under the square – the solution the Los Angeles city administration had implemented at Pershing Square. The project was carried out under the overall control of the Urban Community of Lyon with a private company handling the engineering concerns. The design goal was to create a new place representing the 1990s while respecting the heritage value of the square. *Tout changer sans rien toucher* – change everything without touching anything – was the design principle; water and

light were the design elements. The design team hired by the city comprised Daniel Buren as the sculptor, Christian Drevet as the architect, and Laurent Fachard as the lighting engineer. They were aided by Bruno Bossard and Catalin Badea of Lyon. Matt Mullican and Pierre Favre of Lyon designed the underground garage.

La Place des Terreaux remains a paved space but with some significant changes. The Bartholdi Fountain was moved across the square in order to allow for the installation of 69 mini water and light fountains. The fountains, fed by 17 pumps that spout water to different heights, cross the square in five lines 5.9 metres apart. A row of columns erected across the façade of the Palais St. Pierre is the only change to the enclosing elements of the square. The street on the south side of the square has boundary markers and different surface materials that distinguish it from the remainder of the square. The traffic along this one side continues to add a sense of bustle to the square. The entrances to the car park are outside the enclosing elements of the square and do not affect it as they do Pershing Square. Coffee shops and restaurants on the periphery open directly onto the space. The surrounding buildings are subtly floodlit during the hours of darkness adding to the ambience of the place at night (Figure 5.14).

The square is a centre of tourism with the cafés and restaurants being major attractions for people and the people themselves becoming major attractions for yet others. In addition to the public benches, the edge of the Bartholdi fountain is used for seating. Children (and teenagers) use the 69 fountains and the Bartholdi fountain as a playground.

Critics regard the redesigned square as a great artistic success (Broto, 2000). It has

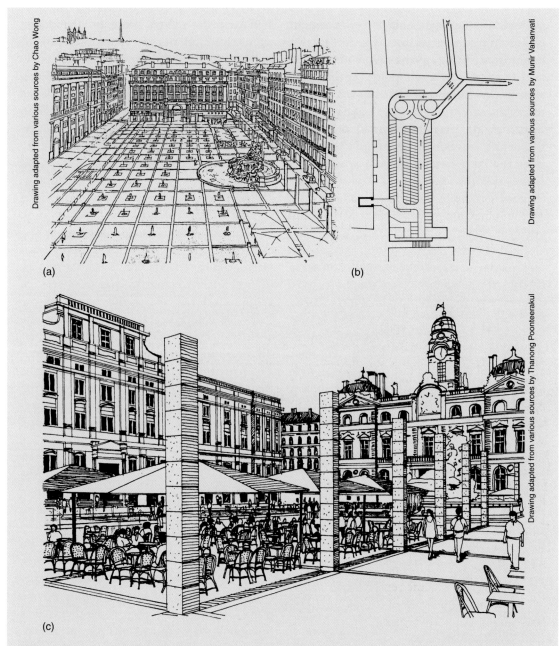

Figure 5.14 La Place des Terreaux, Lyon. (a) A sketch of the square from the top of the Hotel de Ville, (b) the layout of the underground parking and (c) a sketch of the daytime use of the square.

been and remains the centre of Lyon, and is thus an important element, possibly the most important, in terms of giving the city an identity, in the city's public realm. The decision to redesign the Place des Terreaux was certainly one made in the public realm of politics and the square is an urban space. Is it urban design? The design of the parking garage is an architectural and engineering feat, the fountains a work of art and the paving landscape work. Overall the final product is a fine collaborative landscape architectural project in a city.

Major references

Bedarida, Marc (1995). Lione: la politica degli spazi publica. *Casabella* **59** (629): 8–23.

Broto, Carles (2000). La Place des Terreaux. In *New Urban Design*. Barcelona: Arian Mostaedi, 26–33.

Gehl, Jan and Lars Gemzøe (2003). Place des Terreaux. In *New City Spaces* [translated by Karen Steenhard]. Copenhagen: Danish Architectural Press, 156–61.

Streets

The perceived quality of a city is very much dependent on the quality of its streets. Their character depends on the lengths of their blocks, their cross sections (the widths of their roadbeds and sidewalks, the nature of the abutting building setbacks and heights, the frequency of entrances to buildings, the presence or absence of shop windows, etc.). The quality is also affected by the nature and speed of vehicular traffic passing along them, how car parking is arranged, the nature of the ground floor uses of the buildings that line them, and their paving and street furniture. This knowledge is only slowly seeping into design action.

Jane Jacobs described the relationship between the nature of street blocks and the character of city precincts (J. Jacobs, 1961). Allan Jacobs has identified and described a number of 'great streets' of various types around the world (A. Jacobs, 1993). His book along with others (e.g. Southworth and Ben-Joseph, 1997) has focused attention on their importance as elements of urban design. During 2002 a conference on Great Asian Streets was held in Singapore (Low Boon Liang, 2002) This conference was particularly important because in the recent mega-projects in the Asia-Pacific region the establishment of the quality of streets has been seen to be the purview of the traffic engineer. The primary goal has been to allow vehicles to be driven as rapidly as possible. The ambient quality for pedestrians has been neglected.

Much recent urban design has focused on the nature of city streets in strong reaction to the Modernists turning their backs on them. Many urban design schemes nowadays contain guidelines for how the buildings that form streets must meet them, building uses and setbacks (if any), in much the same way as written for the boulevards of Haussmann's Paris 150 years ago. The large-scale all-of-a-piece urban developments, such as Seaside in Florida and Poundbury in England, designed under the banner of the New Urbanism, are being controlled in this manner. The concern here is not, however, with such designs but with the landscape architecture of a street.

Major references

Jacobs, Allan (1993). *Great Streets*. Cambridge, MA: MIT Press.

Moudon, Anne Vernez, ed. (1987). Public Streets for Public Use. New York: Van Nostrand Reinhold.

Rudofsky, Bernard (1969). *Streets for People: A Primer for Americans*. New York: Doubleday.

CASE STUDY

George Street, Sydney, Australia: a street upgrading project (1997–9)

The responsibility for planning and managing change in the City of Sydney (as opposed to the metropolitan area) has been the responsibility of the Sydney City Council since its inception in 1855. The state government, however, has retained its veto power over planning and urban design decisions in the city. The redesign of George Street is an example of a landscape project often referred to as urban design. It was carried out under one auspice even though a number of eminent consultants were involved in dealing with various aspects of the project. They worked as one team under the direction of Margaret Petrykowski of the New South Wales Public Works Department (PWD) who was responsible for the overall design and many of the details. The light pole design was by Alexander Tzanes, Barry Webb and KWA, the landscape architects were Tract Consultants, and Philip Cox and J. C. Decaux Australia designed the street furniture.

George Street is the major street running through central Sydney. It changes character considerably along its course from Sydney Harbour (Port Jackson) in the north to the Central Railways Station in the south (see Figure 5.15a). Until it was refurbished its sidewalks were narrow (3.6 metres wide) and crowded, and their surfaces varied from asphalt to patched concrete and a variety of other paving materials. Few would describe George Street as a great street. *A Statement of Environmental Effects of the George Street Urban Design and Transportation Study* (1993) noted that the street possessed neither visual unity nor did it afford pedestrian amenity. It had been shaped incrementally over its 200-year history by piecemeal design.

In the mid-1990s a decision was made to upgrade the street from Alfred Street at the harbour end to Central Station, a length of 2.6 kilometres (about 1.8 miles). The city council was the client for the project but the PWD had overall responsibility. It delegated the design to its Projects Department in conjunction with City Projects with Petrykowski as designer. Contract drawings were done by Noel Bell Ridley Smith, Architects. During implementation the project architect was Bill Tsakalos of the New South Wales Government Architect's office. The design of the programme, the civil and the electrical

Figure 5.15 George Street Sydney, improvements. (a) The George Street location, (b) George Street North Proposal, (c) a typical intersection detail, (d) a general view towards the south, (e) a detail, (f) the bus station at the southern end.

Figure 5.15 (g) footpath detail at the Town Hall steps.

engineering, and the quantity surveying were all contracted out to private firms. The budget for the whole upgrading was $A75 million (approximately $US50 million in 2000).

The project was developed in three phases. The first two involved the preparation of the street for rebuilding rather than the actual reconstruction. The first step consisted of the removal of the median strips where they existed, the relocating of existing traffic lights and the creation of temporary traffic lanes and other street markings. The second phase involved the installation of mobile barriers between the roadway and the sidewalk to protect pedestrians while the sidewalks were widened by up to 2.5 metres (8 feet) and were prepared for new kerbs and paving. The third and final phase involved the relocation of existing services,

the installation of new services and the preparation of the area for the reconstruction of the sidewalks, their surfacing in bluestone and the insertion of new granite curbed gutters to the street. The installation of a coordinated set of street furniture followed. London Plane trees, chosen because of their resistance to pollution, were planted along the street to give it a sense of unity.

During construction, there was much opposition to the changes being made. There were also some design problems. The kerb cuts, for instance, were too steep for wheelchairs and had to be altered. Disruptions to the flow of both vehicular and pedestrian traffic were frequent. Despite the complaints the project had the continuous support of the major of Sydney, Frank Sartor and the New South Wales State Government.

The result of all the work is a tidier street unified by consistent paving materials and street furniture. Cluttered areas were de-cluttered to give an air of roominess, wider sidewalks were provided and street furniture was made simpler and modern. The changes have not, however, made George Street a great street. Its cross section is given and in the absence of an autocratic power advocating change it will remain much as it is. The George Street upgrading remains a highly competent award-winning landscape architecture project.

The refurbishment of George Street has had a catalytic effect leading to the upgrading of a number of shopfronts along it and, particularly, around Railway Square. In combination with other similar projects and the increase in the number of apartment units in Sydney's central business district (CBD) it has enabled more sidewalk cafés to be located on the city's streets and thus initiated a chain reaction of events that have added to the precinct's vitality. It has also led to the redesign of other city streets. A precedent has been set.

The goal for George Street in the present Central City Development Control Plan is to maintain:

1 the street line and the current building–street relationship;
2 the height of buildings as they abut the street, and to create;
3 continuous colonnading along it.

Doors and entranceways should, according to the plan, be 'emphasized' in any new buildings. In combination the development control plan and the landscaping work on George Street are certainly urban design. One without the other is hardly so.

Major references

Department of Public Works and Services and the Council of the City of Sydney (1997). *George Street and Railway Square Redevelopment: Statement of Environmental Effects*. Sydney: The authors.

Lochhead, Helen (1999). Sydney afresh. *Architecture Australia* **88** (September/October): 68–75.

Urban Projects Unit (1993). *George Street Urban Design and Transport Study – A Draft for discussion with the Sydney City Council*. Sydney: The authors. *http://www.statetrail.nsw.gov.au/Railestate/VOL-UME1/ NUMBER4/5a57f74.htm*

Parks

Park design has been an aspect of the work of landscape architects that often merges with urban design. Frederick Law Olmsted's work during the late nineteenth century included the design of the Columbian Exposition of 1893 in Chicago and a number of suburbs. He is, however, probably best known for the design of New York's Central Park. It is one of the most urban of parks in the world. Parks may form parts of urban design schemes but they themselves are products of landscape architecture.

Parks are designed and redesigned as fashion changes. Many new parks are also being built. They vary considerably in size and the roles they play in the city. The redevelopment of the proposed Shanghai waterfront is an example of an almost seamless melding of buildings and landscape architecture. It has hardly got off the ground. The design of the waterfront in Kuching is one that is very much related to its context – environmentally and socially. In contrast, Parc de la

Villette is very much an object in the Paris cityscape as well as an environment for those who use it. To be urban design, park design and architecture need to be integrated into a single-design approach. Bernard Tschumi did this in the design of the Parc de la Villette. It is, however, still predominantly a landscape architectural scheme containing architectural elements.

Major reference

Baljon, Lodewijk (1995). *Designing Parks*. Amsterdam: Architecture and Nature Press.

CASE STUDY

Kuching Waterfront, Sarawak, Malaysia: a waterfront park as a catalyst for urban redevelopment (1989–93)

Kuching lies on the Sungai Sarawak 20 kilometres in from the sea. The city's riverfront used to be the regional shipping and distribution point of the Malaysian state of Sarawak. It intervened or acted as a seam, depending on one's point of view, between the commercial area on Main Bazaar and the river. The commercial area contained Chinese shophouses, a high-rise hotel and office buildings. The development of a road network and air transportation during the 1960s and 1970s, and the change in shipping technology led to the abandonment of the godowns (warehouses) and the general deterioration of the waterfront. The river wall had deteriorated, mud-flats filled former shipping channels, and squatters had built shacks along the waterfront. At the same time it was a lively colourful area of fishing boats and commerce. The area contained historic buildings, commuter jetties, and government and commercial buildings. It was also a mess.

The client for the redevelopment of the waterfront was the Sarawak State Economic Development Corporation (SEDC), a statutory agency established in 1972 to promote the industrial, commercial and socio-economic development of the state. SEDC's Tourism and Leisure Agency has been responsible for carrying out a number of joint ventures with private developers. These works have included cultural facilities, golf clubs, shopping areas and hotels that cater to tourists from East Asia, in particular. Most of the properties carry international brand names, such as Holiday Inn, Arnold Palmer and Crowne Plaza. In order to upgrade the image of Kuching, the re-invention of the waterfront became a necessity.

In the early 1980s the Chief Minister of Sarawak envisaged a new link between the city and river but it took some time to initiate a project that would achieve this end. In 1989, SEDC was assigned the role of developer of the waterfront by the state's government. The next year it, in turn, hired the project team. The team was comprised of a local and an international consultancy. The former was United Consultants (Kuching) and the international team was Conybeare Morrison and Partners, a Sydney landscape architecture and urban design firm. It was the latter that led the design effort from beginning to end.

Figure 5.16 The Kuching Waterfront Park. (a) Conceptual plan, (b) first phase plan and (c) a view of the waterfront.

A former Colombo Plan Malaysian student who had studied in Sydney was the connecting link between client and the Sydney firm.

The design goal was to provide a mix of facilities along the waterfront that would appeal to both local and international visitors, and establish a specific local sense of place. The desire of SEDC was also to retain the historical and cultural settings of the waterfront but to get rid of the dirt and truck traffic and to link Main Bazaar to the water and views across it. It was to be a showpiece for Kuching and an exemplar for waterfront design in Malaysia. It was perceived to be a 'quality of life project' and well funded.

There were thus several design objectives. One was to open up the riverfront to the city by creating view corridors to the water. Another was to preserve the historic elements in the area and a third was to be 'Kuching in character'. The artworks, and food outlets are hence predominantly local in nature rather than parts of international chains. Indigenous tribal patterns were adapted for the paving patterns. The materials, however, had to be robust and easy to maintain. No local materials that possessed this quality were available so granite stocks were imported from China and mosaic tiles from Ravenna in Italy. A further objective was to remove the mudflats that locals regarded as ugly. The riverfront was extended and parts of the new development are located on reclaimed land. The tidal difference on the Sungai Sarawak was 5 metres. A barrage built down river now keeps the water at a constant height. It also effectively cuts the city off from the sea as far as shipping is concerned and makes the pontoons that form part of the design redundant.

The new waterfront consists of a 1-kilometre (about 3040-foot) long riverside promenade (see Figure 5.16). The promenade was built on piles to prevent settling and lined by tropical trees at 12-metre intervals to provide shade. The landscape architects were under some pressure to build a colonnade but won the argument to keep it as an open walkway. The scheme has a dumbbell design linking the hotel district with downtown Kuching. Between the two ends there are a number of rotundas that serve as rest points and also a series of 'features'. There are food outlets and restaurants, a pavilion for cultural performances, a series of water features and fountains and a 'thematic' playground for children. They are all aimed squarely at the tourist market but they also provide for local residents, Malays, Chinese and minorities alike, so that there is always a mix of people there.

A number of special features give a unique character to the Kuching waterfront. The Courthouse is celebrated with a square in front of it. The former Sarawak Steamship Company headquarters is home to a tourist centre. At the southern end of the board-walk is the Chinese Museum housed in a building erected in 1912 by the Chinese community of Kuching for the Chinese Chamber of Commerce. A Town Square that contains a nineteenth century square tower is the centrepiece of the project. Pools and fountains now flank it. The tower, formerly a gaol, houses an exhibition. It also offers views across the new waterfront to the historic features of the city and river: Malay villages, the Astana (home of the Brooke family, the white rajah's of Borneo from 1837 until the 1950s), and Fort Magherita.

The art works include the Hornbill Fountain, a modern steel sculpture, depicting Sarawak's national bird. The balustrades are finely wrought, the furniture is well designed and the planting reflects the lush tropical environment of Sarawak. It is this integration of buildings, landscape and streetscape that makes this project as much an urban design project as a work of landscape architecture. It was the design work of one firm from the inception of the idea down to the detailing of paving patterns.

The metamorphosis of the waterfront has acted as a catalyst for the redevelopment of adjacent areas. Land values in the neighbourhood of the riverfront have increased substantially and new buildings facing the park have been erected. The old godowns and bond stores on Main Bazaar have become tourist-oriented crafts shops. An unanticipated, but welcome, by-product of the design is that the waterfront draws all elements of the multi-ethnic Kuching population together. It is used by one and all. It received a civic design award from the Australian Institute of Landscape Architects in 1994.

Major references

Breen, Ann and Dick Rigby (1996). Kuching Waterfront development. In *The New Waterfronts: A Worldwide Success Story*. London: Thames and Hudson, 148–51.

Conybeare Morrison and Partners (1990). Kuching Riverfront Masterplan. Sydney: The authors.

Sara Resorts Sdn. BhD (2000). *A tribute to the people: Kuching Waterfront*. http:/www.sedctourism.com/waterfront/

CASE STUDY

Parc de la Villette, Paris, France: a deconstructed park design (1979–97)

The Parc de la Villette has a complex development history. In 1979, the Etablissement Public du Parc de la Villette (EPPV) initiated the development and design process that resulted in the park. The goal, along with that of a number of other contemporary projects, was to make Paris once more the art centre of the world. The specific objectives were:

1 to create a product of international note,
2 to build a national museum of science and technology,
3 to create an urban 'cultural' park.

The site was 55 hectares (136 acres) of semi-abandoned industrial land in the northeast corner of Paris. It included a major slaughterhouse and a cattle hall/ sales yard. A canal divides the site into two and another borders much of the site on the west.

The design of the park occurred in two phases: (1) an international design competition was held in 1982 and the winner announced in March 1983, and (2) the project was further refined by pragmatic changes by the winning team. The French Minister of Culture, Jack Lang, announced the Concours International Parc de La Villette in 1982. The programme included a large museum of science and industry, a *cité* of music, a major hall for exhibitions, and a rock concert hall as well as the park. It required two existing structures on the site to be reused. The park was to reflect 'urbanism, pleasure and experimentation' and was to achieve a unity in its architecture and

105

landscape. The hope was that the development would be a bridge between city and suburb, and act as a 'gateway' to Paris from the east. This design agenda was a pure act of will of the French government rather than one based on a market study. It was developed under the strong influence of the then President of France, Giscard d'Estaing. He had chosen Adrein Fainsilber from amongst 27 French architects to convert the Grande Salle into a science museum.

The competition for the park attracted 472 entries from 41 countries. The team headed by Bernard Tschumi won the competition (see Figure 5.17a). He was then appointed head of the project team to implement it. In 1984, a closed competition for the Music Centre and for four housing schemes on the north side of the park was held (Baljon, 1995). The construction of the park began in 1985 and can be said to have been completed in 1997. The design was conceived so that it could evolve as construction progressed and changes are still occasionally being made. Its 'finished' state is shown in Figure 5.17c.

The design has attracted considerable attention because it was associated with a design ideology derived from contemporary literary analysis. It consists of three largely independent systems superimposed on each other. The first is a series of points at the intersections of a 120-metre (390-foot) grid, eight squares to the north and south and five squares east to west. At the intersections are a series of follies, their structural envelope covered by bright red-enamelled steel sheets (see Figure 5.18a). Tschumi designed them all. The second system consists of a set of lines. These are the paths of pedestrian movement organized in two interconnected systems. One consists of cross axes of covered galleries, and the second of a meandering

'cinematic' promenade presenting a sequential series of vistas and enclosures. The third system consists of the surfaces of the park. In addition, alleys of trees link the major activity sites of the park. The surface materials, grass and paving, were chosen to best afford the activities that were expected to take place in different locations.

The follies are 10.8-metre (36-foot) cubes 'divided three dimensionally into 12-foot cubes forming "cases"'. These cases according to Tschumi 'can be decomposed into fragments . . . or extended through the addition of other elements' (Tschumi, 1987). Certain gardens on the 'cinematic promenade' were allocated to other architects to design. Each garden had, however, to be designed within the framework established by Tschumi.

The park contains of a mix of facilities. The Cité des Sciences, a science and technology museum, is housed in what was the largest of the old Villette's slaughterhouses (see Figure 5.18b). It is 40 metres (133 feet) high and stretches over 3 hectares (7 acres). Adrien Fainsilber (with Peter Rice and Martin Francis) had three major concerns in creating his design: water should surround the building, vegetation should penetrate the greenhouses, and light the cupola. The park also contains La Géode, a giant entertainment sphere with a high hemispherical screen, the Grande Halle, an old cattle shed converted into exhibition space, the Cité de la Musique, l'Argonauts, a navigation museum with a submarine parked outside it, and the Zenith Theatre. The theatre is a polyester tent designed for audiences of 6000 attending pop-music concerts.

During the summer, the Parc attracts as many as 15,000 people a day; during the winter it has about 3000 visitors each day. The French government has achieved its goal. The park attracts international acclaim

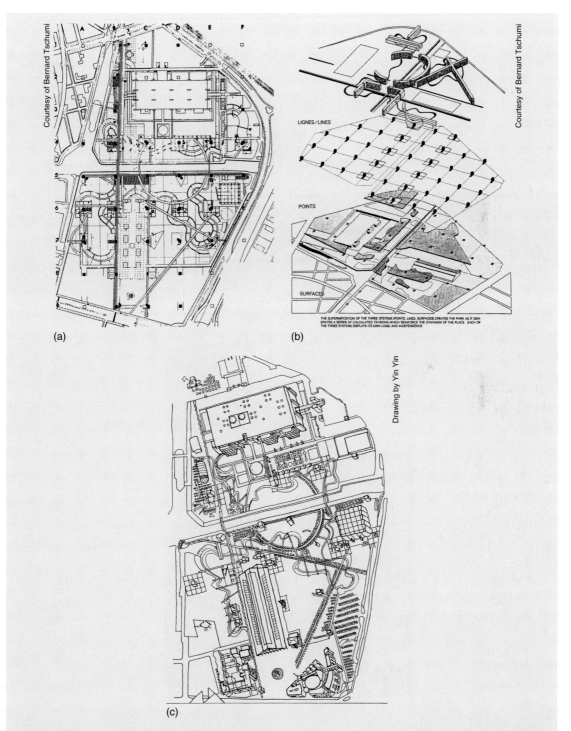

Figure 5.17 The Parc de la Villette, Paris. (a) Tschumi and team's competition winning entry, (b) the design deconstructed and (c) the park as built.

Photograph by Ruth Durack

(a)

Photograph by Alix Verge

(b)

Figure 5.18 Two structures at the Parc de la Villette. (a) A folie and (b) the Cité des Sciences.

and, more importantly, attention. The acclaim that the park has received is based on its intellectual aesthetic ideology as a work of art and its intellectual under-pinning. It has been embraced by the architectural cognoscenti and has been extraordinarily widely published. The ideology has been proven to be difficult to transfer to urban developments. Any such plans, and there are a number of them, have remained on paper. In many ways the Parc de la Villette is indeed an urban design project combining landscape architectural and architectural features into a unified whole.

Major references

Baljon, Lodewijk (1995). *Designing Parks*. Amsterdam: Architecture and Nature Press.

Benjamin, Andrew (1988). Deconstruction and art/the art of deconstruction. In Christopher Norris and Andrew Benjamin, eds., *What Is Deconstruction?* New York: St. Martin's Press, 33–56.

Broadbent, Geoffrey (1990). Parc de la Villette. In *Emerging Concepts of Urban Space Design*. London: Van Nostrand Reinhold (International), 316–9.

Tschumi, Bernard (1987). *Cinégramme Folie: le Parc de la Villette*. Princeton, N.J.: Princeton University Press.

A Note

The Shanghai Waterfront Park, Shanghai, People's Republic of China: a proposed integrated park and building urban design scheme (2000+)

As in many parts of the world (e.g. Battery Park City, Canary Wharf and Darling Harbour described in Chapter 8), the port facilities developed in Shanghai during the first half of the twentieth century have become redundant. With the development of mega-projects in the city – the Pudong in particular – the heavily polluted Huangpu River, wide though it is, instead of being the eastern edge of the city's core, has become a seam for development. The recent abandonment of many waterfront industries has led to a significant improvement in the quality of the river's water thus making land along its banks attractive for development.

In 2000, the Shanghai Urban Planning Bureau organized an international competition for a development plan for both sides of the Huangpu River. The area covered was 2470 hectares (6.3 square miles) and 24.7 kilometres (13 miles) in length extending from the Fu-Sing Island to the south of Ruiz Jin Nan Road. The goal of the Bureau was to use this strip of riverfront for recreational tourism and commercial development. It was also necessary to provide flood control measures and to encompass numerous cultural, historical and economic elements in the design. Three schemes were chosen as finalists: those by Sasaki, the Skidmore, Owings, and Merrill, San Francisco office (SOM), and the Cox Partnership of Sydney. The second of these firms was chosen to proceed with the scheme. Many of the planning principles, such as the network of green links connecting the river to the interior of the site, were adopted from the Cox Partnership plan.

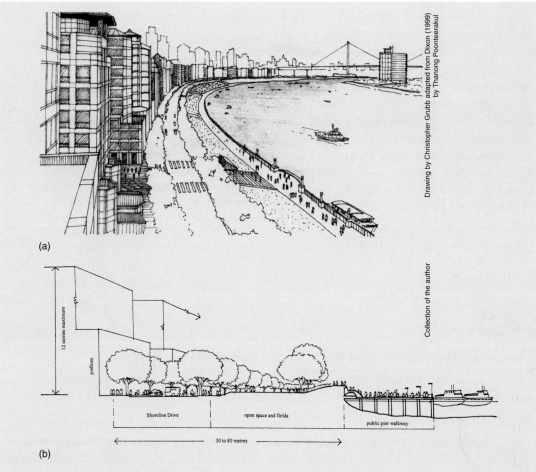

(a)

(b)

Drawing by Christopher Grubb adapted from Dixon (1999) by Thanong Poonteerakul

Collection of the author

Figure 5.19 The Shanghai waterfront proposal. (a) A sketch of the proposed Crescent and (b) A cross section through the Crescent.

As often happens in large schemes, the client changed over the course of time from the one who initiated it. The Shanghai P. & K. Development Company joined the Shanghai Port Authority as the property developer. They became the investment, marketing and the coordinating authority for the scheme. SOM was responsible for the master plan while the Shanghai Urban Planning and Research Institute executed the local planning. The land along the river was rezoned and the area between the proposed new development and the river was designated as parkland.

One of the design goals was to extend the visual linkages between the city and the waterfront. This task is not easy, as the river has high berms to prevent the flooding of the city. The other goals established were to create distinct precincts each with its own identity along the river and to enliven the front. The first goal is to be met by extending the streets down towards the river edge, the second by creating architecturally and activity unified neighbourhoods, and the third by adding to the passenger traffic on the river. Providing a coastal passenger-shipping terminal will augment the ferry services.

A major feature of the park is the Crescent (see Figure 5.19a). The width of the park varies in order to obtain some variety. The planting scheme is also varied with some areas left relatively open for active recreation while others have been designed for passive contemplation. On the landside, the park is proposed to be bounded by mid-rise (up to 12 stories in height), mixed-use, podium-based buildings and a boulevard. The buildings will give a strong definition and a sense of urbanity to the park. The boulevard has been purposefully designed to restrict its use as a major traffic artery. Its width has been kept down to two moving lanes in each direction and frequent pedestrian crossings have been introduced. The waterfront has an esplanade on the river's edge with lawns and trees between it and the boulevard. What is not clear from the sketch but is clear from the cross section is the use of a berm to control flooding. Inevitably it cuts off the visual link between the public pier walkway and the park inland to it (see Figure 5.19b).

The scheme, if completed as now specified, would really be an all-of-a-piece urban design with a major total landscape architectural element. Guidelines have been written for the buildings that will line the park. The goal is to obtain a consistency in façade design with local referents. The buildings will require the investments of a variety of property developers and be designed by different architects. Whether the park itself should be considered to be an urban design is another matter. The design integrates park space and buildings but we shall have to wait and see whether the scheme actually develops as stated here. Parcels of land are being released for competition up and down the river. The analysis of how it turns out will make a worthwhile case study!

Major references

Dixon, John Morris (1999). *Urban Spaces*. New York: Visual Reference Publications.

Marshall, Richard (2001). *Waterfronts in Post-Industrial Cities*. London: Spon Press.

Cox Group (2002). *Shanghai Waterfront masterplan, China*. www.cox.com.au/projects/masterplanning_urban_design/index, html

Some Notes on Detailing the Environment

Much of the detailing of the design of the public realm of cities is a problem of landscape architecture. The quality of the detailing, as displays and as behaviour settings, makes a major contribution to our feelings about places and about the cities of which they are a part. By detailing is meant the small-scale patterns – the kerbs and kerb cuts for making an environment barrier free, the grates and man-hole covers, the paving, the steps and staircases, and the seating designs. The architect Ludwig Mies van der Rohe is often quoted as saying 'God is in the details'. Certainly the quality of the public realm is not simply a function of its overall design but its details. The quality of the 16th Street Mall in Denver, Colorado owes much to its detailing (see Figures 1.1 and 5.20).

Coutesy for the Olin Partnership, Philadelphia

Figure 5.20   The 16th Street Mall, Denver.

The quality of the detailing depends on how the elements are handled, their composition, patterns, colours, the precision of the workmanship and what they afford in terms of human activities. Of particular importance are paving patterns, the nature of illumination, the design of street furnishings and the nature of the signage. What is fashionable can be important for it gives both designers and users of the environment a sense of being up-to-date. What is regarded as fashionable does, however, change. Sometimes a richness in patterning is held in high esteem but simpler patterns seem to be the ones that endure (e.g. Piazza San Marco, Venice; see Figure 5.2).

The manner in which the pubic realm is illuminated – naturally and/or artificially, day or night – contributes substantially to its ambient qualities. The concern is not only for safety but also for aesthetics. The perceived quality of spaces between buildings – streets, alleys, squares and nooks and crannies – is very much dependent on how the architecture and landscape architecture are organized and illuminated. The way façades of buildings are illuminated can enrich the experience of being in places. There are many examples of finely detailed environments but many more that are carelessly designed and deteriorating rapidly. Detailing the environment is a fine art.

Commentary: Are these Landscape Architectural Products Urban Design?

The quality of urban spaces depends on how they are enclosed as much as on their own attributes. Impressive though individual buildings and a city's skyline may be when seen as a panorama, it is the quality of the city's open spaces – the public realm – that defines their nature and their image in people's eyes. The open spaces of a city – their landscape architecture – have been designed by a wide variety of people and during the second half of the twentieth century they went through several fashion cycles within different cultural contexts. It is clear that the quality of the landscape architecture is both the essential ingredient of the case studies included in this chapter. Can it all, or any of it, be claimed to be urban design? Of all the schemes presented in this chapter, the most urban, Pershing Square, is the one that can least be called urban design. Both the SITE and the Legoretta/Olin design focused on the surface of the square. Maybe in the long run the Square will become a true urban place integrated with its enclosing elements. It is not one yet.

Important though the quality of their landscape architecture is, well-designed cityscapes and parks are not the panacea for the ills of cities. They cannot solve social or economic problems on their own. The authorities in Oak Park found that out. Parks and other landscaped areas need to be well located and well designed for specific functions in terms of people's lives as they are lived and also in terms of how the natural world works. These functions need to be understood. Urban design schemes everywhere need to be cared for after completion as well as they are in Singapore. Often the nature of maintenance required is a question avoided in design thinking. As a result many spaces when built soon deteriorate and have a negative impact on their surroundings and a people's self-esteem.

What have not been at all included in this chapter are examples of designing public/open spaces in arid climates. 'Greening the city' is an unfortunate slogan for improving the biogenic quality of cities. Greening cities in arid zones, such as Phoenix, Arizona or Tehran needs to be considered very carefully. Such cities need to be 'browned' as much as 'greened'. Much can be learnt from traditional human settlement patterns in different climatic zones (see, e.g. Rudofsky, 1969). Those settlements, however, were not designed with automobile usage in mind. We need new paradigms addressing the opportunities and problems of our contemporary world.

The products described in this chapter are varied and typically landscape architecture in cities. Where the projects included the framing elements of open spaces and/or contain significant buildings as an essential part of the scheme they surely are urban design. If not they are important landscape architecture projects in cities. Many landscape architects would claim that this distinction is pedantic. The distinction is certainly often blurred. Riverwalk in San Antonio (see Chapter 10) is included in this book under the rubric of plug-in urban design. It could be argued that it is primarily concerned with only the design of the horizontal surfaces between buildings and so is a product of landscape architecture. It did, however, consciously set out to change the three-dimensional world around it and it succeeded in doing so. Whether redesigning elements of the public realm is urban design in it purest sense or not remains an undecided issue. Landscape architects claim it is. If it is then what is landscape architecture?

The products of architecture and the nature of urban design

Most urban design projects are architect led if not initiated. Many architects claim expertise in urban design the day they are graduated with a degree. Their image of urban design varies. Although architects have often been part of the anti-urban intellectual elite (White and White, 1964) a number of prominent practitioners and educators have been vitally interested in cities and city life. Others, while strongly socially aware find that being involved seriously in urban design, as it is described in Part 1 of this book, is just too frustrating. They thus prefer to stick to the design of individual buildings and, sometimes, building complexes. Yet others want cities to be works of art. Few cities are, except in the cumulative sense of being a collage of buildings and open spaces (Rowe and Koetter, 1978).

The Products of Architecture: Buildings

Architects design buildings for individual clients. The buildings serve many purposes but, possibly, the primary purpose is to create a return on capital monies. Property developers have learnt that having a famous architect design their buildings enhances their investment. The public interest is not of concern to them or their architects unless it enhances profitability or if it is encoded in building regulations. A building affords and shelters specific activities but it is also a display of an architect's talents and the best way of displaying a building is as an object in space to be admired.

The borderline between large, multi-building architectural schemes and urban design is often fuzzy. I suspect the designers of Rockefeller Center saw the complex as an architectural project. If the term 'urban design' had, however, been coined in the 1930s, perhaps they would have regarded it as an urban design scheme. Rockefeller Center has been classified as a total urban design in this book (see Chapter 7) but its architects may have seen it as an all-of-a-piece urban design. They may not have liked to have been seen as one team of associated architects rather than a set of creative individuals each producing a building of note. Much the same can be said about the Lincoln Center (see Figure 7.7).

When urban design is considered to be a high architectural art the concern in design is often reduced to how to express in geometrical forms and materials a currently fashionable idea – the focus is on abstract intellectual aesthetic theories rather than life as it is lived. A new norm is appearing in the architecture and urban design of the global commercial marketplace. It is based on producing building forms that are a departure from geometric norms using expensive materials. The results should not be dismissed out of hand as 'glitzy' or 'kitsch' even though much new Asian architecture has been referred to as 'non-judgemental kitsch'.

The architecture versus the city literature is well established. Many of the recent buildings of architectural luminaries have paid little heed to the public spaces they are creating or how the buildings they design help make good streets. They do not relate their buildings to their surroundings other than to use their contexts as a backdrop for a display. Many, if not almost all, architectural critics support this position. They focus on a building as a work of art and many young architects strive to emulate the work. Fine though the Seattle Public Library (completed 2003) designed by Rem Koolhaas might be, it shows a 'disdain for comfortable public spaces' and turns its back on the city; it does not encourage people to hang around and participate in urban life. Nor is the plaza facing the Guggenheim Museum (1997) designed for Bilbao by Frank Gehry a hospitable place. The museum is an exciting building as is his Walt Disney Concert Hall in Los Angeles (completed 2003; see Figure 6.1). Neither adds much to the streetscape. Is this the new urban design as leading architects and their patrons see it?

There are four situations in which the design of individual buildings or individual building complexes seem to be regarded by mainstream architects and architectural critics as urban design. The first is when buildings pay some respect to their built contexts – street alignments, ground floor uses and designs, and overall massing (i.e. they have the same 'texture' as their surroundings). The second is when a building acts as a catalyst for urban development. The third is when the facilities that are traditionally in a neighbourhood or city are incorporated into a single multi-use building, and the fourth is when there are a number of buildings in a complex – large-scale architectural projects.

Contextual Design

One might think that the least obligation of any new building is make its surroundings more commodious and interesting. The trouble is that this obligation often gets in the way of an architect's desire for self-expression in built form. The urban design awards of the journal *Progressive Architecture*, from the inception of the scheme in the early 1970s to the demise of the journal in the mid-1990s, more often than not went to individual buildings. No awards went to completed urban design schemes. In 1999, the Royal Australian Institute of Architects (RAIA) was considering giving an urban design award to a building that complied with the requirements of a master urban design plan. In a field where the individuality of designs is exalted and architects try to find a niche for themselves in the marketplace for services by being different, the willingness to pay attention to the public realm is indeed something to be rewarded. The development of a discrete

Photograph by Kathy A. Kolnick

(a)

(b)

Figure 6.1 The Walt Disney Concert Hall, Los Angeles in 2004. (a) The Concert Hall as object and (b) the Concert Hall in context.

contextual architectural attitude in Barcelona after the fall of the dictatorship of Franco has been little emulated elsewhere and indeed no longer holds sway in that city.

The RAIA gave its major urban design award in 2002 to the refurbishment of an outdoor music bowl. Its secondary award that year went to a new bridge allied to a museum refurbishment. At least the bridge is an element of urban infrastructure. It received the award, however, for being as much an art object as an important urban link (Awards, 2002). It is sad that nowadays the pressures on architects are such that simply designing with a sense of decorum, with respect for the nature of a street or precinct, brings an award.

The issue of how an individual building adds to or makes its context is a fundamental concern in urban design. Should a building meld in with those around it or stand out? Should it be a foreground or a background building? Almost all developers and their architects want their buildings to be foreground buildings and resent any guidelines or other design controls that they see as limiting their imaginative power. Interestingly, major architects seem to have less difficulty in designing background buildings than minor ones striving to make their mark.

CASE STUDY

Pioneer Place, Portland, Oregon, USA: building in context (1979–90)

Central Portland has a number of characteristics that make it unusual amongst American cities. The first difference is that its blocks are small (200 feet square; 61 metres square) and the streets are narrow (60 to 80 feet; 18 to 24 metres) thus providing a pedestrian friendly, easily walkable environment. Secondly, the downtown area has block-sized parks. (There is also a linear park along the western edge of the Willamette River). Thirdly, the city has many older buildings that give it both a sense of history and visual character. Fourthly, sunlight at street level is valued; Portland is cloudier than most North American cities! Fifthly, many of the streets have views to the surrounding hills. In sum, these variables make Portland, well, Portland. They form a well-loved city pattern.

A proposal by property developers Cadillac-Fairview designed by the Zimmer Gunsul Frasca Partnership in 1980 demonstrates the issues that arise in designing in cities when a building complex, architecturally interesting, but paying little respect to its context runs into political opposition. The proposal was for a multi-use four-block scheme that combined four buildings (one on each block) into a single development (see Figure 6.2). The four buildings were to be linked with skybridges such as those in Minneapolis although Portland's climate is considerably less harsh than that of Minneapolis. Unlike the skybridges in Minneapolis that must have glass walls (see Figure 10.22), the ones in this proposed complex were lined with shops that made them wide and opaque. Their function was to make the buildings a unified cluster, an island, largely independent of its surroundings.

Portland is a city with a lively street-life, yet the proposal turned life inwards as if it was a suburban shopping centre. The size of the complex was well beyond that of Portland's block structure; the skybridges blocked the view of the hills and, it was feared, as in Minneapolis, that they would take people, particularly the middle-class, off the streets. The size of the complex would have also dwarfed the adjacent Pioneer Courthouse. The proposal, if built, would have changed its context in a way that was regarded as negative and would probably

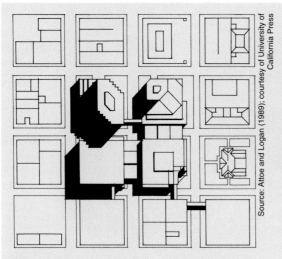

Source: Attoe and Logan (1989); courtesy of University of California Press

Figure 6.2 The Cadillac-Fairview proposal, 5th and Morrison Streets, Portland.

have acted as a catalyst for other similar developments. Portland would no longer be Portland.

Negotiations between the Portland Development Commission and Cadillac-Fairview over the nature of the design broke down and the regional economic climate turned sour so the development was shelved. What it did do was act as a catalyst for other possible ideas for the site so the commission invited other proposals. One presented by the Rouse Corporation was accepted. It was designed by ELS/Elbasani and Logan, Architects. It was regarded as being more in the public's interest. It too evolved as a result of negotiations; failures to attract tenants and eventual successes shaped it.

Named Pioneer Place, the proposal focusing on Morrison Street made the Pioneer Courthouse (currently being revamped in 2004) a foreground building instead of having it dwarfed by high-rise buildings (see Figure 6.3). While the four blocks of the project changed the architectural character of the

city, it maintained the city's nature of small blocks and open spaces. One of the blocks contains a 16-storey office tower with a 60,000 square feet department store – Saks Fifth Avenue, the complex's anchor store. Pioneer Place also contains an internal shopping pavilion of 155,000 square feet. Shops, nevertheless, grace the street frontages. The proposal does retain skybridges but they are smaller and less obtrusive than those in the Cadillac-Fairview proposal. They link the pavilion with Saks Fifth Avenue across the street.

This case study shows that 'context' has to be defined with some precision. Often it is reduced to simply the poorly defined 'visual character of buildings'. It has to do with the way buildings meet the street, their height (especially on their streets façades), their ground floor uses and the distribution of entrances, their materials and fenestration, cornice and roof patterns. Buildings can be designed to either support or change the context. What developers propose, depends on their values and what a society prescribes, if anything. It would have been easy for Portland to think 'We'll take anything' when the economy turned sour. It did not; the Morrison Street scheme is the result. Designing in context can be highly innovative but it does require additional thought. Fiscal conservatives would, nevertheless, question whether the original proposal was not more in the public interest.

Major reference

Attoe, Wayne and Donn Logan (1989). Portland Oregon: A positive catalytic reaction requires an understanding of context. In *American Urban Architecture: Catalysts in the Design of Cities*. Berkeley and Los Angeles: University of California Press, 96–101.

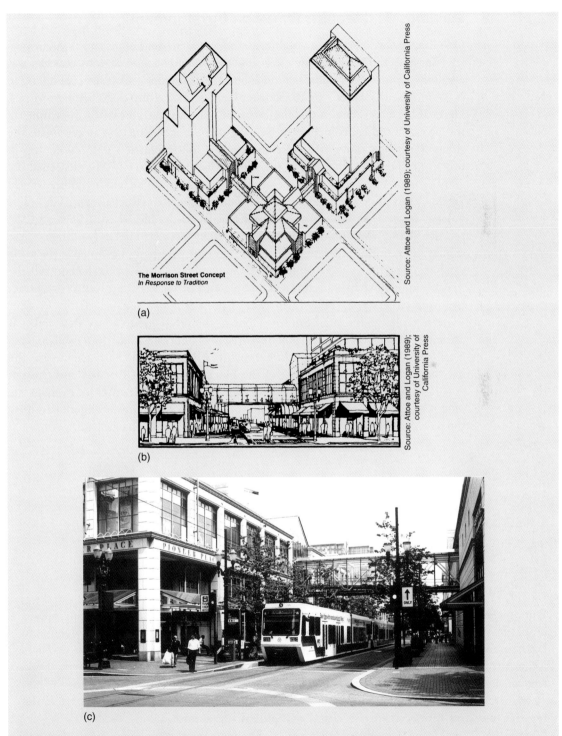

The Morrison Street Concept
In Response to Tradition

(a)

Source: Attoe and Logan (1989); courtesy of University of California Press

(b)

Source: Attoe and Logan (1989); courtesy of University of California Press

(c)

Figure 6.3 Pioneer Place, Portland, Oregon. (a) The Morrison Street concept in response to tradition, (b) an active street-life proposal and (c) the development in 2004.

Buildings as Catalysts for Urban Development

One concern in considering building complexes as urban designs and as public policy issues lies in their catalytic effect on their neighbourhoods. This concern was certainly a motivating factor behind John D. Rockefeller's plans for Radio City in New York (see Chapter 7 on Rockefeller Center). It was also that of Robert Moses, Head of the City Planning Commission of New York in the 1950s in promoting the proposal for Lincoln Center (see Figure 7.7). His goal was to eliminate the slums north of Columbus Circle and build a 'glittering new cultural centre' in order to change the character of the whole west side of the city. He succeeded but 7000 people were displaced by the project (Caro, 1974). The building of the World Trade Center in lower Manhattan had a similar purpose (Ruchelman, 1977). The *Grands Travaux* of French president François Mitterand in the 1980s and the recent (2000–3) development of the Walt Disney Concert Hall in Los Angeles had similar aspirations. The latter, designed by Frank Gehry, hopes to have the same catalytic effect on Grand Avenue as the Guggenheim Museum has had on Bilbao.

All buildings shape the flows of people and of winds, they add to or detract from the streetscape. They form part of the skyline. They can, as the Pioneer Place scheme, result in an improvement of the cityscape in a way that makes it attractive for further development. Museums, libraries, and new well-located retail space can all spur urban development. The Canary Wharf scheme was the lead project in the development of the Docklands area of London and parking garages were in Glendale (see the case studies of both in Chapter 8). Perhaps the most widely publicized building that has acted as a catalyst for development during the past decade has been the Guggenheim Museum in Bilbao, Spain.

CASE STUDY

The Guggenheim Museum (completed 1997) and the Abandoibarra master plan, Bilbao, Spain: a building as a catalyst for development (in progress)

During the 1990s, the city of Bilbao turned a corner. It was a declining port city in the Basque region of northern Spain largely unknown to the world. Today it is very different. A number of major projects developed by the Basque government have regenerated and modernized the city: the Metro, the Euskalduna Congress Hall, the Tramway, the Port of Abra, the Airport and the most important of all in bringing Bilbao to the eyes of the world, the Guggenheim Museum (see Figure 6.4). These projects have, according to the city's mayor, Iñaki Azkuna, elevated the self-esteem of the city and given it confidence to participate in the globalizing world.

The spur for the planning effort that has led to the revival of Bilbao was the flood

Figure 6.4 The Guggenheim Museum in 2004.

of August 1983 that wrought physical and economic havoc. The subsequent 1987 metropolitan plan developed policies for enhancing Bilbao's connections to the external world, increasing mobility within the city, improving environmental and urban quality, investing in human resources and technology and for building a range of cultural facilities. Part of the cultural effort was to create an internationally prestigious museum of modern art. Contemporaneously, the Solomon R. Guggenheim Foundation was looking for a second European site (after the Peggy Guggenheim Museum in Venice) where it could display parts of its collection.

An agreement was reached whereby the Basque administration would pay for the building and the foundation would manage the museum and provide the collection and temporary exhibits. The Solomon R. Guggenheim Museum on Fifth Avenue, New York designed by Frank Lloyd Wright

had set a precedent for having an internationally renowned architect design a building for the foundation. After some debate over whether a refurbished Alhóndiga building in the city could suitably house the collection, a decision was made to have a limited competition for the design of a museum to be located on the banks of the Nervión River. The site was in the centre of a triangle whose vertices were the Arriago Theatre, the University of Deusto and the Fine Arts Museum.

A precedent had been set for the use of limited competitions in Bilbao. The Bilbao Metro (known affectionately as *Fosteritos*) design competition was won by Norman Foster (the other entrants were Santiago Calatrava, Architektengruppe U-bahn and Gregotti Associates). The metro opened in 1995 and is now being extended. The architects involved in the competition for the design of the museum were Arata Isozaki (representing Asia), Coop Himmelblau

(Europe) and Frank Gehry (America). Gehry's design was chosen because it featured an iconic building that might help the Basque people 'communicate an independent identity to the world'. It is a much-admired sculpture of curved volumes made of stone and glass and covered in titanium. On one side is the river and on the other side a large forecourt that sets the building as a sculpture in space.

What impact has the development had? It has surpassed all expectations not only as a work of Art but also as a catalyst for development. The museum drew 4.5 million visitors between 1997 and 2001. They have spent money on accommodation and restaurants that, in turn, has had an impact on the commercial sector of the economy. It is estimated that the museum has added an additional 660 million Euros to the Gross Domestic Product and 117 million to the annual tax base of the city. Over 4000 new jobs have been directly attributed to the development of the museum (Vidarte, 2002). It has spawned new centres of contemporary art in the city – Artium and BilbaoArte (which provides work space for young artists) – and other galleries exhibiting current art. More than anything it has changed the image of the city in the world's eyes. Although it is the jewel in the crown, it is not only the Guggenheim Museum that has resulted in this change. The 'Euskalduna' Conference and Music Centre, the two bridges across the Nervión (the Zubizuri footbridge designed by Santiago Calatrava and the Euskalduna Bridge by Javier Manterola), the new airport terminal designed by Calatrava and the ongoing construction of the Abandoibarra precinct have all had a positive impact on the city's image.

The Abandoibarra plan designed by César Pelli links the Guggenheim Museum, the Fine Arts Museum and 'Euskalduna'. The scheme acts as an extension of the nineteenth century Ensanche, and the public park located on the river. Pelli was elected to do the master plan because of his experience at Battery Park City (see Chapter 8) although he was not the master planner for that scheme and his Abandoibarra master plan depicts a more fragmented Modernist design in which streets are dividers rather than seams of life (see Figure 6.5). The exception is in Pelli's design for the Plaza Euskadi in which the proposed buildings frame the plaza. At the head of the plaza on the axis of Elcano Street to San José Square in the existing central business district will be a 33-storey, 150-metre tower for the provincial Government of Vizcaya designed by Pelli himself. The plaza is to be designed by Diana Belmori.

The Abandoibarra area also contains a Sheraton Hotel (completed in 2004) designed by Ricardo Legorreta, and buildings that will 'emerge like giant doorjambs without a threshold' designed by Arata Isozaki. In addition, Bilbao Ría 2000 (an institution created in 1992 for managing the land of Metropolitan Bilbao) has a public art program to create sculptures in the zone by artists such as Eduardo Chillida and Ulrich Rücheim.

The investment by the Basque government has reversed the economic decline of Bilbao. The city has been transformed from a decaying industrial and port city into a prestigious centre for the arts. It has, however, focused on buildings and not on the quality of the public spaces amongst them despite the new buildings, including the

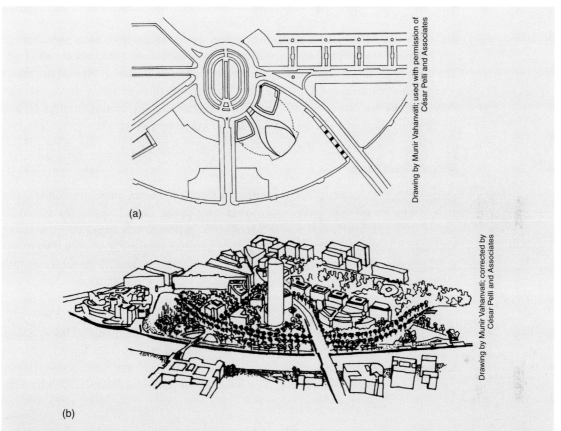

Drawing by Munir Vahanvati; used with permission of César Pelli and Associates

(a)

Drawing by Munir Vahanvati; corrected by César Pelli and Associates

(b)

Figure 6.5 The Guggenheim Museum as a catalyst. (a) The Abandoibarra master plan, 2000 and (b) the proposed Plaza Euskadi featuring the government of Viscaya building, 2004; the Guggenheim Museum is on the left.

Guggenheim, being designed to integrate 'into the city's urban structure'. The spaces lack any human-scale detail and contain no activities that attract people to them. The blank walls of the Guggenheim, for instance, result in no eyes on the open space fronting it. This and such spaces have become havens for negative behaviour. An opportunity for good detailed urban design that enhances the life of the city has been lost. The space in front of the Guggenheim now houses Jeff Koon's mammoth 'Puppy' that helps reduce its visual size. What we do have is a 'cutting-edge' building that many critics see as being a precedent for signature buildings of the twenty-first century.

Major references

Bilbao Ría 2000 (2003), whole issue (December).

Mas, Elías (2002). The Ensanche of Bilbao. In *Euskal Hiria*. Victoria-Gasteiz: Central Publishing Services of the Basque Government, 134–41.

Segal, Arlene (1999). Turning the tide: Guggenheim, Bilbao. *Planning: Architecture and Planning Review for Southern Africa* 163 (May–June): 4–9.

Vidarte, Juan Ignacio (2002). The Bilbao Guggenheim Museum. In *Euskal Hiria*. Victoria-Gasteiz: Central Publishing Services of the Basque Government, 153–8.

123

Buildings as Urban Designs?

Buildings have also been regarded as urban design when they incorporate some mix of those elements that are traditionally regarded as components of cities. They are considered to be vertical precincts. Some individual high-rise buildings contain such elements as a hotel, apartments, shops and a religious facility within them. If they are large enough such buildings are called 'megastructures'. They are cities or precincts of cities within single buildings.

Megastructures

During the 1960s and 1970s a number of megastructures housing various types of facilities were built. Even more were proposed. They include the works of people such as Paolo Soleri whose Arcosanti is painstakingly being constructed in Arizona. Today such large single-structure projects tend to be confined to major suburban shopping centres surrounded by parking for cars. A major twentieth century building type, such centres make a substantial impact on city forms and life. Whether the design of megastructures, by themselves, should be considered to be urban design is open to question.

The *City of the Future* suggested by Hugh Ferris during the 1920s was one precedent for this line of thinking, and Le Corbusier's schemes for Algiers was another. Their deviations from the norms of urban development and design have attracted considerable attention. The schemes include Roadtown (1970) by Paul

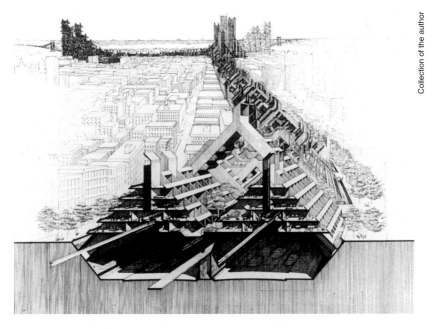

Collection of the author

Figure 6.6 Mega-roadtown, a proposal by Paul Rudolph, 1970.

Rudolph (see Figure 6.6) and a series of explorations by Buckminster Fuller but also earlier proposals in the 1920s and 1930s by Modernists especially expressionists such as Sant'Elia. The 1969 City/State plan for Battery Park City (see Figure 8.33) is very much in this mould. As Rayner Banham suggested almost 30 years ago megastructures are design ideas of the past (Banham, 1976). Their attraction, however, persists. Some early twenty-first century buildings in China are close to the megastructure idea in concept. They strive to be vertical precincts.

Major references

Banham, Reyner (1976). *Megastructure: Urban Structures of the Recent Past*. New York: Harper and Row.

Mansfield, Howard (1990). *Cosmopolis: Yesterday's Cities of the Future*. New Brunswick, NJ: Rutgers University Center for Policy Research.

A NOTE

Arcosanti, Arizona, USA: a prototype for a city in a building: a 'vision' going bad? (1969 – the anticipated completion date is 2030)

Arcosanti, near Scottsdale, Arizona is the brainchild of one person, Paolo Soleri. It is one of the smallest of the generic city-in-a-building schemes that he proposed. It represents the effort to bring to reality one of his many explorations on paper of a design for an energy and resource efficient city. These studies attempted to find an alternative to the consumption of the vast swaths of land taken up by urban sprawl and the resultant energy-consuming long commutes to and from work. (These commutes are considerably longer now than when Soleri was initiating his ideas.) Soleri's solution was to condense cities into single three-dimensional forms. The purpose was to eliminate the space taken up by cars in the typical American suburb. The city of the future, Soleri believed, should be much denser yet possess the social and activity mixture of the traditional city.

Arcosanti (see Figure 6.7) is being built to demonstrate Soleri's ideas. It has been designed to house from 1500 to 5000 people at a density of 215 to 400 people per acre (about 530 to 1000 people per hectare). It is located north of Phoenix on the edge of a valley surrounded by arid land vegetation. Today, the 'city' consists of half-completed buildings: apartments, businesses, production units, education facilities and also agricultural fields. In contrast to Arcosanti, which is modest in size, many of Soleri's proposals are double the height of the Empire State Building in New York and designed to house 500,000 people. They are all based on the concept of *arcology* (architecture + ecology).

Three principles form the basis of Soleri's arcology. He has described them in somewhat esoteric language. The first is *complexity*. Soleri believed that daily activities should

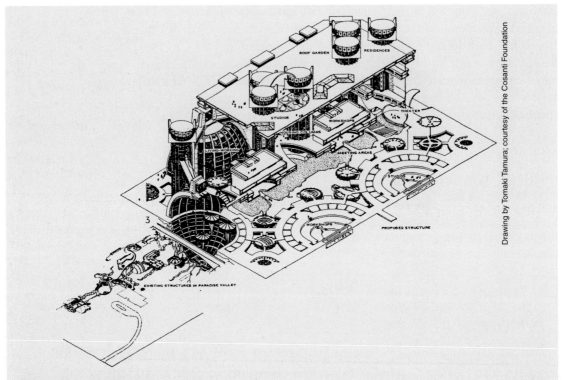

Drawing by Tomaki Tamura; courtesy of the Cosanti Foundation

Figure 6.7 Arcosanti: the proposal.

be clustered together because such cluster-ing represents the processes of everyday life. The second principle, *miniaturization*, sought to integrate resources efficiently by reducing the sizes of spaces and the time to travel between them. The third principle he labelled *duration*. Duration is difficult to understand but has to do with the time consumed in carrying out the activities of life and the goal of 'living outside time' – that is, the capacity to renew oneself and one's surroundings.

To build Arcosanti, Soleri formed the Cosanti Foundation to conduct research and to raise funds from philanthropic organizations, the royalties on book sales and permissions to publish his work and the sale of Soleri-designed bells (forged on site). The foundation also organizes

voluntary student labour during the summer months to build the city. The foundation has about 65 staff members – volunteers and employees. About 150 students work on the project each summer. Arcosanti has become a tourist destination attracting about 50,000 visitors each year.

Arcosanti had its beginnings in 1956 when Paolo and Colly Soleri bought the land that became the home base of the Cosanti Foundation. Soleri's early experi-ments there were with earth structures. He established his first office on site in 1959 and developed an apprentice programme for architects and students. They explored the building of earth-cast apses that became a feature in the design of Arcosanti. The design of the prototype city was developed in 1969 and construction began in 1970. It

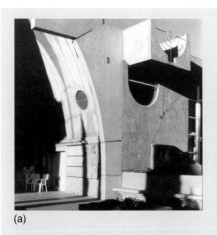

Photograph by Kathy A. Kolnick

Figure 6.8 Arcosanti, Arizona: the progress. (a) A view in 1995 and (b) a view in 2004.

had been given impetus by the success of a touring exhibition of Soleri's proposals. Over 100,000 people in Washington alone visited it.

The first steps in getting Arcosanti built involved the production of the working drawings for the foundry and ceramic workshops. The building of a campsite and drafting room followed. The housing frame was begun in 1973 and step-by-step, apse-by-apse, room-by-room, from year to year, progress is being made. It is slow going. By 2000 the project was 3% built (see Figure 6.8). Its completion date is predicted to be 2030.

Design decisions are very much made from the top down in a largely authoritarian manner. The reason is that an overall ideology, within the rationalist intellectual tradition, guides the design and dictates decisions. The slow construction of the projects and the emphasis on obtaining funds means that those elements that generate resources are built, rather than what is needed to build a residential community – the heart of any city. Few people live there and educational facilities are not available for other than the youngest children.

Arcosanti is a bold experiment. Whether it is as ecologically sound as claimed will be open to investigation as its full character develops. Perhaps it is the basis for future settlement patterns, perhaps not. Much depends on whether the world's population grows substantially and land for building becomes truly scarce. Interestingly enough many of Soleri's concerns are those that the 'smart growth' advocates are raising now. The design patterns they are promoting to deal with those concerns are, however, very different. Arcosanti is, nevertheless, a city design and, sensible a design or not, it is a type of architectural product: a new town in a single building.

Major references

Arcidi, Philip (1991). Paolo Soleri's Arcology: updating the prognosis. *Progressive Architecture* **72** (3): 76–9.

Sherer, Dean C. (2004). Arcosanti: yesterday's vision of tomorrow revisited. *CalPlanner* (March–April): 1, 5, 14.

Soleri, Paolo (1969). *The City in the Image of Man*. Cambridge, MA: MIT Press.

CASE STUDY

Bielefeld University, Bielefeld, Germany: a university campus in a building (1969–76)

A number of universities qualify to be megastructures. Bielefeld is one. The idea of a new university in Ostwestfalen in northern Germany was initiated in early 1965 by a professor of sociology, Dr Helmut Schelksy, together with the Minister of Culture, Prof. Dr P. Mikat. Serious planning began later in that year. In June 1966, it was announced that the university would be located in Bielefeld. The first chancellor of the University, Dr E. Firnhaber, was selected in 1968 and the first provost, Prof. Dr E. J. Mestmäcker, in the following year. The academic structure of the university is the evolving work of many hands. The campus design, however, like almost all buildings, was very much in the hands of one team.

Bielefeld University is located on the periphery of the city. It was the subject of a design competition that received a number of entries from well-known architects. The prize for the concept that formed the basis of the university's design went to a team comprised of Klaus Köpke, Peter Kulka, Wolf Siepmann and Katte Töpper, with Michael von Tardy. That design team in conjunction with university officials and the Quickborner Team then developed the complete space program for the university. The actual final design was begun in 1970. Ground was broken for construction in April of 1971, and the building was completed in 1976 at a cost of DM 623 million. The university now has 14,000 students.

The building is substantial in size (see Figures 6.9a and b). It is 380 metres long and 230 metres in width (1247 feet by 754 feet), and altogether 140,000 square metres (over 1.5 million square feet) in floor area. It is a commuter college with surface parking around it in much the same manner as a suburban shopping centre. Like a shopping centre it has a glass covered central mall, with anchors at the ends and small shops and cafés along its sides. At one end of the mall is a swimming pool and at the other end the main auditorium. The various faculties and schools are located in rectangular blocks perpendicular to the axis of the mall.

In its publicity material the university administration notes that people accustomed to traditional universities 'will appreciate the efficiency' of moving from refectory to classes to the library all under one roof. The layout is said to foster close links between disciplines. The aspiration was also to foster a link between research and teaching following the educational model of Alexander von Humboldt. The mall is described as a vibrant meeting place for students. In the rainy Bielefeld climate, perhaps the greatest asset of the design is that one can walk from place to place without getting wet.

Publicly funded, Bielefeld University is, indeed, very much a single-design effort having been guided step-by-step by one set of planners, designers and university officials working as a team. In contrast to most universities where individual buildings have been located in open spaces, Bielefeld University is in a single building surrounded by parking and sports fields. A small allotment of student housing is on the periphery of the campus. The Teutoburger Wald (woods) lies to the north of the campus.

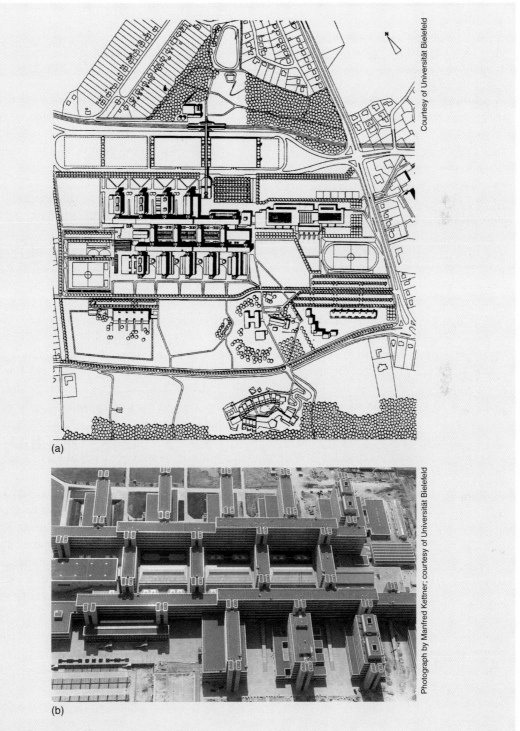

(a)

(b)

Figure 6.9   Bielefeld University. (a) The site plan and (b) aerial view.

Whether or not one regards the campus as an urban design rather than an object sitting in open space depends on one's attitude towards megastructures and towards what constitutes urban design.

Major references

Trott, Gerhard (1985). *Universität Bielefeld*. Bielefeld: Kramer-Druck.

Universität Bielefeld (2004). http://www.uni-bielefeld.de

Neighbourhoods

The planning of neighbourhoods was a preoccupation of city planners and architects for the entire twentieth century and is still a subject of major attention. Debates on the utility of the concept as a unit in urban design continue (Madanipour, 2001). Clarence Perry, a sociologist, developed the idea of the neighbourhood unit as part of the 1927, *The New York Regional Plan*. He proposed that all the facilities of daily life be located within walking distance of a set of residential units. The focus, or the core of the unit, would be an elementary school, shopping facilities, and a community centre (see Figure 6.10). It is a pattern central to New Urbanist thinking today.

The unit is exemplified in the design of Radburn, New Jersey which became a prototype for new residential neighbourhoods around the world (see Stein, 1957). It is the idea behind the Runcorn 'communities'. It has seldom been copied on all its dimensions, but rather only in plan and not in three dimensions. It has had mixed success when applied in plan form only. Le Corbusier also created a neighbourhood type, but it was located in a single building. It is a vertical neighbourhood. He also called it a 'unit'. It, even more so than Radburn, has had mixed success as a prototype.

It must be remembered that communities and neighbourhoods are two different phenomena. A community consists of people who interact with each other; a neighbourhood is a spatial schema. The two can coincide especially if the population is homogeneous and has shared problems and a need for mutual support. The idea that one can create a community through physical design needs to be considered with great caution. The affordances for interaction on a local level can be created but whether residents perceive or use them depends on their motivations.

Major references

Lang, Jon (1994). Meeting affiliation needs. In *Urban Design: The American Experience*. New York: Van Nostrand Reinhold, 252–79.

Madanipour, Ali (2001). How relevant is 'planning by neighbourhoods' today? *Town Planning Review* **72** (2): 171–91.

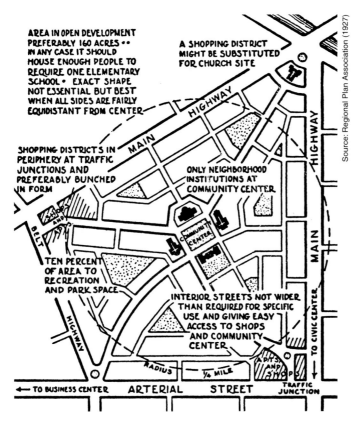

Figure 6.10 The Neighbourhood Unit concept.

CASE STUDY

The Unité d'Habitation, Marseilles, France: a neighbourhood in a building (1946–52)

Le Corbusier produced a number of conceptual designs for cities and apartment blocks during the 1920s and 1930s. Neither he nor others, however, turned his large-scale ideas into built form until the 1950s when the reconstruction of Europe after the devastations of World War II was underway. The Unité d'Habitation is part of one such total urban design scheme that moved from being on the drawing board to being built in the real world. The Marseilles Unité (see Figure 6.11a), located well out from the centre of the city on Boulevard Michelet, was the first to be built. Others followed: Nantes-Rezé (1952–3), Berlin (1956–8: see Figure 6.11b), Briey en Forêt (1956–8), Meaux (1956–8) and Firminy (1961–8). Most departed from the basic model as built in Marseilles in some respect.

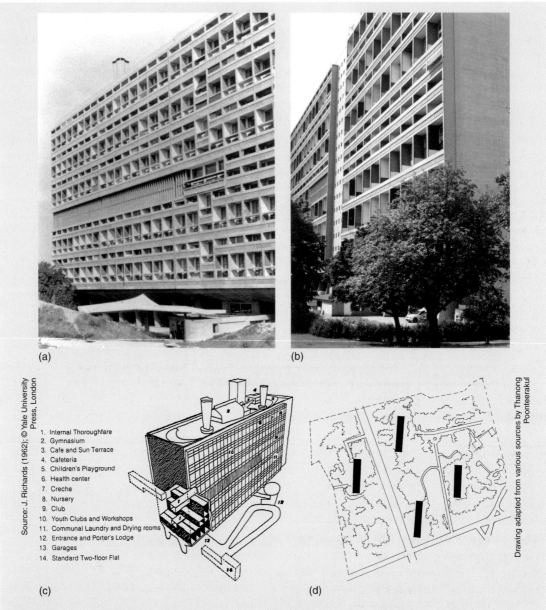

Source: J. Richards (1962); © Yale University Press, London

1. Internal Thoroughfare
2. Gymnasium
3. Cafe and Sun Terrace
4. Cafeteria
5. Children's Playground
6. Health center
7. Creche
8. Nursery
9. Club
10. Youth Clubs and Workshops
11. Communal Laundry and Drying rooms
12. Entrance and Porter's Lodge
13. Garages
14. Standard Two-floor Flat

Drawing adapted from various sources by Thanong Poonteerakul

(a)   (b)

(c)   (d)

Figure 6.11 The Unité d'Habitation. (a) The Unité d'Habitation, Marseilles in 1961, (b) the Unité, Berlin in 2002, (c) cross section through the Unité d'Habitation, Marseilles and (d) the intended site plan for the Marseilles development.

Raoul Dauty, the Minister for Reconstruction in post-war France, commissioned the Unité in Marseilles. The project was, however, supported with greater and lesser enthusiasm through 10 changes in the French government and seven Ministers of Reconstruction. The central government needed mass housing and Le Corbusier sought a vehicle to explore his own ideas. His relationship with the French bureaucracy was sticky because he wished to be free from all building regulations. He was also legally challenged for 'desecrating the countryside' so he saw himself battling for Architecture against great odds.

Le Corbusier's idea for the Unité had antecedents in the nineteenth century utopian principles used in the design of workers' accommodations in the Familistère, Le Cruesot and Mulhouse. The Unité is not a megastructure in a conventional sense, but rather a neighbourhood of what was supposed to be a city of like residential/neighbourhood units. It is a vertical neighbourhood unit housed in a single building set in a park-like setting. A number of these neighbourhoods would form a city or, at least, three or four would form an identifiable cluster. The plan for Marseilles shows Le Corbusier's basic idea (see Figure 6.11d). It was, he believed, the type of environment appropriate for people's lives in the second half of the twentieth century. The Unités that were built are, however, all individual stand-alone structures.

The Unité's footprint is 110 metres by 20 metres (360 feet by 65 feet) in size. It is set on *pilotis* (the columns on which a building stands leaving the ground floor open). It was designed to consist of 337 residential units housing 1000 to 1200 people, a small hotel, retail establishments and communal facilities. The shopping is located on a central floor and areas for a nursery school, jogging track (long before such an activity became popular), and other communal facilities are on the roof. The apartments are each two floors high, with a balcony to provide fresh air and sunlight, primary concerns of Le Corbusier. The arrangement of apartments allows for a skip-stop lift system with stops on each third floor. The ground floor was for the parking of cars in dedicated places, for circulation, and for recreation.

The scheme affords many of the functions of built form shown in Figure 1.6 as Le Corbusier perceived it should. The problem with his design idea is that it is removed from everyday life; the Unité is simply not a large enough unit to sustain much in the way of retail activities. As a result most of the shops have been converted to other uses. Parking is more haphazard than intended. The development is, nevertheless, much loved by those who live in it. It fits their way of life well, but they have chosen to live there. A similar result occurs in the Unité in Berlin which is really simply an apartment building with only a shop and a post office. Elsewhere, however, the Unités stand semi-empty.

A second problem lies in the way bureaucrats and architects think. As Le Corbusier intended public housing agencies and architects around the world from the United Kingdom to Venezuela have regarded the Unité as a prototype to be replicated. They wanted up-to-date designs. The success has been very limited. In the first place the buildings are pale copies of the precedent set by the Unité d'Habitation in Marseilles (Marmot, 1982). In the second, the ways of life of their inhabitants and what the buildings afford are at odds.

Major references

Jencks, Charles (1993). *Unité d'Habitation*. London: Phaedon Press.

Le Corbusier (1953). *L'Unité d'Habitation de Marseilles (The Marseilles Block)* [translated from the French by Geoffrey Sainsbury]. London: Harvill.

Marmot, Alexi (1982). The legacy of Le Corbusier and high rise housing. *Built Environment* 7 (2): 82–95.

Buildings Complexes as Urban Design?

The classification system used in this book is at its fuzziest in dealing with complexes of buildings. Is the new Stata Center at the Massachusetts Institute of Technology (see Figure 6.12) a building, or a series of buildings, or a total urban design project? It is presented as an object in space tied into the university's infrastructure system. Rockefeller Center and Pruitt Igoe have been categorized in the core of urban design, yet here the cemetery at Modena, Kresge College built on a green-field site, and the rehabilitation of the Ghirardelli complex in San Francisco have been classified as primarily architectural works. The logic for locating these three examples outside the mainstream of urban design activity is that they are self-contained professional architectural works. All three are really independent units.

The Ghirardelli Square scheme has had an enormous impact on its surroundings. This multiplier effect was not part of a conscious overall urban development policy but it has shown the potential importance of individual projects of its scale as generators of urban rehabilitation. The cemetery at Modena is a creative adaptation of a building type and Kresge College, has become a precedent for total small college designs but neither has had a catalytic impact on it surroundings. All three are fine examples of the integration of open and enclosed space into a coherent overall design. Much can be learnt from them.

Figure 6.12   The Stata Center, M.I.T. in 2004.

CASE STUDY

The cemetery of San Cataldo, Modena, Italy: a necropolis in a set of buildings (1971–6)

A cemetery in much of the world is a horizontal necropolis, sometimes consuming acres and acres of land. Cemeteries can also be buildings. Either way they are cities of the dead. They have an ambiguous position when it comes to urban design and architecture. The cemetery in Porto Alegre, Brazil (see Figure 6.13) is clearly a building, but that cannot be said for the cemetery at Modena, although its architect said that it was 'considered as a building'.

Aldo Rossi, the Italian neo-Rationalist architect, designed the cemetery of San Cataldo for Modena. Many critics regard it as his masterpiece. It is an extension to an existing cemetery that has an 'elongated east–west courtyard axis surrounded by brick neo-classical ossuaries' designed by Andrea Costa in the mid-nineteenth century. The courtyard of that cemetery is a conventional burial ground.

The new cemetery has an axis to the west of that established by Costa. A Jewish cemetery and central services are located in between Costa and Rossi's designs in a symmetrical pattern along the axis (see Figure 6.14a). Rossi's design picks up on many features of Costa's cemetery: its overall geometry, the termination of walkways at a wall of buildings and the overall composition of objects within a frame. A courtyard surrounded by ossuaries, lies beyond this central axis. These ossuaries are three stories high with external walls. The ground floor windows of the ossuaries are elongated but are aligned with the square windows above them. The ossuary walls are lined with niches. The buildings within the courtyard are symmetrical about a central axis. At the northern end of this axis is a truncated cone and at the southern end a red cube.

The cone is a communal grave, the cube a house for the dead. The cone houses the unclaimed remains of those who have died in hospitals, jails and hospices. At the upper level is an amphitheatre where services can be held. Below is the common grave. The cube is an ossuary. It is built of brick with windows punched into it. Its appearance is that of a semi-abandoned building. It has brightly coloured metal balconies and stairs giving access to burial niches (see Figure 6.14b). It is open to the sky. One of the walls is solid. The square 1-metre by 1-metre windows in the other three walls have neither frames nor panes. The centre of the cube is the location of funeral services.

The 14 buildings lining the central spine within the courtyards have niches on the side so that they face each other across the space they enclose. The southernmost of these buildings forms a large Euclidean U. The height of the buildings depends on their location within the triangular layout. Rossi explained his design using an analogy. 'The longest element is therefore the lowest whilst the shortest is the tallest . . . thus a shape analogous to the vertebrae of some osteological formation results' (Rossi cited in Broadbent, 1990: 188). The cemetery has a second and narrow spine immediately to the west of this group. This spine is raised on two-storey septa (dividing

135

Figure 6.13 The cemetery, Porto Alegre in 1989.

walls) with a single-storey ossuary above. The ossuary has pink walls and square windows with a pitched blue metal roof.

The cemetery is a work of art. Rossi's goal was to create a sense of timelessness. The design concern is centred on the architectural composition in order to achieve a psychological end. The organizing principles are based on the story that Rossi wants to tell. It is an aesthetic idea that is open to interpretation by everyone. The cognoscenti will respond warmly or coldly to it in terms of their acceptance or rejection of the architect's vision. Others will respond to it in terms of what they perceive. Although Rossi considered the cemetery to be architecture and there is little landscape design to it, it is possible to consider cemeteries as a type of urban design precinct.

Major references

Adjmi, Morris, ed. (1991). *Aldo Rossi Architecture, 1981–1991*. New York: Princeton University Press.

Arnell, Peter and Ted Bickford (1985). *Aldo Rossi: Buildings and Projects*. New York: Rizzoli International, 88, 101.

Broadbent, Geoffrey (1990). *Emerging Concepts in Urban Space Design*. London: Van Nostrand Reinhold (International), 186–9.

Johnson, J. Eugene (1982). What remains of man? Aldo Rossi's Modena cemetery. *Journal of the Society of Architectural Historians* **1**: 18–54.

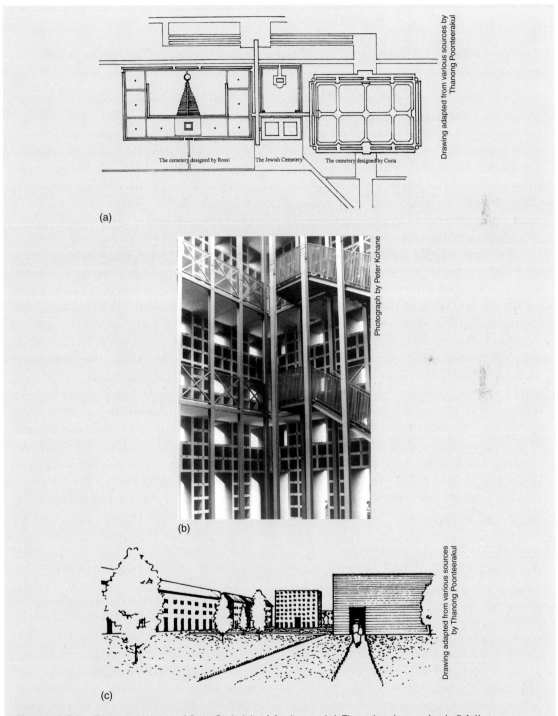

Drawing adapted from various sources by Thanong Poonteerakul

The cemetery designed by Rossi   The Jewish Cemetery   The cemetery designed by Costa

(a)

Photograph by Peter Kohane

(b)

Drawing adapted from various sources by Thanong Poonteerakul

(c)

Figure 6.14 The cemetery of San Cataldo, Modena. (a) The plan in context, (b) the interior of the cube and (c) a view towards the cube.

CASE STUDY

Kresge College, University of California at Santa Cruz, California, USA: a living-studying building/complex (1966–74)

Kresge College is interesting both for its design and the process through which it was conceived. It was initiated at a time when the members of Board of Trustees of the University of California system were worried about the student unrest at the University of California at Berkeley with its main square, Sproule Plaza, giving a focus, a heart, to the university. The master plan for the University of California at Santa Cruz was designed by William Turnbull (of Moore and Turnbull) in 1967 to have dispersed colleges. One of them located on a rugged peripheral site surrounded by redwood trees is Kresge College.

In 1969, Moore and Turnbull had completed a design for a college on the site but state funds were only available for teaching facilities. The idea of an integrated living-learning environment existed in the minds of the provost, Robert Edgar, and assistant provost, Michael Kahn. A donation from the Kresge family (of K-Mart fame) had enabled a college along those lines to function in temporary accommodation. With financial contributions from the state and recognition that ongoing student accommodation fees would have to cover some of the costs, planning went ahead. To aid the programming process, the university ran a course 'Creating Kresge College' and a group of students conducted a survey of their fellows about the types of accommodations they desired. The results were partially incorporated into the design.

The college has antecedents in the Ezra Stiles and Samuel F. B. Morse Colleges at Yale (1962) designed by Eero Saarinen and the colleges at Oxford and Cambridge. The actual design has precedents in similar neighbourhood-like 'village' designs in California. Sea Ranch (1975) by Moore, Lyndon, Turnbull and Whitaker, for instance, is a 2020-hectare (5000-acre) development of clustered units (designed by Joseph Esherick) that exudes a sense of coziness.

For Kresge College, Moore and Turnbull (really Charles Moore) designed a scheme around a 1000-foot (280-metre) L-shaped central open space – a 'street' – that the site allowed (see Figure 6.15). This space is entered from the parking lot through a large gateway. At both ends of the street are 'crowd-pullers'. Along the street the architects placed administrative, academic, residential and social units. The idea is similar, like Bielefeld University, to that of a suburban shopping mall with its anchor stores at both ends and smaller shops in between. It is a powerful geometrical type.

The street has kinks in it to give a picturesque, 'townscape' flavour and it has places for people to meet, sit and chat. It was designed to make the sequential experience of spaces varied and interesting from the moment a person comes through the entrance gate to its termination at a court around which are located a restaurant and the assembly (town) hall. Along the way the vista changes as one changes direction. The street is punctuated with steps, platforms and student speakers' rostrums (above the garbage cans). It is the communal space of the college. The architecture of the built form is stark and contrasts strongly with both the picturesque street layout and the

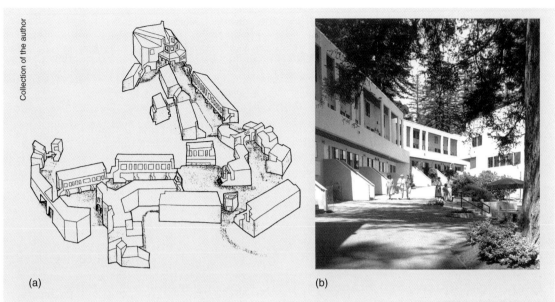

Collection of the author

(a) (b)

Figure 6.15 Kresge College, University of California at Santa Cruz. (a) The college layout and (b) a view of the 'street' in 1993.

redwood trees in the background. Much attention focused on the internal design of the college, what it should and should not accommodate, the appropriate size for student groups using a hierarchy of common facilities, where they would interact, and how teaching and living spaces should be connected.

Those who inhabit the design are generally well satisfied with it as a living and working world. One of the difficulties with the participatory design is that those who are engaged in the programming are not necessarily those who will inhabit the building. The students who participated in developing the program envisaged the showers as communal spaces, but those who have inhabited the scheme have perceived the kitchens to be the locus of daily interactions. Space would have been allocated slightly differently if this behaviour had been predicted. In addition, there is a tendency to over-estimate how much people will go

about changing internal designs to suit their peculiar needs. The students have not changed much. After 30 years of operation the original design has proven to be robust. Some elements of the social and physical program of the college have proven to be expensive to maintain. By 1987 maintenance costs of running the complex had risen from an original \$31 to \$212 per student per annum and have continued to rise. The simplicity of the architecture has, however, survived changes in architectural fashions very well indeed.

What was created at Kresge College is an academic 'village'. As such it is an urban design. As a single work, it is architecture! The focus of attention in developing the design was very much on the interrelation of open and enclosed space, and on the public and the private realms of student life. The concern was with the aesthetic function of the complex as a unifying element. It was designed as much for providing a sense of

139

belonging for students who spend a short but intense part of their lives at the college as for the provision of accommodation for academic activities. It functions well as such.

Major references

Bloomer, Kent C. and Charles W. Moore (1977). *Body, Memory, and Architecture*. New Haven: Yale University Press.

Broadbent, Geoffrey (1990). Kresge College (1966–74). In *Emerging Concepts of Urban Space Design*. London: Van Nostrand Reinhold (International), 254–60.

Floyd, Nubra (1987). Kresge College. *Progressive Architecture* **68** (2): 76–9.

Kresge College. http://www.greatbuildings.com/buildings/Kresge_College.html

CASE STUDY

Ghirardelli Square, San Francisco, USA: recycling a building complex (1962–7, 1982–4)

In 1893, the Ghirardelli family bought a sloping block of land bounded by North Point Street, Larkin Street, Beach Street and Polk Street in San Francisco, and constructed a red brick factory complex to carry on the chocolate making company founded by their ancestor, Domingo Ghirardelli in 1849. The factory complex was built between 1900 and 1916. The family enterprise was bought by the Golden Grain Macaroni Company in the early 1960s and moved to San Leandro, California.

The factory buildings were fine industrial structures, solidly built with well-executed brickwork. They were, however, decaying and the site was abandoned apart from a small segment for a limited continuing operation of the company. The site offered considerable potential for redevelopment. The centre of the complex was open to sunlight and to views of San Francisco Bay. The question then was what to do with it.

The financially rewarding option for a property developer would have been to demolish the factory and build apartment buildings on the site. The constraint was that the zoning code limited the height of buildings along the city's waterfront in order: (1) to prevent any obstruction of the view of the San Francisco Bay from Russian Hill and (2) to maintain the character of the city derived from its rolling topographical contours. Concerned that no public benefit would result from building an apartment complex, William Matson Roth, a public-spirited San Franciscan, and his mother purchased the block with the eye to renovating it. He hired the architectural firm of Wurster, Bernardi and Emmons to carry out a study of possible uses for the complex. In conjunction with landscape architects Lawrence Halprin and John Matthias they developed a program for the block and carried it out. It was a total renovation project.

The project was carried out in two phases. The first was completed in 1965, and with the departure of the remaining chocolate works, the second was finished in 1967. The problem was to fit in 68 retail

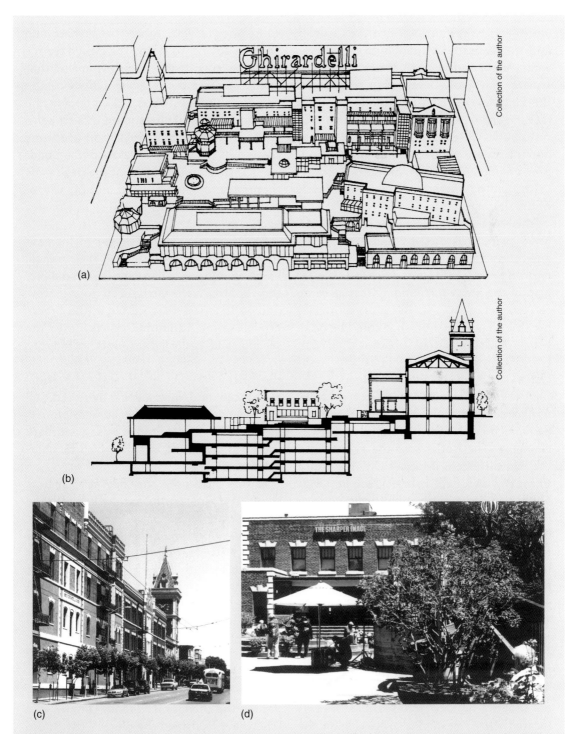

Collection of the author

Collection of the author

Figure 6.16 Ghirardelli Square, San Francisco. (a) The layout, (b) cross-section showing the parking levels, (c) a street view in 2004 and (d) a view of the interior space in 2004.

stores and 15 restaurants into the complex and to create on-site parking for 300 cars while retaining the open character of the square. Placing five levels of parking under the complex solved the parking problem (see Figure 6.16b). The retail stores and restaurants were placed around the square and the square itself was redesigned to contain an interwoven set of plazas, courtyards, and passages on a number of levels of the sloping site.

The renovated complex became a much-loved place well used by San Franciscans and tourists alike. Its economic success also created problems for it. It generated similar uses in the areas surrounding it that came to compete with it. It also, however, became an exemplar of what could be done with robust industrial buildings. In San Francisco itself Joseph Esherick and Associates renovated the nearby Cannery.

By the beginning of 1980, years of heavy use were beginning to take its toll and the demand for the type of retail outlets was changing. The Roths sold the complex to the Northwestern Mutual Life Insurance Company and Real Estate West in 1982. These two organizations hired the Edward Plant Company, a retail leasing and development firm, to manage and upgrade the complex. The owners and consultants formed a team to develop, market and lease the development. William Roth suggested to the Plant organization that Benjamin Thompson and Associates of Cambridge, Massachusetts and Lanier, Sherrill, and Morrison, a San Francisco architectural firm, be hired to design the renovation.

Thompson was a commercial tenant of the square – his Design Research store was located there. He had also served on the honour awards jury of *Progressive Architecture* when Ghirardelli Square received a citation

so he knew it well. Albert Lanier had long been an advisor to Roth. The design team's goal was to provide an environment that would increase the retailing activity on the site. Its objectives were: (1) to update the retailing image of the square, (2) to solve some of the intricate circulation problems created by the variety of levels of the building, (3) to eliminate some of the dead ends that made retailing difficult and (4) to create a 10,500-square-foot (980-square-metre) anchor store.

Shopfronts were redesigned to increase their visibility and modernize their image. Large hand-carved wooden signs and directory boards were introduced to aid way-finding, banners that flutter in the breeze provide some additional visual life to the setting, and neon lighting was introduced to selectively enliven the place. Meanwhile the brickwork was re-pointed, the roofs resurfaced and landscaping restored. All the changes had to be compatible, as deemed by San Francisco's Landmark Preservation Board, with the historic character of the area.

It was not only the design that was changed to enliven the square but also the administration. Special events such as art shows have become a regular feature of life there. New leasing arrangements were made to include more high-fashion stores to appeal to young people and, similarly, more casual outdoor restaurants were added. In short, the 'old-fashioned' image was replaced by a more 'festival market' one. In the space of 4 years the gross retail sales increased by 50% and net operating income by nearly 60%. Some observers decried the changes. Lawrence Halprin said 'They have Rousified the place' – the Rouse Corporation being a major suburban shopping mall developer. Perhaps the greatest success of the Square has, however, been its demonstration that decaying areas on the edge of central cities can be renovated with financial success provided the behaviour of the market is understood. Ghirardelli Square became a precedent that many other designs throughout the world have followed. Both major renovations there were carried out as total collaborative designs. Are renovation/redesign products such as Ghirardelli Square urban design projects? The square's rehabilitation was not a product of public policy-making. It could have been given the public interest concern of the Roths. It, however, was not!

Today (2004), the complex is finding it difficult to compete with the Cannery and with discount stores that offer similar goods at lower prices. Will it be changed yet again?

Major references

Attoe, Wayne and Donn Logan (1989). *American Urban Architecture: Catalyst in the Design of Cities*. Berkeley and Los Angeles: University of California Press, xiii–iv.

Barnes, W. Anderson (1986). Ghirardelli Square: keeping a first first. *Urban Land* **45** (May): 6–10.

Freeman, Allen (1986). 'Fine tuning' a landmark of adaptive use. *Architecture* **75** (11): 66–71.

Urban Objects

The placing of elements in the urban scene has an important impact on cities. They include a wide variety of types. Objects of sculpture (monuments, art works and curiosity objects), clock towers, fountains, and street furniture all add lustre to the cityscape (see Figure 6.17). They can make focal points, terminals to vistas, instantly recognizable places for people to meet, and generally provide an additional amenity to the environment. They can also add unnecessary clutter. As many urban open spaces are boring because they are poorly related to their surroundings, there is a tendency for designers to want to fill them up with something. They become over-designed. The deck at La Défense (see Chapter 8) was improved considerably when sculpture was added to it, but well-designed open spaces (in terms of size and what surrounds them) have no need for much in the way of added elements.

Banners and signs form an important part of cities and the way they are handled often says much about the culture of which they are a part. Architects have generally desired to neaten the environment but the chaotic nature of objects and appurtenances that crowd many lively streets makes one pause to think about the way to move ahead. Recently, large screens, used for advertising, but also for entertainment have begun to appear in public squares. Buildings are now being developed with 'smart skins' that are able to portray images. In some places (e.g. Singapore) great attention is paid to the illumination of buildings that adds much liveliness to the night-time urban environment. The introduction of such items into the city is seen as urban design by some observers. It changes cities.

Collection of the author

(a)   (b)

Figure 6.17   Urban objects. (a) Union Square, New York in 1997 and (b) sculpture by Picasso, Daley Plaza, Chicago in 1993.

Major reference

Robinette, Margaret A. (1976). *Outdoor Sculpture: Object and Environment*. New York: Whitney Library of Design.

Commentary: Are these Architectural Products Urban Design?

Individual buildings are important. The Chrysler Building in New York has shaped people's view of what good urban buildings are as objects and as space making elements. It is a well-fitting design for a city but it was not an urban design project! It is the catalytic effect of the buildings in some of the cases covered here that might make them urban design. Others can be regarded as urban design because they incorporate mixed-uses that are part of the traditional city into a single unit. Most are, however, simply architectural works on an urban scale, as interesting and as important as they may be. Much of the difference comes from the scope of the goals set and the concern or not with their potential multiplier and side effects on their environments.

All the schemes described here have in common a major concern for their geometry, their formal aesthetics. This observation does not mean that the architectural idea has totally led the program rather than come out of it. Kresge College is an example showing a great concern for the development of a coherent behavioural and building program before design began. What all the cases

144

do show is that the quality of the program is crucial to the development of high-quality work.

Three of the schemes included here, Arcosanti, Kresge College and Ghirardelli Square owe much to philanthropic gestures. The Guggenheim Museum, the Unité d'Habitation and Bielefeld University were amongst those publicly funded. What they have in common is that they are architectural works completed by single teams. They have evolved and will continue to evolve as time goes by. Ghirardelli Square has had a formal makeover already. The Unité has seen a reduction in the number of shops it contains. Arcosanti evolves on the drawing board day-by-day. At Kresge College students have added trellises and planting that were not intended as part of the original idea of making a flexible scheme. All of the buildings have shown wear and tear due to use and the effects of the climate.

Designs evolve. Robust buildings and open spaces survive in new guises, adding a sense of place and continuity of spirit to locations. All new buildings change the urban scene when they are built – some radically, some not. Individual buildings are nevertheless, not urban designs as envisaged in this book, complexes of buildings may well be. The projects described here all have strong architectural ideas behind them. However paramount the central architectural idea guiding a design may be, it is essential that the design be based on a multi-functional model of human behaviour and can evolve as the world evolves. Alternatively, it should be designed to be demolished.

Canary Wharf, London in 2004

THE CORE OF URBAN DESIGN WORK: PROCEDURES AND PRODUCTS

PART 3

Specifying what falls within and without the core of urban design work will raise the ire of a number of city planners, landscape architects and architects. Each profession has a broader view of its own work than the view of its work held by people outside it. In order to understand what urban design is in comparison to those activities and products described in Part 2 it is necessary to identify a particular set of processes and products as being the heart of urban design. The position taken here is that those people, architects mainly, whose work in the 1960s and 1970s defined the field 'almost got it right'.

The core of urban design work is defined here primarily in terms of common processes of design and administration. There is a significant intellectual similarity between varieties of products generated by the same generic method within a specific design paradigm. True, it is possible to cut the cake in another direction. An organization based on product types would allow the impacts of differences in methodological approaches to be explicated. It would not, however, show the thought processes, similar though they may be, that differentiate urban design from the traditional practices and views of city planning, landscape architecture and architecture.

Urban design, as stated in Chapter 1, is fundamentally concerned with the design of the three-dimensional qualities of the public realm of human settlements, taking into consideration the fourth dimension – time. Time is a consideration in urban design in many ways. It is both a factor in the way an urban design is experienced and in its relationship to its cultural context at different moments in its history. Some of the projects described in this part of the book have been hailed a great success at one moment and as a failure at another only to be regarded as a success at a third time.

Time is also a factor in the evolution of an urban design project. Many of the schemes included here evolved as perceptions of the nature of the problem being addressed changed in response to shifts in their political and economic contexts. There were five clearly different proposals for the Barbican site (see Chapter 7) and at least six distinct designs were produced for Battery Park City during its 30-year evolution, each based on a contemporary urban design paradigm (see Chapter 8).

Buildings and their context also change from the moment a job is said to be have been completed. The climate and patterns of use – indeed sometimes love – take their toll so projects need to be renovated or demolished. Two of the schemes described here – Pruitt-Igoe in St Louis and Paternoster Square were demolished largely because what is now perceived to have been the wrong paradigm was employed as the basis of their designs. Paternoster Square has since been rebuilt. The first of these projects is described in Chapter 7 and the second in Chapter 8.

In Chapter 2, I described four types of urban design – total, all-of-a-piece, piece-by-piece and plug-in – based on the way a vision for a city or precinct is implemented. A brief recapitulation is in place here to set the framework for this part of the book. The term 'total urban design' implies that the whole scheme is carried out under one auspice and by one hand even if it is a communal hand. Examples are described in Chapter 7. 'All-of-a-piece urban design' is the type described in the statement by Lord Llewellyn-Davies that opens Chapter 1 of this book. It involves creating a vision for a city or one of its precincts and capturing that image in a conceptual design. The conceptual design is then divided into parcels of land each of which is developed and designed by different people in accordance with a set of design guidelines, or directives. A number of such projects are presented in 'Chapter 8: All-of-a-piece urban design'. The two chapters also cover a wide variety of product types that employ a wide variety of paradigmatic approaches. The processes and products described in Chapters 7 and 8 were the traditional core of urban design work.

Saying that 'piece-by-piece urban design' falls within the core of urban design endeavour is more controversial because it does not involve specific physical design projects but rather the design of policies that promote the development of certain building and urban types within specific precincts, of a city. Piece-by-piece urban design involves the use of zoning and other planning instruments to achieve urban outcomes without using site-specific design guidelines or directives. The procedures employed are described in Chapter 9.

The fourth type of urban design that falls within the core of urban design is plug-in urban design. It does deal with specific design projects. It focuses primarily but not entirely, on the design of links between places. Infrastructure elements can also include facilities such as schools, libraries and other public services. The public policy concern is with their catalytic effect. Infrastructure design as urban design is discussed in Chapter 10. Much infrastructure design, however, falls outside the realm of direct urban design interests and is either city planning or civil engineering. It could be argued that the concerns of civil engineering, as much as the other environmental design disciplines, can overlap those of urban design. That discussion is dealt with briefly in 'Chapter 12: Afterthoughts: Urban design – field or discipline and profession?'.

Total urban design

7

Total urban design occurs when an entire project is carried out under one auspice and under the direction of an individual designer or a group acting as an individual. It is completed as one piece of work from property development to design to implementation. The concern is from the broadest policy issues, to the architecture, to the landscaping and to the details of street furniture. Total urban designs include a wide variety of product types: new towns, urban precincts of various descriptions (either as cleared site projects or as partial redevelopments), new suburbs, housing developments, campuses and historical revitalizations. Some projects are mixed types.

The strengths of total urban designs lie in their unity of appearance and, often, boldness of form. To critics this unity is their weakness. There is certainly the danger of them being dull, boring, if sanitary places but that is not necessarily because they are total urban designs. Many have indeed proven to be disappointing once they have been experienced for a short while but it is because of the paradigm followed. Attitudes towards specific total urban designs vary from observer to observer and they change over time. Designs (e.g. the Barbican, London) that were originally praised for the strength of their ideas were then seen to be lacking the diversity, individualism and the complexity that the traditional city offers. The Barbican, amongst other schemes, is now seen as a fine design.

The total urban design schemes, particularly housing projects from the 1950s and 1960s, based on the Modernist ideology that sunlight and air are the crucial variables in urban design are no longer seen as worthy substitutes for the personal identity and the variety of behaviour settings that many seemingly run-down areas of cities possess. Sunlight and air are indeed fundamental human requirements but whether they should override so completely other design considerations (as they still do in many large-scale housing projects in Asia today; see Figure 7.1) has been questioned (Miao, 2003).

It is extremely difficult, for one hand to design for variety. Urban designs schemes carried out all-of-a-piece following New Urbanist ideas have thus become the accepted paradigm of many architects at the beginning of the twenty-first century in the United States and there is considerable sympathy for the ideology elsewhere. Many Modernist design ideas are, however, still alive,

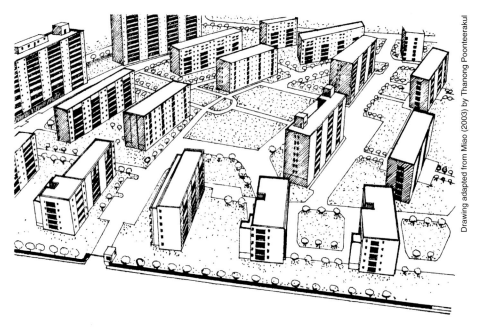

Drawing adapted from Miao (2003) by Thanong Poonteerakul

Figure 7.1   A typical early twenty-first century gated housing scheme in Shanghai.

well and frequently used in practice. No doubt, however, the urban designs qualities that give them critical acclaim in architectural circles will change in a cyclical manner as they have done in the past. Simplicity and boldness will be followed by a demand for complexity and mess followed by . . .!

Major references

Lang, Jon (1994). The nature of urban design today. In *Urban Design: The American Experience*. New York: Van Nostrand Reinhold, 68–100.

Moudon, Ann Vernez and Wayne Attoe (1995). *Urban Design: Reshaping Our Cities*. Seattle, WA: Urban Design Program, University of Washington.

The Case Studies

The case studies presented here include a variety of new towns and precincts of cities. The idea of a new town is widely understood although there are debates over how inclusive and independent a development a new town should be in terms of the activities it affords. They are supposed to include all the aspects of a city so that they can exist as semi-independent units within a regional context. They are seldom as self-contained as the accepted definition suggests.

The way precincts are considered here is complex. Some of the examples are located on what were green-field sites (land formerly unused or used for agriculture); others were built on brown-field sites (those previously built-upon and demolished). In this chapter, a somewhat arbitrary distinction is drawn between those precinct developments on totally cleared brown-field sites (or in the case of the Barbican in

150

London on an almost totally cleared site), and those involving the integration of existing buildings into a new development. Both are examples of urban renewal.

Within the category of precincts a number of distinctions have been made. Housing developments have been organized into a category, as have been campuses and streets. Housing complexes tend to be predominantly single-use areas, campuses have park-like settings, and streets are elements of urban infrastructure. Bucharest's Avenue of the Victory of Socialism is categorized in this chapter as a total urban design because it includes the buildings that line it and frame it. As such it is a very different project to the landscaping of George Street, Sydney described in Chapter 5. It is a design that involved the third dimension of a city not only its ground plane. The Avenue is also an example of autocratic urban design and in many critics' eyes an urban design disaster.

New Towns

There is no census of the new towns built in the world during the second half of the twentieth century. We know that the number is vast. The proportion designed totally by one hand for one public authority or for one private developer is relatively small, but the number is still substantial. Some developments that started out as total urban designs became piece-by-piece urban designs; all have evolved since they were nominally completed. Chandigarh in India, for instance, is seen by many as the work of one man, Le Corbusier, but it has been the work of many people and is becoming more so as time passes. It started out as a total urban design on the drawing board but apart from two precincts it has evolved into a city-planning scheme with a number of urban design projects within it.

The group of total urban designs includes a national capital city, a number of state capitals in their initial stages, many cities built *de novo* to redistribute populations within a country and company towns. Brasília is a national capital, while Chandigarh, the capital of Punjab, Bhubaneshwar, the capital of Orissa and Gandhinagar the capital of Gujarat, all in India, are examples of state capitals that began as total urban designs. The new towns programmes of the United Kingdom and of Soviet Union provided many examples of the second type of new town. Although none are included in this chapter, Runcorn described in Chapter 4 is an example. The Gujarat State Fertilizer Corporation (GSFC) Township in Vadodara in India is both an example of the manifestation of a government redistribution policy and a company town. Only the developments of Brasília and the GSFC Township are described here. They fully exemplify the characteristics of new towns that are total urban designs at a large and small size, respectively.

Capital Cities

Custom-built capital cities are much shaped by the motivation to make them symbols of their country or state. This necessity is particularly strongly felt and displayed in the design of their governmental precincts as is clear in the design of Washington, colonial New Delhi, Brasília, Chandigarh, Islamabad, and, more recently, Abuja and Belmopan. Even more recently, there are the examples of Yamoussoukro in the Ivory Coast, and currently Putra Jaya in Malaysia. The scale of these endeavours varies considerably with Yamoussoukro being the most grandiose and Belmopan, the least. Brasília is the only one that is really a total urban design and then only in its formal area. Chandigarh may have had an over-all total infrastructure design but its components have been carried out piece-by-piece in accordance with general zoning codes and building byelaws. Only its capital and city centre complexes remain total designs. Brasília is *the* exemplar of a total urban design guided by strong political and architectural ideologies. Its urban design process was quite autocratic in nature.

Will new capital cities be designed in the future? The relocation of national and state capitals is still talked about in various countries with varying degrees of seriousness. In 2004 the establishment of a new capital for South Korea was blocked by that country's constitutional court. There are continuing low key discussions of new capital cities for Argentine and Japan, and a state capital more centrally located than Juneau for Alaska. Possibly, the balkanization of regions of the world may result in new capital cities. Presumably when Chandigarh (at present serving as the capital of two Indian states: Punjab and Haryana) becomes solely the capital of Punjab, Haryana will require its own. Much depends on the drive of individual leaders to celebrate their own states and themselves.

Major references

Capital Cities (1989). *Ekistics* **50** (299). Special Issue.

Nilsson, Sten Ake (1973). *The New Capitals of India, Pakistan and Bangladesh*. London: Curzon Press.

Rapoport, Amos (1993). On the nature of capital cities and their physical expression. In John H. Taylor, Jean G. Lengelle and Caroline Andrew, eds., *Capital Cities: International Perspectives*. Ottawa: Carleton University Press, 31–64.

CASE STUDY

Brasília, Brazil: a national capital (1946–70+)

The idea of and the name, Brasília, for a new capital for Brazil goes back to, at least, 1823 when José Bonifcacio suggested that the country's capital should be moved to Goias. The action to actually build a new capital began on 18 September 1946, when using the power invested in it by Article 4 of the nation's constitution, the Brazilian Chamber of Deputies voted to move the nation's capital from Rio de Janiero to state-owned land in the interior. The goal was to open up the centre of the country to significant development. The decision was a bold act of will.

In 1953, the Congress instructed the administration to select a site by 1955. A year later, the aerial photographic and interpretation company of Cornell University

Collection of the author

Figure 7.2   President Juscelino Kubitschek.

professor Donald Belcher was hired to pinpoint a suitable site. The firm recommended one based on its topography, soil qualities, rainfall and winds. It has porous soil and summer rainfall, and is located at an altitude of a little over 1000 metres with a relative humidity varying between 55% and 86% over the course of the year. In 1956, with the site selected, Congress authorized the formation of a company NOVACAP (Nova Capital) to proceed with the development of Brasília. Its only shareholder was the Brazilian Government. The whole process of development was pushed ahead by President (1956–61) Juscelino Kubitschek (see Figure 7.2) and some see the city as a monument to him.

In September 1956, NOVACAP announced a competition for the general plan of Brasília. The requirement was that the entries: (1) show the proposed structure of the city, the location of its precincts, centres and lines of communication at a scale of 1:25,000 and (2) provide a supporting report. The competition was open to all Brazilian architects, planners and urbanists. A considerable body of data was assembled to assist the entrants. The winning entry was to be selected by an international jury (including Brazilian architect Oscar Niemeyer). From 26 entries it selected the scheme (see Figures 2.3 and 7.3a) by Lucio Costa, a consultant town planner, over those by Gonçalves, Millman and Rocha, MMM Roberto (see Figure 7.3c) and Rino Levi (see Figure 7.3b). Costa's selection was controversial because he failed to meet the criteria established by NOVACAP. He, nevertheless, had an idea that captivated the jury and, it seems, President Kubitschek. Oscar Niemeyer became the principal architect.

Costa presented a series of sketches on five cards. His plan was chosen because it was a 'noble diagram' supported by a

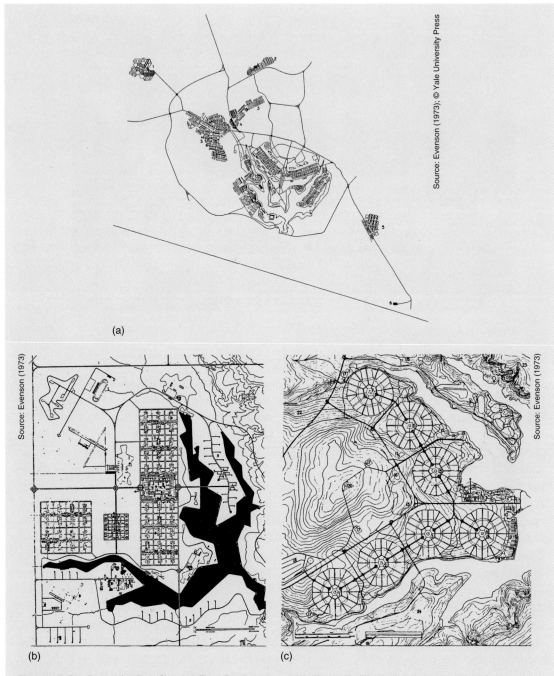

Figure 7.3 Plans for Brasília. (a) The Costa plan with the satellite townships that had grown up by 1967, (b) the Rino Levi proposal and (c) the MMM Roberto firm proposal.

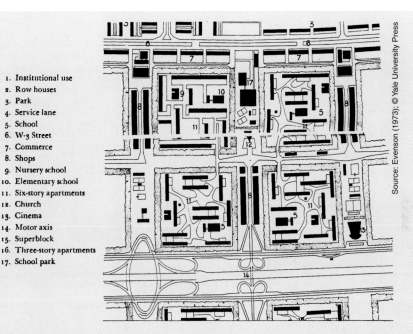

1. Institutional use
2. Row houses
3. Park
4. Service lane
5. School
6. W-3 Street
7. Commerce
8. Shops
9. Nursery school
10. Elementary school
11. Six-story apartments
12. Church
13. Cinema
14. Motor axis
15. Superblock
16. Three-story apartments
17. School park

Source: Evenson (1973); © Yale University Press

Figure 7.4 The plan of the residential superquadras.

convincing report. The scheme featured two great axes. One axis, the monumental, would contain the capital complex; the other, in the form of an arc tied to the drainage pattern of the site, would house the residential and associated sectors. Conceptually the plan had four parts:

1 the government buildings,
2 the residential *superquadras* (superblocks), (see Figure 7.4)
3 the vehicular circulation pattern,
4 the city centre.

In his original report Costa said the lakefront should be reserved for recreation but ultimately the lake divided the totally planned world from that of the private lots on its south (see Figures 3.1 and 7.3a).

The plan has antecedents in two generic city designs of Le Corbusier: the City for 3 Million (1922) and the Radiant City (1930). The dwelling units are of uniform height and appearance, and are grouped into superblocks with communal facilities and gardens. The administration, business and finance towers are located at the central crossing of axes. Thus Brasília was a total urban design north of the lake with NOVA-CAP as the developer, Lucio Costa as planner and Oscar Niemeyer as architect. The team was responsible for the design and implementation of a single-unified product. Beyond the 'plano pilloto', it is a piece-by-piece urban design and satellite towns have grown up somewhat haphazardly plugging into whatever pieces of infrastructure were available (Figure 7.3a).

The funding of the infrastructure and buildings, apart from the foreign embassies and the private lots south of the lake, was provided and controlled by the central government of Brazil. Even so, significant changes were made in the plan due to political and economic

Collection of the author

(a)

Collection of the author

(b)

Figure 7.5 Two views of Brasília. (a) The monumental axis; an early photograph and (b) the residential superquadras; an early photograph.

pressures and other architects became involved but the design team remained in charge and the main goal of making a symbolic centre for Brazil was fully achieved.

Brasília was built from the centre outwards. The first phase involved the design of the monumental axis and adjacent areas to the east and west. When Brasília was inaugurated in 1960, 3 years after ground was broken, the main buildings on the monumental axis, the congress and ministries, the bulk of the highway system and several of the superblocks had been completed. The majority of the citizens of the metropolitan area, however, resided in towns that had sprung up around the construction site and many of the workers lived in construction camps and immigrants from country areas lived in flavellas (shantytowns). The total designed core of Brasília itself became a city for the middle class (Figure 7.5).

As a symbol for the country Brasília has been a great architectural success. The sculptural quality of government precinct has been much photographed. As a demonstration of Modernist ideals it has no peer. Brasília has fostered regional development as intended and has become a major cultural centre. It has become a city. Many people enjoy living there. Brasília, however, lacks the liveliness of Rio de Janeiro or São Paulo. There is little street-life, no street corners as places to hang out. Its streets are not seams for life, but, rather, edges to superblocks and designed for the free flow of traffic. Yet the car ownership level is not what was predicted. The life of the city has become internalized. The city design represents the complete break from tradition, behaviourally and physically, that the Modernists sought.

Major references

Del Rio, Vicente and Haroldo Gallo (2000). The legacy of modernism in Brazil: paradigm turned reality or unfinished project? *Docomomo Journal* 23 (August): 23–7.

Epstein, David (1973). *Brasília, Plan and Reality: A Study of Planned and Spontaneous Urban Development*. Berkeley and Los Angeles: University of California Press.

Evenson, Norma (1973). *Two Brazilian Capitals: Architecture and Urbanism in Rio de Janeiro and Brasília*. New Haven: Yale University Press.

Holston, James (1989). *The Modernist City: An Anthropological Critique of Brasília*. Chicago: University of Chicago Press.

Company Towns

A company town is a planned settlement for workers of a single-industrial organization. Many were built in Western Europe and the Americas during the nineteenth century as a response to the 'coke towns' of the industrializing world. They were predominantly private enterprise developments and every aspect of the physical town, and often life within it, was under company control. Some are well known. Bourneville in England (1879+), Pullman, Illinois (1880–4), the earlier Le Cruesot and Mulhouse in France and the Krupp industry towns in Germany amongst many others had both physical and social objectives in mind and were both autocratic and paternalistic. Such towns are characterized by company-built community facilities and housing. The housing is very much all the same with the more senior staff having the larger abodes. The manager's house is often distinctive.

Other company towns have been resource oriented. Many were located at the sources of mines. Wells, British Columbia (1937–67), for example, served the Gold Quartz Mine and had a population of 4500 at its peak. It was sold off when the mine closed in 1967. It now has a population of 250 people. Nhulunbuy

(1966+) in northern Australia is a town of 4000 people developed to exploit bauxite deposits. It flourishes still. Such towns will continue to be built while the earth's resources that are located away from major centres are exploited.

Most manufacturing-industry-based company towns were and are located in the suburban areas of cities. With the improvement of both individual and mass transportation and the provision of government funded housing programmes during the twentieth century, private enterprise company towns became unnecessary. Manufacturing-based company towns are, nevertheless, like mining towns, still being built. The reason for their existence did, however, change during the second half of the twentieth century. They were part of national policies for redistributing employment opportunities and population.

Internationally known architects designed some company towns. B. V. Doshi designed the GSFC Township described here. It is a thoughtfully considered company town, but many have been designed in a hurried fashion, because they are expected to be short lived. All company towns, whether designed by famous architects or not, have much in common. In particular, it is that design control is centralized. More than any other type of new town they tend to be total urban designs. Some follow the Garden City paradigm; others are Rationalist. Others (e.g. Yorkship Village – now Fairview – in Camden, New Jersey, 1918) are domestic scale City Beautiful schemes. A number, such as Fairview, have survived the demise of their parent company.

Major references

Bucci, Frederico, ed. (1998). *Company Towns*. New York: Princeton University Press.
Crawford, Margaret (1995). *Building the Workingman's Paradise: The Design of American Company Towns*. New York: Verso.
Darley, Gillian (1978). *Villages of Vision*. London: Palladin.

CASE STUDY

The GSFC Township, Vadodara, India: an industrial township (1964–9)

The Indian government has a policy of decentralizing industries. To attract workers to locations outside their home states, townships have to be built to house them at subsidized rates in attractive surroundings. There are many such towns in India providing for a wide variety of industry types. State governments have followed suit. The GSFC is one such organization. Its township on the outskirts of Vadodara (formerly Baroda) is one

such company town. It is an example of an urban design where the architect has tried to deviate from the standard norms of company town design.

Balkrishna V. Doshi, the architect for the township, in writing about the design for company towns, noted:

In large township projects where the government controls finance, there is a definite

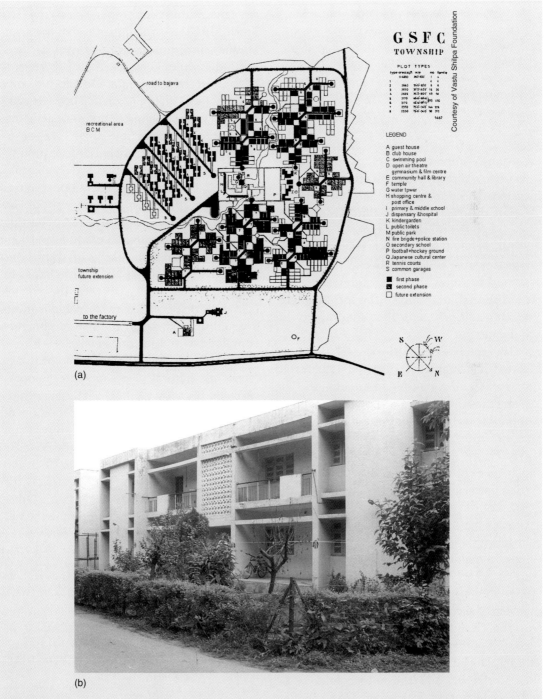

Figure 7.6 The Gujarat State Fertilizer Corporation (GSFC) Township, Vadodara. (a) The site plan and (b) a view of lower-income housing.

pattern of rules and conditions to be followed in spite of local needs or changes in
the cost of materials. The projects usually
emphasize the size and area of rooms
rather than living concepts . . . As a result
housing in India has always remained a
package of boxes and not housing (Doshi
cited in Steele, 1998: 50).

Many company town plans in India are
just taken directly from government specifications without much additional thought.
Often the road hierarchy and widths are
given and the number of units of each type
of housing unit is specified. This was largely
true for the GSFC Township but Doshi
strove to meet local requirements and
paid special attention to the local climate,
local traditions and the adaptability of
buildings.

The total area of the township is 140
acres (56 hectares) of which half is allocated
to parks and a quarter to circulation. The
plan takes the form of a superblock with all
vehicular traffic entering the interior of the
block from a single-circumferential road
(see Figure 7.6a). It is a modified Radburn
plan (see Figure 7.18a). A network of pedestrian paths links the residential areas to the
heart of the site. At the car-free core of the
site are the public facilities: dispensary and
hospital, kindergarten, post office, a primary, a middle and a secondary school, and
some sports facilities. A water tower is a
special design feature giving a point of reference to the core area.

The housing types owe much to
contemporary modern architecture in
India, Doshi's experiences in working with
Le Corbusier, and the antecedents of Le
Corbusier's work in that of Tony Garnier.
The nature of the types and their location
reflects the status and income level of their
residents within the company hierarchy (see
Steele, 1998). At the upper end of the scale
families have houses with private gardens
located in quiet enclaves. At the lower end
of the hierarchy are flats and 'slotted' row
houses (see Figure 7.6b). Their designs
respond to the spilling out of daily activities
into open areas in a manner typical of
Indian life. Doshi paid special attention to
the creation of open spaces with nooks and
crannies. Balconies provide opportunities
for diverse behaviours: sleeping out on
charpoys, parking motor scooters, chatting
and doing light industrial work. In particular, the territorial hierarchy of transitions
from private space to public – from steps to
ledges to the small street to the square
(*chowk*) is respected. The township is given
a visual unity through the use of concrete
combined with thick brick walls.

Doshi, as he freely admits, got some things
(such as natural ventilation techniques)
wrong in his early work. His later townships
(e.g. for the Life Insurance Corporation of
India (LIC) Township at Hyderabad,
1968–71 and for Indian Farmers Fertilizer
Cooperative (IFFCO) at Kalol 1970–3 and
1976) are more sophisticated but follow the
ideas he developed in Vadodara. Other
Indian architects have picked up the themes
much more recently and with greater detail
borrowing patterns from the past in a New
Urbanist manner.

Major references

Curtis, William J. R. (1988). *Balkrishna Doshi: An
Architect for India*. New York: Rizzoli International.
Doshi, Balkrishna V. (1982). *Housing*. Ahmedabad:
Stein, Doshi, Bhalla.
Steele, James (1998). *The Complete Architecture
of Balkrishna Doshi: Rethinking Modernism for
the Developing World*. London: Thames and
Hudson.

Figure 7.7 The Lincoln Center, New York with the Metropolitan Opera in the background in 1993.

Precincts: Green-field and Cleared Brown-field Sites

Most urban design schemes deal with precincts of cities. A wide variety of them have been designed by one hand. They include capital complexes, cultural districts, commercial centres, campuses of many types, and simply thousands of housing developments, urban and suburban. The Lincoln Center in New York (see Figure 7.7), and the Capital Complex (see the Case study below) and the City Centre in Chandigarh (see Figure 2.4) are amongst many well known such developments around the world that were the responsibility of one authority and designed by one architect or one team of architects under a single leader – in the case of Lincoln Center the leader was Wallace K. Harrison. A number of architects worked under his direction. They included his partner Max Abromowitz and Philip Johnson. The Barbican in London is a multi-use complex of the type. In these schemes the borderline between architectural and urban design gets blurred.

The unity of physical texture and aesthetics of such schemes leads them to be, in Kevin Lynch's terms, districts (see Lynch, 1960). Whether districts designed by one set of hands are as desirable as they might have been if different hands had designed them is always open to question and debate. Any evaluation depends on the values deemed to be important at the time of the analysis. At present the lack of visual variety and the boldness of the schemes is generally deemed to be a weakness by those outside the architectural profession. Architects are more divided in their opinions.

161

CASE STUDY

The Capital Complex, Chandigarh, India: a civic design (1953–62+; still incomplete)

Chandigarh, a new state capital, resulted from the partitioning of the state of Punjab partly into India and partly into Pakistan on independence in 1947. The Capital Complex stands outside the main body of the new city itself. Its site is approximately 400 metres north–south and 800 metres east–west in dimension. It was designed by Le Corbusier and superseded an earlier design by Mathew Nowicki who died in an aircraft accident in 1951. B. V. Doshi was the very young site architect. The government of India was the ultimate sponsor of the project while P. L. Varma, Chief Engineer of Punjab, and P. N. Thapar, the State Administrator, were the immediate clients. Prime Minister Jawaharlal Nehru also took a keen interest in the project as a symbol of the newly independent India. If Le Corbusier needed support when his ideas were in conflict with those of local officials, he turned to Nehru.

The Capital Complex as it now exists consists of three buildings and two sculptural structures (see Figure 7.8). Their arrangement stands in strong contrast to the colonial organization of the Capital Complex in New Delhi. The three major buildings: the Secretariat, the High Court and the Assembly building (legislature) are monuments to the democratic principles of the Indian constitution. The Assembly Hall and the Supreme Court are the most prominent facing each other across an extremely broad stretch of concrete paving (455 metres, about 1500 feet, in length, but seemingly farther on a summer day). This arrangement symbolizes the balance of power between the legislature and the courts. The Secretariat is to the rear

and the Governor's palace – the Governor being representative of the central government – to the north. The latter building has never been built. Nehru rejected the idea of its location at the head of the complex as being undemocratic. It reminded him of the location of the Viceroy's palace in New Delhi. The alternative proposal was to have a museum there. It too has yet to be built.

The overall composition is based on two interlocking 400 metre squares. The eastern façade of the Secretariat bounds one edge of the western square and the Assembly Hall and the proposed museum are within it. The eastern square has the Assembly Hall, museum and the High Court within it. The composition also contains a series of gardens, courts, reflecting pools and monuments. The Tower of Shadows, the Monument to the Open Hand and the Pit of Reflection have been completed but other components remain unbuilt.

The largest of the buildings in the complex is the Secretariat located to the side and rear of the Assembly Hall and symbolically subservient to it. It has a north–south axis and defines the western edge of the site. The building itself is based on a grid pattern with small porches on its eastern and western façades. Freer forms break the grid pattern and the status of workers inside is shown on the façade by the size of units allocated to them. The roof of the building houses a seldom-used garden.

The Assembly Hall has a square plan with the hall itself, with seating for 250 legislators, being surrounded by ceremonial space and separate galleries for the press, and for men

Figure 7.8 The capital complex, Chandigarh. (a) Le Corbusier and B. V. Doshi in Paris, (b) the site plan, (c) a view of the capital complex in 1996 with the monument to the Open hand in the foreground and the Assembly Hall and the Secretariat to the rear and (d) the entrance to the Assembly Hall.

163

and for women. On three sides of the building are offices that are protected from the sun by a massive *brise-soleil*. A council chamber with seating for 70 has a pyramided ceiling. The great portico facing the Supreme Court has eight thin piers that support a troughed roof that spills rainwater into a reflecting pool in front of the building. The inspiration of the cooling towers of the power station outside Ahmedabad, is clear in the roof form.

The High Court is an L-shaped building housing the High Court Room and a number of smaller courtrooms equally expressed on the building's façade. A high portico faces the Assembly Hall. The three pylons of the portico that rise 18 metres (50 feet) from the ground symbolize the majesty of the law, the fear of the law and the shelter of the law. A double roof protects the whole building from the power of the summer sun.

The complex as an entity – buildings and landscape – is a powerful symbolic work of art by a single architect. In many ways it formed his international image as an architect of note.

It is a moving composition for many architects and a source of pride for the citizens of Chandigarh. The design illustrates Le Corbusier's exploration of geometrical, cosmological, rural and vernacular themes. It is unambiguously a total, Modernist, urban design project. Few schemes are as clear in their intentions. It was entirely publicly funded. Whether or not so much money should have been spent on a single project is always a subject of debate especially in a country with meagre financial resources.

Major references

Bahga, Sarbijt, Surinder Bahga and Yashinder Bahga (1993). Capitol Complex, Chandigarh (1951–62). In *Modern Architecture in India. Post-Independence Perspective*. New Delhi: Galgotia, 24–7.

Lang, Jon, Madhavi Desai and Miki Desai (1997). *Architecture and Independence: The Search for Identity – India 1880 to 1980*. New Delhi: Oxford University Press.

Nilsson, Sten Ake (1973). *The New Capitals of India, Pakistan and Bangladesh*. London: Curzon Press.

CASE STUDY

The Barbican, London, England, UK: an inner city development (1959–82)

The Barbican development is located on a 62-acre (25-hectare) site in the northwestern corner of the City of London. The site had been almost completely destroyed during World War II. It consists of three components: a 12-acre (5-hectare) site – the Golden Lane Scheme – a southern portion of 10 acres (4 hectares) and a central area of 24.7 acres (10 hectares). It is this central mixed-use but predominantly residential complex designed by Chamberlain, Powell and Bon in 1959 that is the example of a total urban design project described here. The design for the site, however, went through several iterations before that design became the one implemented.

During the 1950s, traffic congestion resulting from the increasing employment in the City was a major problem requiring attention. While the number of jobs located there was soaring, the residential population of the City had plummeted from 125,000 in 1851 to 5000 a hundred years later. One public policy goal of the council was to attract people to live in the City again. The Barbican was a response.

The City Corporation of London (now Corporation of London) was originally the sponsor of the project. It had started purchasing land at the end of World War II and by 1954 had acquired freehold possession of 50% of the site and had taken steps to acquire an additional 25%. It was, however, the London County Council who ultimately promoted the project. In addition, an architectural leader, Sir Gerald Barry, formed the New Barbican Committee as a political pressure group to take the lead in shaping the type of development that was to occur. It was the Committee that developed the first building programme for the site.

The programme specified that a single scheme should be built. It was to provide accommodation, reduce traffic congestion, preserve the few historical buildings that remained on the site, and have generous open spaces and gardens without them being overshadowed by buildings. The goal was to create a 'city monument' (New Barbican, 1954). The programme represented the beginning of a 25-year total urban design effort that involved five major possible designs produced over a 5-year period and the ultimate selection of the last of them for implementation.

Kadleigh, Whitfield and Horsburgh produced the first scheme in 1954 at the behest of the New Barbican Committee. The firm proposed a multi-level, multi-use megastructure that it hoped would capture the public's imagination (see Figure 7.9a). The design consisted of four levels of underground warehousing served by its own road/rail system plus parking for 3000 cars. The historic buildings would be set in parks as objects in space. The already-proposed new highway would be located along the site's southern boundary. A four-storey warehouse podium layered with four-storey terrace houses would surround the complex. Five point-towers, and a trade and hotel/conference centre would act as major landmarks on the site. This bold design succeeded in arousing public interest in the project. The rivalry between the London County Council and the City Corporation led to more radical proposals but the tone had been set for the nature of the project.

The first of the alternative schemes came from the London County Council's Planning Division; it was the Martin/Meade Plan (see Figure 7.9b). The proposal was less controversial than the first scheme. It consisted of a lower-density residential development with office buildings set in parkland, several blocks of building for general commerce and two main office towers. The City Corporation soon came back with an alternative (see Figure 7.9c). Its Planning Division produced a design whose density of development was between the two earlier proposals. It was predominantly a commercial development but included residential buildings and two point towers. Unlike the earlier proposals it had defined streets.

The need for massive public financing led to the involvement of the central government in the project. The then Minister for Housing and Local Government, Duncan Sandys, argued for a residential neighbourhood with schools, shops and open spaces even if it meant 'foregoing a more remunerative return on the land' (Cantacuzino, 1973). His pleading found little support in the marketplace. What did take place was that the responsibility for designing of the

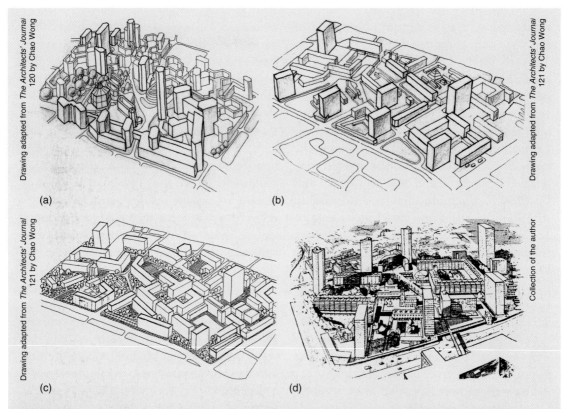

Figure 7.9 Proposed designs for the Barbican, London. (a) The Kadleigh, Whitfield and Horsburgh proposal (1954), (b) the London County Council proposal (1955), (c) the London City Corporation proposal (1955) and (d) the Chamberlain, Powell and Bon scheme.

project was moved from the public sector agencies to private firms.

The next proposal (1955), the fourth, was rejected by the London County Council because of its high densities and despite the amount of open space, the lack of large ones. The scheme, designed by Chamberlain, Powell and Bon, built on the first proposal prepared for the New Barbican Committee. In order to be economically viable, it was a high population density scheme (750 people per hectare). Four-storey buildings were organized in a checkerboard pattern around a series of alternating public and private courts. The firm significantly revised this

scheme in order to meet the approval of both the County Council and the City Corporation. The City Corporation approved the revised Chamberlain, Powell and Bon scheme in November 1959. It is this scheme that is a total urban design although not as totally under one control as Brasília or the capital complex at Chandigarh. The project consists of a multi-level circulation system, tower blocks, a theatre, restaurants, internal lawns and water gardens (see Figure 7.9d).

The history of the proposals and their rejections is not unique to the development of the Barbican. In total urban designs of its nature in democratic countries with different

Figure 7.10 A view from the elevated walkway in 2004. See page 2 for another.

making its original aim of providing for low-income earners difficult to achieve.

The scheme, as built, consisted of 2113 flats, maisonettes and terrace houses, mostly in blocks of six stories high and ranging in size from one to five rooms, the Guildhall School of Music and Drama, the City of London School for Girls, a fire station, the Coroner's Court and Mortuary, two hotels, shops, restaurants and pubs, and sports facilities. It is a complex scheme. Parking, refuse removal and drainage all had to be integrated into a functioning whole (Figure 7.10).

It has been a scheme much praised and much criticized. Today, it does have a somewhat foreboding presence for the visitor and way-finding is not easy, but its detailed landscaping and attention to building finishes at least partially offset the negative. It is a fine legacy of 1950s and 1960s total urban design ideology. The Barbican received heritage listing in September 2001. Critics see it as a subsidized housing development for the wealthy. It has certainly been a popular place to live.

Major references

A great place to live (2001). *The Guardian*. Friday, 7 September. http://www.guardian.co.uk/g2/storey/0,3604,548152,00.html

Cantacuzino, Sherban (1973). The Barbican development, City of London. *Architectural Review* **154** (918): 66–90.

New Barbican (1954). *The Architects' Journal* **120**: 456–66.

interest group struggling for recognition and different approval agencies vying for power, designs evolve. Implementation does not come easily either. The construction of the Barbican took 20 years, during which time the programme and thus the design were altered. Strikes, traffic concerns and changes in the demands of the marketplace continued to affect the scheme. Building costs soared,

Precincts: Urban Renewal

The Barbican was built on a site bombed out during World War II. In a sense it was an urban renewal project. Urban renewal projects, as understood here, however, involve the planned demolition of obsolete and/or decayed segments of cities, in whole or in part, and their rebuilding. The new development may be publicly or privately financed, or some mixture of the two. Often governments use their power of eminent domain to acquire land and to accumulate small sites into single-parcels ripe for redevelopment. Private companies without that power have also succeeded in painstakingly agglomerating individual sites into a large parcel. Much depends on land ownership patterns. In cities such as London, large segments of land are in single ownership and leased out for 99 years. When the leases come to an end, the land is available for redevelopment. In the case of Rockefeller Center in New York a wealthy family purchased a lease from a single landowner and redeveloped the site but had to capture a number of sub-leases.

Whether built on freehold or leasehold sites a wide variety of urban renewal schemes have been completed around the world. The conflicts between different stakeholders can be intense and questions of what really is in the public interest arise. Traditionally strong financial and political forces usually win the arguments but sometimes alliances of weaker forces prevail. In either case the urban design scheme goes through many twists and turns before it is finally built.

Major references

Bentley, Ian (1999). *Urban Transformations: Power, People and Urban Design*. London: Routledge.

Freiden, Bernard J. and Lynne B. Sagalyn (1991). *Downtown, Inc.: How America Rebuilds Cities*. Cambridge, MA: MIT Press.

CASE STUDY

Rockefeller Center, New York, NY, USA: a collaborative design (1928–34; expanded 1947–73)

Rockefeller Center has been included in this collection of case studies because of its precedent setting character. Nowadays it might even be regarded as a Neo-Traditional design in the way its buildings meet and form the street. Its designers would be aghast at hearing such a statement. It was regarded by them as Modernist and still appears so.

The Center was built on land owned by Columbia University. The site is located in the heart of mid-town Manhattan between 48th and 51st Streets, and Fifth and Sixth Avenues. It had been a fashionable residential area during much of the nineteenth century but a series of changes in its neighbourhood had had deleterious effects on the blocks. In 1928 John D. Rockefeller Jr.

bought the lease to the site from the university. His desire was to create a development that would improve an area close to his family home on 54th Street. What was built was the first set of high-rise buildings anywhere forming a single complex rather than a series of independent edifices. It has become a precedent for other such schemes around the world. Few, if any, have proved to be as well loved.

The idea for the scheme began with the search for a new home by the Metropolitan Opera whose building was inadequate and its neighbourhood seedy. In 1928 the Opera under Otto Kahn developed the idea of making the Opera House part of a multi-use complex. A number of potential sites were examined before it was realized that the Columbia University owned mid-town estate was due for re-release. The accumulation of sites held by different lessees proved to be a costly task. The price was 1930$3.6 million plus as much as another million to capture all the leases. The idea for developing the whole rather than part of the site was based on the perception that in doing so a civic space appropriate as a forecourt to the Opera would be financially feasible. The Opera hoped that Rockefeller would be a major benefactor by financing the open space and then by loaning money to the Opera company.

If Rockefeller Center has become a precedent for other designs, it also had precedents. It was inspired not only by Beaux-Arts design principles, but in particular, by the success of Grand Central Terminal, a city within a city. It is, however, a very different complex. Rockefeller first envisaged a commercial centre of three towers with a new Opera House and a plaza as the centrepieces. Designed by Benjamin Morris, it was called Radio City. A second scheme was drawn up by Corbett, Harrison and McMurray, and a third by Benjamin Morris again (see Figure 7.11a). This scheme was developed under the direction of an architectural advisory board operating under the supervision of a realtor, John R. Todd, renowned for his fiscal pragmatism. The scheme did not go ahead as the Metropolitan Opera withdrew from the project and Rockefeller did not control the whole site. Instead what was built is a profit-driven commercial and entertainment centre largely in accordance with Todd's instructions. What endured was the idea of the plaza. It was seen as an extraordinary public gesture because of the price of land but it has proved to be the core of the project and to have increased the profitability of the whole complex.

In October 1929, Todd announced that L. Andrew Reinhard and Henry Hofmeister would produce an overall conceptual diagram (see Figure 7.11b). Their site plan clearly harkens back to the earlier plans by Benjamin Morris. A consortium of architects designed the final scheme. It consisted of Reinhard & Hofmeister, Corbett, Harrison and MacMurray, Raymond Hood, Goodley & Foilhoux, and Edward Durell Stone. The design was, however, very much guided by the aesthetic position taken by Raymond Hood. The overall urban design has Beaux-Arts overtones but the buildings have the streamlined verticality and massing of the Art Deco (see Figure 7.11c). The unity of the scheme is due to Hood's influence and the willingness of the other architects to submerge their own attitudes in order to achieve a single-unified complex. Despite the depression of the 1930s, work proceeded on the project from 1930 onwards. It and the Empire State building were the two major commercial building projects of the 1930s in New York City.

Radio City was able to move forward because of the financial backing of Rockefeller and aggressive marketing. The Center attracted major tenants such as Time Warner and the Associated Press, as well as government offices and consulates of various countries. The complex is a prestigious address and was renamed later the Rockefeller Center. It comprised ten buildings in its initial phase, the last of which was completed in the 1940s. The catalytic building, however, was the RKO motion picture and vaudeville theatre – Radio City Music Hall. Opened in 1932, designed primarily by Raymond Hood but in collaboration with the other firms, it had a full stage and had seating for over 3500 patrons. It is still a major attraction in New York with

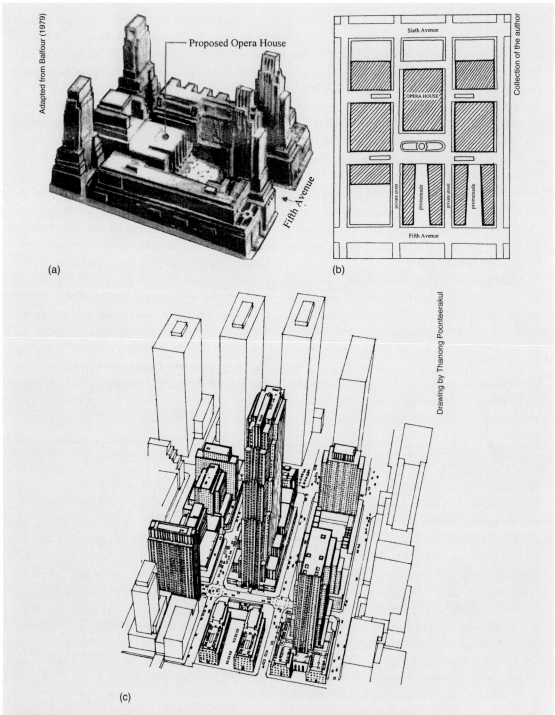

Figure 7.11 Rockefeller Center, New York. (a) The third proposal for the Center, (b) the Reinhard and Hofmeister development plan and (c) the Center as built.

concerts by international celebrities and with its Christmas spectacular. The hall spurred development. Rockefeller Center was completed in the 1960s with the erection of the buildings along Sixth Avenue but adaptations to the scheme continue.

The centrepiece of the public space is a sunken plaza backed by a statue (Prometheus by Paul Manship, 1934; see Figures 7.12 and 7.13) and surrounded now by flagpoles carrying the flags of the members of the United Nations. The plaza is reached from Fifth Avenue by a walkway with well-maintained central planting boxes. There were a number of thoughts about what the plaza should be – a forecourt for the Opera House, a promenade lined with trees, and a raised forum surrounded by shopping – before it took its final basement level form. It like many sunken plazas, was lifeless unable to retain the retail uses around it until a skating rink was introduced during the winter months. Made possible by developments in refrigeration

technology, it was a last-ditch experiment to get some life into the space. It is now a major attraction not only for skaters but also for spectators. It is surrounded at the basement level by restaurants and a lively if rather dreary shopping concourse that links the development to New York's subway system (see Figure 7.14).

The key building of the project is the RCA building. Its shape was dictated by Todd's assessment that all useable space had to be within 30 feet (9 metres) of windows to be rentable in a time of economic depression. Such a slab building had precedents in Frank Lloyd Wright's San Francisco Press building and in 1920s design explorations of architects including Marcel Breuer, Walter Gropius and Le Corbusier. Raymond Hood gave the building its poetic character through a series of setbacks – the first at 100 feet to comply with zoning codes created to ensure some sunlight at ground level. The other setbacks were due to Hood's desire to have all

Figure 7.12 The view towards the Plaza from Fifth Avenue in 1993.

Figure 7.13 Prometheus.

usable space in the building within 22 feet (7 metres) from the windows and for aesthetic effect. There are a number of pioneering aspects to the project. It has an underground parking lot and off-street delivery access. It uses high-speed elevators and is fully air-conditioned. It relied on its own steam and electricity plants. Like many other such complexes it spurred development around it.

In many ways, Rockefeller Center could be regarded as an all-of-a-piece urban design where the design guidelines were set by one firm of architects and followed by different architects designing different buildings. It is considered to be a total urban design here because one development team guided by a strong individual, John Rockefeller, and led by a strong architect, Raymond Hood, put it together. Rockefeller Center today, 70 years later, is 'sparely elegant, modern but civilized and occupying a convenient mid-town location whose horizons embrace both the uptown swells and the more raucous types

Figure 7.14 The concourse level.

downtown' (Mark Steyn cited in Cooke, 2000: 266). The project remains an exemplar of a privately funded development that provides for both private and public activities. There is little more that one can expect of an urban design scheme.

Major references

Balfour, Alan (1978). *Rockefeller Center: Architecture as Theater*. New York: McGraw Hill.

Sharp, Dennis (1991). *Twentieth Century Architecture: A Visual History*. London: Lund Humphries.

Precincts: Historic Preservation and Urban Revitalization

Abandoned buildings have been converted into other uses when they are strategically located and have qualities that can be exploited. Cotton mills in Mumbai have been converted to office buildings, garment factories in Philadelphia and woolstores in Sydney into apartments, and the Ghirardelli chocolate factory in San Francisco (as has already been described) into a shopping and tourist centre. The list can go on and on. Not only do the buildings give a sense of continuity – a sense of history – to a city's inhabitants but also often they cannot be replaced today for financial reasons with ones of a similar quality. Such conversions of individual buildings are not generally regarded as urban design despite the catalytic effect they may have on the development of their surroundings.

Special district legislation and the use of zoning incentives as part of city planning have seen precincts conserved or renovated and, usually, gentrified. The upgrading in financial status of occupants occurred, for instance, in the Marais in Paris, Society Hill in Philadelphia and Duxton Hill in Singapore (i.e. the original population is displaced by one of a higher income as the physical environment and services are improved). The conversion of industrial precincts of cities as single projects into new uses without extensive demolition is less common. Clarke Quay in Singapore is, however, an example. It was totally converted into a new use under the direction of a single team of a developer and an architectural firm.

Major references

Attoe, Wayne (1988). Historic preservation. In Anthony J. Catanese and James C. Snyder, eds., *Urban Planning*. New York: McGraw-Hill, 344–65.

Jacobs, Steven and Barclay G. Jones (1962). *Urban Design through Conservation*. Unpublished manuscript, University of California at Berkeley.

Tiesdell, Steven A., Taner Oc and Tim Heath (1996). *Revitalizing Historic Urban Quarters*. Boston: Butterworth-Architecture.

CASE STUDY

Clarke Quay, Singapore: an abandoned warehouse area (1989–93: 2003+)

Singapore is a city-state with a democratically elected government that is very much involved in planning and development matters. Responsibility for planning and design lies with the country's cabinet. It delegates authority to the Urban Redevelopment Authority (URA) which is the de facto planning department. It has the degree of cooperation between various agencies charged with urban development that many other cities envy. There is thus a high degree of consensus about what schemes should be carried out and how they should be developed amongst the various ministries and agencies of the government. The government strives to keep a balance between private developers' ideas and the overall efficiency of the city.

After independence from colonial rule, the government did not actively work on conservation because of other priorities. Three factors changed this situation:

1 the economic downturn in the late 1970s,
2 the return from graduate education of young architects who had studied preservation projects abroad,
3 the presentations at a conference on heritage tourism held in Singapore in 1983 that convinced the authorities in Singapore of the economic benefits of preservation.

Clarke Quay is an example of the result.

Clarke Quay is a five-block precinct of 23,000 square metres (246,100 square feet) located on the Singapore River about a kilometre from the city-state's central business district. It consisted of nineteenth

century godowns and shophouses, the Merchants' Court, the Cannery and the Whampoa Icehouse (demolished in 1981 for road widening). The Cannery had been erected in 1901 to house a British engineering firm and had later been converted into a pineapple-processing factory. The rows of shophouses and warehouses gave the site its physical character (Figure 7.15).

The traditional southern China terraced shophouses were two or three stories in height and housed working class families on the upper floors and shops facing the street on the ground floor. In Singapore the type had been partially adapted to the tropical climate with high ceilings and a 5-foot wide shaded arcade (a requirement established in the early nineteenth century by Sir Stamford Raffles, founder of Singapore). Second storey jack-roofs allowed hot air to escape from interiors. The long-narrow form of the godowns and shophouses make conversion comparatively easy. Sixty godowns at Clarke Quay have been converted into more than 200 shops, restaurants, bars, etc. as part of the process of revitalizing the Singapore River front. Clarke Quay has also recently been connected by a new station to Singapore's Mass Rapid Transit (MRT) system (see Chapter 10).

Prior to the development of Clarke Quay, the URA had already embarked on a 10-year programme to clean up the highly polluted Singapore River. This clean-up was made possible because, the waterway's traditional commercial role as a transhipment centre had been lost as the result of the development of new shipping technologies.

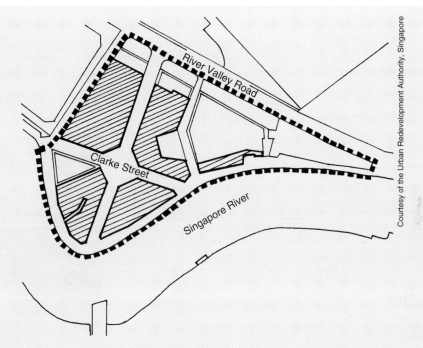

Courtesy of the Urban Redevelopment Authority, Singapore

Figure 7.15   The Clarke Quay Conservation Area, showing the buildings to remain.

Figure 7.16   Boat Quay, Singapore.

The URA began the construction of a highly successful riverside promenade in 1992. Its success was both economic and social with the creation of an *alfresco* dining area on the waterfront at Boat Quay (see Figure 7.16). The promenade was extended along the river past Clarke Quay to Robertson Quay and completed in early 2000. All establishments

175

along it that are designated commercial can set up outdoor eating areas. The guidelines for the design of the promenade were established by the URA and were followed by successful tenders for each project.

The building of the promenade was an all-of-a-piece infrastructure design scheme in which individual developers built pieces according to guidelines (e.g. those in Figure 7.17a).

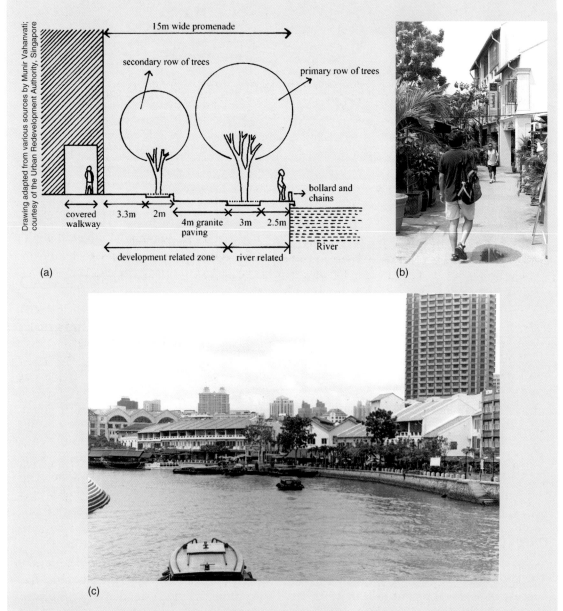

(a)

(b)

(c)

Figure 7.17 Clarke Quay, Singapore River. (a) The design controls for the riverside promenade, (b) the promenade and (c) the Quay in 2003.

The redevelopment process for Clarke Quay began in 1989. The URA gave the Quay heritage conservation status in July of that year. It was designated an area for a combination of adaptive reuses of its warehouses and shophouses. The URA allocated 'historically compatible' activities to each sub-zone. These uses included a hotel, and entertainment, retail and cultural facilities. The project was subjected to a tendering process under the URA's Sale of Sites programme in which the price offered for the land, the proposals and the economics were evaluated as a package.

The winning tender was submitted by DBS Land Ltd. Many designers were involved but their work was highly controlled by a central agency. The architectural and landscape architectural firms included ELS/Elbasani and Logan, RSP Singapore and EDAW from San Francisco. Thus the development team can be regarded as a public–private partnership between the URA, DBS Land, the designers and the Singapore River Business Association. Despite the various organizations involved, the renovation of Clarke Quay was carried out as a single project under one auspice.

The project ultimately consisted of the restoration of historic buildings, the insertion of new buildings and the pedestrianization of the whole site. The property market was allowed to dictate the specific uses. The requirement was that the façades and roof design of buildings be kept. As a result, although the Quay resembles what it was in the past, it has a completely different ambience. It is now an up-market, retail, food and beverage centre – a nightlife area – and a major destination for tourists and locals alike. The transformation cost $S186 million and was completed in 1993.

The historic buildings saved provide Singaporeans with a link to the past. In addition, one of the world's great river waterfronts had an additional element added to it. DBS Land created a promenade, a 10- to 15-metre wide water-edge walkway lined by trees in accordance with the guidelines issued by the URA. The promenade connects a series of plazas, pocket-parks, performance zones and water features thus catering for adults and children, and providing a diverse set of attractions. Encroachments onto the walkway have narrowed the channel for walkers but have enlivened the scene. But not enough!

Places change. The flow of the high-spending European and Japanese tourists of the early 1990s slowed. By 2000 Clarke Quay had a worn-out look. Competition from air-conditioned shopping malls and other similar developments meant that Clarke Quay no longer had a secure niche in the marketplace. In addition, the Quay does not have the shiny new image of the Esplanade theatre complex (designed by Stirling and Wilford) or One Fullerton (the recent redevelopment of a neo-classical colonial building). The Quay's landlord, CapitaLand Commercial, was seeking tenants to draw people back again and hired a British firm headed by Wil Alsop to draft a 'new look' for the Quay. The tenants feared that the change will involve rental increases well beyond the $S13 to $S15 per square metre that they were paying.

Amongst the characteristics of a good design is that it can adapt to change. The future of Clarke Quay is uncertain, but it is likely to retain much of its present form with greater attention paid to the comfort level of people. The physiological and aesthetic predispositions of visitors have shifted, as Maslow would have predicted (see Chapter 2). A shinier, modernistic appearance would probably meet the expectations of tourists and locals alike better than its historic one. We shall soon find out.

Major references

Breen, Ann and Dick Rigby (1996). *The New Waterfront: A World Wide Success Storey*. London: Thames and Hudson.

Heng Chye Kiang (2000). The night zone storyline: Boat Quay, Clarke Quay and Robertson Quay.

Traditional Buildings and Settlements Review **XIX** (Spring): 41–9.

Heng Chye Kiang (2001). Singapore River: a case for a river of life. *Singapore Architect* **211** (September): 90–5.

Precincts: Housing Complexes

Some may argue that the Barbican is really 'just' a housing development but there are thousands of housing schemes around the world that are much more single use in nature. They follow an extraordinarily range of forms based on a variety of antecedent ideas. The Rationalist schemes generally follow models developed at the Bauhaus in Germany and advocated by architects such as Ludwig Hilbersheimer (see Figure 7.18), and by Le Corbusier in his proposals for ideal cities and neighbourhoods that culminated in the building of his Unité d'Habitation (see Chapter 6). Such forms still dominate residential area design in many countries today. Pruitt-Igoe is a 1950s American example.

The Empiricist proposals have either followed Garden City and neighbourhood unit principles or were simply pragmatic, financially driven schemes led by property developers. Private ownership was stressed. Lately many such residential area designs have been driven by New Urbanist ideas. The most important

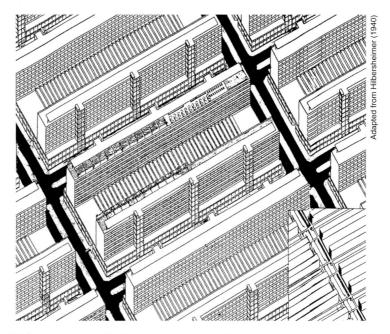

Adapted from Hilbersheimer (1940)

Figure 7.18 A generic Bauhaus-type residential area design as presented by Ludwig Hilbersheimer.

Empiricist model for a residential area design for most of the twentieth century, however, was Radburn, New Jersey (1928+ but never fully completed), a much-loved total urban design scheme (Figure 7.19). The development company failed financially during the recession that followed the Wall Street collapse, but Radburn has been an influential design idea, as can be seen in the design of the GSFC Township in Vadodara (see Figure 7.6a).

Rationalist schemes were built everywhere. Sometimes they were successful in terms of their acceptance by their residents (e.g. in the early new towns of Singapore and in Korea and China), but at other times they have been notorious failures as happy living environments. The experience in the so-called Anglo-Saxon world has been very mixed, with major shortcomings in both social and physical design schemes in the United States, the United Kingdom and Australia. They failed to provide a suitable milieu for the lives of people with low incomes. Pruitt-Igoe has become a name synonymous with this failure. It was one of the spurs to the development of systematic studies of the person–environment relationship as a basis for creating urban design ideas. It also led to the re-recognition that urban design must also be more than simply 'architecture writ large'.

At the beginning of the twenty-first century a wide variety of primarily residential total urban designs are being built. They come in a range of product types. Some are traditional suburban developments; others follow seemingly newer ideas although many of those ideas have been around for almost a century. They include

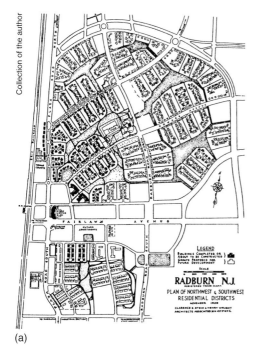

Collection of the author

(a) (b)

Figure 7.19 Radburn, New Jersey. (a) The site plan and (b) a cul-de-sac in 1993.

gated 'communities' and retirement villages. The gated community is a highly contentious type designed to protect those who live within one from crime and the presence of unsavoury characters (Blakely and Snyder, 1997; Minton, 2002; Low, 2003). It is generally associated with wealthy enclaves in the United States, but it is a highly prevalent type for new middle-income housing in cities such as Seoul and Shanghai (Miao, 2003; see Figure 7.1). Raleigh Park included here is a half-hearted example of a gated community. Yet another type is the retirement community (called 'silver towns' in Korea) in which age restrictions preclude the residence of people under a specific age (usually 55 years). The more radical housing types include housing cooperatives, and 'cohousing'.

Cooperatives are multi-unit buildings or estates in which residents have rights to occupy their units by purchasing stock in the corporation formed to develop and own the project. The corporation is the client and an architect designs the project and then the corporation sells the rights to the units. The cooperative is then run and maintained by an elected board of directors who assign running costs to the shareholders. Cohousing complexes may or may not be cooperatives.

Cohousing involves the design of a number of houses, usually 20 or 30, to form a community. The houses are located around a common open space and a common building. The members of the group may share household activities such as cooking and child minding. The idea is primarily European, and Scandinavian in particular, but about 70 cohousing projects have been built in the United States since 1990 and at the time of writing (2004) another 70 were on the drawing boards. Most are designed by a single architectural firm for a single group. The maintenance and other communal costs are assessed against the residents. The example reviewed here is Trudeslund in Denmark. Its form is similar to Kresge College at the University of California at Santa Cruz. I have classified that as primarily an architectural scheme (see Chapter 6)! The distinction is not easy to defend but has to do with the permanency of residency, the communality of decision-making and property ownership. At Trudeslund the community itself made decisions based on a common social vision. At Kresge College a consultative design process was used but decisions were made from the outside from the top down. It is really a single building.

Major references

Franck, Karen and Sherry Ahrentzen (1989). *New Households, New Housing*. New York: Van Nostrand Reinhold.

Hayden, Dolores (1984). *Redesigning the American Dream: The Future of Housing, Work and Family Life*. New York: Norton.

Rowe, Peter (1993). *Modernity and Housing*. Cambridge: MIT Press.

CASE STUDY

Pruitt-Igoe, East St Louis, Missouri, USA: an ill-fated public housing project (1950; proposal to remodel, 1956; demolished 1972)

Pruitt-Igoe, a Modernist public housing complex was a total urban design. It was built on a 55-acre (22-hectare) site and consisted of 2740 units in 33 eleven-storey buildings (see Figure 7.20a). It was the first 'racially integrated' public housing development in the city of St Louis. Twenty buildings were for Afro-Americans and thirteen were racially integrated. It had the capacity to house about 11,000 people but the occupancy rate was often only about 60%. The population density was lower than that of the Barbican (500 people per hectare as against 750) because of the amount of open space between the buildings (220 feet minimum was the requirement based on sun angles). A 'river of trees' was designed to flow through the site. The client for the project was the St Louis Housing Authority and the construction cost was 1960 $US57 million funded through mechanisms provided by the United States Housing Act of 1949.

One design team carried out the whole project on behalf of a public agency. Harland Bartholomew was the planner and the architects were Hellmuth, Yamasaki and Leinweber. The complex was modelled on aspects of Le Corbusier's Unité in Marseilles (see Figure 6.11) and 100 Memorial Drive apartments at the Massachusetts Institute of Technology (Montgomery, 1966). Although the Public Housing Authority insisted on much cost cutting, the scheme was built pretty much as designed.

The buildings had skip-stop elevators that halted only on the fourth, seventh and tenth floors (see Figure 7.20b). Access to the other floors was by staircases from spacious galleries on the stop-floors. These galleries were designed to be playgrounds for children and gathering places for adults. In 1951, the scheme received high praise in an *Architectural Forum* editorial for saving 'not only people but also money'. The editors of the journal saw the complex as being a worthwhile design paradigm for the future. The reality proved to be different.

The household mix was not what was expected. Single-mother, welfare-dependent households overwhelmingly inhabited the complex. In 1965 only 990 of the 10,736 residents of Pruitt-Igoe were adult males. Many of the features praised in the *Forum* were sources of frustration for the residents of the project. The grounds were perceived to be and were unsafe. Access to the buildings could not be controlled. Women had to go on errands and shopping in groups. There was little for children and adolescents to do. Antisocial behaviour followed. The supposed rivers of trees were trashed with glass and rubbish. The mailboxes on the ground floor – a potential informal meeting place – and community rooms were vandalized and the corridors, lobbies and stairs became feared places. Rubbish got stacked up against the malfunctioning chutes. The lack of toilets on the ground floor meant that the children urinated where they could. Pipes burst in winter.

A $US7 million proposal was made in 1956 to remodel the scheme by turning the galleries into conventional corridors. By the mid-1960s the project was in poor shape while the Housing Authority reputedly still owed

Figure 7.20   Pruitt-Igoe, St Louis. (a) Isometric view of the site, (b) diagrammatic cross-section and floor plans, (c) the architect's drawing of the predicted behaviour in a gallery and (d) a gallery in reality.

Collection of the author

Figure 7.21 Pruitt-Igoe prior to demolition.

$30 million for its construction and was seeking funds for its demolition (Montgomery, 1966). By 1970 it was 70% vacant. Demolition took place in July 1972 and was hailed by architectural critic Charles Jencks as the death of Modernist architecture and the birth of Postmodernism. The failure had a major impact on the thinking of architects and city planners. Many in the architectural profession abandoned their social concern. It was just too hard. Many planners turned their attention to the improvement of social and economic issues rather than the character of the built environment (Figure 7.21).

The project, along with the similar British and French examples showed the limitations of architecture and built form as a determinant of social behaviour – good or bad. The necessity for a social support as well as a physical design agenda in urban design became clear. This need was recognized in the 1930s but was forgotten, or disregarded, by the 1950s. It was obvious in retrospect

that much more attention needed to be paid to the space between buildings – to the public realm of large-scale architectural schemes – and to the facilities provided. The design of Pruitt-Igoe was well intentioned but based on a paradigm inadequate for its purposes. Housing and urban design theory has come a long way since then. Practice lags.

Major references

Editorial (1951). Slum surgery in St Louis: a new apartment type. *Architectural Forum* **94** (April): 128–36.

Montgomery, Roger (1966). Comment on 'House as haven in the lower class'. *Journal of the American Institute of Planners* **32** (1): 23–31.

Montgomery, Roger (1985). Pruitt-Igoe: policy failure or societal symptom? In Barry Checkoway and Clive Patton, eds., *The Metropolitan Midwest: Policy Problems and Prospects for Change*. Urbana, IL: University of Illinois Press, 229–43.

Newman, Oscar (1974). *Defensible Space: Crime Prevention through Urban Design*. New York: Macmillan.

CASE STUDY

Raleigh Park, Sydney, Australia: a market-oriented suburban design (1982–2000)

The creation of total urban designs is not straightforward in democratic countries even when there is considerable financial and/or political clout behind their design and development. Raleigh Park is a 30-acre (12.34-hectare) development on a triangular site in south-central Sydney. It is a total urban design – a suburban precinct based on Garden City principles at a neighbourhood scale. It was a brown-field site. The W.D. & H.O. Wills' cigarette factory and workers' recreational facilities occupied it previously. Like Pruitt-Igoe, Raleigh Park received a planning award (from the Royal Australian Institute of Planners) in 1996 and a design award in 1998 (from the Urban Development Institute of Australia), but only after it had been largely completed and occupied. Raleigh Park is a very different place to Pruitt-Igoe for people in very different financial circumstances.

The development was a joint venture of two property development companies: Mirvac Ltd and Westfield Holdings Pty Ltd, designed in-house by Mirvac's HPA Associates (Henry Pollack Architects). It was named after Sir Walter Raleigh who introduced tobacco to Europe from North America. It consists of six residential towers of between eight and thirteen stories in height, three-storey walk-up housing units and 150 houses (well below the legally permitted number of units). The administrative buildings of the cigarette company were preserved as communal facilities and commercial rental space. The history of the development is chequered and the site went

through the hands of a number of potential developers and design firms before the implemented plan was created.

The impetus for the project came from the Labor government in power in New South Wales in 1982, catching the local government, the City of Randwick, by surprise. It announced that the site of the cigarette factory would be converted into a housing development as part of a larger packet of redevelopment aimed at securing its majority in Labor-held seats at the next state election. Local residents and merchants, however, took the proposal to the State Land and Environment Court challenging it on procedural grounds. The case became moot when the government passed a bill validating any invalidity in the planning process! Consequently an approach was made to the Randwick City Council in 1984 by Westfield Holdings (in joint venture with Amatil, the parent company of W.D. & H.O. Wills) to develop the site. The architects were Jackson, Teece, Chesterman, Willis & Partners. The scheme, which seems to have no central idea behind it (see Figure 7.22) did not proceed.

In 1986 Westfield obtained an extension of the development approval deadline and also bought out Amtil's share of the project. Shortly before the new date expired, and after considerable negotiation, the State Government bought the land from Westfield for $A30 million and sought tenders for the development of 1200 to 1400 town house units on the site (excluding a portion where Westfield had

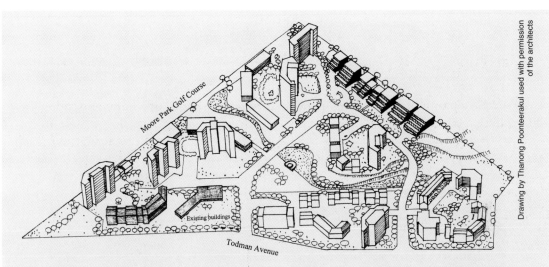

Drawing by Thanong Poonteerakul used with permission of the architects

Figure 7.22   Raleigh Park: the Jackson, Teece, Chesterman and Partners proposal.

already begun constructing 155 units of housing).

In December 1988, the National Trust of Australia (NSW) listed the buildings of the cigarette factory for their architectural importance. The factory complex was at that time leased to Virgo Productions, a film production company, who wanted to establish a permanent location for the making of films and television programmes. Virgo submitted a bid to the government to retain the existing buildings for their own purposes. The proposal failed. Westfield Holdings won the tender for reputedly $A43 million with Mirvac as an interested party.

The design that has emerged consists of a simple loop road with a connecting road in its middle (see Figure 7.23a). There is one 'guarded' vehicular entrance to the site on Todman Avenue and a number of pedestrian entrances (often locked). Apartment blocks line the northern edge of the site facing the Moore Park golf course. The remainder of the site is devoted to single-family homes,

two stories in height in a zipper-lot formation. The architecture is in a typical 1980s post-modern historicism style designed to appeal to the Asian market – much of the housing was sold to investors in Hong Kong. It is the landscaping that gives the site its character (see Figure 7.22b and c). Mature trees were preserved and much planting was added to give a high-quality, oasis-like atmosphere. A central park acts as a flood control device. The cigarette factory's administration building has been preserved as private offices and provides a sense of historic continuity to the site.

The scheme, after some early problems due to the economic recession of the 1990s, has been a marketing success. Early purchasers of housing units made sound financial investments. Raleigh Park has become an exemplar of a total urban design in Sydney where developer, urban designers, architects and landscape architects were one team. The project has spurred other similar developments. Worries do exist about the

(a)

(b)

Figure 7.23 Raleigh Park, Sydney. (a) A model of the scheme as built and (b) a view of the landscaping.

concept of gated communities (see Blakely and Snyder, 1997; Low, 2003) although at Raleigh Park there is seldom anyone manning the gate.

Major reference

Mirvac/Westfield (1997). Raleigh Park. A report prepared for the Urban Development Institute of Australia. Sydney: The authors.

CASE STUDY

Trudeslund, near Copenhagen, Denmark: a cohousing development (1978–81)

Trudeslund is situated in the town of Birkerød north of Copenhagen. It is a total urban design of a small residential community (for a full description, see McCamant and Durrett, 1993). The design brief was based on a social ideal that is manifested in its physical design. In 1978, 20 families came together to form a cooperative society in which a number of household activities and responsibilities of daily life would be shared. The focus of concern amongst those shown in Figure 1.6 was thus on patterns of life that both provided for a sense of individuality and a sense of community. The families' immediate objective was to get permission to build a cohousing development on land that was zoned for detached houses. The speed required to process their application for a zoning change led to a lack of clarity of social goals amongst the members of the group, resulting in half of the families withdrawing from the scheme. The group restructured itself and formed a clear statement of its intentions.

The process of moving from an agreed on agenda to a completed project was arduous and time consuming as decisions were made democratically with all members of the cohousing group participating. As with all interactive open-ended decision-making processes it was truncated only by some external circumstance. In this case it was the fear of interest rates escalating (in 1980–1 they rose to 21%). The group asked four architectural firms to submit designs for their consideration and decided to proceed with the one prepared by Vankustein Architects. Interestingly it was the architects who strove for a greater degree of integration and

communal activities than the community members themselves wanted. The members were very conscious of their individual identities and of houses as financial investments and wanted the designs to be non-controversial and less obviously communal. If the community collapsed, they wanted the houses to be easy to sell on the open market.

Trudeslund ended up comprised of 33 residences and a common house. The community is laid out on two pedestrian streets lined with row houses in an L-shaped plan (see Figure 7.24a). An L-shaped common house with a small square in front of it is located at their intersection. There are two children's playgrounds – one halfway down each street. In addition, the wooded areas outside the community act as a playing area for children. Each house has a small front garden abutting the street. The parking space for cars is on the outside.

An area of programming conflict arose over the design of the kitchens of each house. Should the house designs be standardized for economic reasons? As each family had its own ideas the kitchens of each unit are unique (all 33 of them). The houses range in size from 90 to 140 square metres (970 to 1500 square feet) and cost from between 77,000 to 1 million Danish Kroner ($US91,400 to $US117,600 in 1980 dollars). The price included a financial share in the common house.

The streets act as communal areas especially for children, but it is in the common house that the communal life of Trudeslund takes place. It contains kitchens and dining rooms; much communal

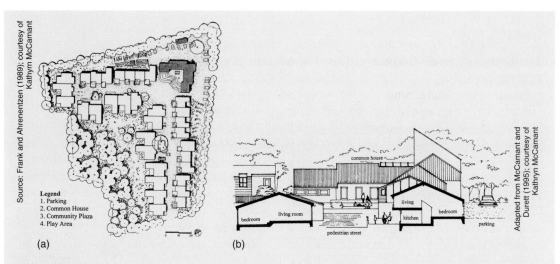

Figure 7.24 Trudeslund, near Copenhagen. (a) The site plan and (b) a cross-sectional view of the street.

meal-preparation and dining takes place there. One of the responsibilities of residents is to cook communal meals on a rotational basis. Some members eat together frequently in the common dining room, others less so. The common house also has facilities for housing visitors, for children and teenagers, and a library, photographic darkroom, workshops, laundry and a store. It really is the heart of the community.

Cohousing projects such as Trudeslund illustrate the diversity of total urban designs. Many total urban designs have resulted from highly autocratic decision processes but Trudeslund is an example of a highly participatory programming and design activity. There were many hands making the broth but, communal effort though it was, it was one project carried to conclusion by one architectural firm under one auspice. Its goal was to provide a rich social life for its members, children and adults alike. Much of life is shared. There are other types of cohousing developments (e.g. for the

elderly) but the philosophy and development process behind them all is similar.

A clearly articulated behavioural brief based on a set of mutually agreed on expectations dictates much about the design. This observation holds particularly strongly for the semi-public spaces (the 'street') and the semi-private, or private to the group, spaces (the internal communal rooms). In much urban design the behavioural assumptions underpinning the design of the public realm are, at the best, based on observations. They are thus more speculative than in this case. There is, nevertheless, often a slip between what people say about how they will behave and what they do.

Major references

Franck, Karen (1989). Overview of collective and shared housing. In Karen Franck and Sherry Ahrentzen, eds., *New Households, New Housing*. New York: Van Nostrand Reinhold, 3–19.

McCamant, Kathryn and Charles Durett (1988). *Cohousing: A Contemporary Approach to Housing Ourselves*. Berkeley, CA: Habitat Press/Ten Speed Press.

Precincts: Campuses

The term campus was first applied to layouts of universities. The idea of a unified campus in a rural setting away from the realities, and temptations, of everyday life in cities is a peculiarly American ideal but was derived from and has been much copied elsewhere. Since the 1980s, the label 'campus' has been extended to cover a variety of types of development other than universities: medical facilities, office complexes and even industrial sites. Although some critics may distinguish between campus design and urban design, the issues addressed are largely the same. Many campuses are small cities. The university campuses that were total urban designs were substantial in number particularly in the years immediately after World War II. Today many are in developing countries. Often, however, the term 'total' can only be applied to the first stage of their development.

Many of the first set of post World War II universities were strongly influenced by Modernist design principles (e.g. The Punjab University in Chandigarh, designed by Pierre Jeanerret and B. P. Mathur and the Universidad Central de Venezuela described below). A number of more recent ones (e.g. the Catholic University at Louvain la Neuve in Belgium) have followed New Urbanist ideas, even though they were conceived before the term 'New Urbanism' was coined (Figure 7.25). They attempt to integrate town and gown into one settlement. They are generally all-of-a-piece designs. Perhaps the majority of campuses have little urban design thought behind their site designs. Their buildings, often individually well designed are simply located within greenery in a modified English landscape design setting.

The two examples of university campuses included in this chapter are both Modernist in nature but follow different design ideas. The Universidad Central de Venezuela follows Le Corbusian principles; the State University of New York (SUNY) in Albany is more in line with its own architect's prior work. The former now has world heritage listing. Universities continue to be built around the world especially in developing countries. More attention seems to be given to the architecture of their individual buildings than to their overall site design. This lack of concern for campus design is unfortunate. The university years are influential ones for those people who have the privilege of tertiary education. The environment in which that education takes place can have a lasting impact, for good or ill, on their attitudes towards design quality.

Major references

Dober, Richard P. (1992). *Campus Planning*. New York: John Wiley.
Turner, Paul V. (1984). *Campus: An American Planning Tradition*. Cambridge, MA: MIT Press.

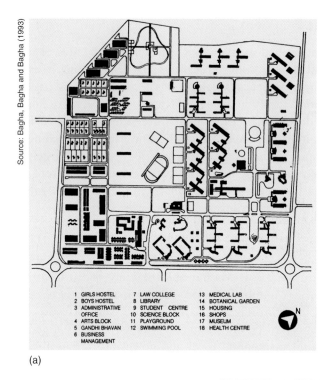

Source: Bagha, Bagha and Bagha (1993)

1	GIRLS HOSTEL	7	LAW COLLEGE	13	MEDICAL LAB
2	BOYS HOSTEL	8	LIBRARY	14	BOTANICAL GARDEN
3	ADMINISTRATIVE OFFICE	9	STUDENT CENTRE	15	HOUSING
4	ARTS BLOCK	10	SCIENCE BLOCK	16	SHOPS
5	GANDHI BHAVAN	11	PLAYGROUND	17	MUSEUM
6	BUSINESS MANAGEMENT	12	SWIMMING POOL	18	HEALTH CENTRE

(a)

(b)

(c)

Figure 7.25 Modernist and Neo-Traditionalist campuses. (a) The plan of Punjab University, Chandigarh, (b) a model of Louvain-la-Neuve and (c) the spine of the Catholic University of Louvain-la-Neuve in 1979.

CASE STUDY

Universidad Central de Venezuela, Caracas, Venezuela: a Modernist campus (1944–77 and continuing)

In October 1943, General Isaías Medina Angarita, the democratically elected President of Venezuela, under pressure from the then rector of the Central University of Venezuela, Dr Antonio José Castillo, announced the decision to build the university anew. It would be a University City on a new site on the old Ibarra Estate located at the edge of central Caracas. The Ministry of Public Works made the choice under pressure from Dr Armando Vegas who recognized the potential of a central site with good foundation conditions as better than the others available at that time. Carlos Raúl Villanueva (see Figure 7.26), Paris educated and Venezuela's leading Modernist architect,

was brought on board the planning team almost immediately. The development and implementation of the master plan was almost entirely in his hands, but marked by rivalries amongst politicians, university officials and designers. One of the problems was that although the project was initiated under Medina Angarita, its development took place under the dictatorship of General Marcos Pérez Jiménez and many people involved in the university did not want to be seen to be associated with his regime.

Villanueva's first scheme for the university (1944) was a symmetrical, axial Baroque one based on the classical discipline of his education in Paris (see Figure 7.27a). At the

Figure 7.26 Carlos Raúl Villanueva.

Source: Leal (1991); courtesy of the Archivo Fundación Villaneuva

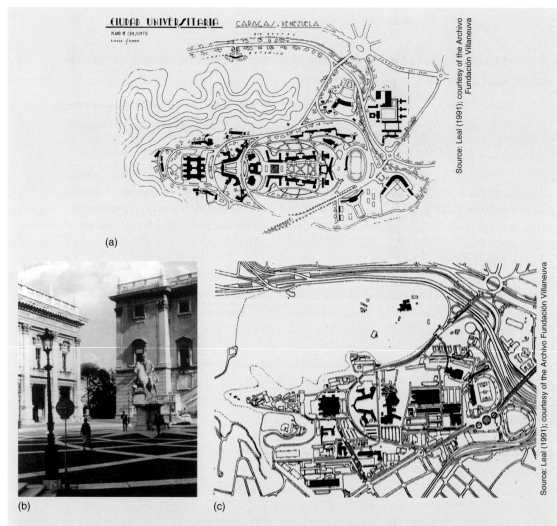

Figure 7.27 Two plans for the Universidad Central de Venezuela. (a) The 1944 site plan, (b) the Campidoglio (the Capital Piazza), Rome and (c) the 1952 plan.

head of the scheme is the University Hospital, in front of which he proposed a trident based on Michelangelo's Campidoglio in Rome (see Figure 7.27b). Buildings for Anatomy and Pathology that formed part of the trident framed the University Plaza. The academic buildings were arranged on the sides of the axis with the sports complex at its end. The proposed architecture of this design was heavily influenced by the Art Deco.

Villanueva's revised scheme (1952) retained many components of his original design in approximately the same locations (compare Figures 7.28a and c). The Clinical Hospital and the trident with the schools of Anatomy and Medical Research (1952–3) remained, as did the major elements of the sports complex, but the strong axiality of the original gave way to a Modernist idea of siting buildings semi-independently in space.

Collection of the author

Figure 7.28 An aerial view of the campus in 1960.

The Covered Plaza (1953) links them. The potential axis is taken up in an asymmetrical manner with the Main Auditorium (Aula Magna) and the Library (1953). To the east of this combination are the Faculties of Law (1954) and of Engineering with the School of Architecture (1956) beyond them. The eastern end of the campus retains the sports complex with the Olympic Stadium and the baseball stadiums being the major features. The workshops for the School of Industrial Engineering (1964) and the Faculty of Economic and Social Science (1977) came later.

Perhaps the major feature of Villanueva's design is the integration of works of art and architecture. He never articulated an ideological position behind his selection of works of art other than to mix the work of Venezuelan with international leaders. There were 105 major murals and sculptures on the campus. The walls of the plazas have murals by artists such as Oswaldo Vigas,

Fernand Leger and Pascual Navarro; the interior of buildings arts works by Héctor Poleo and Pedro León Castro amongst others. Sculptures by artists such as Henri Laurens, Jean Arp and Antoine Pevsner adorn the plazas. The main auditorium (Aula Magna) has Alexander Calder's Flying Saucers as 'acoustical clouds' hanging from the ceiling (Figure 7.29).

When completed the campus was a veritable display of Modernist architecture (albeit by one set of hands) and art. Since 1970, bits and piece have been added to the campus so that it has lost the integrity of the ideas of its author. The political upheavals in Venezuela of the period from the 1960s to the 1990s saw much degradation of the art works. Murals were covered with graffiti and sculptures abused. They had become a symbol not of progress but of the political *status quo*. Changes in the campus meant that some of the murals were 'walled up' as new buildings were erected.

(a)

Photograph by Giancarlo Cerutti di Ludovico

(b)

Figure 7.29 Two views of the art of the Universidad Central de Venezuela. (a) The Rectorate Plaza in 1998 with the mural 'Static Composition–Dynamic Composition' by Oswaldo Vigas and (b) the 'Aula Magna' in 2004.

As early as the mid-1970s an effort was made without much success to clean up the murals and to protect the sculptures. In 1981, Villanueva's dining complex was demolished to make way for a new one and a porcelain mural by Francisco Navies was largely destroyed. In reaction, the Rector of the University, Dr Carlos Moros Ghersi created a Unit for the Preservation of the Artistic Patrimony of the Central University of Venezuela. It was headed until 1990 by a sculptor, Miguel Borrelli. The artwork is celebrated again but only a discerning eye can still see the total urban design effort of Villanueva. It no longer dominates the layout of the campus; his individual buildings still do.

Major references

Larrañaga, Enrique (undated). The University City and the architectural thought in Venezuela. In *Obras de Arte de la Cuidad Universitaria de Caracas/Works of Art of the University City of Caracas*. Caracas: Universidad Central de Venezuela, 45–62.

Leal, Ildefonso (1991). *Historia de la Universidad Central de Venezuela*. Caracas: Ediciones del Rectorado, Universidad Central de Venezuela.

Moholy-Nagy, D. M. A. Sybille, P. (1964). *Carlos Raúl Villanueva and the Architecture of Venezuela*. London: Tiranti.

Villanueva, Paulina (2000). *Carlos Raúl Villanueva/ Paulina Villanueva/Macía Pintó*. New York: Princeton Architectural Press.

CASE STUDY

The State University of New York at Albany, New York, USA: a university as a superblock (1960+)

The G.I. Bill for education in the United Sates resulted in a massive increase in the demand for tertiary education amongst World War II veterans – a demand that increased with the arrival of the 'baby-boomers' on the American scene. During the 1960s, SUNY expanded rapidly in various locations in New York State, including Albany, its capital. Being a public institution the development of SUNY was very much affected by political infighting in the state legislature.

It was a Republican Governor of the state, Nelson Rockefeller, who had the initiative and energy to shape the development of the state's university system. When he came to power, the state college system was in disarray with a poor academic reputation and various departments and schools scattered across the state. Past decisions had been made for political rather than academic reasons. Rockefeller and his family had a long-held interest in the physical development of cities and their architecture. He put his interests in education and in architecture to work for the state.

The first step in Rockefeller's plan was to establish a fund – the State University Construction Fund (SUCF) – to pay for new facilities that would attract more and higher-quality students to the state system. Raising the status of the university would, in turn, act as a catalyst enabling better facilities to be built. Parallel to this step was the establishment of a scholarship fund to provide educational opportunities for financially disadvantaged students.

195

SUNY Albany was in the centre of the city in a series of overcrowded university and other buildings such as warehouses that had been co-opted to provide teaching facilities. The SUCF was used to overhaul the educational programmes and facilities of such state institutions. The architects of the State's Division of the Budget made some preliminary sketches for a new Albany campus and consequently a site of 290 acres later expanded to 360 acres (145 hectares) that had housed the Albany Country Club on the outskirts of the city was chosen for the new campus rather than one of three more central sites. These urban sites were rejected because of their high cost and the necessity for the removal of family homes before construction could begin.

The members of the country club were opposed to the state's acquisition of the land and politicians feared that moving the university out of the city would further lead to the decline of central Albany. The former were placated by the price paid for the site and the latter by the decision, again led by Rockefeller, to build a new state government centre and plaza adjacent to the existing state buildings in the centre of the city. It was subsequently built, designed by Harrison and Abromovitz and now named after Rockefeller (see Figure 7.30).

The initial goal for the university was to provide for 10,000 students with about half living on campus. Edward Durrell Stone was hired to be the architect of the university after Wallace Harrison, the original master planner, withdrew from his role. Stone's scheme is simple (see Figure 7.31). All the academic buildings are clustered and united by a huge podium and continuous roof – a sort of megastructure. The purpose was to reduce the cost of roads and utilities and to provide a reasonably comfortable environment during the severe upstate New York winters. (Unfortunately the configuration of buildings leads to a harsh environment in the winter by channelling winds into the complex's open spaces.) The dormitories were clustered in four groups around the main podium to form a pedestrian precinct that can be crossed on foot in 5 minutes. Each dormitory cluster was located around a quadrangle formed by a three-storey podium. Within each quadrangle a 23-storey tower housing 1200 students was located. Facilities were provided for recreation and parking on the perimeter of the campus (Birr, 1994).

Stone had recently completed the Institute for Nuclear Science and Technology in Rawalpindi and he adapted features of that design to the Albany campus. The campus is a symmetrical complex decorated with colonnades, domes and fountains. In the middle of the central podium is a tower set in an open space that acts as a node. The rectilinearly planted trees enhance the formality of the composition. Students gather here for many events, planned and spontaneous. At a lower level there is a fountain and reflecting pool. The main architectural experience comes from the sequential set of vistas one sees in moving from the periphery to the centre of the complex.

Stone created a superblock with a pedestrian environment within it. New buildings, however, fall outside this block. A 1999 analysis of the campus by the Hillier Group found that first time visitors were much confused by the university's layout. No landmarks give a sense of direction and the symmetrical design makes it difficult to relate one's location to specific destinations.

Figure 7.30   The Nelson D. Rockefeller Empire State Plaza, Albany, New York.

Source: Turner (1984)

Figure 7.31   The State University of New York at Albany.

197

The scheme is a total urban design with Rockefeller as Governor, the President of the State University System and the architect working hand in hand with the SUCF. The new campus met its goal of giving SUNY, as a whole, a higher profile and enabled it to compete effectively with private universities for well-qualified staff and students.

Major reference

Birr, A. Kendall (1994). *A Tradition of Excellence. The Sesquicentennial History of the State University of New York at Albany*. Virginia Beach, VA: Donning.

Precincts: Streets

There have been many street improvement schemes around the world. They have generally been landscape architectural projects that have not dealt with the enclosing elements that make a street a street. Baron Haussmann's redesign of Paris under Napoleon III's patronage was very much a three-dimensional design. Although the streets were designed as a unit, the buildings that form them were built by different developers. Haussmann's Paris was clearly a large all-of-a-piece urban design following strict guidelines but those later inspired by his work forgot this point.

Albert Speer's work under another dictator, Hitler, never came to fruition but it was boulevard-based total urban design on a large scale for Berlin. It was very much concerned with the three-dimensional qualities of the street. Monumental in nature it was designed to impress. So was the Avenue of the Victory of Socialism in Bucharest. It was built, entirely with state funds. Many less-ambitious street designs have also been built as total urban designs. The cul-de-sac in Radburn is part of larger total residential neighbourhood unit design (see Figure 7.19b). In recent times the *woonerf* (or what are now being called 'home zones', a combination of a multi-use street and adjacent houses) has captured the imagination of many architects. It is designed both as a play space for children and a place for parking cars (Biddulph, 2002). The cul-de-sacs in Radburn function in much the same way although they were not intended to do so. The example of a street chosen to be described here is at the opposite end of the scale. It is mammoth. Will it be regarded one day as a great street? It is considered to be ghost town today.

Major references

Biddulph, Mike (2002). Towards successful home zones in the UK. *Journal of Urban Design* **8** (3): 217–41.

Jacobs, Allan (1993). *Great Streets*. Cambridge, MA: MIT Press.

Moudon, Anne Vernez, ed. (1987). *Public Streets for Public Use*. New York: Van Nostrand Reinhold.

CASE STUDY

The Avenue of the Victory of Socialism, Bucharest, Romania: a government precinct (1977–89 but continuing)

After World War II a communist dictatorship was established in Romania under President Nicolae Ceausescu. Ceausescu initiated a number of large-scale urban design projects as part of his programme to turn Romania into a modern country. These efforts focused on Bucharest, a city that was badly damaged by a major earthquake in early 1977. In rebuilding the city Ceausescu announced that new buildings would have to be designed along modern lines. He also seized the opportunity to demolish many structurally sound areas to enable him to build a new government complex. The complex was to be a celebration of his new political order. It was also an opportunity to get rid of a quarter of the city that was full of single-family houses belonging to the old power and intellectual elite. As Ceausescu proclaimed:

> I am looking for a symbolic representation of the two decades of enlightenment we have lived through; I need something grand, something very grand, which reflects what we have already achieved (Ceausescu cited in Cavalcanti, 1997).

The public interest was defined in Ceausescu's own terms.

Ceausescu's chief architect, Dr Alexandru Budisteanu, believed that the development of monumental boulevards was the way to create a beautiful city. Like other architects working for dictators he had Paris in mind. One of Ceausescu's desires was to build a Victoria Socialismului (Victory of Socialism) civic centre in Bucharest. To achieve it he worked outside the existing legal framework for city planning in Romania by establishing a new law and building regulations governing the reconstruction of cities in the country to suit his purposes. The aim was to demolish villages (urban and rural) and replace them with his own view of modern urban design and modern architecture. Any remark he made was taken as a design directive. Architects who protested lost their jobs.

The site chosen for the civic centre project was in the Uranus district of the city because of its historic importance and elevated location. A competition for the design of the civic centre was held in 1978 in order to give the appearance of democratic decision-making. It was a sham. The programme was announced verbally and Ceausescu chose the winner, Anca Petrescu, despite the presence of jury members drawn from the nation's architectural elite. Demolition of the site began in 1978 with many of the inhabitants being given only 24 hours notice to vacate their houses. Forty thousand people were displaced and relocated on the outskirts of the city. Their departure impoverished the social and intellectual life of central Bucharest because the displaced included artists, professors, writers and many craftspeople.

A grand boulevard, the Bulevardul Victoria Socialismului (Avenue of the Victory of Socialism, but now Bulevardul Unirii), 3.5 kilometres in length (purposefully longer than the Champs Elysées in Paris) and 92 metres in width was driven through parts of the historic core of the city and lined with 'North Korean' style Socialist buildings (see

Drawing adapted from Calvacanti (1997) by Chao Wong

(a)

Photograph by Ruth Durack

(b)

Figure 7.32 The Avenue of the Victory of Socialism, Bucharest. (a) The plan showing the building footprints and the area demolished and (b) the view up the Avenue towards the Casa Republicii.

Figures 7.32a and b). Fifty thousand dwelling units were demolished to make way for it. Many historic buildings were destroyed in the process. The old city is now dwarfed by all the new construction.

The programme for the buildings lining the avenue was never clearly articulated. They were built to give the street its frame. They are of uniform height being about 10 stories high and neo-classical in appearance. At the head of the street is the Casa Republicii, or House of the People, reputedly the second largest building in the world in term of space (the Pentagon in Washington being the largest), the tallest in Bucharest (86 metres and, reputedly, the same below the ground), and 276 metres long. Designed to be the government centre (and as a Palace for Ceausescu), it now houses the Romanian Parliament. The building is now called the Palatul Parlamentului (Palace of Parliament). It has 700 offices, meeting rooms, restaurants, libraries and assembly halls for 1200 people (the 66-metre by 30-metre Romanian Hall, the 55-metre by 42-metre Banquet Hall and the 64-metre in diameter cylindrical domed Congress Hall (Cavalcanti, 1997: 98). The architect of record for the Casa Republicii is indeed Anca Petrescu. She designed a simple modern building for the site but it was superseded by Ceausescu's own 'New Romanian Architecture'. He inspected its construction on a weekly basis and made many on-site design decisions. Models were made for him so he could understand proposals. Unlike Hitler and Mussolini, he could not read drawings.

In front of the building is a semicircular plaza, the Piata Semicirculara capable of holding a crowd of 500,000 people.

Monumental buildings frame it. The centre of the boulevard is lined with fountains, commemorative arches and columns, and sculptures. They stand in an 8-metre wide green strip that they share with a variety of tree species. Designed to be a celebration of socialism, the buildings lining the boulevard now house international capitalist organizations – banks and insurance companies. The western end is largely deserted and dilapidated; the fountains have not played for a decade.

The project required so great a capital investment that it bankrupted the state (although the actual total cost is unknown). The boulevard remains a major axis with lengthy vistas. It celebrates its developer, President Ceausescu. He had the political and financial control to develop his idea, hire architects, and supervise the construction of the project. Professionals followed his directives. Unlike Paris or the work of Mussolini in Rome, the only consideration in the design of the Avenue of the Victory of Socialism was Ceausescu's own aesthetic ideal. Little attention was paid to the non-symbolic functions of the built environment.

Major references

Cavalcanti, Maria de Betânia Uchôa (1997). Urban reconstruction and autocratic regimes: Ceausescu's Bucharest in its historic context. *Planning Perspectives* 12: 71–109.

Petcu, Constantin (1999). Totalitarian City: Bucharest, 1980–9, semio-clinical files. In Nigel Leach, ed., *Architecture and Revolution: Contemporary Perspectives on Central and Eastern Europe*. London and New York: Routledge, 177–88.

Stamp, Gavin (1988). Romania's New Delhi. *Architectural Review* 184 (10): 4–6.

Commentary

These case studies show that considerable power, financial and/or political, is required to build total urban designs on any large scale. Although such designs are easier to implement in totalitarian societies, they have been carried out in vastly different legislative, legal and administration systems. The degree of singular control over the property development and design process varies considerably from case study to case study. On one hand there are schemes such as Rockefeller Center, Brasília and Avenue of the Victory of Socialism in which much was designated by a central authority – private in the first case, public in the latter two – without much outside interference. On the other hand Raleigh Park, although the product of one organization, was very much battered by city politics and the conflicting requirements of local community groups. There were two major designs and a number of other proposals for the Raleigh Park development. There were half a dozen for the Barbican.

The quality of the schemes described in the case studies varies considerably. Some of them, such as SUNY, Albany are regarded as 'powerful architectural statements' others less so. Many total urban designs are admired for their geometrical boldness. The buildings at Brasília and in Chandigarh are much photographed as abstract sculptures. Such environments, however, are often devoid of the urban elements that support life generously.

Strong geometrical ideas are more appropriate in some types of developments (such as capital complexes) than in others. Powerful symbolic statements are important for they boost our self-esteem. Problems, however, can arise: (1) when the symbolic statement is perceived by people to present a poor image of them, it has negative associations and (2) when art substitutes for life, where geometrical cleverness is the prime design criterion. Both can happen more easily when design power is centralized. The lesson of Pruitt-Igoe that there is often a gulf between what politicians, developers and architects want and what people want is still to be learnt not only in the United States but elsewhere (Michelson, 1968). The French experience, for instance, is illuminating.

Val-Fourré, a *banlieue*, the largest of 1100 such housing estates in France, houses well over 30,000 people (28,000 officially) in 1960s and 1970s tower blocks. Located 85 kilometres (about 50 miles) from Paris, its inhabitants in 2004 were drawn from almost 30 different ethnic groups, mainly recent immigrants. Such estates may work well in China for middle-income people and are being built at varying sizes but they do not do well for socially and psychologically dislocated people with many children who have nothing to do. Val-Fourré is called a *banlieue sensible* (sink estate or trouble spot) or pejoratively a *cité* or HLM (cheap rent homes). The 23 de enero estate in Caracas, Venezuela (see Figure 3.4) consists of 30 slab blocks and is equally notorious. It is amongst many other similar estates around the world. Philadelphia alone had a dozen such large-scale housing projects. The last of them, the Martin Luther King Jr. Housing, was demolished late in 1999.

The decisions to build such housing developments were well intentioned but no public consultation, empirical information, or market forces dictated the urban design and architectural forms in which they were built. It is not only housing projects that were approached in this fashion but the problems associated with them in democratic societies were dramatic. Total urban designs can be based on consultation with the stakeholders involved. The design of the programme and housing at Trueslund demonstrated this although it could be argued that it is a deviant case both in terms of product type and size of development. It is small.

Some of the schemes included here, although total designs, rely heavily on the market to decide uses (e.g. Clarke Quay) even though the decisions to build them were public policy ones; others were centrally decreed (e.g. Brasília and the GSFC Township at Vadodara). In the case of the Avenue of Victory of Socialism, no clear image related to reality was specified for the occupation of the buildings that line the boulevard. It was the theatricality of the setting that was deemed important. Market forces are now dictating building uses. Much is still unoccupied.

The successes and failures result not from the schemes being total urban designs but from the goals set and the nature of the programme assumed. In some cases a grand scheme does celebrate civic pride for a people and enhances their self-image. Certainly the capital complex in Chandigarh does this. In other cases it is the creators who have set out to celebrate themselves. Some schemes suffered from severe financial constraints; others were just shortsighted. In addition, all urban designs have failings on one dimension or another. It is impossible to meet all the requirements of all the people who inhabit or use, or are affected by a project equally well.

The case studies included in this chapter, although varied in nature, have at least one thing in common. Each was conceived and carried out as one project and cut from a single piece of cloth. They are total urban designs. The time taken to implement them varied but each was conceived to be completed within a short time-frame. Brasília took only 5 years to build. When the decision-making power is centralized actions can be taken rapidly.

8

All-of-a-piece urban design

To many observers, organizing urban design projects to be carried out building-by-building, and landscape-by-landscape by a number of developers according to an overall conceptual design is *the* core of urban design work. Many architects see all-of-a-piece urban design as inferior to total urban design because it is less a work of individual art. They believe projects would be better if dreamt of and designed by one hand as in Le Corbusier's design for the capital complex in Chandigarh or Oscar Niemeyer's work in Brasília. Others, however, believe that it is only through all-of-a-piece urban design that both a unity and variety can be captured in large project design today.

Procedurally, all all-of-a-piece designs are similar following approximately the structure shown in Figure 2.6. The degree of control over what is to be designed, however, varies considerably from highly controlled designs to those in which considerable freedom of action is given to the developers and designers of the various components of a scheme. The products of all-of-a-piece urban design run the gamut of design types: new towns, new precincts and urban renewal schemes. Few all-of-a-piece urban designs are as 'theatrical' as many total urban designs although Haussmann did very well in Paris! Their focus of attention depends on the nature of a culture and the nature of the priorities established by the stake-holders concerned. Each of the schemes described in this chapter focuses on some of the functions of the built environment identified in Figure 1.6 more than others. In each a number of concerns arise that are not characteristic of total urban design.

The source of funding is always a concern but a special set of issues arises with all-of-a-piece urban design in capitalist countries. How are the pieces going to be implemented? Is the infrastructure to be built by the public sector? Or by the developer of the overall project? Or by the developers of individual sites? Is the public sector to subsidize the work? Who is to oversee the development? Some public authorities or a private developer? All-of-a-piece urban designs vary considerably in dealing with all the concerns implicit in these questions.

The second issue deals with a series of design questions about the conceptual design or master plan. Are there some buildings that are to be regarded as fore-ground buildings and others as background? What is to be the degree of design control over the work of an individual developer or architect and/or landscape architect? Is it to be an ordered scheme or a chaotic one? There is considerable experience in doing the former, very little in dealing with the latter. How does one write guidelines to ensure well-functioning organized chaos? The nature of the design guidelines used to shape an urban design scheme is central to all-of-a-piece urban design work.

Design Guidelines

Clare Cooper Marcus (1986) has written about design guidelines as a link between research and practice. The most general such urban design guidelines are contained in the directives established by Christopher Alexander and his colleagues in their pattern language (Alexander *et al.*, 1977). Such guidelines are generic statements that specify the goals, the design pattern for achieving them and the evidence supporting the linkage between goal and pattern. In all-of-a-piece urban design the concern is with writing directives that ensure that the intent of the conceptual design is met. The focus here is thus on project-specific guidelines, or what have been called 'design directives' for completing the components of an all-of-a-piece urban design.

The fundamental nature of design guidelines has changed little over the centuries. Façade guidelines prescribing the nature of fenestration to be incorporated on new buildings can, for instance, be traced back at least to fourteenth century Italy. What has changed and will no doubt change in the future are the perceptions of the mechanisms that achieve the design goals and the types of guidelines that are used to ensure those mechanisms are incorporated in a design.

There are three types of design guidelines used to implement urban design objectives: prescriptive, performance and advisory. They may be specifications for open spaces – that is streets and squares – and/or for the buildings that frame them. Prescriptive guidelines describe the pattern that a building complex, building, or building component must take (e.g. all buildings must have purple stringcourses of brickwork at every 5 metres of height). Performance guidelines specify how a building should work (e.g. no shadows can be cast on a particular open space during the hours 11.00 a.m. to 2.00 p.m. at the winter solstice). Property developers overwhelmingly prefer the first because they state the design forms required without any ambiguity. It is easier to create enforceable guidelines when a public authority has a legal stake in the development (e.g. is a land holder or is contributing to the project's financing), or by creating covenants or other requirements in giving property developers permission to build. Advisory guidelines are suggestive in nature whereas prescriptive and performance are mandatory if they are adopted into law for specific constitutionally acceptable purposes. There is no legal requirement to comply with advisory guidelines.

The three types of guidelines are often used together. The case of the Dallas Arts District is outlined in Figure 8.1. The conceptual diagram is illustrated in Figure 8.1a. The guidelines in Figure 8.1b are of three types: prescriptive (the

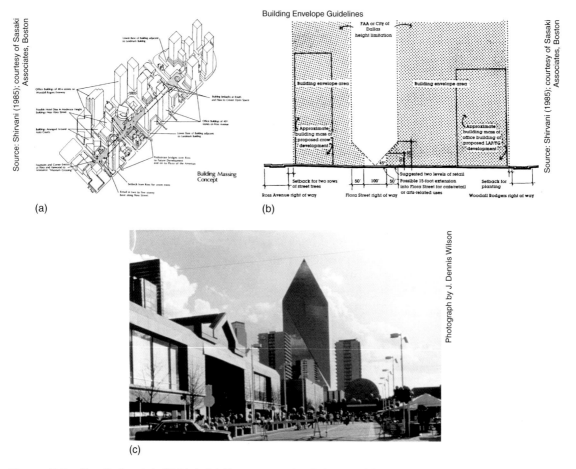

Figure 8.1 The Dallas Arts District. (a) The conceptual design, (b) the building design guidelines and (c) the district in 1993.

building envelope), performance (setback for two rows of trees) and advisory ('suggested two levels of retail'). The solar access diagram shown in Figure 8.2 may specify a performance but it is highly prescriptive. The façade guidelines in Figure 8.3 are clearly advisory but had considerable clout in the way they were administered.

Guidelines that can be defended in court contain three parts: the objective, the pattern required to achieve it and the argument for the pattern based on empirical evidence (Stamps, 1994). If they do not, they are easy to challenge and to be dismissed in the courts and administrative tribunals of democratic societies.

All all-of-a-piece urban designs involve the specification for individual buildings to some extent. The most global requirement is for building uses but many other factors can be stipulated for building and open-space design (see Figure 8.4a). One application of a number of guidelines is shown in Figure 8.4b. The degree to which building designs should be controlled is open to debate. The urban

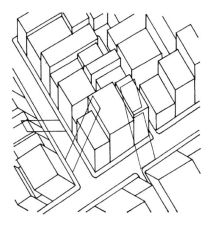

Figure 8.2   A solar access diagram.

OBJECTIVE 15

TO CREATE A BUILDING FORM THAT IS VISUALLY INTERESTING AND HARMONIZES WITH SURROUNDING BUILDINGS.

POLICY 1

Ensure that new facades relate harmoniously with nearby facade patterns.

When designing the facade pattern for new buildings, the pattern of large nearby existing facades should be considered to avoid unpleasant juxtapositions. Incongruous materials, proportions, and sense of mass should be avoided.

As a general rule, facades composed of both vertical and horizontal elements fit better with older as well as most new facades.

Courtesy of the Department of City Planning, City and County of San Francisco

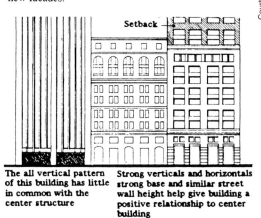

The all vertical pattern of this building has little in common with the center structure

Strong verticals and horizontals strong base and similar street wall height help give building a positive relationship to center building

Figure 8.3   Guidelines for new buildings in context, San Francisco.

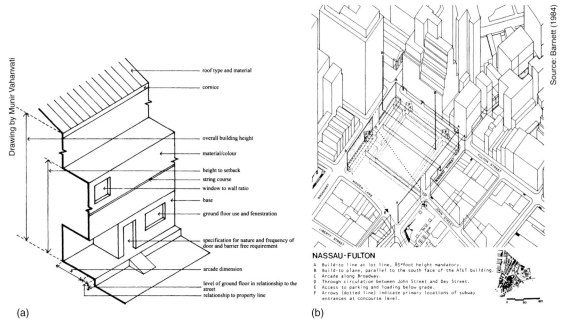

Figure 8.4 Building design guidelines. (a) Possible variables for building design guidelines and (b) an example: Nassau-Fulton, New York.

design objective has been to define the character of the public realm – streets, squares and other open spaces – and to obtain a sense of unity and/or diversity.

Major references

Barnett, Jonathan (1982). Designing cities without designing buildings. In *An Introduction to Urban Design*. New York: Harper and Row, 76–152.

Cooper Marcus, Clare (1986). Design guidelines: a bridge between research and decision-making. In William H. Ittelson, Masaaki Asai and Mary Ker, eds., *Cross Cultural Research in Environment and Behavior*. Tucson: University of Arizona, 56–83.

Cowan, Robert (2003). *Urban Design Guidance: Urban Design Frameworks, Development Briefs and Master Plans*. London: Thomas Telford Ltd.

Punter, John (1999). *Design Guidelines in American Cities: A Review of Design Policies and Guidance in Five West Coast Cities*. Liverpool: Liverpool University Press.

Shirvani, Hamid (1985). *The Urban Design Process*. New York: Van Nostrand Reinhold.

Watson, Ilene (2001). An introduction to Design Guidelines. *http://www.plannersweb.com/wfiles/w157.html* accessed on 9 January 2004.

The Case Studies

The case studies focus almost entirely on precinct design. It is at this level that the nature of urban designing is clearest. The one new town that is included,

Seaside, is smaller than many of the precincts studied here. The cases cover a wide variety of product types and have been organized in approximately the same sequences as those in the previous chapter on total urban design.

A large number of projects on green-field and cleared brown-field sites in a number of countries have been included. Developed at various times during the past half-century they reveal a wide array of attitudes towards ways of life and aesthetics. The schemes are all well known. The two urban renewal schemes – Charles Center and Central Glendale – are fine examples of their type although many other projects in countries other than the United States of America could have been selected to demonstrate the same concerns. Two types of campuses – a university and a business centre – illustrate two very different aesthetic philosophies while the one housing case study – Stadtvillen an der Rauchstrasse – stands in strong contrast to both of them and to Pruitt-Igoe and Raleigh Park. The final case study included is an example of urban renewal but is classified here as an example of a festival market development. As such it is a descendant of Baltimore Inner Harbor.

New Towns

Most new towns in capitalist countries have turned out to be a collage of all-of-a-piece and *laissez-faire* urban designs. The exceptions are those company towns that start off, as noted in the previous chapter, as total urban designs. The genuine all-of-a-piece new town designs are few in number and small in size. They do have the process of development and design in common. Most such new town design processes start off with some vision of how the city will function, instrumentally and symbolically. The question then, as in all all-of-a-piece urban designs, is: 'Once one has a guiding vision, how does one get it implemented?'

Case studies of all-of-a-piece new town design are difficult to construct after implementation in comparison to total urban designs. They tend to be long drawn out affairs involving many stakeholders. Each person involved remembers the process in a unique way, often highlighting his or her contributions to it. What might appear to be an all-of-a-piece design turns out to be either total urban design as in the centrally controlled Soviet new towns of the 1960s, 1970s and 1980s, or much more fragmented efforts focusing on the design of the infrastructure as an armature for development.

Seaside in Florida, small though it is, and followed by many other designs, is *the* exemplar of an all-of-a-piece new town design. The description of it presented here relies heavily on secondary sources and interviews. It is an important case study because it demonstrates the essence of urban design procedures. It also raises questions as to how far one should go in prescribing the design of individual buildings.

CASE STUDY

Seaside, Florida, USA: a seaside vacation town (1981 to the present)

Seaside is an example of a tightly controlled all-of-a-piece urban design. It is also an example of what was called Neo-Traditional urban design but now goes by the name of the New Urbanism. The developer was and is Robert Davis who inherited 80 acres (32 hectares) on the panhandle (Gulf of Mexico) coast of Florida from his grandfather in 1970. Davis wanted to create a vacation town based on his memory of those he knew and loved as a boy. He recalls: 'The idea of Seaside started with the notion of reviving the building tradition of Northwest Florida which had produced wood-framed cottages so well adapted to the climate that they enhanced the sensual pleasure of life by the sea' (Davis, 1989: 92). He engaged Andres Duany and Elizabeth Plater-Zyberk to design the town.

Seaside has become an important case, for good or ill, of urban design because it asserts the primacy of the public realm over the private (Katz, 1994). It is a resort community with a small, but increasing, number of permanent residents. The master plan – a layout with a small-scale City Beautiful core and with an emphasis on access to the beach – was drafted in 1982. Construction has proceeded since then. Today Seaside is a fully functioning town with a town hall, school, chapel, post office, retail stores and commercial tenants, and a wide variety of housing types.

The site has an irregular shape with a county road running across it almost adjacent to the waterfront (see Figure 8.5). The guiding objective in the design is that everything residents could want on a daily basis should be within a 5-minute walk of their homes – a hallmark of New Urbanism.

The core of the plan is a 'semi-octagonal' square where the post office, shops, library and other communal facilities are located. This area is connected to a square to the northwest where the town hall is located. The link is the town's main commercial thoroughfare. The plan consists of a hierarchy of street sizes depending on their perceived functions in a concentric network that spreads out from the centre and links it with the neighbouring town of Seagrove. While the plan, building codes and design guidelines for the buildings are clearly the work of Duany and Plater-Zyberk, the ideas were framed during a 2-week-long charette with other designers, local officials and consultants. The construction of houses had actually begun before the master plan was completed; by 1994 the first phase of Seaside was 70% built. It continues to evolve.

The public buildings and spaces of Seaside include pavilions on the beach, buildings in the central square, the town hall and buildings on the periphery of the town. The pavilions sit on the southern (beach) end of each north–south street. The private building types include a number of mixed-uses: residential/retail/lodging, residential/retail/office and residential/workshop. Seaside also has a special district (large lots to the south of the county road that could contain a variety of uses) and two types of residential development. These types are not necessarily restricted to a specific zone but are scattered throughout Seaside. The code also includes the building design guidelines.

Davies sold the plots at Seaside to individual purchasers who could build what they

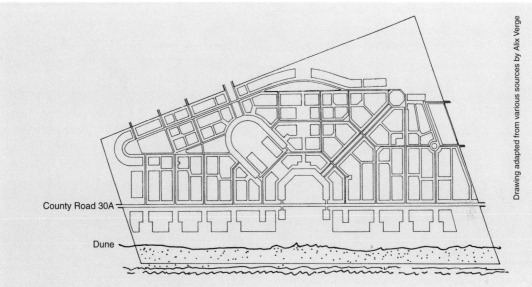

County Road 30A

Dune

Drawing adapted from various sources by Alix Verge

Figure 8.5 The Seaside, Florida plan.

liked provided it met the requirements of a stringent code. The Urban Code of Seaside specifies the requirements for eight types of buildings, explicitly enough to create a visual unity in the development, but flexibly enough to give architects creative freedom (see Figure 8.6). Type 1 is for those lots that define the central square or are located on the main streets throughout Seaside (see Figure 8.8). Similar specifications exist for the other seven types of buildings.

Each residential building must have a porch facing the street (see Figure 8.7a and b). The goal was to have residents using them and being aware of passers-by in the hope of establishing acquaintances. Each house must have a roof of wood shakes or be of metal. Most residential buildings must have white picket fences and on any given street the fence must be different from all the others. Garages must be in the rear of buildings. The gardens should contain no sod; only indigenous plants are allowed. In all, there are 19 general construction requirements that specify design

details from wall cladding to the location of house numbers. These specifications have not stopped houses from running the full range of present-day styles. Internationally renowned architects designed many of them. A sense of unity is, nevertheless, clearly achieved because the design guidelines were clearly written with that goal in mind.

Seaside has been a marketing success. It is increasingly a resort for wealthy people. Land prices have soared well above inflation levels. Lots purchased in 1982 for $15,000 commanded $300,000 in 2001. Beachfront lots go for as much as $1.5 million. Home prices are approaching the $1 million mark. As an urban design, it has become an icon of the New Urbanism, striking a balance between the needs of vehicle drivers and those of pedestrians. It demonstrates that an approach to design integrating planning, landscape architecture and architecture can result in fine living environments. Critics find the town 'too cute' but they are outsiders not residents. It is well loved by the latter.

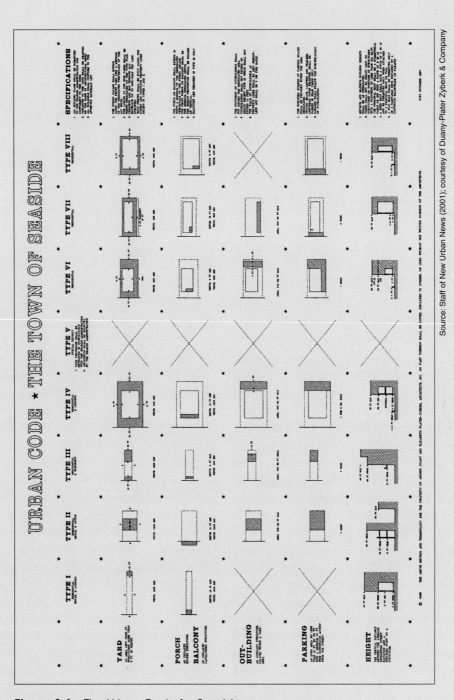

Figure 8.6 The Urban Code for Seaside.

(a)

(b)

Figure 8.7 Two views of Seaside. (a) View from the northeast looking west and (b) a general view of the housing.

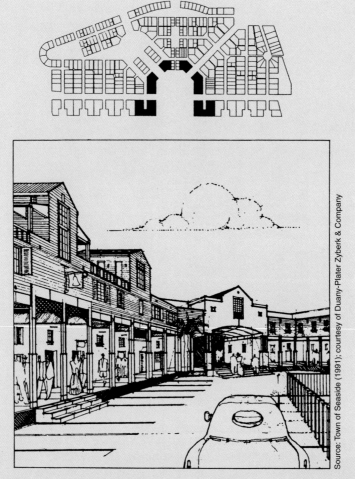

Source: Town of Seaside (1991); courtesy of Duany-Plater Zyberk & Company

Figure 8.8 The specifications for Type 1 buildings (housing above shops) for the central area (see upper drawing).

Seaside is the antecedent of a large number of later developments. Celebration in Florida is Seaside writ large! There have also been attempts in other countries to look at their own traditions and to take what has worked in the past and adapt those patterns to deal with the present and the future. Poundbury on the outskirts of Dorchester in England, for instance, draws heavily on the design patterns of the traditional Dorset village.

Major references

Davis, Robert (1989). Seaside, Florida, U.S.A. *GA Houses* **27**: 90–123.

Duany, Andres and Elizabeth Plater-Zyberk with Jeff Speck (2000). *Suburban Nation: The Rise of Sprawl and the Decline of the American Dream*. New York: North Point Press.

Katz, Peter (1994). *The New Urbanism: Toward an Architecture of Community*. New York: McGraw Hill.

Mohney, David (1991). *Seaside: Making an American Town*. New York: Princeton University Press.

The Town of Seaside (1985). *Center* **1**: 110–17.

Precincts: Green-field and Cleared Brown-field Sites

Many cities around the world have precincts that have been largely abandoned; there are many yet-to-be-built-on areas on the periphery of cities that are ripe for development as cities expand. The former sites are primarily the results of changes in the technology of manufacturing and transportation, but the desire to upgrade areas has also been a motivating factor in their renewal. Port areas with their finger wharfs and/or small docks have been abandoned in cities across the world: Baltimore, London, Cape Town, New York, Rotterdam and Sydney amongst them. The same cities and many others have abandoned railyards, often extensive in size, close to their cores. Military establishments such as naval yards and barrack areas have become redundant and their sites available for redevelopment.

Ten schemes are presented here to illustrate the diversity of urban design. One, the Citizen Centre in Shenzhen is presented as a brief note as it is still under construction. It stands in strong contrast to total civic urban design projects. Four of the schemes set out to be new business districts to rival those already existing in their cities. They are, in approximately chronological order, La Défense in Paris, Canary Wharf in London, Euralille in Lille and the Lujiazui area of Pudong in Shanghai. Each follows a different design paradigm. The first two were planned to retain Paris and London's pre-eminent places in the world. Euralille and Lujiazui have been designed to join the club. From a design point of view they are interesting because of the different ways in which they handle traffic. The purpose of the sixth scheme, Battery Park City, was to enliven the Lower Manhattan business area in New York by injecting new housing into it and opening up the Hudson River waterfront to the public. The Paternoster development, the seventh example, was built on a bombed out site in London in the 1960s following Modernist principles. It was deemed to be boring and dreary. It was demolished in the 1990s, rebuilt and completed in 2003. The eighth scheme, Pariser Platz in Berlin, has had a very different purpose; it has been to recapture the sense of place it had in its citizens' hearts before having been destroyed in World War II and left that way for 40 years in a divided Berlin. The final scheme, the Potsdamer Platz district, also in Berlin, has a very different character. Its nodes are inside buildings not open-air squares. A note on the proposed World Trade Center site in New York has been included to bring this set of examples up-to-date. What it will end up being like is open to conjecture.

The development of only a couple of these ten schemes has taken place in a straightforward linear step-by-step manner. Most have tangled histories although the central idea behind each (with the exception of Battery Park City) has remained remarkably intact. Each shows the impact of politics and politicians and world and local economic conditions on their histories. They also show the debates that took place amongst stakeholders over the appropriate architectural paradigm to employ. The longer the development period the more marked are the ups and downs of the implementation process. This reality is something that theories of architecture seldom reveal. Case studies yield a truer picture.

A NOTE

The Citizen Centre, Shenzhen, People's Republic of China: a new civic design (1994+)

The Citizen Centre complex in Shenzhen is in the process of construction. It has followed a very different process of design than the capital complexes at Chandigarh designed by Le Corbusier and Brasília designed by Oscar Niemeyer. As a complex it will be an all-of-a-piece urban design. Following a typical procedure used in China the design results from a process of consultation/competition. This system is used to generate interesting potential solutions but it can also result in eye-catching designs with short-run futures. In 1995, a number of architects were asked to submit designs for the Citizen Centre. The best of them was deemed to be that by John M. Lee/Michael Timchula Associates based in the United States. It remains to be seen how the Citizen Centre complex turns out as design decisions are still being finalized (Figure 8.9).

The new heart of Shenzhen is organized along the central green zone of the city designed largely to a plan by Kisho Kurokawa of Japan. The site is 1.9 kilometres wide and 2.2 north-to-south with Lotus Hill to the north. It is laid out in a grid bisected by the east-to-west Shennan Avenue. The commercial area lies to the south of the Avenue, and the government and cultural zone (a 180-hectare site) to the north.

The landmark building of the government complex is the City Hall designed by John Lee. Its roof has an eye-catching form like the wings of a roc. It is equipped with solar voltaic panels as part of the effort to reduce energy consumption and costs. Below the roof the building is divided into two almost symmetrical parts containing the various administrative functions of the city. In front of the building is the 'Crystal Island', a transparent steel and glass structure, and a green zone that extends to Lotus Hill.

The green zone is flanked by a number of buildings that will be built by a number of

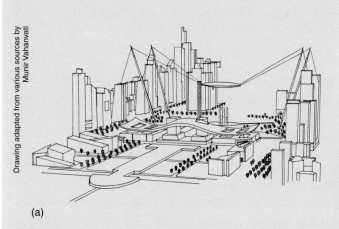

Drawing adapted from various sources by Munir Vahanvati

(a)

(b)

Figure 8.9 The Citizen Centre complex, Shenzhen. (a) The conceptual site in its proposed context and (b) the Citizen Centre.

developers on behalf of the city to the city's requirements and designed by different architects. The Cultural Centre of Arata Isozaki lies on the left of the City Hall facing Lotus Hill. It consists of the Concert Hall and Library with an elevated deck between them. The fronts of the buildings will have pleated glass walls. Directly across the green area from them is the Children's Palace. A level of unity will be achieved through the massing and colour of the buildings that were subject to control. The

result is a complex of three buildings and a park (a strong contrast to Le Corbusier's concrete deck at Chandigarh) designed in accordance with a site plan within a larger master plan for the city.

Major references

Chen Yuan (2000). The course of SZD planning and design. *World Architecture 2000* (Suppl.): 5–9.
Kurokawa, Kisho (2000). Urban design of the public space system along the central axis. *World Architecture 2000* (Suppl.): 29–36.

CASE STUDY

La Défense, Haut-de-Seine, France: a new 'central' business district (1958–90 and to the present)

La Défense, Paris's new business district is located on a site of 750 hectares (2.9 square miles) west of the Seine just outside the city's jurisdiction. The name comes from the statue, 'La Défense de Paris', erected in the area in 1883 to commemorate the war of 1870. For prestige reasons the precinct does retain 'Paris' as its mailing address but as it is legally located outside Paris, it is not subject to the stringent planning controls within the *boulevard périphérique* developed under pressure from President Valéry Giscard d'Estaing after Paris's first 1960s towers (particularly the 56-storey Tour Montparnesse) shocked the citizens of Paris and tourists alike. The height of buildings within the city became restricted to 31 metres. This policy is now (2004) under review as pressures for higher densities of development are arising. It suffices to say that La Défense is an 'edge city' visually and

symbolically connected to the heart of Paris by the Champs Elysées, Paris's historic boulevard spine, the Métro system, the regional express line (RER) and the A-14e motorway. It was designed to be and is a different world to Paris.

The conception of La Défense can be traced back to the 1920s but it was a long pregnancy. Regional plans and a 1931 competition for the *Voie Triomphiale* [Triumphal Way] from the Etoile to La Défense gave impetus to the idea for the location of a new business district for Paris on its periphery. A 1956 *Regional Development and Organization Plan* proposed that the population density of the inner city be reduced and that nodes be established on its periphery – something that has subsequently happened to cities in many countries as a result of market forces not regional planning policies (Garreau, 1991). There was a felt need to maintain the character of the historic core of Paris as it was and as it exists in people's imaginations. It is what the 25 million tourists who come to Paris each year desire to see and enjoy. The result was the moving of some services to the periphery of the city and the building of a series of new towns around it.

By 1956, a number of office towers had already been located in the vicinity of La Défense. In 1958, EPAD (Establissement Public pour l'Amenagement de la Region de la Défense) was formed and progress started on what we now know as La Défense. An EPA is a public body that works with private companies to acquire land and prepare it for development. It links the efforts of local and national governments with those of private sector developers. EPAD thus had the power to expropriate land, establish a development zone and expedite construction. EPAD bought the land, rehoused about 25,000 people, demolished 9000 dwellings and several hundred industrial and light-industrial factories, and set about developing an office estate. The development spans four decades of fits and starts with the major periods of inaction being prior to 1964, between 1974 and 1978, and again between 1992 and 1998.

An early proposal (1964) consisted of two rows of skyscrapers equal in height (100 metres) surrounded by housing and with an esplanade covering the roadways. Little came of it. A more serious proposal for the site was instigated in 1971 by President Georges Pompidou, and a third a few years later by President Giscard d'Estaing. The third proposal is essentially what we see today.

President d'Estaing and Prime Minister Raymond Barre had intervened in 1978 because, in spite of state funding, the economic future of La Défense was uncertain. New development was being carried out at a slow pace. EPAD was in a poor financial state as its resources came from the sale of construction rights. It had a deficit of 680 million francs. Under d'Estaing's leadership the central government put in additional resources drawn directly from publicly owned savings banks. Additional restrictions were also placed on building within Paris by a national government authority DATAR (Délégation à l'Aménagement du Territoire et à l'Action Régionale) and a differential tax rate was put in place to encourage development at La Défense.

The construction of the infrastructure was the major enabling step because it allowed buildings to be plugged into a vehicular, rail and pedestrian transportation network. This network is organized into a multi-layered structure segregating the different transport modes with a vehicle-free 40-hectare (100-acre) pedestrian deck, or esplanade, being the top layer. Vehicular traffic is kept on the periphery of the superblock (see Figure 8.10). The original conceptual design builds on Le Corbusier's idea of what a modern city should be. As the scheme evolved it has become denser to stimulate some sense of urbanity and liveliness. The Centre National de Industries et Techniques, with its triangular roof, was one of the first landmark buildings in the area. It acted as a catalyst spurring further development (see Figures 8.11–8.13).

The partial termination of the axis from the *boulevard périphérique* today is the La Défense Arche designed by Danish architect Johan Otto von Spreckelsen who died before construction was completed. The Arche was the winning entry in a design competition held under the auspices of

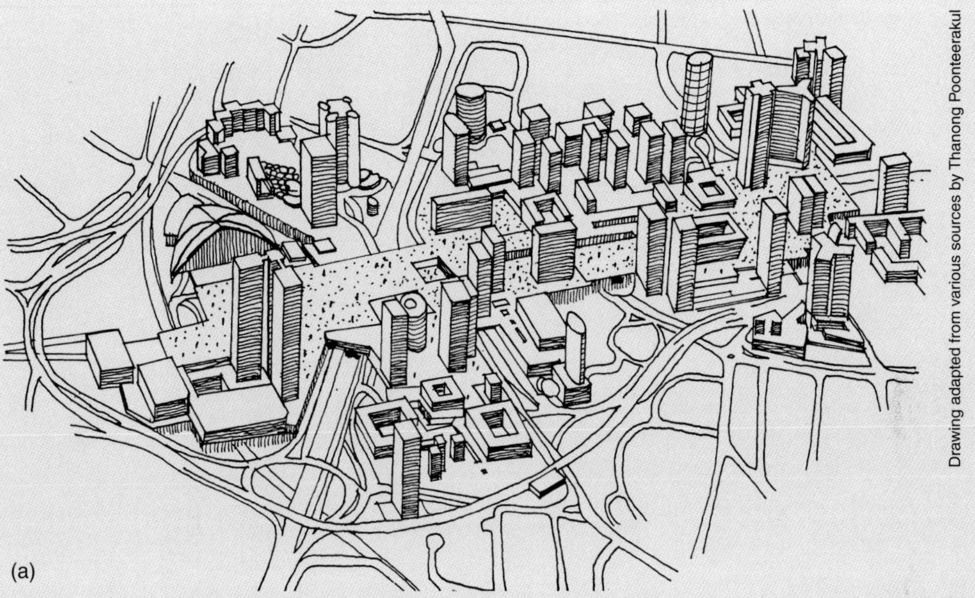

(a)

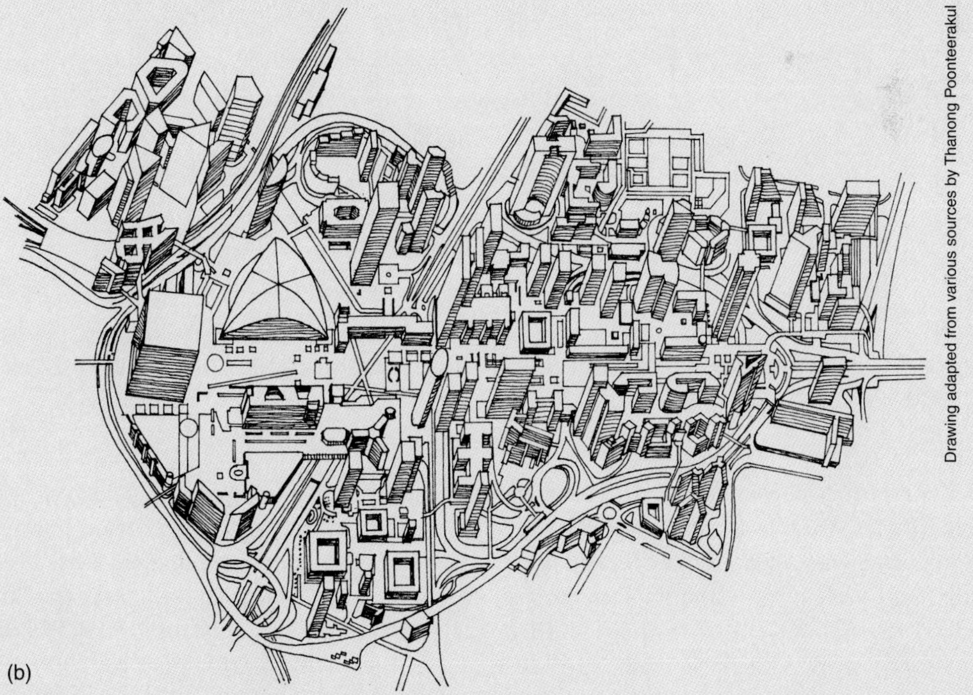

(b)

Figure 8.10 La Défense before and after the building of the Arche. (a) The predicted massing diagram in 1970 prior to the idea of La Défense Arche and (b) the massing diagram in 2003.

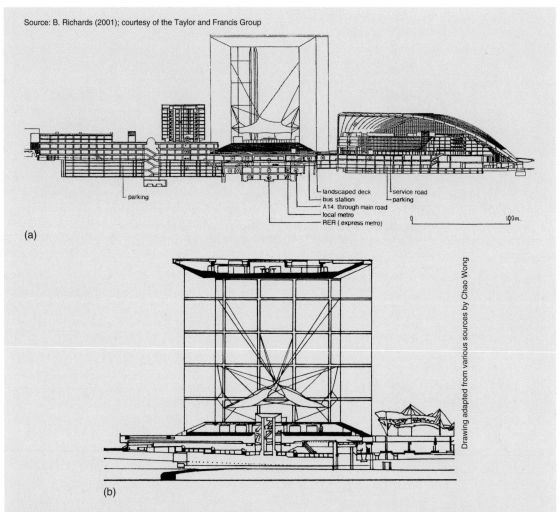

(a)

parking
landscaped deck
bus station
A14. through main road
local metro
RER (express metro)
service road
parking

0   100 m.

Drawing adapted from various sources by Chao Wong

(b)

Figure 8.11 Sections through the deck, La Défense. (a) Cross-section and (b) partial longitudinal section.

President François Mitterand. It was part of his *Grands Travaux* (Great Works) programme that was primarily concerned with preserving Parisian monuments such as the Grand Louvre but it also helped finance major new works such as the Cité des Sciences in an old slaughterhouse at Parc de la Villette (see Chapter 5). A decked bridge west of the Arche continues the axis to St Germain-en-Laye.

The Arche was designed in 1983 and completed in 1989, a century after the Eiffel Tower. Various earlier schemes by I. M. Pei, Emile Aillaud and Jean Willerval had been rejected. The Arche is an office building, 35 stories (100 metres) high by 100 metres wide (the size of the Caré le Cour, or Square Courtyard, at the Louvre and large enough to accommodate Notre Dame). It is slightly skewed to the axis and in the

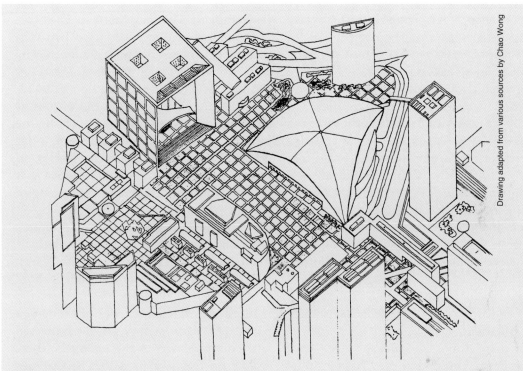

Drawing adapted from various sources by Chao Wong

Figure 8.12 The western end of La Défense.

Photograph by Tata Soemardi

Figure 8.13 La Défense with the Grande Arche in the background and the Centre National de Industries et Techniques on the right.

form of an arch. It is topped by an art gallery and viewing platform. The competition for the Arche site attracted 424 entries. An architectural jury selected four finalists. They were submitted anonymously to Mitterand who selected Spreckelsen's entry. Today the Arche is a major tourist attraction and gives La Défense a sense of place in Paris. It also allows for the further extension of the axis starting with the Champs Elysées and continuing through the Arche to the far distant Versailles. The landscape between the Seine and the Grand Arche – the D'alle Centrale – is to the design of Dan Kiley, the North American landscape architect. Working in 1978, Kiley sought a classical modernism of fountains and art works. Four long lines of pollard London Planes reinforce the visual axis.

In many ways La Défense might have been better included in the Chapter 10 as a plug-in design where buildings of various types and architecture, ranging from Modernist to post-modern with neo-classical overtones are plugged into a framework. It has turned out to be a poorly organized all-of-a-piece design. The conceptual diagram and how to achieve it were never carefully articulated. The building guidelines varied over time as the result of political pressures and economic necessity. The scheme was much affected by successive presidents of France, each attempting to leave his imprint on Paris.

The first set of design controls limited height and sought an architectural unity for the precinct. As the design evolved the specifications of what should be built were loosened in order to get some life into the scheme. A *laissez-faire* attitude ultimately prevailed. By the early 1970s companies were encouraged to build distinctive *gratte-ciels*

(skyscrapers). They have done so. Each corporation has tried to outdo the others with its building. Yet few buildings are touched by post-Modernist design patterns. The result has been a haphazard collection of buildings that are perceived to be out of context with the dignity and grandeur of the *axe historique*. EPAD appears not to care. It has created the premier business district in Europe and has the statistics to prove it. It is the landscape that ties the complex together (Figures 8.14 and 8.15).

Has La Défense been a success? Admirers regard it as a modern day Utopia; detractors think it is part of the Brave New World. It has been dismissed as a 'business slum' (Eriksen, 2001). Despite efforts to rectify the design it remains a series of Modernist parts. The open spaces are disconnected and poorly related to the buildings; there is little on the deck to attract pedestrians. Although it is relatively free of air pollution, the high winds on the deck level promoted by the tall buildings make the pedestrian environment particularly inhospitable in winter and even on some summer days. EPAD has made a valiant effort to make the esplanade more attractive by adding trees for aesthetic reasons and also to ameliorate the wind conditions. It has increased the amount of shopping, and promoted the development of art galleries, as well as including more sculptures to make an open-air museum. A carousel has become a permanent feature.

From a business point of view La Défense is a resounding success. Fourteen of France's top 20 corporations are located there. In 2000, 130,000 people worked in the precinct for 3600 companies. Over half of the people employed have been described as 'executives'. Those two figures are indicators of one measure of success. They are what

Figure 8.14 La Défense: typical commercial buildings with a stabile by Alexander Calder in the background.

Figure 8.15 Office workers and tourists looking down the axis towards the Arc d'Triomphe from the steps of the Grande Arche.

impressed visiting politicians such as the United Kingdom's Prime Minister, Margaret Thatcher and Shanghai's Mayor (later premier of the People's Republic of China), Zhu Rongji. Canary Wharf and Lujiazui are the children of La Défense and the scheme for Hanoi North a grandchild (see Marshall, 2002). If Haussmann's Paris was the model for earlier generations of political leaders, La Défense is for today's.

Major references

de Graveline, Frederique (2002). *La Défense, Les Villes et Leurs Projects: Projets Urbain en France*. Paris: Editions du Moniteur.

EPAD (*c.* 2002). *La Défense*. EPAD.

Lowe, Garrard (1996). Urban lessons from Paris. *Urbanities* **6** (1): 1–6. http:www.city-journal.org

Torres, Felix (1987). *Paris La Défense: Métropole Européenne des Affaires*. Paris: Editions de Moniteur.

CASE STUDY

Canary Wharf, Isle of Dogs, London, England, UK: the urban design of commercial pragmatism? (Primarily 1985–98 but continuing)

Canary Wharf, the centerpiece of the London Docklands redevelopment, is an offspring of La Défense. The government of Margaret Thatcher had been encouraged by that scheme's success as a commercial venture to pursue a similar policy in London. Following the example of La Défense, Canary Wharf has been designed to cater to the commercial development of London outside its traditional commercial centre, the City. It is located on what was once a thriving port site abandoned as the result of changes in the size of ships and the nature of transportation technology, particularly the development of containerization. For all intents and purposes this brown-field site had been totally cleared except for the remnants of the docks.

Today, the area comprises 18 office buildings, a retail centre, hotels, a conference and banqueting centre, five parking stations (in addition to the parking below the office buildings) and landscaped open space. It is served by a light-rail system and, belatedly in 2000, by an underground railway station on the Jubilee Line (see Chapter 10). The site extends over 86 acres (34.4 hectares) of which about 20% is landscaped open space. To get to this state has been a harrowing experience.

In the 1980s, the British government under Thatcher took over control of the Docklands area from the five local borough governments responsible for it and established the London Docklands Development Corporation (LDDC). The LDDC's task, as stated in 1981 by the then Environment Secretary, Michael Heseltine, was to 'bring these barren areas back into more valuable use'. The Corporation encouraged a market-led approach to design but it also created an enterprise zone that offered tax incentives for firms to locate at Canary Wharf. The Docklands' statutory regulations were

Figure 8.16 A model of the SOM proposal for Canary Wharf.

also suspended. Much was left up in the air. There were, for instance, no specific regulations about building developers' contributions to the cost of the infrastructure or landscape architecture. Decisions were made on an *ad hoc* basis.

In 1985 an American entrepreneur, G. Ware Travelstead, proposed a 35-hectare commercial development designed by Hanna–Olin for the Canary Wharf site but in the same year Skidmore, Owings and Merrill (SOM) was commissioned to produce a master plan and design guidelines for the area (see Figure 8.16). The present layout retains the essential feature of that plan. The

design has a City Beautiful/Beaux-Arts axis terminated by a landmark building (see Figure 8.17). The area was divided into 26 building sites and formal landscaped gardens. The design guidelines – prepared by SOM and the LDDC – specified height limits for the buildings in order for the central towers to be landmarks, and also the requirements for the materials to be used in order to establish a sense of unity. Development proposals that conformed to the guidelines did not require LDDC approval. Anything that deviated from them did. The guidelines turned out to be quite prescriptive giving architects little design leeway.

In 1987, the developers Olympia and York, earlier a key investor in Battery Park City (see later in this chapter), inherited the master plan. The company was part of the Reichmann family real estate empire in Canada. Otto Blau, a key member of the company advised against investing in Canary Wharf because of its location. Paul Reichmann, who had developed a close relationship with Margaret Thatcher, was persuaded to go ahead by her personal promises that an underground rail connection to the site would be built in order to make the site commercially viable. By the time she left office in 1990 no progress had been made on the line.

The development of Canary Wharf, like that of La Défense, has not been smooth sailing. £1.3 billion was quickly invested between 1981 and 1986. After those years of speculation and development, bankruptcies in the 1990s saw the financial collapse of the development. The commercial rental market was severely depressed. No leading tenants had signed leases. This lack of demand for commercial office space had

Photograph courtesy of the Olin Partnership, Philadelphia

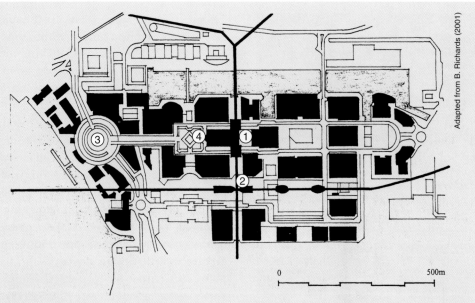

Adapted from B. Richards (2001)

1.Canary Wharf Light Rail station; 2. Jubilee Line station; 3. Westberry Circus; 4. One Canada Place

Figure 8.17 The Canary Wharf plan.

a major impact on Canary Wharf because it was not a mixed-use development. Olympia and York went into receivership in 1992. It owed substantial sums to 91 lending banks that had invested money largely on Paul Reichmann's enthusiasm for the project. Three years later Canary Wharf was sold to an international consortium of which Paul Reichmann is a leading member for £700 million. In 1995, Prince al-Walid bin Abdul Aziz of Saudi Arabia helped bring Canary Wharf out of bankruptcy. The development was not helped by the Irish Republican Army's car bomb attack of February 1996 causing £50 million worth of damages and killing two people. In 1999, the consortium became a public company with shares selling at £3.30.

With the rise in demand for office space in the mid-1990s much has now been built.

Building-use programme changes have enriched the development mix. It was expanded to include more restaurants, clubs, hotels, and leisure and entertainment facilities. The only residential development consists of luxury apartments at Wood Wharf but more apartments are in the offing nearby. The LDDC having completed the regeneration programme closed in 1998. A Canary Wharf Group now promotes the development. In 2002, Canary Wharf was 99.5% leased. It has a working-day population of 55,000 people and new buildings are being erected in adjacent areas. Canary Wharf is, however, still in financial trouble.

In late 2003, the Canary Wharf Group had £3 billion debts. Efforts were being made to sell-off the company. The downturn in the London office market resulted in the

Figure 8.18 Three views of Canary Wharf. (a) A view from the ferry wharf, 1993, (b) a view on axis towards One Canada Place, 2004 and (c) a view from the south, 2004.

company's shares trading at £2.43 in November 2003 having dropped to as low as £2.20 earlier in the year. The financial difficulties were being compounded by tenants whose leases were coming up for renewal seeking lower rates than they were currently paying to remain at Canary Wharf (Timmons, 2003). The physical environment is, however, there for everybody to see.

The architecture of the buildings has been described as 'post-modern classical'. Marble, limestone, brick, steel and glass are the primary building materials. A unity of design is achieved through the round corner towers at the entrances to the squares, the pedimented façades facing the Thames, the window grid applied and the attic story setbacks. The buildings were designed by major global architectural practices such as Kohn Pederson Fox, I. M. Pei, Troughton McAslan and César Pelli. Pelli (Architect of the World Financial Center at Battery Park City) was hired by Olympia and York to design the key building, One Canada Square, which is one of three landmark towers that can be seen from a distance. It is a relatively plain 800-foot (245-metre) Modernist building of stainless steel and glass with a reconstituted limestone base. It is an architecturally subdued building. It is distinguished primarily by its location at the end of the axis and by its height (see Figure 8.17).

The design controls have resulted in Canary Wharf being considerably less flamboyant than much commercial architecture of the 1990s. Contemporary critics saw this character as negative but it seems to be aging well in our contemporary critics' eyes. An important urban design difference between Canary Wharf and La Défense is that the buildings have street addresses so they can be reached from the street. At La Défense the pedestrian zones are largely undifferentiated. Perhaps this detail is something that SOM brought with them from their American experience (Figure 8.18).

The project has been both damned and praised. The lack of concern for the infrastructure necessary for the working population, particularly in public transportation, was severely criticized by all and sundry. The problem has now been largely addressed. A direct link to Heathrow airport and Liverpool Street station is still at the proposal level and Canary Wharf firms are lobbying hard for it. There is also a proposal for a monorail connection to the heart of the City. Canary Wharf has been criticized for its bland, cheap, hermetically sealed architecture and finishes. It has been unfairly dismissed as the 'architectural expression of Thatcherism'. There are, however, problems. The sick building syndrome has, apparently, been common. The office monoculture that isolated the development from the social difficulties of people in its surroundings has also been the subject of negative commentary. Outsiders regard Canary Wharf as a private estate.

On the positive side the master plan has been praised for the quality of its landscaping: its circuses, squares and tree-lined streets. The individuality of the buildings designed by different architects (i.e. its all-of-a-piece urban design quality) has also been regarded as an achievement of merit. The overall success of the endeavour remains to be seen. It has, nevertheless, already achieved its primary goal of relieving, but not eliminating, pressure on the City.

Major references

Edwards, Brian (1992). *London Docklands: Urban Design in an Era of Deregulation*. Oxford: Butterworth Architecture.

Hoyle, Brian S., David Pinder and M. Sohail Husain (1994). *Revitalising the Waterfront: International Dimensions of Dockland Redevelopment*. Chichester: John Wiley and Sons.

Meyer, Han (1999). *City and Port: Urban Planning as a Cultural Venture in London, Rotterdam and New York*. Utrecht: International Books.

Ogden, Philip, ed. (1992). *Update: London Docklands, the Challenge of Development*. Cambridge: Cambridge University Press.

Powell, Ken (2000). *City Transformed: Urban Architecture at the Beginning of the 21st Century*. London: Laurence & King.

CASE STUDY

Euralille, Lille, France: a new city heart (1987 to the present)

In 1994, Rem Koolhaas and his Office of Metropolitan Architecture (OMA) prepared a master plan for the centre of Lille. Its aim was to create a new city in the heart of the old. The necessity of doing so had been the subject of considerable political negotiation. The growth of the European Union, the development of the Channel tunnel, and the desire to extend the North European line of France's TGV (*Train à Gran Vitesse*) had placed Lille, a city with a declining industrial base, at the centre of the London–Brussels–Paris business triangle. The city is strategically placed having a population of over 100 million people living within a radius of 300 kilometres (200 miles). It is, however, perhaps too close to Brussels to become a major centre.

The SNCF – the French national railway – in looking to develop its network north had proposed a stop in Seclin, a Lille suburb. It had calculated that the cost of running the line through central Lille would be 1.9 billion francs above the cost of running it through the outskirts of the city. In 1985 Lille's Deputy Mayor, Pierre Mauroy (Prime Minister of France from 1981 to 1984) started to pressure the French government to have the train station in the centre of the city. In 1987 he had success. Mauroy went on to form a development management organization, Lille Metropole, to implement the project. Jean Peyelevade, a close associate, was placed in charge of raising funds. Lille Metropole with the regional office of the SNCF and the Regional Chamber of Commerce formed a public–private partnership to steer the project. The core shareholders were five major French banks.

Lille Metropole invited four French and four foreign architects to submit master plan proposals for the site. The French architects were Claude Vasconi, Jean-Paul Viguier, Yves Lyon and Michel Macary while the international ones were Norman Foster, Vittorio Gregotti, O. M. Ungers and Rem Koolhaas. The last mentioned's plan was accepted and the OMA became the master planner for Euralille. An all-of-a-piece urban design approach was followed with a number of illustrious architects working on the individual buildings in accordance with the master plan.

229

The prime consideration in the development of the urban design concept was its symbolic aesthetic character as a futuristic new business centre for Europe (see Figures 8.19 and 8.20). The central ideas of the scheme were those of Koolhaas as presented in his book *Delirious New York* and his theories of 'bigness', 'commercialism', 'exhibitionism' and 'density without architecture' (Koolhaas, 1978). Selective voids to create a complexity of geometry and monumental architecture are the essential ingredients of the scheme. Philosophically, despite Koolhaas' observations in New York it is closer to the Rationalist tradition than the Empiricist.

The scheme has five major components:

1 The TGV station used by London–Brussels trains.

2 A triangular forum outside the station (an 'expression of the conceptual opposition of history–future').
3 Le Corbusier Street (the main traffic thoroughfare linking station, business centre, the edges of Sant-Maurice and Le Corbusier Square where old and new cities meet).
4 The park.
5 The Convention and Exhibition Centre.

The whole is framed by the edges of the neighbourhood of Sant-Maurice. The Convention and Exhibition Centre is a 300-metre (1000-foot) long multi-functional structure designed to link the fragmented parts of the scheme. The TGV line runs on the surface through the city opening it up to view and views from it.

Implementation of the project took place over a decade in two phases. Phase One (1991–5) involved the acquisition of land and the building of the TGV line and station

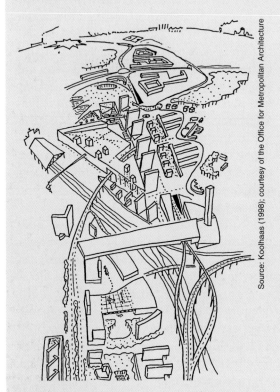

Source: Koolhaas (1998); courtesy of the Office for Metropolitan Architecture

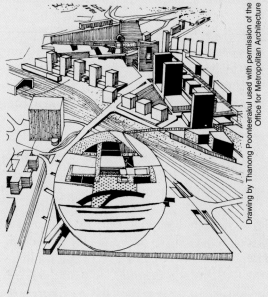

Drawing by Thanong Poonteerakul used with permission of the Office for Metropolitan Architecture

Figure 8.19 Rem Koolhaas' concept for Euralille.

Figure 8.20 Massing drawing of the development.

Photograph by Tata Soemardi

(a)

Photograph by Tata Soemardi

(b)

Figure 8.21 Two images of Euralille. (a) The link between the old station and the shopping centre and (b) The Credit Lyonnais tower.

(designed by Jean-Marie Duthilleul). The land available for development had been owned by the French military and had been a *zone non-aedificandi* – not available for development. The relevant legislation needed to be changed and had already been during the premiership of Mauroy. Progress on the implementation of the Koolhaas proposal was, however, hampered by the real estate crisis of Europe that also affected La Défense and Canary Wharf. A number of key investors abandoned the project leading to the dropping of some elements of the scheme (e.g. the four-star hotel). Phase Two (1995–2000) saw some amendments to the master plan but brought the project to semi-completion. The key buildings were an office tower for Credít Lyonnais (designed by Christian de Portzamparc and known locally as 'the boot'; see Figure 8.21b), the World Trade Centre (Claude Vasconi, Arch-itect), a shopping and office centre (by Jean Nouvel), and Congress Centre and Rock Concert Hall designed by Rem Koolhaas him-self. Seventy per cent of the building rights for the town centre had been sold by 2002 and Euralille2, a more suburban type mixed-use development is on the drawing boards.

The urban design is very much a personal statement of Rem Koolhaas. It has been attacked and defended largely on those grounds – as a work of art – in which the individual buildings are objects to be admired as signature statements. The objective has been to attain a high level of prestige for the development. It has been an extraordinarily expensive endeavour that demonstrates the interconnections amongst politics, ambi-tions for one's own city, urban design and architectural ideologies. It is Pierre Mauroy's dream and it was his arm-twisting that enabled Euralille to go ahead. The scheme also shows the importance of grand archi-tectural ideas as a catalyst for business development. Le Corbusier would have been proud of the audacity of the project.

Major references

Goldberger, Paul (2000). *The Architecture of Rem Koolhaas*. Los Angeles: Jensen and Walker.

Koolhaas, Rem (1998). *1987–1998, OMA Rem Koolhaas*. Madrid: El Croquis Editorial.

Spaans, Marjolein (2004). The implementation of urban regeneration projects in Europe: global ambitions, local matters. *Journal of Urban Design* **9** (3): 335–49.

CASE STUDY

Lujiazui, Pudong, Shanghai, People's Republic of China: a global business precinct (1990+)

The Lujiazui (also sometimes spelt Lu Jia Zui) Finance and Trade Zone in Pudong, Shanghai is not only a good example of an all-of-a-piece urban design with highly *lais-sez-faire* overtones, but also a good example of the urban design and architectural values being displayed in China and many other Asian countries today. (In China similar efforts can be seen the Fu-tian new district in Shenzhen and the River North area of

Chongqing.) Lujiazui is the largest single-construction site in the world. Nearly 160 foreign banking institutions are already located there. By 2005, 12 million square metres of office space will have been built. As yet, however, no significant international organization has set up its headquarters in the precinct.

Pudong was partially a green-field site of agricultural land but it also contained ship-building works, petrochemical plants and other industries along the river. The land is publicly owned. In April 1990, the government of the People's Republic of China announced its plan to develop the Pudong New Area as part of its economic reform effort to attract foreign investment. The goal of the development is to turn Shanghai into a global commercial centre by creating a precinct of prestigious modern buildings and manicured open spaces with a coordinated infrastructure and communications network. One hundred and eighty-two other Chinese cities are reputedly hoping to attain the same end but only the major ones are serious contenders. Shanghai is much better placed than its competitors to achieve its goals.

The overall plan of Pudong contains four special development zones: the Lujiazui Finance and Trade Zone, the Jinqiao Export-Processing Zone, the Waigaoqiao Free Trade Zone and the Zhangjiang High-Tech Park. The first of these is the focus of attention here. Suffice to say that Jinqiao is to be an industrial area of 9.6 square kilometres (5.8 square miles) located in the centre of Pudong, the Waigaoqiao Zone, China's first free-trade precinct, is to be located on the estuary of the Yangtze River, and the Zhangjiang High-Tech Park is to emphasize science and education. The last mentioned is to be 17 square kilometres in size and located in the eastern part of the Pudong New Area. It is planned to be the location of computer software companies and precision medical apparatus manufacturing industries.

The Lujiazui Finance and Trade Zone is planned to be the new commercial heart of the whole city, and an extension of the Bund – the financial core of Shanghai that lies across the Huangpu River from Lujiazui. Lujiazui covers an area of 6.8 square kilometres (4 square miles). The zone is planned to house financial, information and real estate consultancy organizations. It is also part of the plan to link Pudong with Puxi, the city precinct west of the river that is undergoing considerable urban renewal. The basic infrastructure of Lujiazui has already been built and the new buildings are being plugged into it with great rapidity. Publicly owned, the land is leased for 99 years at 50% of the predicted value it would have when developed.

The full-scaled planning effort for Lujiazui began in 1992 when the Shanghai government under the leadership of Mayor Zhu Rongji, set up the Senior Consultants Committee (SCC) to initiate development. The committee was comprised of local officials and professionals, and also four foreign design teams. The international teams were from France (Dominique Perrault, designer of the glazed towers of the Bibliothèque Nationale in Paris, 1992–6), the United Kingdom (Sir Richard Rogers, known for his high-tech architecture), Italy (Massimiliano Fuksas, whose schemes for high-rise buildings were attracting attention) and Japan (Toyo Ito, whose ITM building in Matsuyama (1993) exploits the characteristics of many varieties of glass). The selection of these architects illustrates the type of architectural imagery sought for the district. The hope was that through the act of design creative future possibilities would emerge. The Shanghai Urban Planning and Design Institute submitted a fifth scheme (see Figure 8.22c).

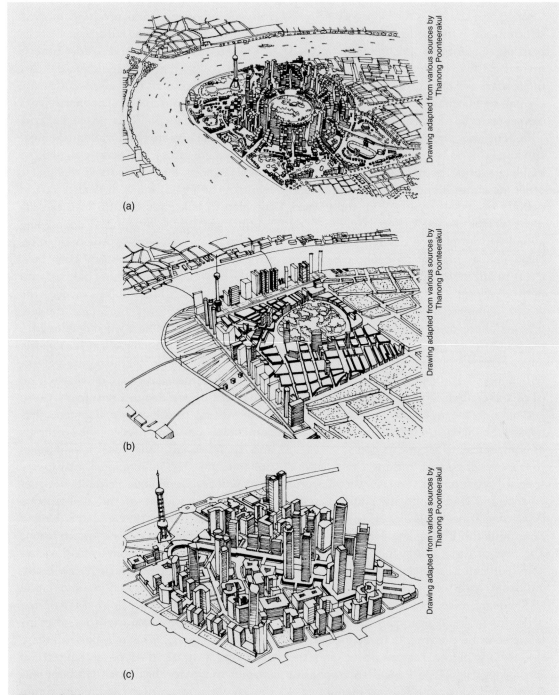

(a)

Drawing adapted from various sources by
Thanong Poonteerakul

(b)

Drawing adapted from various sources by
Thanong Poonteerakul

(c)

Drawing adapted from various sources by
Thanong Poonteerakul

Figure 8.22 Three of the five proposals for Lujiazui. (a) Richard Rogers' scheme,
(b) Dominique Perrault's scheme and (c) the Shanghai Urban Planning and Design
Institute's scheme.

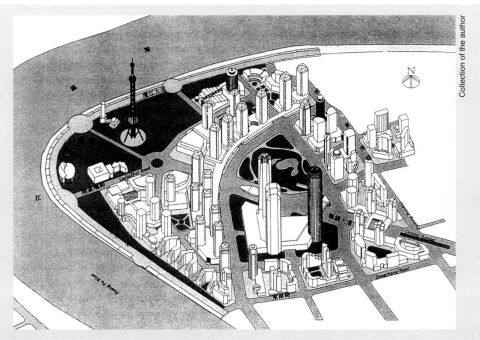

Collection of the author

Figure 8.23 The master plan for Lujiazui prepared by the Shanghai Urban Planning and Design Institute.

The five schemes were presented to the SCC as a set of potential ideas for the site. After deliberating on the schemes the SCC proposed:

1 a major development of the transportation infrastructure with new tunnels across the river and an underground rail system;
2 the development of parkland along the river;
3 that super-high landmark buildings should be located in the core area with lower buildings near the river;
4 that the development of infrastructure should be phased so that any proposed developments could go ahead without stretching financial resources or causing a delay.

In 1994, the municipal government of Shanghai and a new corporation, the Lujiazui

Finance and Trade Zone Development Company, invited the Shanghai Urban Planning and Design Institute to do the urban design plan for the area by adapting the five schemes presented to the SCC. The result was a variation of the Institute's own model. The plan divided the area into three sub-areas, proposed an underground pedestrian network, a park along the river and a set of foreground buildings. The desire was also to create a mix of uses so that Lujiazui would not be simply a 9.00 a.m. to 5.00 p.m. office zone (Figure 8.23).

One of these sub-areas was proposed to be a district of high-rise buildings – the higher the better – with a central park. Another was proposed to be a commercial district, located on the west side of a central avenue, and the third was proposed to be a waterfront precinct to contain cultural and entertainment facilities, gift shops and the pre-existing

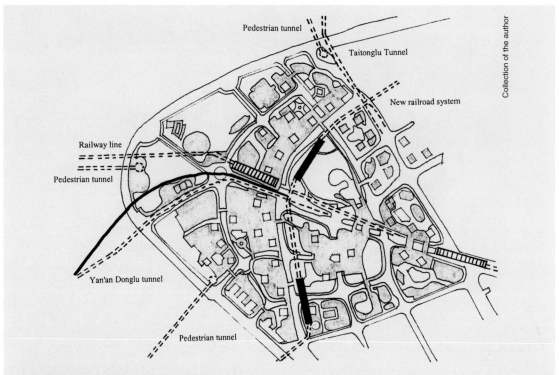

Collection of the author

Figure 8.24 Lujiazui: transportation links.

Oriental (or Eastern) Pearl Television Tower. An underground pedestrian network would unite these three parts of Lujiazui. A central avenue would link the waterfront and the central park. The major transportation interchange would also be located on the central avenue.

Today the road network consists of two major components: the central avenue and a ring road. The central avenue is the powerful coordinating element of Lujiazui. It is a two-way arterial boulevard, consisting of eight lanes and includes a road divider planted with grass and trees, and with a continuous water feature along it. Not only is the avenue to be the major road transportation route but also a visual corridor linking the three sub-districts of Lujiazui. It has grade-separated interchanges connecting it to the

roads that serve the interiors of the sub-districts. The ring road has six lanes and bounds the central area of Lujiazui (Figure 8.24).

The most visible landmark of Lujiazui is the Oriental Pearl Tower, an over 400-metre (1260-foot) high spire. Symbolizing the resurrection of Shanghai as a leading player in world trade, the tower is comprised of 11 red spheres – two large ones and nine smaller ones of up to 50 metres in diameter supported on 9-metre diameter columns. The Shanghai World Financial Center (Shi Mao) was planned by Kohn Pederson Fox to be 488 metres in height topping the Petronas Towers in Kuala Lumpur. Construction on the building was started in 1997 but Asia's economic crisis halted work on it. Concerns about terrorist activity not withstanding, the Mori Building Company of Tokyo has (at the time of writing) changed the planned height to make it even taller in order to top the 508-metre Taipei Financial Centre being built in Taiwan. The design at present shows it to be a metallic, wedge-shaped tower with a hole at the top. It will overshadow its neighbour, the 88-storey, 420-metre tall Jin Mao Tower (1993–9) that sits on a six-storey podium. Designed by the Chicago office of SOM in a fusion of Art Deco and a touch of traditional Chinese types, the Jin Mao Tower is the third tallest building in the world. It was unknown at the time of writing whether the World Financial Center design will change again as the result of the announcement by Emaar Properties that its Burj Dubai on a 20-acre (9-hectare) site was designed to an unspecified but taller height.

The design guidelines for the buildings of Lujiazui consist of height controls and a series of more detailed site-by-site requirements. In the core area, the landmark tri-towers were stipulated to be a minimum of 360, 380 and 400 metres in height. The area around them is to be a linear high-rise zone with buildings stepping down from 220 metres in height to 160 metres on the waterfront. In this linear zone the design guidelines stipulate building setbacks, building envelopes, the height of podiums, materials and the height of colonnades (Figures 8.25 and 8.26). The profile sought is shown in Figure 8.27.

The expenditure on the first step of the Pudong development was estimated to be about $US10 billion obtained from the central government in Beijing, the Shanghai Municipal government, the Asian Development Bank and the World Bank. The total cost for the whole development spread over 30 years will probably be in the region of $US80 billion. Half of this sum is expected to

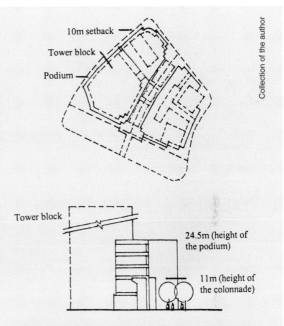

Figure 8.25 Central area design guidelines.

Figure 8.26 An artist's impression of Century Avenue, Lujiazui.

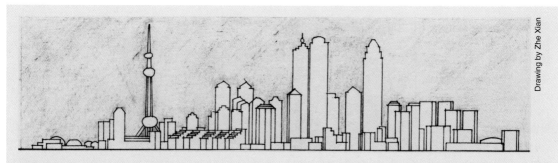

Drawing by Zhe Xian

Figure 8.27 The proposed skyline, Lujiazui.

Figure 8.28 Lujiazui as seen from The Bund in 2004 (for another view see page 358).

come from foreign investment. To attain this goal a number of incentives are being offered to investors:

1 a reduced (15%) income tax rate;
2 exemption from duties on export-oriented imports;
3 tax relief for construction and infrastructure projects;
4 land leases for 50 or 70 years.

   The whole process of development has been organized into a number of phases. The first phase was the development of the

Figure 8.29   The architecture of Lujiazui from Century Avenue, 2004.

road links, telecommunications facilities and energy systems. This investment allowed building construction to begin. The second phase involved the development of the regional infrastructure to support the development of Shanghai as well as, more specifically, the Pudong area: airports, telecommunications centres, the subway system extension, the external ring road, the international conference centre, etc. These two stages provided the essential infrastructure for further development (Figures 8.28 and 8.29).

The sites have been leased to or are being leased to different property developers by the development company. What is emerging is a spacious, 'glitzy' area of high-rise buildings designed by internationally renowned architects. It presents a panoramic skyline outrivaling Manhattan for architecture grandeur and variety of forms (see Figure 8.28). The open spaces give an image of luxuriousness but they are also large and unfriendly to pedestrians. The width of the central avenue (now called Century Avenue) at 100 metres provides a strong visual link between the river and the core of Lujiazui, but it is also a substantial divider between the area's components. Five kilometres long, it serves local vehicular traffic and pedestrians below the ground and it has a new subway line that provides public transport. Whatever the quality is perceived to be, Lujiazui sets a precedent for China, both in process and product, as a symbol of modernity. In 1999, 70% of the office space in Pudong was estimated to be vacant because of the gross over-supply but by 2004 this figure had reputedly dropped to 15%.

The project is not simply market-driven but rather driven by the aspirations of a people as represented by their government officials. Its architecture has been called 'non-judgemental kitsch' in which diversity is exciting, everything is possible and everything is acceptable. It is a hybrid architecture reflecting concepts of individualism, modernity and tradition. Lujiazui is evolving into a piece-by-piece design of separate buildings each striving to be a foreground building barely within the constraints imposed by the design guidelines.

Major references

Balfour, Alan and Zheng Shiling (2002). *World Cities: Shanghai*. Chichester: Wiley-Academic.

Lim, William S. W. (2004). *Have You Been Shanghaied? Culture and Urbanism in Glocalized Shanghai*. Singapore: Asian Urban Lab.

Marshall, Richard (2003). *Emerging Urbanity: Global Projects in the Asia Pacific Rim*. London: Spon Press.

Olds, Kris (1997). Globalizing Shanghai: the 'Global Intelligence Corps' and the building of Pudong. *Cities* 14 (2): 109–123.

Wang, An-de, ed. (2000). *Shanghai Lujiazui Central Area Urban Design*. Shanghai: Architecture and Engineering Press.

CASE STUDY

Battery Park City, New York, NY, USA: a 'new town in-town' (1962 to 2002, but continuing)

Whether or not one cares for the design of Battery Park City, it is arguably *the* exemplar of an all-of-a-piece urban precinct design in the United States. Chronologically, it predates Canary Wharf, Euralille and Lujiazui but it is very different. It was not seen as a new business district but as an adjunct to an existing one. Now almost completed (and repaired after the events of 11 September 2001 when it was much damaged; see page 379 for a 2004 view) Battery Park City's development history is lengthy. The undertaking was embroiled in political infighting (particularly between politicians and bureaucrats of the State and the City of New York) and battered by the fluctuations in New York City's economy and the corresponding demand for property development. Political and civic leaders and architectural critics (particularly Ada Louise Huxtable of the *New York Times*) wielded considerable influence on the proposals for the scheme. What we see today on the site is a product of the 1979 master plan, but the process of planning for Battery Park City began in the early 1960s.

Like many other river ports throughout the world, the finger wharfs on the Hudson River became obsolete in the 1960s. In Lower

Courtesy of the Olin Partnership, Philadelphia

Figure 8.30 The site in 1977 with the World Trade Center towers in the left background.

Manhattan 20 piers that had once busily handled produce had fallen into disuse and became decayed. They were owned by the city and run by its Department of Marine and Aviation. The river could legally be land-filled to pierhead-line and the 37-hectare (92-acre) site so created used for develop-ment (see Figure 8.30). The Department wanted to build a new shipping terminal with an industrial esplanade along the edge, with housing blocks behind (see Figure 8.31). These blocks were proposed to be located, in the Modernist manner, as objects in space. This plan, presented in 1962, was poorly received by the press, the public and by government officials.

A series of alternative proposals followed. The governor of the state, Nelson Rockefeller, wished the development to be a compre-hensive community built over a base of light

industry. He asked Wallace K. Harrison of Harrison and Abromowitz, who had worked for him before, to prepare a plan. In 1966, the firm produced a poorly received orthodox Bauhaus/Le Corbusian scheme (see Figure 8.32). Like the 1962 plan no implementation procedure was designed along with the urban design. Implicit in both proposals was that they were total urban designs to be imple-mented by a single developer. Proposed fund-ing procedures were never worked out.

The City responded to the State's plan with one of its own. Mayor John Lindsay hired the firm of Concklin and Rossant to do the job. As a compromise the firm worked with Harrison and Abromowitz (and with Philip Johnson as a broker of ideas), to pro-pose another scheme. It was presented in 1969. The conflict between the city and the state over control of the project was finally

Figure 8.31 The New York City Department of Marine and Aviation proposal, 1963.

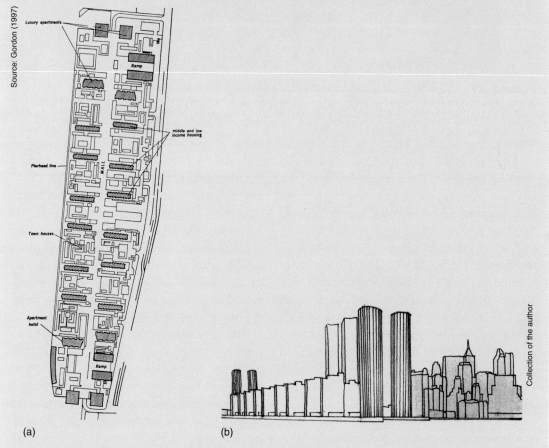

(a)

(b)

Figure 8.32 The Harrison and Abromowitz plan (Governor Rockefeller's proposal). (a) The plan and (b) massing diagram.

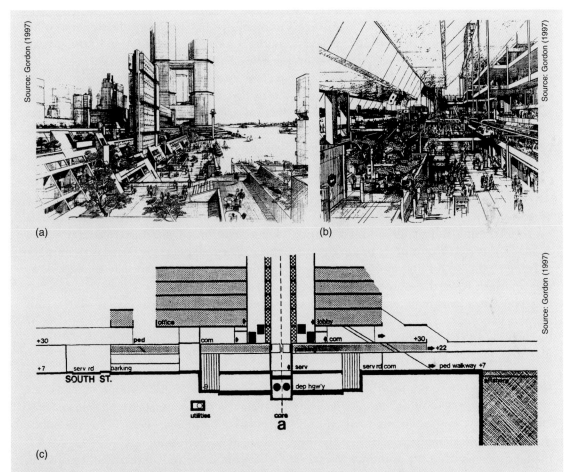

Source: Gordon (1997)

(a)

(b)

(c)

Figure 8.33 Battery Park City: the City/State plan of 1969. (a) General view along the Hudson River, (b) internal view of the proposed spine and (c) cross-section through the spine.

resolved with the formation of the Battery Park City Authority (BPCA) in 1968. The authority was given considerable freedom of action. It has had a chequered career but has seen the project through to completion.

The 1969 proposal was well received by press and public as appropriate for Manhattan. It was radically different to its predecessors consisting of a seven storey, partly enclosed, partly open interior-mall containing a variety of urban functions and amenities – shops, restaurants schools, parks,

recreation facilities, access from transit lines and utilities (see Figure 8.33). It ran the length of the Battery Park City site. The scheme also proposed the decking over of the West Side Highway to link the site directly with the rest of Lower Manhattan. The City's planning department translated the scheme into a voluminous zoning code. The problem was money. Who would finance the project?

The 1973 recession and the close-to bankruptcy conditions of the BPCA and of the City of New York did not encourage investment in such a mammoth project. Subsequent plans for the precinct were thus more down to earth. A 1975 proposal was pragmatically related to how developers finance their projects. It divided the whole site into a number of residential clusters or pods that could be developed independently. The pods turned in on themselves to create isolated, controllable middle-class worlds. The pods were to be linked by elevated walkways with traffic moving underneath, but the idea was abandoned as too costly. It was a sort of plug-in urban design although who would finance the walkways was not clear. Nevertheless, one of the pods, Gateway Plaza, was built. It took a number of years to complete being finished in 1982. By then the BPCA had abandoned the pod plan and another master plan was in place.

Until 1979, the land was leased to the BPCA. The parlous financial state of the 1970s led to New York State's Urban Development Corporation stepping in and the title was transferred to the BPCA. Having the land title enabled the authority to make decisions rapidly. One of the first decisions it made was to adopt a conceptual plan radical in its simplicity (see Figure 8.34a). The conceptual design and master plan were the work of Alexander Cooper and Stanton Eckstut. Produced in 1979, the scheme's intellectual foundation was a precursor to the ideas of the New Urbanist movement in urban design.

This new plan was developed under considerable time and political pressure. Richard Kahan, Director of the BPCA at that time, faced considerable constraints. Payment on a $200 million bond issue had to be made in 90 days and a plan requiring the approval of the New York State legislature had to be made within that time. It also had to be something that property developers could understand. The parcelization of the overall scheme had to be fairly standard.

The plan proposed that up to 14,000 housing units be built on the site, that commercial facilities be incorporated as an integral part of the scheme, and that 6 million square feet (557,000 square metres) of office space be located opposite the World Trade Center. Thirty per cent of the site would be squares and parks and an esplanade would run along the Hudson. The streets consumed another 16% of the site space. The new plan was based on a number of objectives. Battery Park City should:

1 be an integral part of Lower Manhattan so the street pattern of Manhattan ought to continue through the site;
2 have circulation at ground level;
3 have its aesthetic qualities based on New York's architectural heritage;
4 have the commercial complex as its foreground buildings, with the other buildings as background;
5 have its uses and development controls flexible enough to respond to changes in the marketplace.

The northern end of the site was to be a park, now named for Governor Rockefeller. Public art would terminate the vistas from the centre of the island on each street in order to provide elements of interest and act as symbols of 'class' – high status.

The master plan specified the sites for buildings and the design controls to be applied to each. The building design guidelines were based on the buildings in well-loved parts of New York such as Gramercy Park and Morningside Heights. The guidelines stipulated the nature of materials, the

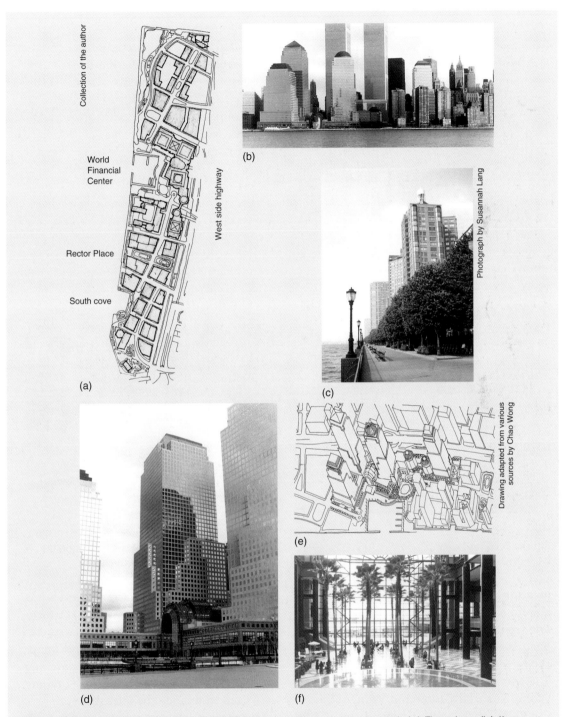

Figure 8.34 Battery Park City: the 1979 master plan as developed. (a) The plan, (b) the view from across the Hudson in 1993, (c) the esplanade in 2003, (d) the World Financial Center layout in context, (e) a view towards the Winter Garden and (f) the Winter Garden in 1993.

Figure 8.35 Rector place, Battery Park City. (a) The design guidelines, (b) rector place as built and (c) the park.

location of stringcourses, that buildings should have articulated bases and cornices and specific window-to-solid-wall ratios. Each building was designed individually as can be seen in Rector Place (see Figure 8.35). The commercial space was taken up by the World Financial Center and Winter Garden (1980–3) that were designed by César Pelli as foreground elements. The esplanade was designed by Hanna–Olin a landscape architectural firm. Its hierarchy of levels has become a model for subsequent waterfront walkways. The BPCA built the public spaces to high standards to ensure a good financial return for the sites. Bonds matching long-term financing with capital funding were used to finance the infrastructure.

The implementation process was considerably less complex than that proposed for the 1969 megastructure proposal (see

Table 8.1 Plan implementation comparison

1969 Master Development Plan			1979 Master Plan	
Physical Design Concept				
Megastructure			Extension of Manhattan Grid	
Public Circulation Spine			Streets	
7 Pods			36 Blocks	
Open-Space Decks			Public Parks	
Planning Controls				
City Ownership			BPCA Ownership	
Master Lease			City Repurchase Option	
Master Development Plan			Master Plan	
Special District Zoning			Urban Design Guidelines	
Site Improvement Cost Estimates				
	$1973	$1979*		$1979
Utilities	14.1	25.2	Utilities	8.5
Civic Facilities	41.1	73.6	Civic Facilities	3.0
Streets, Spine	58.3	104.4	Streets	13.7
Foundations	19.2	34.4	Foundations	N/A
Architecture and Engineering	26.0	46.5	Architecture and Engineering	Inclusive
Contingency	15.8	28.3	Contingency	Inclusive
Total ($ million)	$174.5	$312.4	Total ($ million)	$53.2
Implementation process				
1 BPCA designs service spine			1 BPCA prepares design guidelines	
2 PARB reviews spine design			2 BPCA designs streets and parks	
3 City Plan Commission Amendments			3 BPCA selects developer(s)	
4 Board of Estimate Amendments			4 Developer designs buildings	
5 BPCA starts spine construction			5 BPCA reviews designs	
6 BPCA selects pod developer			6 BPCA builds streets and parks	
7 Developer designs pod platform			7 Developer builds building	
8 BPCA reviews pod/spine connect				
9 Developer designs towers				
10 BPCA approves tower design				
11 PARB reviews pod design				
12 CPC amends MDP (if required)				
13 B of E amends MDP (if required)				
14 Developer builds pod platform				
15 Developer builds first building				

Source: Gordon (1997); courtesy of David Gordon
*1973 Costs inflated to $1979 using CPI (1973 = 128.4; 1979 = 230.1).

Table 8.1). The first phase of constructing the project involved the building of the World Financial Center with Olympia and York as developer. It was a financial success at least partially due to government commitments being fulfilled – an expectation that Paul Reichmann carried with him to London and the development of Canary

Wharf. Then the tactic was to build towards the north and south of the site (i.e. from the centre out). The first residential pod, Gateway Plaza, remains a relic of the previous plan.

The project as it has emerged, is very much part of New York and not nearly so much part of the global architectural scene as are La Défense and Lujiazui. Battery Park City has ended up being an all-of-a-piece urban design almost as rigidly controlled as Seaside but following very different design guidelines. It shows what can be accomplished, particularly in times of high demand for development, through carefully conceived urban design rather than *laissez-faire* planning. At the same time critics feel that the architecture's focus on the appearance of New York – on its visual aesthetic character – has led to a lack of the behaviour settings that characterize New York. It is also not the

type of architecture sought by the global economy. Yet, by all reports, it is well liked as a place to work by office workers and a place to live by its 25,000 residents. It is estimated to have cost $US4 billion to create.

Major references

Alexander Cooper Associates (1979). *Battery Park City: Draft Summary Report and 1979 Master Plan.* New York: The authors. *http://www.batteryparkcity. org/guidelines.htm*
Barnett, Jonathan (1987). In the public interest: design guidelines. *Architectural Record* **175** (8): 114–25.
Gordon, David A. (1997). *Battery Park City: Politics and Planning on the New York Waterfront.* London: Routledge, Gordon & Breach.
Russell, Francis P. (1994). Battery Park City: an American dream of urbanism. In Brenda Case Scheer and Wolfgang Preiser, eds. *Design Review: Challenging Urban Aesthetic Control.* New York: Chapman and Hall, 197–209.

CASE STUDY

Paternoster Square, London, England, UK: a second go at an important urban precinct (1956–2003)

Paternoster Square is the only case study in this book where one new urban design project was demolished and replaced by another. The precinct's history highlights: (1) the necessity to take market conditions into consideration in designing complexes of buildings, (2) the danger of embracing a currently fashionable design paradigm that is inappropriate for dealing with the task at hand and (3) the impact of changing clients on the urban designing process. In addition, designing a complex adjacent to a major historical landmark raises a host of

deeply felt emotional concerns for a large dispersed community.

Sixteen years after the devastation of the area north of St Paul's Cathedral in the City of London by German bombing in 1942 during The Blitz, Sir William Holford prepared a proposal for the redevelopment of the precinct. The site stretches from St Paul's Cathedral to Newgate Street. Holford's scheme was a total urban design, Modernist in its layout and architecture. It was built between 1961 and 1967. The client was the Central Electricity Generating Board (CEGB)

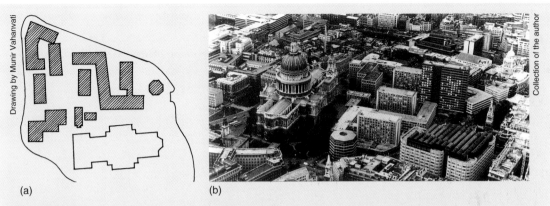

Figure 8.36 The Paternoster development: Lord Holford's design, 1967. (a) The figure–ground relationship and (b) a bird's eye view.

which had obtained a long-term lease of the site from the Church Commissioners of the Church of England.

The Holford scheme consisted of narrow rectangular, slab, commercial buildings set within an orthogonal site geometry (see Figure 8.36). Their height was restricted by their closeness to St Paul's – a control imposed by the Church Commissioners and one that still exists. They were designed to provide good light to office interiors. The buildings in day-to-day operation proved to be less than functional. Their shape did not meet the deep-plan requirements for commercial space at the time. Many critics and lay-people thought the development was lifeless and boring – a grim pedestrianized piazza. It was considered to reflect the functional theories of the Bauhaus Rationalist design ideology not British values. Much was shoddily built. During the 1980s the precinct became increasingly abandoned and the site came up for redevelopment.

In 1986, the site ownership (except for Sudbury House) passed from CEGB to a consortium consisting of Stockly, British Land, Unilever and Barclays Bank on a 250-year lease from the church. A year later the Mountleigh Group acquired Stockly (and its portion of control over the site) and then sold it on to Cisneros of Venezuela. The transactions reflected the buoyancy of the London property market at that time. The search for a design more appropriate for the site than that of Holford began in earnest. Ownership of the lease subsequently changed hands 'promiscuously' several times over the next 10 years (1995–2004). Greycoat and Park Tower acquired the property to be later replaced by Mitsubishi Estates (MEC).

An architectural competition organized by Stuart Lipton, a developer, on behalf of the Mountleigh Group was held in 1986. The figure ground studies of the proposals of the seven shortlisted architects are shown in Figure 8.37. Arup Associates was selected to proceed. Their design was a complicated neo-Rationalist one proposing the use of abstract historical referents in the buildings that formed it. The buildings were also designed to meet the commercial need of the marketplace for deep, highly serviced space. The proposal was criticized by Prince Charles whose views were widely supported by the lay-public. He argued for a more classical approach to design. John Simpson completed another

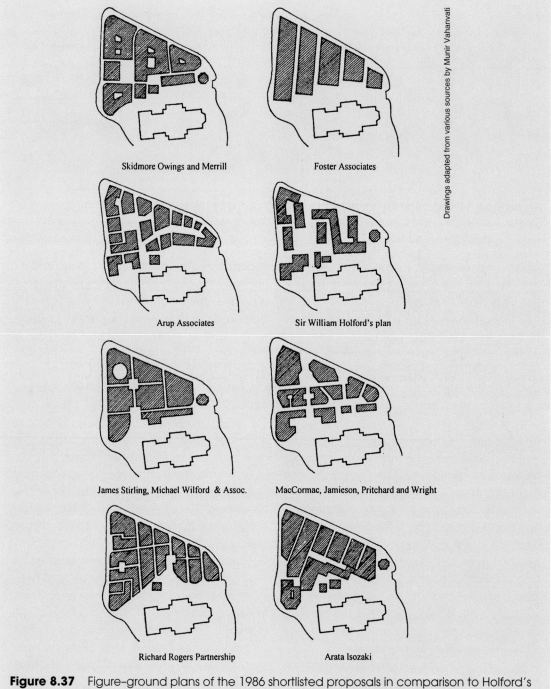

Drawings adapted from various sources by Munir Vahanvati

Skidmore Owings and Merrill

Foster Associates

Arup Associates

Sir William Holford's plan

James Stirling, Michael Wilford & Assoc.

MacCormac, Jamieson, Pritchard and Wright

Richard Rogers Partnership

Arata Isozaki

Figure 8.37 Figure–ground plans of the 1986 shortlisted proposals in comparison to Holford's scheme.

scheme proposed by Prince Charles' advisors Dan Cruickshank and Leon Krier.

The Simpson scheme was also a competition winner. In this case the sponsor of the competition was a newspaper, *The Evening Standard*. Simpson tried to combine 'functional' requirements in a complex consisting of an underground shopping mall and office buildings with classical façades. It was part of the Classical tradition in English architecture. His design went through several changes. A joint John Simpson/Terry Farrell scheme proposed in conjunction with a number of renowned classical architects (e.g. Allan Greenberg, Hammond, Beeby and Babka, and Quinlan Terry) was submitted unsuccessfully for planning approval. The recession of 1993 appears to have killed the possibility of implementing it. While it initially received Prince Charles' approval, the scheme was widely dismissed by critics as a 'pastiche'. While the proposed implementation process is unclear, it was presented as a single comprehensive product (Figure 8.38).

In 1995, MEC bought out its partners and appointed William Whitfield as master planner for the site. His scheme was adopted in 1996; demolition of the Holford project proceeded over the next 3 years and the new project was completed in October 2003. The scheme is an all-of-a-piece urban design and Neo-Traditional in character. The master plan strove to achieve a visual integration with the architecture of St Paul's by picking up on the stone and brick of Christopher Wren's design for the Chapter House of the Cathedral that now forms part of the scheme. Today the precinct contains 1 million square feet (110,000 square metres) of offices and shops (but no housing) in a number of independent buildings.

The London Stock Exchange, Goldman Sachs International and CB Richard Ellis are major tenants. The site plan consists of a large central square and pedestrian ways that link it to St Paul's, to the underground station and to Newgate Street. In the centre of the square is a 23 metre-high column topped by a gold-leafed copper finial that is floodlit at night. A statue of a man driving sheep – the area was once a livestock market – stands at one entrance to the square (Figure 8.39).

Five different architects designed the buildings following specific guidelines that have ensured a unified yet diverse design. The firms involved were MacCormac, Jamieson Prichard (Warwick Court), Eric Parry Architects/Sheppard Robson (10 Paternoster Square), Allies & Morrison (St Martin's Court), and Whitfield Partners with Sidell Gibson and Sheppard Robson (the buildings along St Paul's Churchyard). The results have been both praised and criticized. The site design has been praised for its plaza and links to its surroundings but the architecture has been criticized as banal (Glancey, 2003). The fundamental controversy remains. Is it better for a new complex to reflect its surroundings or be in contrast with them when it is adjacent to a major, psychologically important building such as St Paul's? Many people now think that the position of contrast taken by Holford was the correct position. It is a pity that his design was so bleak and an eyesore to so many.

Major references

Buchanan, Peter (1989). Paternoster pressure. *Architectural Review* **185** (1107): 76–80.

Freiman, Ziva (1990), Controversy: Paternoster Square. *Progressive Architecture* **71** (3): 115–16.

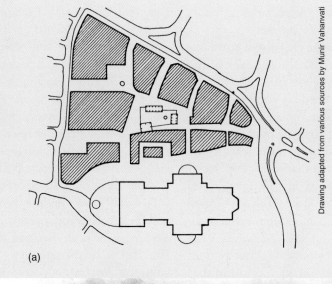

Drawing adapted from various sources by Munir Vahanvati

(a)

Collection of the author

(b)

Figure 8.38 The Hammond, Beeby & Babke, Porphyrios Associates and John Simpson & Partners design. (a) The Figure–ground plan and (b) the image sought.

Glancey, Jonathan (2003). It's a jumble out there. *The Guardian* (3 November). *http://www.guardian. co.uk/arts/critic/feature/0,1169.1076585.html*

Papadakis, Andreas C., ed. (1992). *Paternoster Square and the Classical Tradition*. London: Academy Editions.

Paternoster Square: *http://www.paternosterlondon. co.uk*

Weston, Richard (2001). The end of the affair. *RIBA Journal* **108** (4): 13–16.

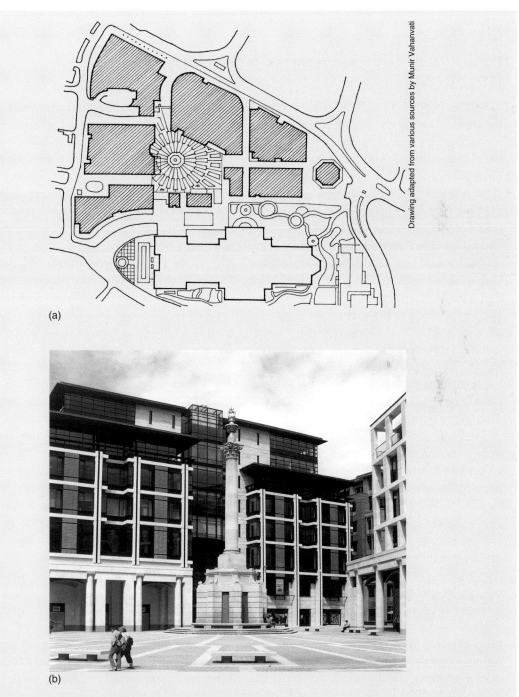

(a)

(b)

Drawing adapted from various sources by Munir Vahanvati

Figure 8.39 Paternoster Square: the Whitfield design. (a) The plan and (b) the square with Warwick Court in the background and 10 Paternoster Square on the right.

CASE STUDY

Pariser Platz, Berlin, Germany: an historic square revived (1992 to the present)

After the reunification of Berlin in 1989, and the dismantling of the wall that ran through it dividing East and West Berlin, Pariser Platz became available for reconstruction. It had been lying empty since being destroyed in World War II. During this period it lay in the East Berlin, or Russian sector, of the city that served as the capital of the Deutsche Demokratische Republik (GDR). The square is bounded on one side by the Brandenberg Gate which terminates the vista down Unten den Linden the ceremonial axis of Berlin. Before World War II the then great powers of the world, the United States, Great Britain, France and Austria had established their embassies on the square or in its vicinity. In addition, the Adlon Hotel and several prestigious apartment and commercial buildings enclosed it (see Figure 8.40).

The Square had originally been constructed in 1734 to the plans of the chief royal architect, Philip Gerlach. The construction of the present Brandenburg Gate (1789, designed by Carl Gotthard Langhans and inspired by the Propylæa in Athens) established the importance of Pariser Platz. The gate lies on the western side of the square and was part of the customs wall that surrounded the city in the eighteenth century. In 1880 Herman Mächtig, the city garden director added two ornamental parterres with fountains dividing the square into symmetrical halves. After the reunification of Berlin there was a universal desire to re-establish the importance of the square to that of its glory days of the period between 1871 and 1933. The question was, 'How?' There was no consensus.

Planning responsibilities for the site were divided. The [Berlin] Senate Department of Urban Development is responsible for overall urban design, zoning controls and landscape design concerns in Berlin but the individual city districts are responsible for local zoning, local development and landscape plans. The latter controls the development and building application process. The form that the restoration of Pariser Platz should take was very much a subject of debate amongst politicians, design professionals and the general public. Some people wanted the square resurrected as it once was; others wanted a *laissez-faire* collage of 'up-to-date' buildings. In addition, the site consists of 11 parcels of land and thus 11 individual owners whose possession dated to the time before the GDR had expropriated the land (see Figure 8.41). They had to be placated.

The outline of the square had been totally obliterated during the war. Archaeological research undertaken in 1992 revealed the square's outline and the locations of the fountains. The open area of the plaza was restored later in the same year. The redesigned plaza thus retains the square's historical outline and includes the foundations of the old water basins and remnants of the fountains. Hans Stimmann who believed that the buildings facing the square should 'combine conservative and modern elements' established the design goal.

A number of regulations and controls guarded the design of the buildings enclosing the square. One of the regulations of the Berlin Municipal Government is that

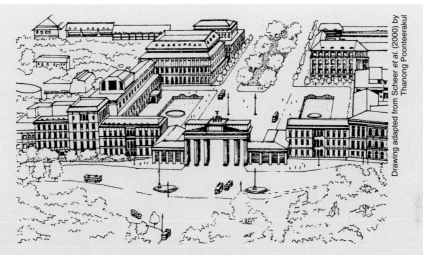

Drawing adapted from Scheer *et al.* (2000) by Thanong Poonteerakul

Figure 8.40 Pariser Platz as it appeared before World War II.

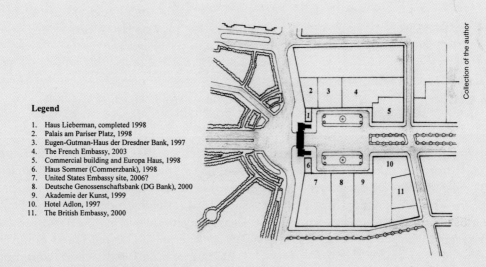

Collection of the author

Legend

1. Haus Lieberman, completed 1998
2. Palais am Pariser Platz, 1998
3. Eugen-Gutman-Haus der Dresdner Bank, 1997
4. The French Embassy, 2003
5. Commercial building and Europa Haus, 1998
6. Haus Sommer (Commerzbank), 1998
7. United States Embassy site, 2006?
8. Deutsche Genossenschaftsbank (DG Bank), 2000
9. Akademie der Kunst, 1999
10. Hotel Adlon, 1997
11. The British Embassy, 2000

Figure 8.41 The Pariser Platz development sites.

20% of any new development in the city must be devoted to housing. The purpose is to have some life in every precinct all day and to have streets and open spaces under natural surveillance (i.e. to 'have eyes on the street'). The aesthetic goal for Pariser Platz was to have buildings that were architecturally of Berlin. The design guidelines (of the 1999 Development Plan I-200) specified that buildings were to be no more than 22 metres in height, sandstone range in colour corresponding to the Brandenberg Gate, and with no more than 50% glazed area on the façade, all in keeping with Berlin traditions. They also had to be built to the property line with no setbacks and have their lower façades

255

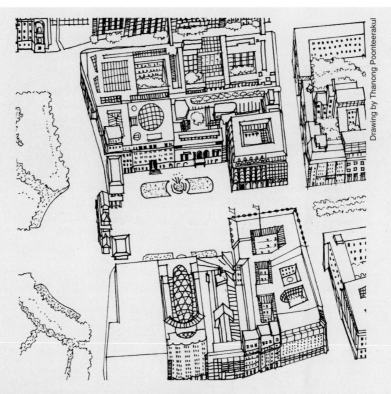

Drawing by Thanong Poonteerakul

Figure 8.42 Pariser Platz as developed by 2002.

(4–6 metres from the ground) visually differentiated from the floors above. The goal was to prevent the square becoming a 'playground' for a set of haphazard architectural ideas. Most of the buildings have complied with the regulations in a direct manner.

Starting in the north western corner, the square is enclosed by Haus Libermann (1996–8), Palais am Pariser Platz, the Eugen-Gutmann-Haus der Dresdner Bank (1996–7), the French Embassy (two-storey in appearance but of more floors in reality) designed by the Christian de Portzamparc Atelier, a residential-cum-commercial building, the Hotel Adlon (the hotel of the past on a new site, designed by Patzcheke, Klotz and Partners), the Akademie der Künst of the Senate of Berlin (2002, designed by

Günter Behnish that leads through to Behren Strasse to the south) and the Deutsche Genossenschaftbank (DG Bank) (a pale sandstone building designed by Frank Gehry and completed in 2000). Adjacent to it is the site for the United States Embassy. Haus Sommer and Haus Libermann, both designed by Josef Paul Kleihues have identical façades and with the Brandenberg Gate enclose the western end of the square. Figure 8.42 shows the plaza as reconstructed. The gate remains the centerpiece of the composition.

Gehry negotiated a 10% increase in the allowable area of glass on the façade of the DG Bank Building (see Figure 8.43b). His success shows both the political power that major architects can have and their desire

(a)

(b)

Figure 8.43 Two views of Pariser Platz in 2002. (a) Pariser Platz under (re)construction and (b) the DG Bank Building with the United States embassy site beyond.

to do things differently. His building is still sedate on the façade with greater exuberance in the internal court and on the rear of the building. The apartments are relegated to the rear so that the objective of having eyes on the square in non-business hours is not met, although there are always many tourists in the area to add some life to

257

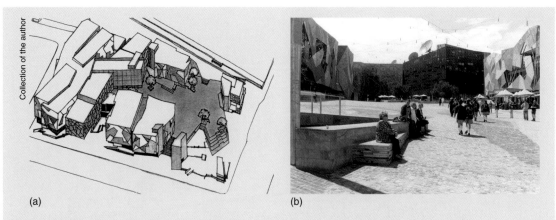

(a)

(b)

Figure 8.44   Federation Square, Melbourne. (a) The plan and (b) a general view.

the open space. This neglect of the intentions of a design directive shows that unless they are highly specific they can be easily avoided.

At the time of this study (2004) the last remaining open site on the Platz is that occupied by the United States Embassy before World War II. A design for the site (by Moore Ruble Yudell of Santa Monica and Gruen Associates of Los Angeles) was proposed but for security reasons, after the 1998 bombing of the United Sates Embassy in Nairobi, the United States Government does not wish to meet the requirement of building to the property line – a requirement put in place to make the square an enclosed space. It wanted a 100-foot setback. Negotiations have taken place between embassy officials and the Berlin administration to resolve the impasse. Both groups wish to have the embassy in its traditional location to add prestige to the Platz and vice versa. Given this situation the Embassy has had the upper hand in the negotiations. A settlement has been reached whereby the setback will be considerably smaller than the United States government wanted and it will pay for the consequent design and

construction changes required in the surroundings.

The reactions to the square are mixed. Many architects (and the lay-public, I suspect) would have preferred to have had the modern glazed global glitziness of Potsdamer Platz. Perhaps the image sought by these critics was more like that of the Federation Square (completed in 2002; see Figure 8.44) in Melbourne (Dovey, 2004). That square is a *total* urban design in which formal and technonic inventions reign supreme within an anti-classical composition. Frank Gehry has found the Pariser Platz to be a little bit like a stage set' (Gehry, 2001). Daniel Libeskind was more scathing. He considers the guidelines to be 'anti-democratic' and 'authoritarian' and the results 'banal'. He does not seem to have commented on the square as an urban place or node. What the design does do is put the Brandenberg Gate on centre stage and makes the other buildings background. Few architects want to be painters of the background. The clash of values represents the conflict between private desires to be self-expressive and public interests in all urban design work.

Major references

Gehry, Frank O. (2002). Building at the Pariser Platz – remarks on the new Berlin. *Casabella* **66** (704): 4–11, 100–2.

James-Chakraborty, Kathleen (2000). *German Architecture for a Mass Audience*. London: Routledge.

Scheer, Thorsten, Josef Paul Kleihues, Paul Kahlfeldt and Andrea Bärnreuther, eds. (2000). *City of Architecture of the City: Berlin 1900–2000*. Berlin: Nicolai.

Schneider, Bernhard (1998). Invented history: Pariser Platz and the Brandenberg Gate. *AA Files* (Autumn): 12–16.

CASE STUDY

Potsdamer Platz, Berlin, Germany: a 'cutting-edge vision' for a consumer society (1991+)

Before World War II Potsdamer Platz was the major node of Berlin and the termination of the railway line to Prussia. Like any node its quality was a function of its surroundings. They were diverse making an activity-rich area of hotels, cafés, art galleries and artists' workspaces. The war changed all that. The area was demolished by allied bombs and divided by the partitioning of Berlin that the end of the war brought. Only the Esplanade Hotel and the Weinhaus Huth survived the bombardment. They stood in a wasteland between the occupied zones of Berlin.

The precinct now consists of or, rather, will consist of three portions: the Leipziger Platz and its enclosing buildings, and the two areas that are the subject of this study. The one north of the Neue Potsdamer Strasse is now known as the Sony site and the other that lies across the road from it is known as the Debis site. In 1990, the land-owners hired Richard Rogers to make a proposal for the area (see Figure 8.45). In 1991, the Senate (i.e. government) of Berlin held a widely publicized design competition for the whole South Tiergarten area. It attracted 16 entries from internationally renowned architects. It was won by Heinz Hilmer and Christoph Sattler (see Figure 8.46). Helmut Jahn won a similar competition for the Sony site but that was sponsored by the corporation. Giorgio Grassi was appointed architect for the strip of land on the east side of the site. He kept to the principles of the Hilmer–Sattler design.

The Hilmer–Sattler design was restrained and essentially a New Urbanist one. It sought to recreate the complex, tight patterns of the traditional European city. The height of buildings was restricted to 22 metres with setback roof structures rising to no more than 30 metres. It had to follow the rule that at least 20% of each new development had to be allocated to housing. The design followed an approach called 'critical reconstruction' in which the stand taken is that the identity of a city is established by its history and does not need to be reinvented simply because that identity is something from the past. It repudiates the ideology of Le Corbusier as represented in the post-war developments in West Berlin (e.g. the Interbau at the Hansaviertel) and in the East Berlin of the GDR where massive buildings were located as objects in space. Opposing critics see critical reconstruction as a romantic attempt at turning back the

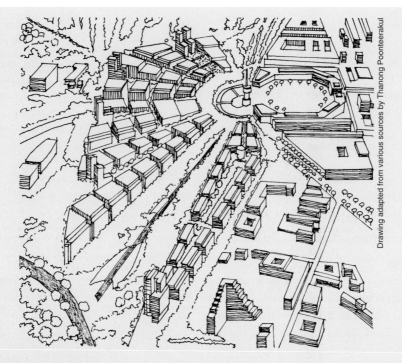

Figure 8.45 The Rogers proposal.

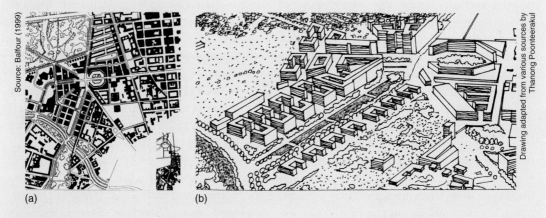

Figure 8.46 The Hilmer and Sattler Berlin Senate competition-winning scheme.
(a) Figure–ground study and (b) aerial view.

clock. Economics overtook the debate. Critical reconstruction was not what the major corporations wanted. The last thing they wanted was to be discrete.

When the wall dividing East and West Berlins was demolished in 1989, the land parcels were made available for sale and were snapped up by major corporations at

260

what were seen by many at well below market rates. Sony and Daimler Benz were the purchasers of the two significant parcels but other multi-national corporations hold land as well. There were 17 sites in all. They were attractive because the area is easily accessible – a number of subway and bus lines have their junction at Potsdamer Platz – and because of the Platz's past history. The Platz itself is on the periphery of the scheme and remains a traffic intersection. Perhaps it will become a place in itself when the development at Leipziger Platz and the Lenné-Dreieck site are completed.

The Berlin-oriented Hilmer–Sattler scheme gave way to a more global corporate one designed primarily by Renzo Piano and Christoph Kohlbecker. It resulted from a competition organized by Daimler Benz. The design includes high-rise corporate towers at both ends of the site but generally retains the build-to-the-property line requirements and height limits of the Hilmer–Sattler scheme. This new plan specified wide sidewalks, ground floor arcades and façades made of materials such as terracotta, limestone or clinker (reddish-brown bricks). At the same time much of the life generally associated with squares was internalized within the buildings.

Neue Potsdamer Strasse is a weak seam for the overall area and divides the site into two major parts with the Sony site, an island complex of eight buildings, to the north and the remainder of the site, the roughly pie-shaped 50-hectare part containing 19 buildings, to the south. This southern portion is an irregular grid of 10 streets, some new and some revived. At its centre now is the Marlene-Dietrich-Platz. Many of the corporations holding land organized their own design competitions within the general principles of the overall urban design but boosted by their own corporate interests. The result is a well-crafted set of prestigious buildings designed by internationally renowned architects. The Sony Center (2000) was designed by Helmut Jahn, the Hotel Grand Hyatt (1998) by Rafael Moneo, the Berlin Volksbank (1997) by Arata Isozaki and the Potsdamer Platz Arkaden (1997–8) – another example of internal, quasi-public space – by Richard Rogers amongst others. Renzo Piano designed six of the buildings himself (Figure 8.47).

The Sony Center (a 26,500-square metre site) consists of seven buildings with the interior Forum as its heart (see Figures 8.48 and 8.49). The Forum is an oblong plaza with a central fountain. It is covered by a tented, glass canopy supported on steel beams rather like the spokes on a bicycle wheel and surrounded by five buildings, all but one of which have concave façades encircling the Forum. The public space that was outside in both the Rogers and the Hilmer and Sattler schemes has become internalized and privatized (or, perhaps, private space has been made public). Shops and restaurants surround the Forum and the buildings include the Film Museum and the Esplanade residence (which consists of the breakfast room and the Emperors' room of the Esplanade Hotel which were moved 70 metres from their original location on air cushions). The upper floors of the buildings consist predominantly of offices and expensive apartments. On the interiors facing the internal court the surfaces are clad with mirrored glass. On the corner of the site, as a largely separate entity, is the 100-metre tall Sony Tower. Across the road from the Sony Tower is the 22-storey office and retail building, the Bürohochhaus am Potsdamer Platz,

Drawing by Thanong Poonteerakul

1. Sony Center
2. Bürohochhaus
3. IMAX Cinema
4. Marlene-Dietrich-Platz
5. Debis Haus
6. Tiergarten Tunnel access
7. National Library
8. Potsdamer Platz Arkaden
9. Philharmonic Hall
10. Musical Theatre

Figure 8.47 The Potsdamer Platz precinct in 2002.

designed by Hans Kolhoff. The two buildings form a high-rise entrance to Potsdamer Platz.

The Kohlhoff building steps down to a lower height away from the platz. Across Alte Potsdamer Strasse are the Weinhaus Huth and a complex of three office–commercial–residential buildings designed by Richard Rogers. The 3-storey Potsdamer Platz Arkaden, links them. Daimler City is a complex of buildings including an IMAX Theatre, the DaimlerChrysler Services Building, a Musical theatre, the Berliner Volksbank and the Neue Staatsbibliothek (National Library).

The district draws in 100,000 people daily and tourists flock there. It is a very different place to the conventional European square and represents a new type of increasingly common civic space – one controlled by private interests. While the buildings are clearly part of the global economy and architecture, considerable effort has been made to make them environmentally responsible. Roofs are grassed, rainwater is used to irrigate the landscaping and some grey water is recycled. The buildings have been designed to consume 50% less energy than conventional air-conditioned buildings.

(a)

(b)

Figure 8.48 The Sony Centre, Berlin. (a) Exterior view on Neue Potsdamer Strasse and (b) the Forum.

Figure 8.49 A view south towards Marlene-Dietrich-Platz with the Arkaden in the foreground.

As a feat of urban and architectural design, an extraordinary amount of coordinated work was accomplished in only 10 years. It is difficult in any urban design project to create the animated type of environment built piece-by-piece over a century or two, but the work of different architects gives a sense of variety to the Potsdamer Platz district. Is it, however, simply a twenty-first century Times Square, New York? (Rossi, 2000).

Major references

Balfour, Alan (1999). Octagon: the persistence of the ideal. In James Corner, ed., *Recovering Landscape: Essays in Contemporary Landscape Architecture.* New York: Princeton University Press, 87–100.

Davey, Peter (1998). Potsdamer Platz: development in Berlin. *Architectural Review* **205** (1223): 31–4.

James-Chakraborty, Kathleen (2000). *German Architecture for a Mass Audience.* London: Routledge.

Ladd, Brian (1997). *The Ghosts of Berlin: Confronting German History in the Urban Landscape.* London: Chicago University Press.

Scheer, Thorsten, Josef Paul Kleihues, Paul Kahlfeldt and Andrea Bärnreuther, eds. (2000). *City of Architecture of the City: Berlin 1900–2000.* Berlin: Nicolai.

A NOTE

The World Trade Center site development, New York, NY, USA: an architectural product or an all-of-a-piece urban design? (2002 – due for completion in 2011)

The political and design history of the World Trade Center as designed by Minoru Yamasaki with Emory Roth and Sons as a consultant has been ably documented (e.g. Ruchelman, 1977). So too has its highly innovative structural systems that collapsed under the impacts of the attack of 11 September 2001. The proposal for the World Trade Center site after the devastation represents contemporary architectural spatial thought. It is, however, premature to present a case study of the redevelopment of the site as the timeline for completion now extends to 2011. Given the number of changes that have already taken place in the short period of the scheme's design history, the project's implementation is likely to be subjected to more as unforeseen technical problems arise and political attitudes shift. In addition, many problems, such as dealing with the climatic conditions of Lower Manhattan, have yet to be resolved. The proposal does, however, represent our contemporary concern with the architecture of globalization and individual rights.

The diverse controversies of how best to create what is essentially a large architectural and landscape architectural project in an urban environment displays the multitude and complexity of factors and emotions that come to play at the intersect of the traditional design fields and urban design work. The final product, as a set of buildings, links and places, will be both cluster of individual objects in space and have an impact on its surroundings. The goal is to link the development of the Trade Center site to a series of 'vibrant, mixed-use communities'. Its ultimate catalytic effect is difficult to assess at present.

The design for the site already has a complex history. Max Protech, an art dealer, almost immediately after the destruction of the twin towers took the initiative and asked leading architects to submit proposals. The resulting exhibition drew thousands of visitors and ensured that 'design quality' became an important consideration in any proposal for the site. The Lower Manhattan Development Corporation (LMDC) in partnership with the Port Authority or New York and New Jersey has played a coordinating role. Their goal has been to have an 'open and inclusive' design process. In July 2002, the LMDC and Port Authority (with Bayer, Blinder, Belle and others as consultants) proposed six initial design elements for the development of the 16-acre (6.5-hectare site): a memorial plaza, a memorial square, a memorial triangle, a memorial garden, a memorial park and a memorial promenade. Two well-attended public hearings, an exhibit and the solicitation of comments resulted in over 12,000 responses. Some respondents wanted to keep the site empty but not rebuilding has not been a seriously considered option (Figure 8.50).

The LMDC and the Port Authority proceeded with selecting firms interested in doing the design for the site. Four hundred and six submissions were received of which seven teams were selected based on their perceived talents and reputations. Their charge was to create a 'soaring vision' for the site. Nine schemes were submitted and publicly exhibited drawing over a million visitors. After both a qualitative and quantitative analysis by the LMDC, the Port Authority and a number of consultants the number was reduced to two (the Memory Foundations scheme of Studio Daniel Libeskind and the World Cultural Center designed by THINK, a team led by Shingeru Ban, Frederick Schwartz, Ken Smith and Rafael Viñoly). The Mayor of New York and the Governor of the State of New York selected the scheme produced by Studio Daniel Libeskind as the winner in February 2003 overruling the jury selection of the THINK team proposal.

THINK proposed a cluster of facilities built around and above the footprints of the Trade Center towers. Two open lattice structures in their design were to have created a

Figure 8.50   Ground Zero: the World Trade Center site in May 2004.

base for soaring Towers of Culture. The transportation centre was located between the towers. The towers were proposed to rise from large reflecting pools that would allow light to penetrate into a retail and transit concourse. Shops were proposed for both the concourse and street levels to relate to and act as a seam with the surrounding community. A number of distinctive buildings would be designed by different architects: a Memorial, the 9/11 Interpretative Museum, a performing arts centre, an international conference centre, an open amphitheatre, viewing platforms and public facilities for education in the arts and sciences. Eight mid-rise office buildings and a hotel on the perimeter of the site were included in the programme in response to a perceived market demand.

The Libeskind design (with Gary Hack and Hargreaves Associates), 'Memory Foundations', unlike the World Trade Center, which had been an island, picked up on the grid pattern of Manhattan. It left a portion of the slurry wall exposed, as a symbol of strength, and included a memorial museum and cultural spaces, the 1776 feet (541 metres) with its spire tall 'Freedom Tower' (in form echoing the Statue of Liberty) as an element marking the spot of the terrorist act on the New York skyline and a variety of activity spaces below. A refined master plan was presented to the public in September 2003 (see Figure 8.51). It included commercial office space, retail development, its integration with the transportation network and public spaces and a new park. The new proposal replaced 1.34 million square metres of space in six buildings with 1 million in five, plus another million square metres of retail space and the same amount of space for a convention centre plus a September 11 Museum. The memorial forms the centre of the composition. An open competition was held for it drawing 5201 entries from professionals and lay-people. They ranged from

266

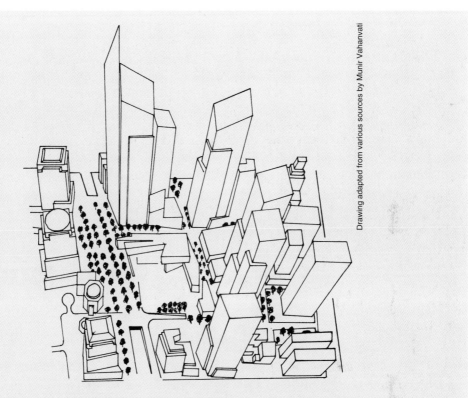

Drawing adapted from various sources by Munir Vahanvati

Figure 8.51 The refined Studio Libeskind master plan.

scaled down twin towers, to classical revival schemes, to parks.

The memorial commemorates the lives lost in the explosion of 26 February 1993 as well as those on 11 September 2001. The winning design, 'Reflecting Absence', selected by a jury headed by Vartan Gregorian formerly Director of the New York Public Library and including Maya Lin, Enrique Norton and David Rockefeller, is by Michael Arad, an Architect with the New York City Housing Authority assisted by Peter Walker, an internationally renowned landscape architect. It consists of two large voids containing pools with the ramps around them encompassing the footprints of the twin towers. The memorial is set in a field of deciduous trees, their coming into leaf each spring symbolizing the revival of spirit of New York. The Arad/Walker design eliminates the wedge of light and a cultural building that formed part of Libeskind's original scheme. Different architects will design other elements of the overall scheme (Figure 8.52).

Santiago Calatrava, selected unilaterally by the Port Authority from potential consultants who responded to a solicitation of credentials, has designed the $US2 billion PATH terminal. The design has soaring wings and a cathedral like space. It represents both architecture as high art and the architecture of structural dexterity. It, like the memorial, is very different to the design in the Libeskind competition-winning scheme. For example, it is a freestanding object in space rather than an attached building making a street line. It will be joined to a new transit hub designed by

Courtesy of the Lower Manhattan Development Corporation

Figure 8.52 The project with the memorial in place as proposed in 2004. Battery Park city is on the left.

British high-tech architect Nicholas Grimshaw. It is hoped that this hub of transit lines will spur adjacent developments in much the way that the renovation of Grand Central Station did in mid-town Manhattan.

Much has changed and continues to change. As Libeskind had no experience in designing skyscrapers, the Governor of New York State, George E. Pataki, and the developer insisted that his firm work with

David M. Childs of SOM, an expert on office building design. Working independently of Libeskind and with Guy Nordeson, Childs produced a number of designs including a 2000-foot high tower. He was, however, forced by Pataki to adopt part of Libeskind's ideas. The Freedom tower design is now considerably 'fatter' than in the original garden-filled design. The resulting collaboration seems to have been reasonably well received. The tower is now essentially a generic 70-storey office building in plan, 1500 feet in height with a 276-foot mast above it.

After all the law suits over insurance payments brought by Larry A. Silverstein who acquired a 99-year lease of the site only 6 months before the towers were destroyed, the jurisdictional battles, and international design competitions – a messy process (although not atypically so) – a final design seems to have emerged. There is a street-bounded complex of:

1 the Freedom Tower to replace the World Trade Center towers on the New York Skyline;
2 a multi-tiered train station;
3 a public park and memorial to the victims of the 2001 attack.

In addition, four adjacent city blocks have been allocated to office towers. This design opens up the site to views of the Hudson River and the Winter Garden of Battery Park City. Unlike Battery Park City it is designed as a series of architectural objects in space in opposition to the existing street-building pattern of New York City.

What kind of urban design is this new development? Is it an urban design at all? The THINK proposal was clearly an all-of-a-piece design. The Studio Libeskind design is partly an all-of-a-piece urban design with some components being designed by others and independently plugged in. It can also be considered to be a scheme plugged into an existing urban fabric with transportation routes linking the site to subway and suburban train routes, ferries and the southern tip of Manhattan. The idea of what was once an overall urban design scheme seems to be getting broken down into fragments. Thus in some ways, it is a design in which the components are being built separately according to the Studio Libeskind master plan but subject only to standard New York building codes.

How much the design will change between now and the date of completion is open to conjecture. The present design is considerably different to Libeskind's winning scheme of February 2003. The design guidelines submitted by Libeskind and urban designer Gary Hack in November 2003 have had little binding power as the four major clients have not been able to agree on them. Thus the Memorial, the Freedom Tower, the PATH Terminal, etc. are proceeding in their own ways bound only by the new streets and blocks created as part of the scheme. The desire not to be another collaborative design like Rockefeller Center, as popular as that urban place is, will certainly be fulfilled.

Major references

Forgey, Benjamin (2004). World Trade Center plans, rising above the squabbles. *Washington Post* (Sunday, 18 April): 1.

Goldberger, Paul (2003). *Up form Ground Zero: Politics, Architecture and the Rebuilding of New York*. New York: Random House.

Knack, Ruth (2003). Up close at the World Trade Center. *Planning* **69** (4): 11–13.

Libeskind, Daniel (2004). *Breaking Ground*. London: John Murray.

Stratis, William (2004). *World Trade Center – Memorial and Reconstruction Plans*. Corte Madera, CA: Ginko.

Precincts: Urban Renewal

Many total urban designs such as the Barbican or Rockefeller Center can be regarded as urban renewal projects and in the 1960s many 'slum' clearance and mass housing schemes certainly were. The concern here is for the schemes that involved the all-of-a-piece development of an existing urban precinct under one aegis without wholesale demolition. Such urban renewal processes generally involve the selective acquisition of properties by a municipal agency using the government power of eminent domain, the accumulation of small parcels into larger ones, and the selling of the parcels to a number of property developers for redevelopment according to specified guidelines. Sometimes, however, it is a private developer who has organized the accumulation of sites.

The power of governments to lead such activities varies from country to country. Much depends on the laws specifying how land is owned and can be acquired. In democratic countries the government power to acquire land is very much restricted by law but in totalitarian countries it is absolute. In many places a *laissez-faire* attitude towards development prevails. The two examples included here, however, represent coordinated efforts to enhance the quality of urban precincts.

The first case study is of a superblock scheme and the second the upgrading of a traditional suburban downtown. The first, Charles Center in Baltimore, is important because not only did it show what can be done in American cities in crisis but also because it had a major catalytic effect on the development of central Baltimore. The second, Glendale in California, shows what can be achieved by a couple of tenacious people with a vision of what might be and the stamina required to push ahead to fulfil it. It is also part of a larger phenomenon.

Many metropolises during the last quarter of the twentieth century experienced the development of the new suburban downtowns or 'edge cities' (Garreau, 1991). These developments were spurred by changes in accessibility based on new highways in particular, but also subway systems and now, reputedly, e-mail. Some of them have involved the redevelopment of suburban shopping streets into major centres (e.g. Bethesda, Maryland, and Walnut Creek, California). Others have seen the intensification of existing suburban shopping malls until they have the mixed-use attributes, and even the density, of existing downtown centres. Glendale is an example of an all-of-a-piece transformation of a decaying suburban centre into a lively 'downtown'.

Major references

Frieden, Bernard J. and Lynne B. Sagalyn (1991). *Downtown, Inc.: How America Rebuilds Cities*. Cambridge, MA: MIT Press.

Garreau, Joel (1991). *Edge Cities: Life on the New Frontier*. New York: Doubleday.

Melnick, Scott (1987). The urbanization of the suburbs. *Building Design Construction* **28** (3): 70–7.

Case Study

Charles Center, Baltimore, Maryland, USA: a central city redevelopment (1954–70)

It is difficult to imagine how later developments such as Inner Harbor (1968 to the present; see Figure 8.72) and the even later baseball stadium (1988) could have taken place without the earlier development of Charles Center. By 1994, Charles Center's success as a catalyst in spurring other developments meant that it was no longer the heart of Baltimore. Few urban redevelopments can claim that type of success. It is also an example of an urban renewal project that did not begin by totally clearing the site and then rebuilding it *de novo*.

Baltimore, like many other American cities, found itself facing strong competition from suburban centres from the 1950s onwards. Department store sales in the city dropped 10% between 1952 and 1957. There was a similar decrease in tax revenues. The office space occupancy rate was, however, healthy (97%) suggesting that the area had potential for renewal if problems with the aging infrastructure and decaying buildings could be addressed. No new building of consequence had been erected in the downtown area for 20 years.

In 1954, the business community formed the Committee for Downtown, Inc. A year later the Greater Baltimore Committee, Inc. (GBC), a private business group was established. The groups merged to form a non-profit, private-planning group, the Planning Council of the GBC. It became, in essence, a planning consultancy. Being a private and local group not only was it removed from much political infighting but it knew Baltimore. It also had considerable energy, if for no other reason than it saw the future

of the investments of its members at stake. The Planning Council hired Dr David Wallace, later a principal in the Philadelphia urban design firm of Wallace, McHarg, Roberts and Todd, to develop a design for a sloping, 33-acre (13-hectare) area in the heart of Baltimore linking the retail, financial and government districts of the city. He, in turn, brought on board other consultants such as George Kostritsky and Dennis Durden.

The GBC was aware of the work of Victor Gruen in Rochester, New York and his proposal for Fort Worth in Texas (Gruen, 1964). The latter design consisted of a ring road around the centre of the city with parking garages feeding off it (see Figure 8.53). The whole area within this loop was proposed to be a car-free pedestrian precinct. The GBC wanted something similar but implementable, financially and politically. On a smaller scale they got it.

The goal of the GBC team was not only to revitalize the blocks that were to be later called Charles Center, but for any developments there to also encourage investment on adjacent sites. The objective was to have a project large enough to have a significant impact, but not large enough to fill all the potential demand that might be generated by an improved physical environment. By 'improvement' was meant that access to downtown offices and shops had to be clear and easy, that parking had to be convenient to destinations and that the buildings had to be both modern and look modern.

The legal responsibility for achieving the specified development goals lay in the

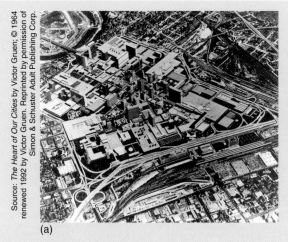

Source: *The Heart of Our Cities* by Victor Gruen; © 1964 renewed 1992 by Victor Gruen. Reprinted by permission of Simon & Schuster Adult Publishing Corp.

(a)   (b)

Figure 8.53   The Fort Worth plan of Victor Gruen, 1958. (a) A bird's eye view and (b) a ground level view.

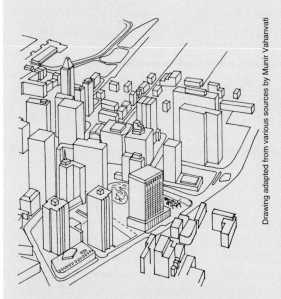

Drawing adapted from various sources by Munir Vahanvati

Figure 8.54   The site before development seen from the north.

hands of the Baltimore Urban Renewal Agency. The redevelopment was designated a Title I project requiring supervision by a number of Federal (central government) agencies. The project was, however, run by an office directed by J. Jefferson Miller. It evolved

into the Charles Center-Inner Harbor Management team responsible for the coordination of the actions taken by government agencies and by private property interests. It was the first such organization in the United States. The design ideas came mainly from Wallace.

Five important buildings on the site were retained (three office buildings, a hotel and a parking structure representing 47% of the assessed value of the site). Business in them continued while redevelopment took place. The remainder of the site was divided into 16 parcels large enough to appeal to a broad range of potential property developers. In order to assemble the parcels 148 separate acquisitions involving 216 different parcels had to be made. Three hundred and fifty businesses involving 8789 jobs had to be relocated. Some organizations were relocated to other buildings on the site and then moved back to newly erected buildings; for others temporary accommodations were found off the site (Figure 8.54).

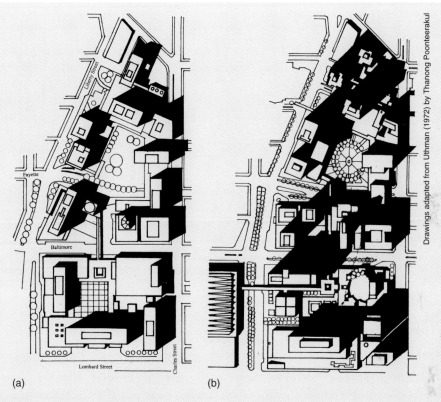

(a)   (b)

Figure 8.55 Charles Center site and plans. (a) The 1957 proposal and (b) the site as developed by 1972.

The site is bisected by Fayette Street (later partially bridged by a building and deck so that two superblocks were linked into one to form the basis of the design). The original design (1957) had clear Modernist overtones with its considerable amount of parks and plazas (see Figure 8.55a), but the one that evolved by 1972 (see Figure 8.55) was significantly denser. Forty changes, each approved by the City Council, were made to the original conceptual design based largely on a more thorough understanding of the property market.

The components of the site were linked by an elevated walkway – a skyway – made possible by the 60-foot (18-metre) slope of the site. At the same time, buildings were built to the property line on the streets so that Charles Center was both an island and integrated with surrounding areas. The sites were disposed of in a number of ways: competition based on team credentials, land price competition, negotiated sales and negotiated leases. Each site had guidelines and controls written in a section of a legally adopted plan titled, 'Aesthetic control and approval of plans and specification' (Baltimore Urban Renewal and Housing Agency, 1959). The controls stipulated the building use, the maximum bulk and the height of each development (see Figure 8.56 for one important block). Some flexibility in terms of the modification of site boundaries was allowed but none in terms

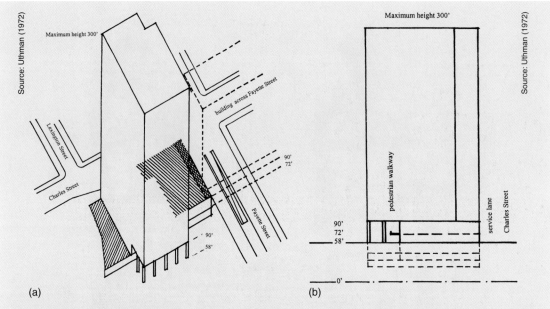

Figure 8.56 Building control envelope for the building at the corner of Fayette and Charles Streets. (a) Isometric drawing from the northwest and (b) view from the west.

of height and bulk. These controls became the basis for specific agreements with individual developers. In the negotiated dispositions many changes took place but in design competitions few. Much depended on what an architectural review board decided.

The first office building was selected by competition. The goal was to have an internationally renowned architect design the scheme in order to set a high standard. The winning entry (of six) was that proposed by Metropolitan Structures of Chicago. The architect was Ludwig Mies van der Rohe. Later developments were selected in a number of ways: by design competition and review, by displaced site tenants, by government agencies or by owner-builders. They included a variety of building types – hotels and housing – but they were mainly commercial structures. The most adventurous building was the Mechanics Theatre, seating 1800 people, designed by John Johansen.

By the late 1960s, Charles Center was largely built-out. It included 1.8 million square feet of office space, 800 hotel rooms, the Mechanics Theatre, 367 apartment units and parking for 4000 cars. The number of jobs increased to 17,000 creating a spin-off in terms of shopping demand. Perhaps the greatest success was that 93% of the businesses in Charles Center were relocated without liquidating. The project, as intended, also generated considerable growth around it – apartment buildings and offices. One of the companies that lost out on the original design competition for a building simply crossed the road and built a building for itself. The process by which Charles Center was implemented also demonstrates how public–private partnerships in redevelopment can be best achieved. Unfortunately Baltimore did not learn as much from Charles Center as it might have done. Some of the excesses of 1980s and early 1990s

(a)

(b)

Figure 8.57 Charles Center. (a) An early model viewed from the north and (b) Hopkins Plaza in 1993, part of the skyway system can be seen on the right.

275

development led to the construction of buildings that were (and are) much under-occupied (Figure 8.57).

Although it remained remarkably intact for 40 years, the scheme has been altered in a number of ways since it was completed. The weakest point of the design has been the sky-way system. Some seldom-used parts have been demolished. It still remains the most efficient way to move around the site, but efficiency is not necessarily what people seek in moving around downtowns unless they are drivers! People prefer to walk at ground level where the life of the city is. Other changes have also taken place. The section of the building spanning Fayette Street has been demolished and all three plazas are being redesigned. The goal is to enhance their utility and their use. The strongest part of the scheme was its financial success; the city's bond rating was increased from A to A1. As an architectural work it was very much a product of its time. Wallace was the recipient of the American Planning Association's Distinguished Leadership Award in 2003.

Major references

Baltimore Urban Renewal and Housing Agency (1959). *Charles Center Urban Renewal Plan*. Baltimore: The Agency.

Blumberg, Andrew (2003). *Big Dreams, Great Vision*. Johns Hopkins Professional Studies Web Edition.

Millspaugh, Martin, ed. (1964). *Baltimore's Charles Center. A Case Study in Downtown Development*. Washington, DC: The Urban Land Institute.

Uthman, Fuad A. (1972). Charles Center, Baltimore: a case study of architectural controls through mandatory design review with an examination of architectural controls within the urban renewal process and through regulation. Philadelphia, PA: Unpublished doctoral dissertation, University of Pennsylvania.

Wallace, David (1964). The planning process. Baltimore's Charles Center – a case study of downtown renewal. *ULI Technical Bulletin 31*. Washington, DC: The Urban Land Institute.

Wallace, David (2004). *Urban Planning/My Way*. Chicago, IL: American Planning Association.

CASE STUDY

Central Glendale, California, USA: a traditional suburban downtown turned into an edge city (1975–90, 1994 to the present)

Glendale is a suburb of Los Angeles lying at the base of the Verduga Mountains. It has a population of about 200,000. Its central district is located on Brand Boulevard just off the Ventura Freeway that connects it to the region. The boulevard is a broad street that once had streetcars/trams running down its centre. Developed by Leslie Carlton Brand in the 1920s it was lined by 2- and 3-storey mixed-use buildings that by the 1950s and 1960s had deteriorated due to the lack of entrepreneurial spirit and absentee landlordism. Land values dropped to as low as $6 to $7 a square foot. The total land value of the Central Business District of Glendale decreased from $31.2 million in 1950 to $20 million in 1970 despite inflation and even though Glendale was and is a relatively affluent city.

The City Redevelopment Agency was founded in 1972. Its actions received strong support from the city council; its board membership consisted of the councillors! Despite the citizenry's strong opposition (in the name of private enterprise) to a redevelopment project in downtown Glendale and to the use of the city's power of eminent domain to acquire land, the agency moved ahead. The initiative seems to have resided in two sets of hands: those of Jim Rez, the city manager and executive director of the Glendale Redevelopment Agency and Susan F. Shick, his deputy, a transplant from the east coast. The city council was the sponsor of the redevelopment of Glendale.

The city used its power of eminent domain to assemble a 20-acre (8-hectare) site on Colorado Street, which runs across Brand Boulevard at the southern end of Glendale's CBD, for the Glendale Galleria, a major shopping centre. As an incentive for the development the city took two actions:

1 it built a 4400-spot parking garage;
2 it created a tax increment financing district.

These actions encouraged a property developer (John S. Griffith Company, later Donahue Schribner) to build the Galleria, a shopping centre. It was constructed in 1976. The Galleria was then a catalyst for other development and the company insisted that later developers and their architects toe the line in meeting design guidelines in order to maintain a high level of aesthetic and general environmental quality in the precinct. The tax increment going to the Redevelopment Agency in 1985 was $5.5 million. This sum could be leveraged 8:1 in the bond market for financing public projects in the downtown area. This meant that the revenue from sales taxes could be spent on the remainder of Glendale.

A CBD study, initiated by Rez in 1975, led to a plan for a rejuvenated Brand Boulevard.

The Redevelopment Agency began to aggressively acquire land for possible redevelopment. New office buildings attracted to the location began to be built at the northern end of the boulevard off the Ventura Freeway. At the southern end, Galleria 2 was built and proved to be highly successful. These successes led to ELS Architects of Berkeley being hired to develop a conceptual design and design guidelines to achieve it. ELS received a 1986 Design Award from *Progressive Architecture* for its work in Glendale.

Through a series of public workshops, ELS Architects and the Glendale Redevelopment Authority identified 10 goals for the district. The 10 goals were: to create a downtown identity, to encourage mixed-uses, to enhance cultural facilities, to encourage pedestrian movement, to create open space, to control vehicular movements, to promote public transit use, to provide a wide range of development opportunities, to make the development economically sound and to increase the tax base of the city. Perhaps, above all, the goal was to give visual coherence to the development. ELS Architects produced a conceptual plan (see Figure 8.58) and design guidelines (see Figure 8.59 for an example) that would achieve the ends specified. The Redevelopment Agency created a strategic plan to market the area.

The conceptual design became the development control plan in conjunction with detailed plans. The plan divided central Glendale into three sections with Brand Boulevard as the backbone. The two roads parallel to it form a loop circulation system off which the parking garages are located. A major financial centre has developed in the northern third. It consists of high-rise bank buildings housing corporations such as Sears Savings Bank, American Savings,

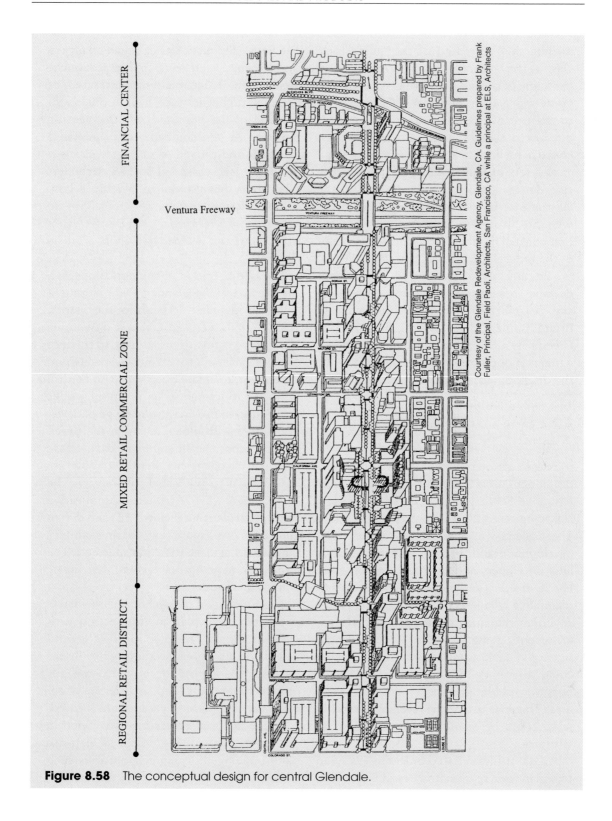

FINANCIAL CENTER

Ventura Freeway

MIXED RETAIL COMMERCIAL ZONE

REGIONAL RETAIL DISTRICT

Courtesy of the Glendale Redevelopment Agency, Glendale, CA. Guidelines prepared by Frank Fuller, Principal, Field Paoli, Architects, San Francisco, CA while a principal at ELS, Architects

Figure 8.58 The conceptual design for central Glendale.

Courtesy of the Glendale Redevelopment Agency, Glendale, CA. Guidelines prepared by Frank Fuller, Principal, Field Paoli, Architects, San Francisco, CA while a principal at ELS, Architects

DEFINITION OF OPEN SPACES

Use buildings, arcades and landscaping to create strongly defined edges and a sense of three-dimensional containment for urban open spaces and plazas.

Discussion

Open spaces, plazas and courtyards in cities take their definition from the strength of their edges. If the edges are weak, the spaces seem to be amorphous or to lack focus. Streets alone do not define an urban open space. The most memorable and successful open spaces are those defined most strictly by the facades of buildings, bosques of trees, garden walls, arcades or other elements having strong character and clear geometry. Examples of historically successful spaces of this type are Piazza San Marco in Venice, Rockefeller Plaza in New York, Union Square in San Francisco, Arco Plaza in Los Angeles and Los Angeles County Art Museum Plaza. It is difficult to think of any successful urban spaces that lack this definition. In fact, it seems that without such definition we tend not to recognize that the space exists.

Space definition and enrichment within open spaces can be achieved by the use of landscape, hardscape and water features. Fountains, pools and defined waterways can be combined with planting and pavement areas to visually and functionally define and enliven urban open spaces.

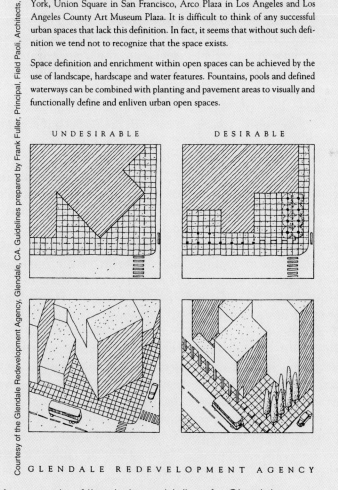

UNDESIRABLE   DESIRABLE

GLENDALE REDEVELOPMENT AGENCY

URBAN DESIGN GUIDELINES

Figure 8.59   An example of the design guidelines for Glendale.

the First Interstate Bank and Valley National Bank. They are clustered around a plaza a block off the Ventura Freeway. The central third is mixed-use. Retail shops, offices, hotels and housing are located on Brand Boulevard with the parking garages behind them. The adjacent streets have bungalows opposite the parking garages. They house professional offices as well as being residences and act as a buffer between the busyness of Brand Boulevard and the residential areas on either side adjacent to the urban core of the city. The southern third of the area is a major regional retail district. It houses the Gallerias, major department stores and smaller-scale retail buildings.

A number of urban design issues were addressed. These included how the street edge could be defined, how open spaces could be enclosed, how shelter could be provided for pedestrians, how the apparent bulk of tall buildings could be visually reduced, how street corners could be enhanced, how blank façades at ground level could be avoided. The design guidelines were advisory in nature but gave the Redevelopment Authority bargaining power in evaluating and deciding on design proposals. The goal of obtaining a high-quality landscape was emphasized throughout the design and construction process. Brand Boulevard today shows it (see Figure 8.60b). The original design standards set a precedent so the design review process allowed no major exceptions from them. Property developers and their architects know this situation so their demands to do things in their own way have been low. Delays in obtaining approval for their proposals are costly.

Much development took place in Glendale during the late 1970s and 1980s. By mid-1985 downtown property values had soared to $470 million (from $99.7 million in 1972) and 9000 new jobs had been created. The demand for development in Glendale remained high throughout the 1980s. The area has had its ups and downs since then as competition from surrounding areas has increased. The Redevelopment Authority in Glendale had, however, moved early and had to a large extent captured the market.

How well has all the effort put into Glendale worked out? Today Brand Boulevard is a quietly successful destination, comfortable, lively and safe. The Galleria was amongst the most successful shopping centres in the United States between 2000 and 2004. In early 2004, a proposal was made to build yet another shopping centre in the area that would be in direct competition with the Galleria if it goes ahead. So in these terms the urban renewal work in Glendale has been highly successful.

The Glendale experience shows a number of things. A handful of people with strong marketable ideas can achieve much. Clear design guidelines, logically derived and based on empirical evidence are powerful tools in helping to achieve a high-quality environment. Tax increment financing can be used effectively to generate the finances needed to develop and, above all, in some cases maintain a well-designed public environment and facilities. Perhaps most of all, a streamlined approval process encourages development. These are powerful lessons. Yet lives change and places change. Plans cannot be static. A slowdown in office development spurred new actions under a new Planning Director, John McKenna.

In 1994, Alexander Cooper, of Cooper Robertson based in New York, was hired to develop a strategic plan for Glendale based on Cooper's successful efforts at Battery

(a)

(b)

Figure 8.60 Glendale in 1993. (a) The Glendale skyline and (b) Brand Boulevard.

Park City and his work for the Disney Corporation. The client in this instance was the City and Glendale Partners, a consortium of corporate executives. After considerable public consultation a plan for the city has been developed. What this effort demonstrates is that cities are constantly in flux if they are doing well economically and the urban design process is not a one-shot deal. As part of a city's development process urban designing is a continuous activity as pointed out in Chapter 5.

Major references

Attoe, Wayne and Donn Logan (1989). Phoenix and Glendale: catalytic design is strategic. In *American Urban Architecture: Catalysts in the Design of Cities.* Berkeley and Los Angeles: University of California Press, 106–17.
Crooks, Cheryl (1985). Glendale's surprising rebirth. *Los Angeles* (July): unpaginated reprint.
Glendale Redevelopment Agency (1986). Urban design information. Glendale: The Agency.
Lewis, Sylvia (1996). Mr. Precedent. *Planning* **62** (8): 10–15.

Precincts: Campuses

Many of the myriad new campus designs of the second half of the twentieth century were haphazard affairs. Some of them underwent a transition during the 1990s as university administrators tried to make them attractive places for students (and for their parents who were paying to send them there). Some were total urban designs; others were all-of-a-piece designs. Sometimes it is difficult to tell. The Universidad Nacional Autónoma de Mexico (UNAM) (see Figure 8.61) is an example.

Originally founded in the 1550s, the present UAM campus was built between 1950 and 1953 by a design team headed by José García Villagrán, Mario Pani and

Figure 8.61 The Universidad Nacional Autónoma de Mexico with the library on the left with mosaic façades by Juan O'Gorman.

Enrique del Moral. It is a more purist Modernist spatial design than Universidad Central de Venezuela with buildings located within an overall orthogonal geometry. The design of the buildings involved over 150 architects but whether the result is a total or all-of-a-piece urban design is open to debate based on perceptions of whether it was really one large team that designed it or a variety of architects. The State University of New York (SUNY) at Purchase is clearly an all-of-a-piece design although some observers might regard it as a plug-in urban design.

The term 'campus', as has already been observed, has been applied to other development types than universities. In common with universities they consist of sets of buildings located in landscaped, park-like surroundings. They may be located in the heart of cities or on the periphery. The Denver Technology Center (DTC), on the outskirts of the Denver, Colorado metropolitan area is one of those developments on a green-field site that is often considered to be a campus. DTC and SUNY at Purchase are the examples of campus planning and design that are included here.

CASE STUDY

The State University of New York, Purchase, NY, USA: a university campus (1967 to the present)

Purchase College is one of SUNY's 64 tertiary educational institutions. It is located 30 miles (50 kilometres) from New York City near White Plains and New Rochelle on what was a 500-acre (200-hectare) farm. The college has a general education programme but it is best known for its conservatory programmes in theatre arts, film-making and music, and the visual arts. The first students were admitted in 1968 into the Continuing Education Program; juniors were admitted in 1971, and the first freshmen in 1973. The development of the campus has gone in fits and starts; enrolments have fluctuated and so has its funding.

Purchase is a product of the expansionist education policies in New York State under the leadership of Governor Nelson Rockefeller. While SUNY Albany was a total urban design, SUNY Purchase is an all-of-a-piece one with a strong basic infrastructure as a point of departure. Like SUNY Albany, its central idea is that of an internationally renowned architect. In this case it was Edward Larabee Barnes. He was appointed to be the master architect, but other equally well-regarded architects designed many of the individual buildings following specified guidelines. Barnes, himself, designed a number of the buildings as well. The capital cost to the state was $US87 million but additional funds were obtained from private donors such as Roy A. Neuberger whose art collection forms the backbone of the Museum of Art at the university (Figure 8.62).

Barnes' master plan placed the main buildings along a 900-foot (274-metre) court. The central buildings are on a raised platform that crosses a road, Lincoln Drive.

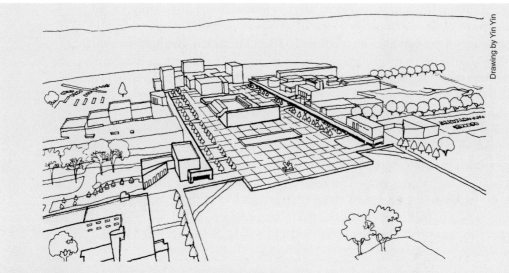

Drawing by Yin Yin

Figure 8.62 A bird's eye view of the massing of the SUNY at Purchase.

Terminating the axis at one end is a gymnasium and at the other is the Performing Arts Center (see Figure 8.63). In between are a rectangular meadow, the Great Court and the library. Perpendicular to the platform and at regular intervals are 30-foot (9-metre) wide pedestrian streets. Between them are the academic buildings. The buildings are partially connected by 'colonnades' lined by trees. Thus in the plan their sites were defined by the circulation network provided by the colonnades that some critics find akin to those of Thomas Jefferson at the University of Virginia.

The design guidelines allowed each building to be designed as an individual commission. They had, however, to front the colonnades for the distance between streets (i.e. 130 feet; 40 metres). The main design control was in limiting the exteriors of the buildings to three materials and colours: grey-brown brick, grey-tinted glass and dark grey anodized aluminium. The last was, at that time, the material of modernity.

The architects were given complete freedom to create any geometric form they desired providing the programmatic requirements were met. The overall result is that the site has the rigidity of Mies van der Rohe's Illinois Institute of Technology but not its rigidity of building forms.

The major building on the campus is the Performing Arts Center designed by Barnes. It has a cluster of four theatres with fly towers rising above the campus. They are a Concert Hall (seating capacity of 1372), the PepsiCo Theater (seating capacity of 713; designed by Ming Cho Lee), the Recital Hall (seating capacity of 680), the Abbott Kaplan Theater (seating capacity of 500) and the Organ Room (seating capacity of 225). The complex hosts about 600 performances a year attracting 125,000 visitors. The list of architects who designed the other buildings is impressive. The Humanities and Social Sciences Building (1974) was designed by Robert Venturi of Venturi and Rauch. Paul Rudolph designed

(a)

(b)

Figure 8.63 Two views of the Purchase campus. (a) The colonnade and (b) a view of the deck with the Performing Arts Center on the right.

the Natural Sciences Building, Gawthmey, Henderson and Siegel the dormitory, Gunnar Bierkerts the School of Dancing building (1977) and Philip Johnson and John Burgee the Neuberger Museum of Art (1971). Despite this diversity of design talent, the campus has a remarkably severe character! In addition, the cheap materials

285

(a)   (b)

Figure 8.64   The architecture of the Purchase campus. (a) The Natural Sciences Building and (b) the Social Sciences Building, both seen from one of the colonnades.

chosen because of the desire to reduce upfront costs have proven to be a burden on operating expenses (Figure 8.64).

Whether or not universities should be located on greenfield sites poorly related to an urban area is another question. They are certainly easier to build and it is certainly easier to provide parking for cars in such locations than on an urban site. They can be designed to be spacious and SUNY Purchase certainly is. It also provides outstanding educational programmes but it can be a dull place to be. It stands aloof from its immediate surroundings. Is that a worthwhile educational objective?

In 1998, a second master plan was developed. It reflected changes that had taken place since the first one was produced 30 years earlier. Kevin Horn and Andrew Goldman, architects, designed it. This plan was drawn up through much greater consultation with department heads and teaching staff than the original one and is more flexible than it. It appears to have little relationship to the original plan's central ideas. Instead, in rather a Modernist fashion, it will fill in open spaces with display buildings. The new plan has, however, to deal with the changing economic conditions in the provision of higher education. The university is under increasing pressure to become financially independent. The implications for its future development and design are unclear. What is clear is that the design philosophy behind the Barnes scheme has set a precedent for other universities to follow (e.g. the University of Miami in Coral Gables). Purchase itself is not one of them. Short-run capital costs and donors' wishes will dominate the physical development of the university.

Major references

Dober, Richard P. (1992). *Campus Planning*. New York: John Wiley, 120–1, 130–1.

Goldberger, Paul (1997). *The Architecture of Purchase College*. Purchase, NY: Neuberger Museum of Art.

Case Study

The Denver Technological Center, Denver, Colorado, USA: a business campus for the automobile age, a 'downtown' in a park (1964 to the present)

The DTC is one of the first and largest sub-urban office parks in the United States. George M. Wallace, a property developer, initiated the project on I-25, the major highway along Colorado's Front Range, where it intersects with I-225 south of the city of Denver (see Figure 8.65). The site also has convenient access to Denver International Airport. Originally a 40-acre (16-hectare) site bought by Wallace for $80,000 in 1964 in order to relocate his office from central Denver, it is now 884 acres (355 hectares) in extent. It expanded in a piecemeal way over the years. Wallace, marketing aggressively, attracted key companies (e.g. Honeywell and Control Data) to locate in the park in 1965. He also heavily promoted the development of nearby Arapahoe County Airport. By 1981, 5 million square feet (460,000 square metres) of buildings had been completed. Much development occurred subsequently. By 1997, DTC had over 600 companies, large and small, located there and an employment figure approaching 20,000 people. The density is thus low by urban standards.

The DTC has had much more thought put into its design than most such parks. It has been and is an all-of-a-piece development rather than a *laissez faire* one. The original designer was Carl A. Worthington, an architect whose offices were located in Boulder, but after 1990 many other consultants have been involved. Five major parkways with landscaped medians provide the armature for the design. The site was then divided into 12 superblocks of mixed-use development. The highest density of development is at the centre of each superblock around a pedestrian open space. Each building has its own parking lot under it or in a surface lot surrounded by landscaped berms. The purpose was to make vehicles easily accessible but also unobtrusive. No on-street parking is allowed.

Each superblock is about 30 acres (12 hectares) in size – the equivalent of 16 to 20 city blocks. The development of each has started from the periphery and worked towards the centre which becomes a pedestrian square surrounded by buildings. The areas between the superblocks are parks with ponds and pedestrian tracks. In total, the open space comprises about 40% of the land area of the development. Most of the buildings are office buildings but hotels, retail shops and residential buildings are concentrated at important locations.

Each site is sold by the developers to private organizations that build their own buildings using their own architects. The site infrastructure is built and maintained by DTC Development Properties from taxes raised through a Special Taxing District whose boundaries are conterminous with those of the DTC. Sub-developers are required to build the internal infrastructure of their sites as well as the sidewalks and streetscape. The ease of access and strict design guidelines ensuring environmental quality appear to have been major attractions for corporations to locate in the DTC. All construction proposals have to be reviewed by an Architectural Control Committee that has six regular members all of

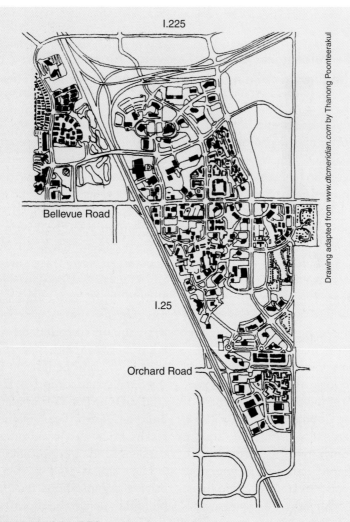

Drawing adapted from *www.dtcmeridian.com* by Thanong Poonteerakul

Figure 8.65 The plan of the DTC.

whom are planning and/or design professionals. They strive to ensure new buildings
are well designed.

The design guidelines specify that each
site should have a minimum of 30% open
space. Parking space cannot comprise more
than 40% of the site and the building no
more than 40%. The purpose is to ensure
the park-like setting. Pedestrian and vehicular access has to be segregated on each site
with the entrances to buildings being

obvious. The major aesthetic control is in the
height of buildings. Many suburban areas
in the United States (and many other countries) have a great fear of high-rise buildings
because they are seen to be representing
the traditional city centres that many suburban residents of the era fled. In the DTC
the height of buildings is restricted to eight
stories. The result is that the buildings are all
built to that height with flat tops and have a
block-like appearance (see Figure 8.66).

Figure 8.66 The architecture of the DTC.

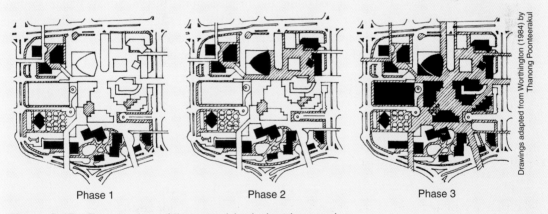

Phase 1   Phase 2   Phase 3

Drawings adapted from Worthington (1984) by Thanong Poonteerakul

Figure 8.67 The phasing of the superblock development.

Each development node is built phase-by-phase (see Figure 8.67). In Phase One, the key buildings within a superblock are constructed and connected to the overall road network. Phase Two involves the building of the sidewalks along the streets and Phase Three, the building of the superblock plazas and pedestrian malls.

Unlike Brasília and Battery Park City, the phasing of the development of the super-blocks has been from the outside inwards.

As the DTC development is on a green-field site it did not involve all the machinations of redevelopment in built-up areas of cities. It was, however, and still is, fought by local residents who perceive that they will be affected by the changes taking place. In addition, the DTC site is under two different political jurisdictions. The planners and developers of the DTC seem to have played the tax benefits accrued to each administration as bargaining tools with great success. One of the catalytic effects of the DTC has been to drive the growth of Denver south along the I-25 corridor. With Denver's CBD as one anchor and the DTC as the other, there has been considerable infilling between the two. The side effects of increased traffic,

air pollution and haphazard development have yet to be addressed. The question is: 'Whose responsibilities are they?'

Major references

Leonard, Stephen J. and Thomas J. Noel (1990). *Denver: Mining Camp to Metropolis*. Niwot: University of Colorado Press.

Worthington, Carl A. (1984). The Denver Technological Center: evolution of a pedestrian oriented community. *Ekistics* **51** (306): 260–6.

Precincts: Housing

Large-scale housing projects tend to be total urban designs. They are certainly the ones that have attracted the most attention from the architectural press. A few high profile, all-of-a-piece housing designs have been carried out. The housing areas of Seaside have already been mentioned. A few of the best-known examples were developed under the auspices of the Internationale Bauausstellung in Berlin during the 1980s (e.g. at Tegler Hafen and Stadtvillen an der Rauchstrasse). The case study here is of the second of these examples. Led by Rob Krier strong building design guidelines shaped it.

Major references

Kleihues, Josef Paul (1987). *Internationale Bauausstellung Berlin 1987: Projektübersicht*. Berlin: IBA.

Minton, Anna (2002). *Building Balanced Communities*. London: Royal Institute of Chartered Surveyors.

CASE STUDY

Stadtvillen an der Rauchstrasse, Berlin, Germany: a demonstration project (1980–6)

The Stadtvillen an der Rauchstrasse, located in the southern Tiergarten neighbourhood of Berlin, was carried out as part of the Internationale Bauausstellung. The developer was Land Berlin with Sozialer

Mietwohnungsbau financing the project. The overall urban design plan was developed by Rob Krier who also wrote the design guidelines for each of the buildings located on the site. In many ways the project is a

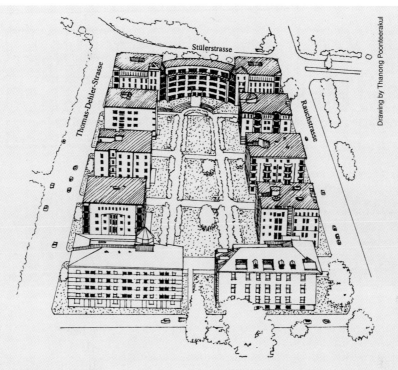

Drawing by Thanong Poonteerakul

Figure 8.68   A bird's eye view of the Stadtvillen an der Rauchstrasse.

response to the massive, Pruitt-Igoe type housing schemes of the 1960s and 1970s in Germany (particularly in East Berlin).

Nine new buildings form the group with the tenth being the previously existing Norwegian Botschaft that encloses the southwestern corner (see Figure 8.68). Each building is slightly set back from the street with a lawn and avenue of trees on the street front. The 1-metre high and 4-metre wide slopes around each building site provide a platform for the apartment blocks and privacy for the ground floor apartments. The ratio of distance between buildings and building height is 1.3 to 1.5. The purpose was to balance the privacy and natural surveillance requirements of the residents. The buildings are situated around a rectangular internal garden of lawns, trees and a children's playground. A rectangular pathway

with a semi-circular end parallels the buildings and loops around this internal court. Pedestrian/vehicular roads cut across the court in a north–south direction.

The buildings of the complex are a variation of the historic building types – embassies and expensive villas – that had existed on the site before the war. Other than the building in the northwestern corner that matches the Norwegian Botschaft in massing and the 'headhouse' designed by Rob Krier all the other six buildings are variations on a specified building envelop in the form of a cube. They were designed by renowned architects: Henry Nielebock, Giorgio Grassi, Brenner/Tonon, Francy Valentiny/Hubaert Hermann, Hans Holein and by Rob Krier himself. The headhouse consists of two cubes linked by a curved component concave to the interior of the block. The main entrance to the

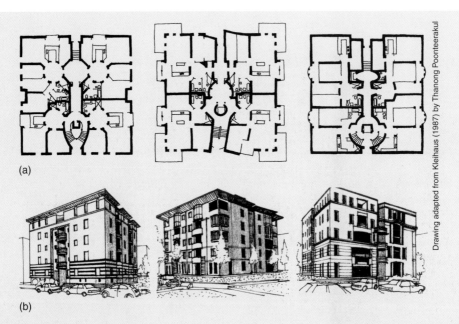

Drawing adapted from Kleihaus (1987) by Thanong Poonteerakul

Figure 8.69 Examples of the villas; Stadtvillen an der Rauchstrasse. (a) Floor plans of villas by Francy Valentiny/Hubaert Hermann, Hans Holein and Rob Krier and (b) sketches of the villas by Francy Valentiny/Hubaert Hermann, Hans Holein and Rob Krier.

Figure 8.70 View of the interior park in 1989 with the villa designed by Brenner/Tonon on the left and the Stülerstrasse building by Rob Krier on the right.

and Preiser, 1994). In this case, however, the individual architects had considerable freedom of aesthetic action within the cube form dictated by Krier. The disposition of apartment units was also a constraint. What the individual architects could not do is have geometric forms that deviated from that cubical form. Critics attack such controls on the grounds that it reduces architectural design to simply the treatment of façades. Krier purposefully set out to achieve a unity in his design in keeping with the tradition of much neighbourhood design. He achieved it.

Financially, it would have made more sense to have increased the total built area on the site. It is a complex well loved by its residents and much visited by architectural tourists. On a small site it displays the work of some prominent architects. The fragmented nature of the adjacent developments means that the streets act as boundaries to the complex rather than seams joining it to the Tiergarten neighbourhood. The scheme is, nevertheless, a good example of all-of-a-piece urban design. It is also a good example of Rob Krier's approach. It is repeated in other very different projects such as the high-density, high-rise De Resident (1989–2001) in The Hague. Architects as famous as those who worked on the Rauchstrasse project designed parts of the overall scheme there. They included Sjoert Soeters, Adolfo Natalini, César Pelli and Michael Graves (Figure 8.71).

Photograph by Jusuck Koh

Figure 8.71   De Resident, The Hague in 2004.

interior park of the complex passes underneath this building (Figure 8.69).

All the architects have stuck to the cube in their individual building designs. All the buildings have similar floor plans with four apartments per floor being served from a central core. The building with the greatest variation is that designed by Hans Holein (see the central images in Figure 8.70). An angled staircase and walls set at an angle in the centre of the façade break the strictly cubical form. The result is a simple, highly unified, internally focused scheme containing 239 apartments.

The rigidity of design guidelines prescribing the aesthetic characteristics of buildings is often challenged by architects (see Scheer

Major references

Broadbent, Geoffrey (1990). *Emerging Concepts in Urban Space Design*. London: Van Nostrand Reinhold (International), 303–5.

Kleihues, Josef Paul (1987). Stadtvillen an der Rauchstrasse. In *Internationale Bauausstellung Berlin 1987: Projektübersicht*. Berlin: IBA, 30–3.

Rauchstrasse, Berlin (1980–5). Masterplan, selected buildings. *www.krierkohl.de/projects/rauchstrasse. html*

Precincts: Waterfront Festival Markets

There are many kinds of waterfront developments. Battery Park City, on the Hudson River, with its central commercial area and residential background buildings, is one kind. The Singapore River, which was once a major transshipment location, has new pedestrian walkways on both sides of it. Kuching's docks are now a waterfront park. The preservation and redevelopment of finger-wharfs into mixed-use developments is yet another product type. Such developments tend to be total urban designs (e.g. Pier 39 in San Francisco, Walsh Bay in Sydney and De Boomjes in Rotterdam). A frequent type of redevelopment of pocket harbours has been into what have been called 'festival markets'. There are a number of them around the world.

The precedent for the festival market type of development was set with Baltimore Inner Harbor (1965 to present; see Figure 8.72). Others soon followed. There are a number of examples in the United States (e.g. Norfolk, Virginia and Miami, Florida); in South Africa there is Cape Town's Victoria and Alfred Docks, and in Australia there is Darling Harbour in Sydney. Cynical (and somewhat snobbish) critics say that they are all the same. They do indeed include many of them same uses – major attractions such as museums and international brand shops – and they are all on waterfronts. The successful ones, and there is a high

Collection of the author

Figure 8.72 The Inner Harbor, Baltimore.

success rate, all attract local, out-of-town and international visitors. It is this mix of visitors that is also a major attraction for visitors. Darling Harbour, somewhat shaky financially but surviving, may well be the best of them. It certainly had the opportunity to learn from a number of antecedents.

Major references

Breen, Ann and Dick Rigby (1996). *The New Waterfront: A Worldwide Success Story.* London: Thames and Hudson.

Craig-Smith, Stephen J. and Michael Fagence, eds. (1995). *Recreation and Tourism as Catalysts for Urban Waterfront Redevelopment: An International Survey.* Westport, CN: Praeger.

CASE STUDY

Darling Harbour, Sydney, Australia: a fragmented development (1984 to the present)

Darling Harbour is an example of urban design by default as much as careful design. The harbour was once Australia's busiest seaport, but although updated in the 1960s, by the 1970s, it was a series of empty Victorian warehouses and rarely used railway tracks. Only an occasional ship used its wharfs. By the end of the decade it was derelict. Its location adjacent to the city centre, however, presented a major opportunity for redevelopment.

In May 1984, the New South Wales State Government announced its intention to redevelop the harbour. Much earlier – during the 1970s – the state government had initiated studies of investments in the area. The Rouse Corporation in the United States (the developers of Baltimore Inner Harbor) was invited to submit a master plan for the area and the government built the Sydney Entertainment Centre and later the Power House Museum in it. These two developments were catalysts for the further exploration of uses for Darling Harbour. Another impetus came from the development suggestions of Lawrence Halprin, the influential American landscape architect. Baltimore Inner Harbor was clearly the model in mind throughout the development of Darling Harbour but considerably more has been achieved.

Late in 1984, the Darling Harbour Act was legislated by the state parliament under the forceful leadership of politicians Neville Wran and Laurie Brereton. The goal was to create a major development by 1988, the bicentennial of European settlement of Australia (or invasion, as perceived by indigenous populations). The act established the Darling Harbour Authority with the Project Design Directorate (later assigned to the MSJ Group) and the Managing Contractors (later Leighton Contractors) under its wing. The Authority was given the task of taking the development forward. Darling Harbour was thus planned in the speculative era of the late 1980s to be a major commercial, entertainment, recreational and residential area that would enhance the economic state of the city and place it more firmly on the world map, as the Opera House had done at mid-century.

The decision to go ahead with the project was based on consultants' feasibility studies that were presented to the State Government, the Sydney City Council, statutory bodies and municipal utility authorities for review. A joint government/private enterprise team oversaw the process of development. The first step involved the resolution of the financial and administrative basis for the project. The second step involved getting the government-owned land released for the development and purchasing land parcels from private owners. It also required the land to be cleared so that it could be a construction site. The third step was to seek expressions of interest from developers and the selection of worthwhile projects. Individual developers making proposals were required to present architectural and engineering drawings and impact analyses of their schemes. Negotiations then took place between the Authority and the developers over their applications. Approvals for road closures, the use of air rights, as well as for the construction of buildings had to be obtained and agreements had to been made with utility providers. Once these steps had been completed, tendering for construction work took place. By 1985, most of the site had been cleared. No specific master plan was adopted but an early one (see Figure 8.73) has guided the development and formed the basis of successive plans of the Darling Harbour Development Authority. In 1985, construction began on the Sydney Convention Centre (designed by

John Andrews) and Exhibition Centre (publicly funded and designed by Philip Cox with Arup Associates as engineers). The process was carried out in haste in a piecemeal manner in order for the scheme to be sufficiently advanced by 1988 to be seen as a functioning entity.

When it became clear what was occurring in Darling Harbour, there was considerable political and public opposition to the development. It was perceived that the money could be better spent on hospitals and other public facilities rather than something frivolous. There was particular strong opposition to the building of an elevated monorail circuit that cuts across the façades of buildings in the central area of the city before looping around Darling Harbour. With the award of the landscape design contract to Regal Landscape, public opinion, however, started to be supportive as the full nature of what Darling Harbour would be became apparent.

The design charge for the site was to create spaces with flat surfaces avoiding slopes. Elongated spaces were to be avoided unless they were terminated by a visible and desired destination. Imposing significant buildings should be contrasted with smaller buildings and accreted around open spaces to give them a sense of enclosure. By 1987 a master plan had evolved.

The site today extends seamlessly under two major highways with a mixture of hard surfaces in its heavily trafficked pedestrian core areas and grassed areas to the south (see Figure 8.74). The buildings are arranged in a horseshoe manner around the harbour which is now partially a marina and partially a site for water entertainment events. The design is anchored at its ends by the National Maritime Museum (with a submarine and

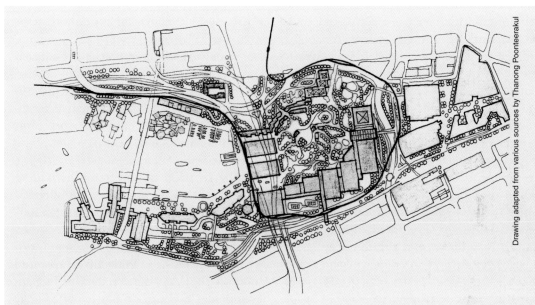

Drawing adapted from various sources by Thanong Poonteerakul

Figure 8.73 Darling Harbour: an early plan.

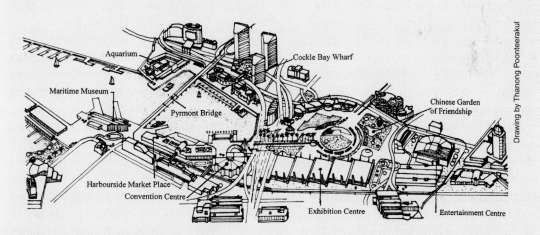

Drawing by Thanong Poonteerakul

Figure 8.74 Darling Harbour in 2003.

destroyer in the water adjacent to it) and a privately developed aquarium that has been successful enough to be extensively enlarged. Both these buildings were designed by Philip Cox. Today, Darling Harbour includes the Exhibition Centre, the Sydney Convention Centre (completed in 1999), the Harbourside Markets (designed by RTKL Associates, Inc and Clarke Perry Blackmore) and, on the city side of the harbour, Cockle Bay Wharf (a restaurant and entertainment area, completed in 2001). Towards the south are a Panasonic IMAX Theatre, Palm Grove (a waterplay area), the Chinese Garden of Friendship, children's playgrounds, amphitheatres, water features and parks. The old

297

Pyrmont Bridge has been converted to a pedestrian way but still opens for high-masted boats to pass under it. Underneath the highways are buildings such as information centres.

Few guidelines shaped the development. In many ways the process has followed a piece-by-piece iterative *ad hoc* approach 'rather than [being] a product design wherein everything is determined before implementation took place' due to the exigencies of time (Young, 1988) and shaped by political forces. As Philip Cox noted: 'Politics and unions take up so much time today . . . I have to get involved in politics because politics determine what the end product will be' (Cox cited in Towndrow, 1991: 257). Debates led to the overall project being fragmented with the landscape being used to coordinate the plan. The outdoor spaces of the precinct gain a sense of unity through the similarity of their surface materials, the use of linking elements such as the water features, the unified design of streetlights, seating and rubbish bins, and the vegetation. Tree species were selected for the microclimate conditions and the functions they are to serve. For instance, a row of palm trees in Palm Grove gives a strong axis to the water. In other places the trees provide a canopy for seating areas. The height of buildings within the harbour zone is restricted to four stories and the height of those immediately adjacent to it on the city side to 15 stories. The height of those on the other side is supposed to be related to the height of the old woolstores. The former regulation allows for good light and a spacious design, the latter allows views of the city's skylines. That three of the major buildings were the product of one architectural office, Cox, Richardson and Taylor

and many of the smaller incidental items of another, McConnel, Smith and Johnson, also helps to add some unity to the development (Figure 8.75).

The development at Darling Harbour occurred in two phases: the rushed development of the 1980s and the work after 1988 – the bicentennial year. The first phase established the character of the scheme with the creation of the basic landscape, the Convention Centre, the Harbourside Markets, the Exhibition Space and the waterfront. The second phase occurred between 1996 and 1998 with a burst of primarily private investments: Sega World, the Aquarium extension, the IMAX theatre, the Darling Park development and Cockle Bay Wharf. Public investment continued with the extension of the Convention Centre and the building of an extensive children's playground.

One of the reasons for public investments in urban designs is to use them as catalysts for development. To date private investment in Darling Harbour has outstripped public three to one with over $A1.5 billion being spent on recent projects alone. Darling Harbour has spurred considerable development around it. The new buildings include hotels and residential units. Warehouses have been converted to apartments, and new commercial buildings are linked to the harbour. Waterfront housing is being developed to the north of the immediate site at King Street Wharf. The Sydney Casino is nearby. A light-rail system (developed by the Light Rail Consortium backed by the State Government) located along an abandoned rail track links the city's Central Station to inner western neighbourhoods and passes by Darling Harbour.

Darling Harbour possesses a vibrant mix of uses and attracts widely different people.

Figure 8.75 Three views of Darling Harbour in 2004. (a) A view southwest from Pyrmont Bridge, (b) a view looking southwest under the highways; the IMAX Theatre is on the left and (c) the landscape features running south under the highways.

Today, of the 14 million or so visitors a year 55% are Sydneysiders and 22% are foreigners. At the time of writing, the exhibition space at the Convention Center was being increased by 10,000 square metres (107,000 square feet) with the building of two new warehouse-type structures to make a total of 40,000 square metres (428,000 square feet) of convention and exhibition space. Financial assistance from the government was reduced from $A17.6 million in the 1996–7 fiscal year to nil in 1999–2000. Still, questions are asked as to whether a stronger overall architectural image could have been obtained with some additional forethought. Similar questions are asked about the links between Darling Harbour and its surroundings. In many ways it turns its back on them. The site was dealt with as an island by a single authority.

Major references

Darling Harbour Authority (1985). *Darling Harbour Draft Development Plan and Strategy, Planning Report*. Sydney: The authors.

Kozloff, Howard (2001). Sydney's Darling Harbour. *Urban Land* **60** (11–12): 82–6.

Project Sunrise Pty., Limited and Sunrise High Technologies and Design Pty., Ltd. (1983). *Urban and Landscape Design Report*. Sydney: The authors.

Towndrow, Jennifer (1991). Darling Harbour. In *Philip Cox: Portrait of an Australian Architect*. Ringwood, Victoria: Viking, 254–64.

Young, Barry (1988). Darling Harbour: a new city precinct. In Peter G. Webber, ed. *The Design of Sydney: Three Decades of Change in the City Centre*. Sydney: The Law Book Company, 190–213.

Commentary

A wide variety of urban design products have been produced through the procedures of all-of-a-piece design. Both public and private interests have initiated them. Increasingly they have involved close cooperation between the two sectors of the economy. Given an overall vision, the degree of control over the design of their individual components has varied considerably. Tight building design guidelines were used in places such as Seaside and Paternoster Square; much looser ones were applied in schemes such as Darling Harbour, and largely advisory ones in Glendale. The goal of all of the guidelines has been to create some level of visual unity, and pedestrian and other user amenity while allowing for diversity.

The quality of urban designs varies considerably. Market-driven schemes such as La Défense and Canary Wharf are based on ease of development within the framework of an international money market largely uninterested in local concerns. They have proven good enough to sell once some basic design flaws were eliminated but they have also missed opportunities. With the wisdom of hindsight it is clear that they have incurred substantial opportunity costs – other designs could have met their ends better and, at the same time, have catered to a wider range of needs. The designs meet their goals but how good were the goals? Should one of the goals of these two projects have been to provide a greater variety of uses from the outset?

A recent study drawing on considerable empirical evidence (i.e. from Garvin, 1995; Punter and Carmona, 1997; Punter, 1999, 2003) has attempted to develop a

Table 8.2 A model describing the likely degree of implementation of urban design guidelines

| Level of clarity | Steps in guideline development and application | | | Effectiveness | Example |
	Formulation	Communication	Administration		
High	Clear, operationally defined objectives and evaluation criteria based on empirical evidence	Written and illustrated guidelines that are publicly reviewed in meetings prior to acceptance	Single authority, legally empowered to enforce regulations, in control	Likely to be implemented and less battered by power relationships amongst stakeholders	Battery Park City
Medium	Objectives and evaluation criteria specified in general terms using words such as appropriate	Written and illustrated and placed on public display in exhibitions. Feedback in written form	A centralized agency or well coordinated multiple agencies under single authority	Partially implemented but subject to the whims of political change	Lujiazui
Low	Advisory guidelines without operational definitions	Written and illustrated but not subject to any public review	Multiple agencies at the same time or in sequence	Loosely applied depending on architects' and developers' values	Darling Harbour

Adapted from Soemardi (in progress).

predictive model of the context in which urban design guidelines are implemented or not (Soemardi, in progress). The level of clarity in formulating, communicating and administering the guidelines defines whether guidelines will enable the objectives of a scheme to be met. Political pressures and governmental corruption can be intervening variables.

Table 8.2 defines the characteristics of guidelines by level of clarity at each phase of their use in urban design projects. Those projects that are high on all three dimensions are those that are implemented while those that are low are unlikely to be implemented in accordance with stated objectives. Those that are a mixture of high, medium and low levels of clarity will be partially carried out and will partially fall by the wayside. Much, however, depends on the strength of the design ideas, the distribution of power amongst the stakeholders involved and the perceived necessity for coordinated action.

All the case studies presented in this chapter were a response to a perceived need for some level of coordinated action. The goal has been not only to have economic growth and design quality in mind but also to manage that growth.

Development can be managed through the creation of special districts, the selective use (in existing areas) of building moratoria, land-use controls, design guidelines and/or controls, and through the design review process. In commenting on the Rauchstrasse scheme, Rob Krier wrote:

> In order to achieve a coherent total image in an urban development plan of this size, the concept of the block must be clearly formulated in geometrical terms and should not embody exaggerated structural fantasies that represent only an individual artistic conception. For the sake of unity, each of the architects taking part must [exert] as much discipline as possible (Krier, 1988: 83).

The case studies show that internationally renowned architects are willing to work within strict guidelines if their purpose and the overall project's objectives are clear and make sense. The guidelines have to be based on a clear logic and on empirical evidence that they will work in achieving a design's objectives. Creating a sense of unity through controlled chaos is more difficult than a sense of unity through similarity!

There are a number of expressions of concern about the degree of control that exists in some of the all-of-a-piece urban designs included in this chapter and, in particularly the seeking of unity in designs. Many of the best-loved areas of cities in the world with extraordinarily high property values have a remarkable unity in design but to many critics this search for unity today represents an old-fashioned idea in an era of individualism. In terms of the total production of new segments of cities, business areas and new residential suburbs, the number that falls into the all-of-a-piece urban design category is low. One critic (Postrel, 2003) suggests that 'if you get the lots right, and the blocks right and the street right and the setback right, somebody can build a crummy' building and the ensemble is still fine. She is probably correct. I would add 'if you get the nature of ground floor uses right!'

The question comes back to the rights of individuals to do their own thing in democratic societies. In looking back at the turbulent history of his master plan (and implicitly the nature of all-of-a-piece urban design) and the evolving design of the World Trade Center site, Daniel Libeskind notes:

> Although [the site design is] not literally what was in my original images, it [i.e., the original design] shows a robustness and a new kind of idea about a master plan . . . It's the reverse of the Potsdamer Platz in Berlin, which is just a bunch of architects following exactly what was on paper . . . the superficial has changed not the principles. . . This is the art of making a master plan rather than an 18th century plan that is obediently followed. We're not living in Haussmann's Paris. We have a pluralistic society . . . I'm not [even] the architect of [Freedom] Tower [after the collaboration with David Childs] (cited in Lubell *et al.*, 2004).

Architectural style does not really matter in the design of cities, the urban character does. No doubt this position will be open to debate (see Chapter 11).

The mechanism to achieve a sense of unity is primarily the Gestalt law of similarity although the other Gestalt laws of visual organization can also be applied (see Lang, 1987). In urban design similarity has generally been assumed to be a matter of style. It has, however, been suggested that instead of a 'skin-deep' stylistic unity that there should be a 'critical reinterpretation' of the 'underlying system' of unity in each building (Mitchell, 2003). The trouble is that unless this is explained to observers, the unity is not seen. There is, however, a unity in chaos too!

9 Piece-by-piece urban design

The overlap between city planning and urban design occurs when the mutual concern is with the three-dimensional physical design of the environment, the detailed activities it should house, and with the nature of the milieu as a public display. In the case of master planning, city planning and urban design may sometimes coincide (as in the case of Runcorn). Thorough comprehensive plans have a set of clear urban design schemes within them – the whole system being held together by the armature of the plan's infrastructure. When planning gets down to the precinct level with clear specifications for the activities that should characterize an area and the building and/or infrastructure types required to afford them, it becomes concerned with urban design.

Piece-by-piece urban design is one method for improving the quality of precincts of existing cities. It does not, like all-of-a-piece urban design begin with a specific concept plan showing the desired physical end state of a precinct. Rather it begins with a generalized mental image of how an area should perform and what it should contain to get that performance. It is an alternative view of what urban design is.

Planning Districts and Urban Design

Kevin Lynch identified districts as one key factor in the cognitive map people have of cities (Lynch, 1960). A district, well bounded or not, is a precinct that is characterized by a similar texture of buildings in terms of their massing. It is frequently an area that houses a particular set of activities. Most cities have a clear central business district; many have clear shopping and entertainment districts. Some have areas dominated by ethnic minorities. Consider all the cities around the world that have Chinatowns. On a smaller scale many have, for instance, a jeweller's row. The mix of these elements gives a particular city its peculiar identity. In many places these districts are under threat due to changing land values as the result of technological or social change. Piece-by-piece urban design addressing the particular problems of a district is one way of shaping a district's nature in a particular direction.

Piece-by-piece urban design differs from city planning in its use of zoning. Whereas zoning controls are generally used to protect citizens from the negative effects of building, in piece-by-piece urban design it is used to encourage the construction of specific building types and/or other facilities within a particular precinct. Such areas are designated 'special planning districts'. Incentives are drawn up for the sought-after buildings or facilities to be built, not in any specific location but somewhere in the district. In this way the district either retains its existing character or attains a new one. As it does not involve the design of specific buildings on specific sites or elements of the public realm, many people would not regard such an activity as urban design but rather as some aspect of planning. Jonathan Barnett refers to it as 'building cities without building buildings' – urban design as public policy (Barnett, 1974, 2003).

Another special type of planning district is a Business Improvement District (BID). There are over 1000 in North America and hundreds more elsewhere. In Britain they are called Town Centre Management Programs. Business people create such districts to enhance the locations where they conduct business. The goal is to make being in the district for work, shopping or entertainment a pleasant experience in safe, congenial and well-maintained surroundings. Legal mechanisms have to be established at some governmental level to enable business people in a precinct to tax themselves in order to: (1) improve the ambiance of their districts, (2) run special events to attract people and (3) maintain the district after improvements have been made. Much of the design work involves landscape architecture – improved street lighting, better paving, the inclusion of trees and other planting, coordinated signage, etc. The objective is to improve the area piece-by-piece through direct action and indirectly through the catalytic effect of an improved physical environment on enhancing investment opportunities.

Three case studies of piece-by-piece urban design are presented here. They are very different in character. One has received widespread publicity – the special districts of New York City. They were first established in the 1960s when it was feared that the character of specific precincts of the city would change as the result of investment pressures. It was expected that if unchecked the result would be a significant loss of what makes New York 'New York'. The second is closer to traditional concepts of urban design and could be regarded almost as an all-of-a-piece urban renewal scheme. It deals with the central core area of Bellevue in Washington State. The public policy goal was to make it a more traditional pedestrian-friendly city centre. The third case study requires some imagination to be included as an urban design project in the terms described in this book. It is a BID dealing with central Philadelphia.

Major references

Barnett, Jonathan (1974). *Urban Design as Public Policy*. New York: McGraw Hill.
Houston Jr, Lawrence O. (1997). *Business Improvement Districts*. Washington, DC: Urban Land Institute.
Houston Jr, Lawrence O. (2004). Capitalist tool. *Planning* **70** (1): 26–9.

CASE STUDY

The Theater and other districts, New York, NY, USA (1967–74)

In 1961, a comprehensive zoning revision in New York City introduced the use of zoning incentives to create specific physical designs. The goal was to encourage property developers to build plazas as part of any new development. Having more open space within the dense environment of Manhattan was perceived to be in the public interest. Crowding and high population density (by no means synonymous) were perceived to be major urban problems. Given a society based on democratic principles and individual property rights, the new zoning code involved the bargaining over the provision of public open space between city officials with incentives and property developers with a desire to build. The hope was that piece-by-piece more open space would be created. There was also an aspiration to get high-quality architecture and to offer developers space bonuses for 'good design'. The legal problems in defining 'good design' operationally proved too great and the thought was not pursued.

In changing the zoning ordinance those professionals involved in designing cities were working in a new way. They were policy designers working at the precinct level rather than urban designers working on specific conceptual designs or master plans. They were working as 'merchants of allowable building space' trading public interest needs for allowable floor space in the private rather than the public realm. They were not, however, dealing with the whole range of problems of the declining hearts of cities that John Lindsay and city planners had to face when he became Mayor of New York in 1966.

The 1960s and 1970s were a period of turmoil in the United States. Inflation rates were high by North American standards, major labour disputes slowed progress, and racial riots demonstrated the frustration of minority groups. Homosexuals and civil libertarians battled for gay rights. The morality of the Vietnam War and political assassinations sent the citizens of the United States and many other people around the world into much soul searching. The physical fabric of the cores of cities in the country was in rapid decline as people and industries moved to the suburbs and to other parts of the continent. It was felt that urban polices had to be developed for specific precincts of cities in order to make a difference. In New York urban design became policy-based and the distinction between urban design and standard physical (and, indeed, social and economic) planning became blurred.

John Lindsay was a two-term mayor of New York, holding office from 1966 to 1974. He had a deep-seated belief that the future of the United States lay in 'bustling, diverse and dynamic cities' and that market forces would neither shape cities positively nor stem their decline. He also realized that attempting to compete against market forces was foolhardy; they had to be harnessed. In harnessing them he felt that the ideas of community groups also had to be considered. Planning had to be at the district level. Importantly, in terms of this book, he established an Urban Design Group to initiate projects that would stop the 'haemorrhaging' of the city's life. Lindsay gave the group unequivocal support during his term in office.

The major products of the group's efforts were the creation of a series of 'special districts' in the city and the elaboration of the incentive zoning codes developed in 1961. The special districts included the Theater District, the Lincoln Square Special Zoning District, the Fifth Avenue District, the Greenwich Street Special District in Lower Manhattan, and the Lower Manhattan Districts of Battery Park City (see Chapter 8) and Manhattan Landing.

The 1961 zoning regulation allowed up to 20% more floor area than the codes allowed if an approved plaza was included in the design of an office or residential building. It was based on the popular myth that any open space in a city is a good thing. This thought was reflected in contemporary Modernist urban design paradigms. The

popularity of the new regulation with property developers led to less than desirable outcomes. Buildings became isolated towers surrounded by unconnected and largely purposeless open spaces unrelated to street fronts or sun angles (e.g. on Sixth Avenue; see Figure 9.1; see Kayden, 2000 for other examples). The continuity of the street as the basis of the life of the city was lost. The lesson learned was that the design of elements of the public realm of cities has to be conceived within a larger urban design vision and plan. The special district legislation was a response.

The special districts were established from 1967 onwards. The Theater District was the first. It extended from Sixth to Eighth Avenue east to west and from 40th Street to 57th Street south to north (see Figure 9.2). Faced

Figure 9.1   Discontinuous plazas on Sixth Avenue, New York in 1993.

with a booming market for commercial office space, traditional legitimate theatres were not an attractive financial investment for developers nor were existing theatres generating enough return on capital invested to warrant their retention in the face of potential profits from the investment in office space. Yet, what would New York be without Broadway and its theatres as an attraction? The Urban Design Group set about the task of devising mechanisms to keep the character of the area based on the assumption that it was in everybody's interest to have theatres in the district. The means had to be found to keep them and/or build them when it was in no investor's direct financial interest to do so.

The Group developed a modified incentive zoning method. It is a simple mechanism but involved many debates before it was established. The legislation had to be passed by the Planning Commission and the city's Board of Estimates. Rather than being a blanket citywide policy, the incentives were tailored made for each district. In the case of the Theater District the objective was to make an investment in a theatre commercially viable for property developers. As in the 1961 legislation, a 20% floor area bonus was offered to a property developer in exchange for building a theatre within a new building (see Figure 9.3). In this way the arts would be indirectly subsidized by the private sector. The test case was the old Astor Hotel site. Mayor Lindsay himself was directly involved in the negotiations with the property developer and the success of the process was largely due to his personal intervention. A new theatre was built. Others followed.

Each of New York's planning districts served a different purpose and thus had different regulations and incentives. Even if somewhat unkempt, Fifth Avenue is one of the great shopping streets of the world. The goal of planning for this district was to have a lively environment around the clock and to protect the profitability of the large department stores located along Fifth Avenue. The strategic location of these stores made the smaller shopfront stores selling a broad mix of retail goods economically

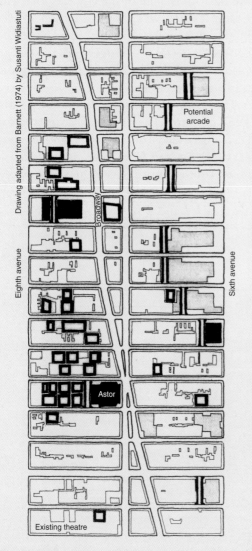

Figure 9.2 The Theater District, New York established in 1962. (New theatres are solid black)

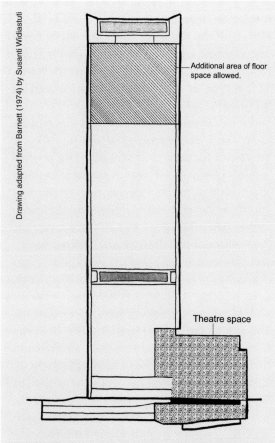

Additional area of floor space allowed.

Theatre space

Drawing adapted from Barnett (1974) by Susanti Widiastuti

Figure 9.3 One Astor Place showing the new theater and the extra floor space allowed.

viable. A continuous line of shops fronting a street with a minimum of intrusion of plazas, bank and office-building entrances provides an ideal shopping and

window-shopping environment. As a result, unlike the 1961 zoning ordinance, the legislation for the Fifth Avenue District *prohibited* the provision of plaza space on the street. It also broke away from traditional one-use zoning classes to include mixed-use zoning that encouraged a combination of residential, office and retail space within single buildings.

The success of such efforts was mixed. Nevertheless, Broadway is still 'Broadway'; Fifth Avenue is still 'Fifth Avenue'. By the mid-1970s four new theatres had been built in the Theater District. They are shown in solid black in Figure 9.2. The hope was that by 2000 another half a dozen would be added piece-by-piece. This has not happened. Today Broadway, nevertheless, remains a theatre district and the work of the Urban Design Group led to further innovative schemes. The Times Square district, for instance, was upgraded in the late 1990s and early 2000s.

Major references

Barnett, Jonathan (1982). The evolution of New York's special zoning districts *In An Introduction to Urban Design:* New York, Harper and Row, 77–93.

Kayden, Jerold S. (2000). History. In *Privately Owned Public Space: The New York City Experience.* New York: John Wiley, 7–19.

CASE STUDY

Central Bellevue, Washington, USA: a new suburban downtown (1980 to the present)

The City of Bellevue lies 10 miles (15 kilometres) east of Seattle across Lake Washington. The cities are linked by two floating bridges. A city of 90,000 people, Bellevue is strategically located in the centre of a rapidly growing region of 380,000 people (in 2000).

In the 1950s, it had a traditional suburban centre of two-and three-storey buildings along its principal streets.

During the 1960s and 1970s Bellevue's central business district (CBD) acquired a standard regional shopping mall and a haphazard sprinkling of six to thirteen storey office buildings generally set back from the streets in a Modernist fashion. By the mid-1970s the area had taken on a design totally oriented to the ease of automobile use. By the 1980s walking in the area had become demanding and unpleasant. The residential areas adjacent to the CBD felt threatened by the increase in automobile traffic and pollution and faced a potential future of being dwarfed and overshadowed by what was perceived to be out-of-scale development. In addition, residents feared that new office buildings would also 'pop-up' in the residential neighbourhoods of the city. On the outskirts of the city in King County of which Bellevue is a part, strip shopping was being developed. It was perceived to be a threat to the economic viability of Bellevue's CBD.

In the mid-1970s there was a proposal to build a super-regional shopping centre in King County outside Bellevue. The proposal was rejected in accordance with Washington State's strong Environmental Policy Act on the grounds that it would lead to environmental degradation. A non-design tool was thus used to reinforce the viability of Bellevue's downtown. At the same time a positive effort was required if the CBD was to be made attractive. The Bellevue City Planning Commission drew up sub-area plans to halt any potential rezoning of residential areas to commercial use. No buildings outside the downtown were allowed to have a Floor Area Ratio (FAR) of more than 0.5 (i.e. the useable floor area of a building

could be no more than half the site size). This FAR did not stop development of commercial space but led to campus type development along the highways outside Bellevue. It is a type of development that citizens of the city found acceptable.

From the early 1980s onwards much planning (and development) effort in Bellevue has been focused on the CBD. The professional planners of the Bellevue Planning Commission made a decision to encourage all major developments in Bellevue to locate in the CBD. The goal was to have a vibrant 'even discordant' downtown of mixed-uses – a high-density urban place with pedestrian walkways, a revamped transit (bus) system, and parking as part of buildings. One of the planning objectives was to encourage the use of the transit system. The Bellevue City Council adopted this goal as policy in 1981. A central transfer centre (designed by Zimmer Gunsul Frasca) built at a cost of $US5 million was included in the city centre plan to encourage transit use. The next step was to develop design guidelines for new development based on the desire to make the district pleasant for pedestrians.

A number of steps were taken. Parking requirements for each building were reduced from 5 places per 1000 square feet (about 100 square metres) of development to 3. An incentive zoning scheme was developed whereby buildings were allowed to be taller than specified in the plan in return for ground level amenities. In 1984 the Bellevue City Council adopted a stepped, or wedding-cake, zoning configuration which controlled the height of buildings, the tallest being in the centre to the lowest (single-family homes) on the periphery adjacent to residential neighbourhoods (see Figures 9.4, 9.5 and page 396).

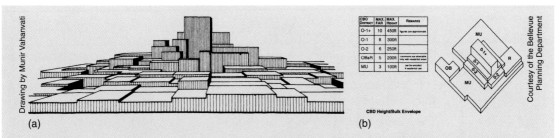

Figure 9.4 The use of the stepped height-bulk zoning ordinance in Bellevue. (a) A typical 'wedding-cake' building height profile and (b) the building height regulation for Bellevue.

Figure 9.5 Downtown Bellevue in 1993.

One of the amenities that the planners sought to put in place was a pedestrian corridor running right across the centre of the city. It was felt that mid-block pedestrian ways were needed to give access to it because the blocks were 600 feet (180 metres) long. All new developments in the downtown area are required to provide links to this corridor. The guidelines for these links by type of street were developed collaboratively by a committee consisting of all those people who held property along the corridor and the staff of the City Planning Commission (see Figure 9.6). The guidelines have no legal basis but are advisory and regarded as 'inspirational'. The hope was that piece-by-piece, as the result of individual developers building individual structures, a new CBD would be created along the lines proposed by the City Planning Commission. The details of all proposals for new buildings have to be submitted by their architects for review and the ability to enforce the design guidelines comes from the threat of delaying

311

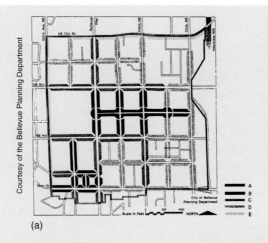

Courtesy of the Bellevue Planning Department

(a)

Courtesy of the Bellevue Planning Department

'A' Rights-of-Way

Intent:

Rights-of-way designated 'A' shall have the highest orientation to pedestrians. This shall be achieved by emphasizing the designer relationship between the first level of the structure and the horizontal space between the structure and the curb line. This relationship should emphasize to the greatest extent possible, both the physical and visual access into and from the structure, as well as the amenities and features of the outside pedestrian space. In order to achieve the intended level of vitality, design diversity, and people activity on an 'A' right-of-way, retailing or marketing activities shall be provided for in the design.

Guidelines:

1. Street level edges of the entire project limit shall incorporate retail activities.

2. The following characteristics shall be incorporated into the design of the structure:

    Windows providing visual access
    Street walls
    Multiple entrances
    Differentiation of ground level
    Canopies, awnings or arcades

3. The following characteristics should be incorporated into the design of the sidewalk:

    Special paving treatment
    Seating

4. These Guidelines for 'building/sidewalk relationships' are to be used in conjunction with other guidelines adopted by the City. In the event the guidelines conflict with more specific guidelines adopted for Old Bellevue, the Major Pedestrian Corridor, or the Major Public Open Spaces, the more specific guidelines, now or as amended in the future, take precedence.

(b)

Examples:

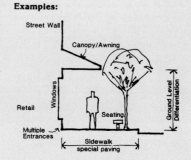

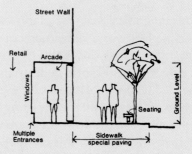

Figure 9.6 Design objectives and guidelines for central Bellevue streets. (a) The CBD street plan and (b) the guidelines for Street Type A.

approvals for building development. Delays cost developers money.

The guidelines were based on a series of propositions: the elements of the downtown should be part of a system; building frontages should be 'pedestrian-oriented' (see Figure 9.7). This latter objective could be met by having places to sit, by adjacent places being complementary, by having protection from the weather, by having focal/curiosity points along the way, by having nighttime activity, etc. Twelve sets of guidelines were developed. They were for primary paths and secondary paths, for corridor walls, linear sectors, the continuity of elements, elements of diversity, vegetation, street crossings, the massing of abutting structures, and for the management of the

system (Hinshaw, 1983). Such terms are usually undefined in planning studies but in the guidelines for central Bellevue they were given operational definitions.

To enhance the quality of Bellevue's central area, a new park was proposed. The hope was to have it funded by municipal bonds issued by the city. The referendum on the bond issue, which required a super majority (i.e. 60%) to pass, was narrowly defeated. The push to build the park was taken up by a citizens' committee and largely privately funded. It was developed according to a design by Beckley/Meiers, Architects.

What has been the result of all these efforts? The development of central Bellevue is often held up as an exemplar of public/private partnership in development. Much

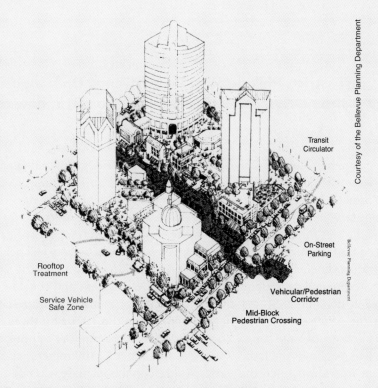

Figure 9.7 The vehicular-pedestrian corridor, central Bellevue.

commercial development has taken place in Bellevue as a consequence of these efforts. By the mid-1990s there was 10 million square feet of commercial space and over 30,000 jobs in the downtown area. Land prices have escalated resulting in increased tax revenue to the city. A side effect of these successes and the concomitant rise in land prices is that unsubsidized housing in the CBD (a goal of the plan) seems unattainable. The parking restrictions and the prohibition on entrepreneurial parking lots has meant that some potential project developers have invested elsewhere but also that 15% of workers use the transit system and another 13% use car pools. These figures may seem low but for suburban United States they are high.

Major references

Hinshaw, Mark L. (1994). Transforming suburbia: the case study of Belleveue, Washington. In Brenda Case Scheer and Wolfgang Preiser, eds., *Design Review: Challenging Urban Aesthetic Control*. New York: Chapman and Hall, 111–18.

Miles, Don C. and Mark L. Hinshaw (1987). Bellevue's new approach to pedestrian planning and design. In Anne Vernez Moudon, ed., *Public Streets for Public Use*. New York: Van Nostrand Reinhold, 221–31.

Punter, John (1999). The city of Bellevue. In *Design Guidelines in American Cities: A Review of Design Guidelines and Guidance in Five West Coast Cities*. Liverpool: Liverpool University Press, 57–65.

CASE STUDY

The Center City District, Philadelphia, Pennsylvania, USA: a business improvement district (1990 to 1995, continuing to 2015; now continuing to 2025)

Central Philadelphia, known as Center City, is defined as the area between the Delaware and Schuykill Rivers, the Vine Street Expressway and South Street – an area falling within about a 20-minute walk of City Hall. The historic core of the city (and of the founding of the United States) falls within it. The area did not see the overwhelming economic and physical environmental degradation that many downtowns of United States cities experienced in the 1960s but it had been stagnating. The construction of a new convention centre was begun in the late 1980s and has been in operation since the early 1990s. This hotly disputed initiative had been part of the effort to revitalize Center City. This development and a number of earlier urban design/planning efforts served as precedents on which the city could build.

Aggressive city planning/urban design under director Edmund Bacon had led to the revitalization (and gentrification) of the severely decayed Society Hill neighbourhood and other inner city areas, the unification of the railway system and the development of the Gallery, an internal centre city shopping mall. From the 1970s on there has been an increase in the number of households living within a mile (1600 meters) of the City Hall (although this increase was not accompanied by an equally significant increase in population). The population, itself was generally wealthy, and a disproportionate number (37%) walk to work and 60% do not own a car. Despite these successes the center of the city, apart from some well-loved places and streets, was still seen as dirty and poorly maintained. In addition, many locally owned national and international conglomerates with little interest in Philadelphia other than as a source of revenue were buying up major locally owned businesses (Lehman, 2000). The city government was perceived to be incapable of making improvements. What then do to about it?

The Center City District (CCD), a municipal authority, was formed by city officials and the business community in 1990. In accordance with state law if more than 30% of the property owners objected it would not have been possible to do so. The proportion in opposition did not reach this figure. The formation of the CCD was also supported by the City Council who authorized its operation until 1995 by a 14 to 1 vote. This authorization was extended in 1994 until 2015 and again in 2004 to 2025. The CCD is headed by Paul Levy, a one-time academic at the University of Pennsylvania, and has a 23-member board. The board has the power to chase the small proportion of property owners who fail to pay their dues. The CCD's budget (about $14 million from a levy on the property tax) first went to the provision of sidewalk cleaning (provided by a private contractor) and public safety. The scope of its concerns expanded later. The goal was 'to increase the number of people on the streets – workers, residents, shoppers, tourists, conventioneers and people drawn for entertainment – to recreate 1948 (Levy, 2001: 190).

In 1991 the board solicited proposals and received 75 responses from individuals

Figure 9.8 Market street in the Philadelphia Center City BID in 2004.

and groups for the security and cleaning programmes, including graffiti removal, that it felt was necessary to improve the quality of the precinct under its jurisdiction. The success of the effort gave the board and its members confidence in its activities. In the fifth year of its existence, the Board felt comfortable enough to start on a street upgrading programme. A 20-year $US21 million bond was raised to finance capital improvements of the streetscape. The city contributed about $5 million. The goal was to establish a 'new look' in order to raise the prestige level of the city. The look was created through new 'pedestrian-scaled' lighting standards, new street trees, new pedestrian maps and signage, the repaving of streets, making the environment easy to use by people in wheelchairs, and by adding new kerbs. The CCD board also took over the maintenance of the existing street trees, many of which were languishing, from the city administration (see Figures 9.8 and 9.9).

In all these efforts, the concern with the third dimension of the city has been restricted to creating advisory guidelines for how property owners might: (1) improve the façades of their buildings and (2) how they might convert disused or underused buildings to other, predominantly residential, uses. In this way the district would be improved piece-by-piece over time. Each improvement would act as a catalyst for further improvements by the property owners themselves. The objective is for property owners to benefit from increased income, the city to have an increased tax-base, and for citizens to have a district of which they are proud and to which they like going – a place to have fun in safety.

Has the programme been successful? Retail occupancy increased from 80% to

Figure 9.9 A uniformed street maintenance worker, Market Street, Philadelphia in 1993.

almost 90% over an 8-year period but there are still many underused buildings in the city. According to a survey most people were aware of the CCD programme. The presence of customer service representatives with radios and of street cleaners providing a sense of security was particularly noted and appreciated. The city is still full of panhandlers and the homeless but the central precinct certainly looks better. Has there been a catalytic effect on building? Not much! Perhaps that is still to come. Tax incentives may have their impact. Certainly the conversion of old industrial and commercial buildings or their unused parts to residential has progressed and is encouraged by the CCD. Overall the CCD is seen as 'hugely successful' in doing what the city administration seemed incapable of doing – improving the quality of Center City.

Major references

Houston Jr, Lawrence O. (1997). Center City District. In *BIDs: Business Improvement Districts*. Washington, DC: The Urban Land Institute, 133–49.

Lehman, Nicholas (2000). No man's town: the good times are killing off America's local elites. *The New Yorker* (June 5): 42–9.

Levy, Paul R. (2001). Downtown: competitive for a new century. In Jonathan Barnett, ed. *Planning for a New Century: The Regional Agenda*. Washington, DC: Island Press, 135–76.

Commentary

A number of major lessons for urban design have been learnt about special districts and zoning from the experience of New York, Philadelphia, and other cities (Lai, 1988; Vossman, 2002). The first lesson is that the image and character of a place should be identified based on an empirical analysis based on community values (Stamps, 1994). The second is that top-down decisions without political and civic commitment are likely to lead nowhere – indeed 'most people do not want what architects want' (Michleson, 1968). The third is that design controls must be enforceable; legislation must precede or accompany the development of regulations. The potential problem with incentive zoning is that it can soon become urban design by negotiable zoning control. It is open to mismanagement and corruption as property developers seek ways to achieve additional benefits for themselves if they are to provide public benefits. Clear channels of legal and administrative action must thus be established.

There was a much broader lesson too. The urban design task is to create salubrious environments for life, to upgrade the behavioural opportunities for people, and to enhance their self-images (to lift their spirits) through environmental improvements. Zoning districts and zoning modifications may create opportunities for achieving these ends but in many instances the zoning tools that are legally available to urban designers are, by themselves, not strong enough. BIDs, a gentle and more inclusive approach to urban upgrading, may achieve more. A high-quality public realm can be good for business.

10 Plug-in urban design

Infrastructure design concerns in urban development vary in extent from the regional scale to the city, to the neighbourhood and to the complex of buildings scale. Regional and urban planning concerns are beyond what one generally regards as urban design. The destructive effect that much highway design has had on the neighbourhoods and lives of inner city residents in many cities of the world (see Figure 10.1 for an example) has led to much more careful analysis of the impacts of new infrastructure components on their environments and the employment of urban designers to deal with them.

Plug-in urban design focuses on the strategic building of infrastructure components of a city. In the case of new towns it is the whole capital web of infrastructure that is important. How this web of capital investment decisions affects

Figure 10.1   A highway plugged into a neighbourhood, Baltimore as existing in 1993.

and can be used to affect the physical nature of cities has long been of interest to urban designers (see Crane, 1960, for instance). But what is urban design about those decisions? And what do we mean by infrastructure when it comes to urban designing? Do we simply mean the roads and other site services, or does it also include facilities such as retail shops, schools, libraries and information technology networks? There is an increasingly heeded demand by ecologists that the infrastructure of cities include natural corridors of vegetation to decrease the heat-island effect and to increase the biodiversity of cities. Infrastructure in this book refers to: (1) elements such as streets and services that make a development possible, and (2) the investment in certain building types (e.g. museums, parking garages and schools) that are expected to have a multiplier effect on investments in their surroundings.

Plug-in urban design refers to the design and construction of the infrastructure of a development site to bind it into a unit and as an incentive for individual owner-builders or property developers to invest in new buildings. Alternatively, it can mean the plugging in of new infrastructure elements into existing built-up areas in order to bind them into a unit and boost their amenity level and thus competitive advantage. The cost of the new elements may be borne by the overall project developer, public or private, as represented in the master plan for a site or by the developers of individual buildings.

Plug-in urban design product types vary in the extent of the infrastructure provided. In terms of links, is it just the roadway or other means of access that are provided? Those components plus a surrounding fence or wall may do for the most basic of churchyards and cemeteries (see Figure 10.2). The facility needs of the visitors, mourners or tourists, are minimal. What is plugged into the paths of cemeteries by way of grave markers and mausoleums varies from culture to culture and from religious group to religious group. What is symbolically important is that the criteria for what makes an acceptable place to bury one's dead within a culture are met.

In designing the everyday environments for the living the question is: 'What range of products does plug-in urban design cover?' At one end of the financial scale we have publicly funded sites-and-services programmes that have the objective of providing the water supply, drainage, sewerage, latrines and road systems of a development in order to provide low-income residents with an incentive to build or upgrade their residences. Much suburban development for wealthier families is similar but much more generous. Sites may be allocated to other than residential uses through the implementation of a zoning ordinance based on a land-use plan. At another level of complexity we have the system of vertically segregated transportation links, walkways and decks, as in La Défense in Paris. Perhaps most importantly, in terms of this discussion is the idea of plugging in.

Major references

Grava, Sigurd (2003). *Urban Transportation Systems: Choices for Communities*. New York: McGraw-Hill.

Figure 10.2 The tomb of architect Colonel John Garston plugged into Park Street Cemetery, Kolkata.

Guy, Simon, Simon Marvin and Timothy Moss, eds. (2001). *Urban Infrastructure in Transition: Networks, Buildings, Plans*. London: Earthscan.

Southworth, Michael and Eran Ben-Joseph (1997). *Streets and the Shaping of Towns and Cities*. New York: McGraw-Hill.

Plugging-in as an Idea

In urban design, the plug-in concept has emerged from two streams of thought. The first has been the down-to-earth use of the infrastructure of cities as a catalyst for development or for unifying developments; the second is that associated with the Archigram group in the United Kingdom in the 1960s and 1970s. It is the former concern that is of interest here, but the latter cannot be allowed to pass unmentioned because its ideas rather than its designs remain of importance in the development of urban design ideology.

The Archigram group observed that many of us live in throwaway societies. Certainly all kinds of products from tissue paper to automobiles to computers are

Source: Cook et al. (1991)

Figure 10.3 The Archigram Group's 'Walking City' plugged into Manhattan, New York.

discarded with remarkable ease once their utility or 'use-by' dates are past. The group suggested that components of cities could be considered in the same manner. Precincts of cities could be plugged into the existing framework of a city as needed and moved away to another location as needed (see Figure 10.3). This idea is far fetched for the present except on a small scale for temporary accommodations. What is important, however, is the thinking behind the idea.

The closest design to the Archigram idea is the serviced campground. Vacationers drive up in their camper vans for a stay and then move on to another location or return home. Trailer parks are similar except the trailers once plugged in never move. Temporary townships for pilgrims, such as to the Kumbh Mela in India, are more about infrastructure design than anything else (see Figure 10.4). The design of such settlements is not generally regarded as urban design but it is. Emilio Ambasz's design for the 1992 Seville World's Fair recognized that once such fairs are over the pavilions of exhibitors are 'thrown away' and he designed it accordingly (see below).

Cities are indeed ever changing. Buildings and precincts will be demolished and rebuilt. The cities of Asia and Latin America are going through rapid changes with high rates of rural–urban migration. Others are changing more slowly. Some company towns may be abandoned. Housing areas will continue to be built on a mammoth scale. Traditional residential suburbs of single-family homes catering to the middle class will be built. Many 'suburbs' around the world will be erected by squatters with whatever materials are at hand.

Figure 10.4 The Kumbh Mela township, Allahabad in 1996.

Figure 10.5 A squatter settlement, Ahmedabad in 2001.

Newcomers will simply plug their huts into the infrastructure available (see Figure 10.5).

Major reference

Cook, Peter, Warren Chalk, Dennis Crompton, David Green, Ron Herron and Mike Webb (1991). *Archigram*. Boston: Birkhäuser.

The Case Studies

This chapter includes a number of case studies that demonstrate a variety of plug-in urban design types. It begins with examples of infrastructure design at the citywide level. This set is divided into two parts: (1) where the infrastructure has preceded building and (2) where it has been plugged into an existing built environment. The second set of case studies deals with infrastructure design at the precinct level. It is subdivided in the same manner. There is only one example of the third set which deals with plugging in specific building types into a precinct to act as catalysts for development. It is included as a note rather than a case study because its impact is yet to be seen. It is the case of the use of schools as infrastructure elements in Chattanooga, Tennessee.

Urban Links: Binding Cities into Units

The design of the links between precincts of a city might be expected to fall outside the purview of urban design, and be a regional and city planning or civil engineering endeavour. Much new town design, however, starts out by working out the infrastructure pattern as Le Corbusier did in promulgating his design for the restructuring of Antwerp in the 1930s (see Figure 10.6) and certainly it was the approach applied in Runcorn.

Links can be highways or roads, heavy- or light-rail links, and pedestrian and cycle-ways. Many cities in the world from Johannesburg to Los Angeles to Kolkata (formerly Calcutta) had extensive light-rail (or tram/trolley) systems until the 1940s or even later. Lobbying from motor organizations and motorists had many of them ripped up because they inconvenienced automobile drivers. There are, however, about 350 such systems now operating in the world; approximately 60 have been introduced since 1975. Los Angeles and San Diego initiated their new systems in the 1980s. Strasbourg opened its in 1994. These new networks are restricted in their range but plans for extension are numerous. In addition, many older systems are being rebuilt to operate in a more luxurious and smoother running fashion. Designers today are paying special attention to the landscaping of streets and public squares along the trolley routes to ensure that they are aesthetically acceptable components of the urban scene. Though all these networks may be important, roads and pedestrian paths remain the major structuring elements of urban form.

Three case studies of citywide infrastructures design that have strong urban design overtones have been included here. The selection of Curitiba in Brazil is arbitrary but it is internationally considered to be a good example of master planning and a relatively inexpensive plug-in urban design. It serves well as an example of how the infrastructure and urban design projects can go hand in hand. The other two case studies deal with mass transit heavy-rail systems. The first of these two is one that was largely, but not entirely, considered prior to urban development taking place. The second is a subway system put into place in response to potential demand but also as a catalyst for local urban renewal projects in areas of

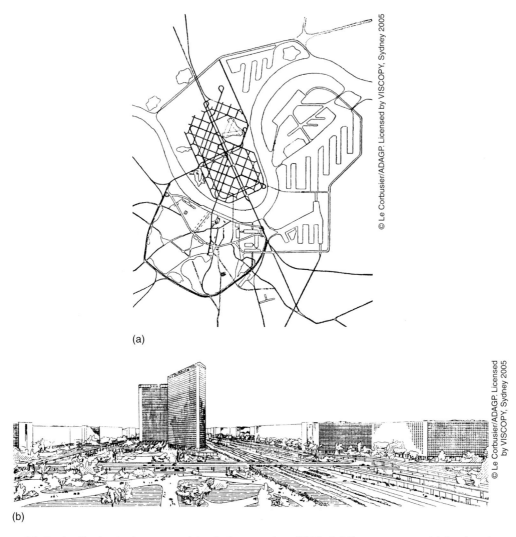

© Le Corbusier/ADAGP. Licensed by VISCOPY, Sydney 2005

(a)

© Le Corbusier/ADAGP. Licensed by VISCOPY, Sydney 2005

(b)

Figure 10.6 Le Corbusier's proposal for Antwerp *circa* 1935. (a) The movement infrastructure system and (b) the proposed image of the city.

a city undergoing rapid transformation. The first of them is the Mass Rapid Transit (MRT) system of Singapore and the second is the Jubilee Line extension in London. The building of the line is no unique occurrence. Many more extensive systems are being built. Delhi, for instance, opened its Metro Rail in December 2002. It is planned to be a 241-kilometre system with 90 stations by 2021. It is being built to hold together the existing parts of a fragmented and rapidly growing city with car ownership reputedly the equivalent of the rest of India together (to say nothing of the city's 47 other modes of road transportation from buses to elephants to rickshaws to human-drawn carts). Bangkok has an elevated system running at the fifth floor level through the city. It is, however, Curitiba that is the exemplar of planning for a system in an existing, rapidly growing, urban environment.

CASE STUDY

Curitiba, Brazil: master planning and plug-in urban design (1965–98)

During the second half of the twentieth century the city of Curitiba, capital of Paraná province in southern Brazil, saw its population grow from 120,000 people in 1940 to about 1.4 million with over 2.5 million in its metropolitan area today. In the early part of this period of growth Curitiba's development was guided by a master plan developed in 1943 by a French urbanist, Alfred Agache. With a population growth of 5% a year in the early 1960s, and contemporaneously with the excitement generated by the design and development of Brasília, the municipality felt that a new plan was needed and

organized a competition to generate ideas for what the city should be. At that time Curitiba had a population of 470,000.

The Agache plan had proposed that growth should take place in a concentric manner from the centre out. A zoning map was drawn up accordingly. In 1965 a new master plan was proposed as the result of the competition. The winning scheme of Brazilian Jorge Wilheim proposed that growth should take place in a radial, linear manner spreading out from the centre so that transportation routes could be most easily be integrated with new development

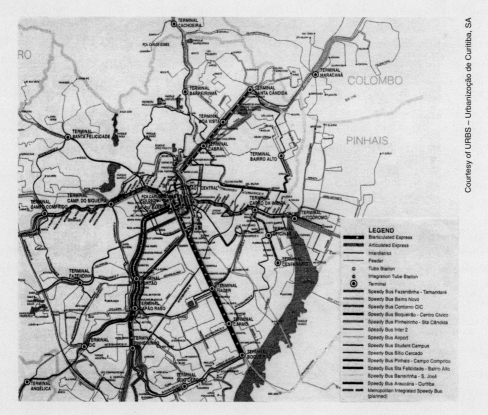

Courtesy of URBS – Urbanizoção de Curitiba, SA

Figure 10.7   The integrated transportation network following the 1965 plan.

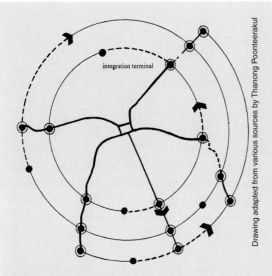

Drawing adapted from various sources by Thanong Poonteerakul

Figure 10.8 The integration concept.

and vice versa (see Figures 10.7 and 10.8). The *Plano Diretor* changed the growth pattern of Curitiba. It also focused on the promotion of industrial development and simultaneously on the enhancement of the environmental quality of the city. The implementation of this vision took place through a large number of architectural and urban design projects that were plugged into the transportation system.

The city has achieved much in improving environmental quality in a way that few, if any, cities in the economically developing world have succeeded in doing. These changes are also highly visible involving the engineering and architectural design of many elements of the city. The planning effort focused on land-use strategies and the use of non-physical design procedures to achieve physical design quality ends. These procedures included the use of the transference of development rights from historically sensitive to other areas of the city and incentives to preserve natural areas

and buildings of significant cultural value. They were also designed to attract developers to build affordable housing and other amenities deemed to be in the public interest.

The programmes for building housing for low-income people were financed by the National Housing Bank but on its demise a Municipal Housing Fund was established. It is financed by taxes on real estate transfers of property, by funds from the municipal budget and by income from the sale of building incentives. These incentives allow building rights in excess of zoning regulations. Other housing projects are really sites-and-service schemes.

The most important infrastructure elements were the 'structural axes' of transportation radiating from but running tangentially to the city centre, the transfer terminals and trinary traffic system (see Figure 10.9). They have provided the armature for plugging in a broad array of urban design projects: high-density nodes, well-detailed stations and bus stops, 'lighthouses of knowledge' (libraries), 'citizenship streets' (community centres, see Figure 10.10) and the strategic locating of accessible museums, theatres, parks and recreational facilities. In addition, and symbolically most importantly, the focus of the transportation routes on the city centre enabled the core of the city to be completely revitalized and modernized through the erection of new buildings and the refurbishment of old. The location of the major transit lines on the periphery of the Central Business District (CBD) allowed the creation of what are called 'boulevards' – pedestrian streets within it. Thus associated with the transportation network were a large number of architectural, landscape architectural and urban design projects

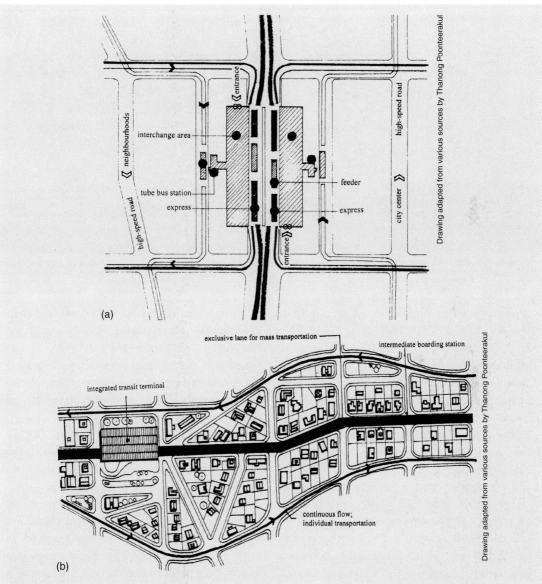

Figure 10.9 The transportation infrastructure in Curitiba. (a) A conceptual diagram of a transfer terminal and (b) the trinary traffic system in the structural avenues.

that have transformed the city. How was this end achieved?

The Institute for Research and Urban Planning of Curitiba (IPPUC) was formed in 1966 to implement the master plan. Zoning laws were passed to increase the density in areas of the city linked to transportation and a public works programme was initiated. During the early 1970s the structural avenues were developed with Federal Government funding. The major transit line began to operate in 1974. The industrial development

327

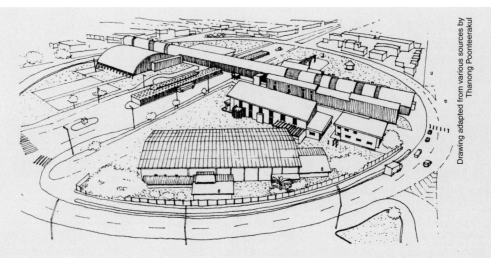

Drawing adapted from various sources by Thanong Poonteerakul

Figure 10.10 A community centre – a 'citizenship street' – plugged into the transportation system.

programme was implemented through the creation of Curitiba's Industrial City (CIC). The CIC has proven to be of great economic importance to the city, contributing significantly to the city's Gross Domestic Product of $8.26 billion in 1995. Twenty per cent of the city's workers are employed there. Without the infrastructure development, the industrial development would have been impossible.

The so-called 'above-ground underground system' has attracted great international attention. The separate express bus lanes and the 'tubular stations' at each stop with platforms that enable passengers to enter a bus without climbing up steps and having already paid for the trip (see Figure 10.11) do operate much as in a subway system. The network carries 1.3 million riders a day. Paralleling the transit system is a hierarchy of roads with each level having a designated purpose. In addition to the efforts to deal with transportation is the desire to create an ecologically sound city. The area in parks has been substantially increased (from 0.5 to 52 square metres per person), over 1.5

million trees have been planted and 145 kilometres of cycle-ways have been built. Recycling programmes have been established and educational programmes increasing environmental awareness have been implemented. What, however, amongst all these activities is urban design?

The design of the transit system can be regarded as plug-in urban design and the community centres consisting of a number of buildings might be regarded as total urban designs. This type of endeavour has traditionally been called physical planning. Such an effort in Curitiba has resulted in a large number of specific design projects, which, fragments in themselves, are part of a well-coordinated larger system. A number of observers regard such work as 'urban design at the city scale'. The lessons of Curitiba do apply to many urban design projects. The question is: 'How was Curitiba's success achieved?'

A recent study (Irazábal, in progress) suggests that there were three major contributions to the success of the 'hegemonic planning project' that was undertaken

Courtesy of Vicente del Rio

Figure 10.11 A tubular bus station.

between 1965 and the end of the twentieth century. In the first place, the power elite rallied around specific schemes. Secondly, the media wholeheartedly supported the work and widely disseminated images of proposed schemes. Thirdly, the lower-income groups could see clear, if small, material gains. In combination these three factors proved to be powerful forces ably harnessed at the mayoral level. The leadership of Mayor Jaime Lerner was particularly important in establishing the transit system in the early 1970s and overseeing the planning process. Despite these achievements, today all is not well.

Over the last decade, the planning process in Curitiba has run into problems. The basic issue is that the citizenry has not been actively involved in the decisions that affect their lives. The middle classes have been favoured. There has been little that celebrates the plurality of views (although recently ethnic memorials have been erected in the city). Many politicians and a diversity

of citizens groups are calling for change. The question now being asked is: 'How do we move ahead?' The city can rest on it laurels, but in a few years its infrastructure will start to decay and what has been achieved will be largely forgotten. New ways will have to be devised to develop the city's competitive advantage over its rivals.

Major references

Del Rio, Vicente (1992). Urban design and conflicting city images. *Cities* (November): 270–9.

Hawken, Paul, Amory B. Lovins and L. Hunter Lovins (1999). Weaving the web of solutions: the Curitiba example. In *Natural Capitalism: The Next Industrial Revolution*. London: Earthscan, 288–308.

Irazábal, Clara (in progress). The politics of development and urban design in Curitiba. In Vicente del Rio and William Siembieda, eds., *Beyond Brasília: Contemporary Urban Design in Brazil*.

Mello, Terezna Carvalho de and Paulo Henrique Battaglin Machado (1999). *Do Desenvolvimento Urbano a Sustentabilidade: From Urban Development to Sustainability*. Curitiba: IPPUC.

CASE STUDY

The MRT system, Singapore: an outstanding rapid transit system (1967 to the present and continuing)

The idea of the Mass Rapid Transit System (MRT) in Singapore goes back to the very earliest conceptual plan designed for the development of the island state after independence. In 1962, Emile E. Lorange, in a study sponsored by the United Nations, made broad recommendations for an action plan for the highly crowded central area of Singapore but he said it should be seen within a larger regional context. The following year a team consisting of Otto Koenigsberger, Charles Abrams and Susume Kobe stressed the need for a unified approach to the location of jobs and housing, and to urban renewal. Further support came from a transportation study, also sponsored by the United Nations, conducted by Britton Harris and Jack Mitchell, that recommended that Singapore have a clear transportation structure plan before major development took place. The study also doubted that a road-based system would be able to handle all the traffic that would be moving along the central circulation route. This series of recommendations resulted in the initiation of a United Nations Urban Renewal and Development Project.

The project's goals were to: (1) establish a long-range physical plan for the republic, including a transportation plan, (2) recommend policies and schemes for the central area, (3) recommend the type of mass transport system to be used, (4) assist in the preparation of specific projects and (5) develop a fully operational agency that could develop the plan further, and implement it. Crooks, Mitchell, Peacock and Stewart, a consulting firm based in Sydney, conducted the study between 1967 and 1971 when the population of Singapore was 2.07 million people and that predicted (with reasonable accuracy) being 4 million in 2000. The long-range proposal for Singapore was presented in a concept plan.

The concept plan is simple but powerful (see Figure 10.12). It was selected from a number of possibilities based on the need for an efficient transportation system. It consists of a loop MRT with seven major nodes/new towns varying in size from 100,000 to 400,000 people, being plugged into it. Accompanying the MRT would be an expressway system, with graded interchanges, and other major roads. It was also recommended that a restriction be placed on the number of cars entering the CBD. (An Area Licensing Scheme now operates and charges a fee for cars entering the district.) The success in developing and implementing the plan has been due to the efficiency of the Singaporean civil service.

The concept plan had, and has, no legal standing. The master plan of 1958 had statutory authority and accordingly was amended (and has been every 5 years since) within the specifications of the concept plan. The concept plan was revised in 1992 and again in 2001, but the basic principles behind the 1971 plan have been retained. Queenstown (1965), the first of the new towns, had already been completed and the second Toa Payoh was completed in the year of the publication of the concept plan. It was not until 1981 that the Singapore government committed itself to building the MRT. Construction began in 1983 and

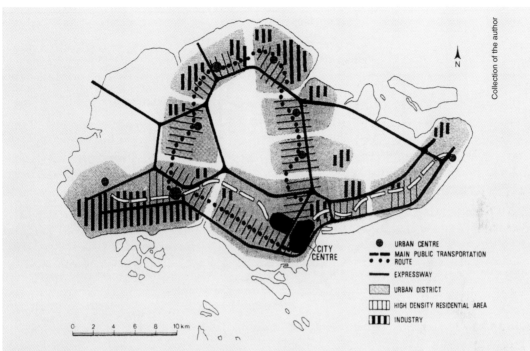

Collection of the author

Figure 10.12   The 1971 Concept Plan for Singapore.

has been the largest construction project in Singapore ever since then.

The first 67 kilometres of the system with 42 stations opened step by step between November 1987 and July 1990 at a cost of 1990$S5 billion. A spur was built in 1996 to form a loop connecting Woodlands in the north to new towns and industrial areas in the southeast and southwest. The system (see Figure 10.13) now has a route length of 89.4 kilometres and has 51 stations (16 underground, 34 elevated and one – Bishan – at ground level). The lines run underground in the central area for 23.3 kilometres (14.5 miles), above the ground for 62.3 kilometres (38.7 miles) and at ground level for 3.8 kilometres (2.4 miles). The new 20-kilometre (12.5-mile) long, 16-station North East Line was completed in April 2003. It is predominantly an underground line linking the

CBD (Harbour Front) to the Singapore Exposition Centre and Pungol. It was built at a cost of 2000$S4.6 billion. The 2001 Concept Plan contains a new orbital route and a radial MRT network. The total length of the MRT lines will be expanded to as much as 500 kilometres (310 miles) in the future to keep pace with and shape the location of Singapore's growth.

Construction has not always been easy. Perhaps not typical, but illustrative nevertheless, has been the construction of the new Chinatown station. Tunnelling had to be below existing buildings and streets. Complex traffic flows had to be maintained at ground level and major utility lines – water, sewage, telecommunications and electricity – all had to operate while construction took place. Links to existing routes and platforms had to be built at interchange stations.

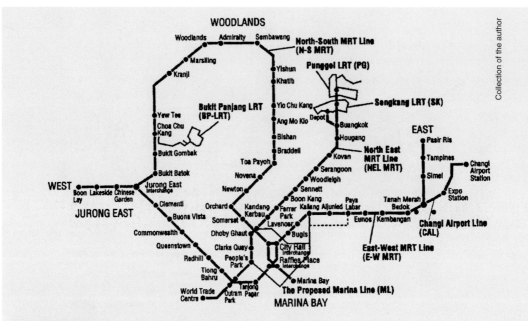

Figure 10.13 The structure of the present MRT lines.

Singapore's Land Transport Authority was created in 1995 and is now the owner and developer of the system. The operation and maintenance of the system is licensed to Singapore MRT Ltd., SBS Transit Ltd. and SLRT Pte. Ltd. under the Rapid Transit Systems Act. The goal of the organizations is to provide a service that can compete effectively with the private automobile as the transportation mode of choice. What differentiates Singapore's MRT system from many others is that its development has been linked to precinct/new town development every step of the way. The key agency in expediting the concept plan has been the republic's Housing Development Board (HDB), a statutory body established in 1960–1. It has had the responsibility for designing and building the new towns. The sheer mass of housing produced since independence led the way in deciding what elements of the transportation and industrialization programme

should be implemented. The HDB has played the major role in determining what land should be made available for transportation routes, where MRT stations should be located, where expressways should be built and how the entire network of infrastructure – water, sewers, power and telecommunications – should be developed.

As time has gone by, more and more attention has been paid to the comfort level of users of the system. Special attention has been paid to the design of subways and stations. The goal has been to make the stations column-free and have sufficient gates to handle rush hour pedestrian traffic with ease. Ticket vending is automated. Extensive pedestrian networks giving as easy an access as possible to the stations have been built. Raffles Place and Orchard Stations have extensive pedestrian networks connecting the station to surrounding buildings. In addition, local bus routes and (in the case of Chua Chu

Figure 10.14 Dover station with links to the bus station and technical college (extreme left).

Kang, Sengkang and Pungol) light-rail systems are tied into the MRT stations.

Dover station (opened in 2001) is a recent addition. Its site was long planned but the station was not built until a critical mass of potential users existed. The adjacent, recently built polytechnic and new housing plug into the station making it economically viable. The station also represents a new design attitude (see Figure 10.14). The stations are to be more individualistic in appearance. Designed by RSP Architects and Planners, a Singapore firm, with Goh Hup Chor as project leader, it is an eye-catching structure that competes effectively with that by Norman Foster at the Expo (Singapore Exposition Centre) Station (1997).

Changing concepts of the public interest have posed great challenges for designers. The new demands, in terms of the functions shown in Figure 1.6, range from those dealing with access for the handicapped to those of attaining prestige through the employment of high-style aesthetics. The new stations on the North East Line have been designed to be barrier free to give access to people in wheelchairs and have been provided with tactile guidance systems for the blind. Travellators have been introduced to speed up pedestrian movement where underground links are lengthy. Art works by world-renowned artists are being added to the stations to provide a feeling of luxury. As Lisia Ecola (2004) has noted:

> Singapore's MRT is simply the crème de la crème of transit: high-tech, spacious, efficient, and spotlessly clean. If Americans knew that transit could be this good, we wouldn't put up with anything less.

The catalytic effect of the MRT stations was both foreseen and exploited by planners and urban designers in Singapore. The construction of stations, for instance, led to a proposed surge of high-density, high-rise development in the CBD and on Orchard Road. The Jurong industrial area was not doing very well until workers had access to it via the MRT. Development around the stations is now being intensified. In 2001, the Ministry of National Development established new guidelines for stations to have convenient and comfortable underground links with shopping areas. An environment of which one can be proud is seen as essential for transit systems to compete effectively with the pleasure of driving oneself about the city. While the MRT is a good example of plug-in urban design, it can also be seen as an all-of-a-piece urban design or as a straight planning project depending on

what about its development one stresses. It is the necklace on which the new towns and the central district of Singapore are strung.

Major references

Attoe, Wayne, ed. (1988). *Transit, Land Use, and Urban Form*. Austin, TX: University of Texas Press.

Chew, T. C. and C. K. Chua (1998). Development of Singapore's Rapid Transit System. *Japan Railway and Transport Review* **18**: 26–30.

Crooks, Mitchell, Peacock, Stewart (1971). Report. *The Urban Renewal and Development Project*, Singapore. Prepared for the United Nations Development Program Special Fund. Sydney: The authors.

Vuchic, Vukan (1999). *Transportation for Livable Cities*. New Brunswick, NJ: Center for Urban Policy Research, Rutgers University.

SMRT. Moving with our customers. www.smrt.com.sg/smrt/index.htm

CASE STUDY

The Jubilee Line extension, London, England, UK: an underground rail link as a catalyst for urban revitalization (*c.* 1974–2000)

The Jubilee Line in London was built both to enhance accessibility to existing areas of London and to spur new development. Like most infrastructure projects, the line had a precedent that it both followed and from which it departed. It sought the environmental quality of Singapore, the efficiency of the Hong Kong Mass Transit Rail (MTR) system and both of those systems' extensive new property development adjacent to each station but with a greater architectural flair in its design. The link between Hong Kong and London is not surprising because the Chairman of London Transport at the time, Sir Wilfred Newton, and the chief architect whom he brought on board,

Roland Paoletti, were both involved in the planning and designing of the MTR system in Hong Kong. Like most such developments, the extension of the Jubilee Line was long in gestation and its conception difficult to date. First talk of it was in 1949 but no action followed.

By the early 1970s, the London Docklands, as noted in the description of Canary Wharf, had become abandoned and the London docks shifted down the River Thames to Tilbury. Much of East London was undergoing substantial population change accompanied by the degeneration of its physical fabric. Plans for extending the London transit network into the area had long been considered but neither political nor financial support was sufficient for it to be furthered. The situation started to change with the formation of the London Docklands Joint Committee of the five Boroughs into which the area fell and a parallel decision made in 1978 to build an underground line to the east from Central London.

The new line would extend the existing Jubilee Line (completed in 1977) that ran from Charing Cross to Stanmore in London's northwestern suburbs. A change of government, however, shelved the project. In 1981 it established the London Docklands Development Corporation (LDDC) and the need for a transportation link to the Docklands became urgent. Lack of funding for a heavy-rail system led to the building of a light-rail line to the Docklands from the City. It has a capacity of 27,000 passengers a day and was completed in 1987.

The system was rendered inadequate by the Olympia and York's proposal for Canary Wharf (see Chapter 8). It projected a working population of 50,000 people at Canary Wharf with a substantial number of other visitors to the site each day. To operate well as a location for commerce and prevent traffic chaos Canary Wharf needed access via a major mass transportation connection. The proposal for the Jubilee Line was supported politically by the British Prime Minister, Margaret Thatcher, who promised to get the project funded. Olympia and York chipped in £400 million ($US1 billion) towards the cost of this infrastructure item. Government support was, however, very slow in coming and came too late to encourage companies to move to Canary Wharf and thus to save Olympia and York from bankruptcy. It was not until 1996 that ground was broken for the scheme. The extension of the Jubilee Line links two main railway stations (Waterloo and London Bridge) with existing centres in East London (see Figure 10.15) that were and still are in various degrees of squalor and gentrification. It also gives access to other urban regeneration projects (such as the Tate Modern art gallery designed by Herzog and de Meuron near Southwark station).

Paoletti and his team of architects completed the design of the line in 18 months. It is comprised of 12.2 kilometres of twin tunnels and a dozen stations (six completely new). The tunnels are relatively deep (from 15 to 20 metres) because they run under existing buildings and also under the River Thames (four times). Constructing it was a major engineering task because the new stations and line had to be plugged into the tunnels and concourses of existing stations. It costs £3.5 billion (US$8 billion). The line was sufficiently complete to be opened in late 1999 although work on it continues. Its programmed opening date of 1998 was highly optimistic as was its predicted budget (£2.5 billion).

The design goal was to create an efficient system with good platform-to-ground connections, good links to other modes of transport (including other underground lines and the light-rail system). The stations would be architecturally distinctive. A different architectural team, most of them with high-tech aesthetic and engineering backgrounds, designed each station except a team under Paoletti that designed the stations at Waterloo and Canada Wharf. No strict design guidelines for unifying the architecture of the different stations were established. Some details that serve a visually unifying purpose were, however, specified: the floors of the concourses, the nature of the escalators, the glass doors and the signage.

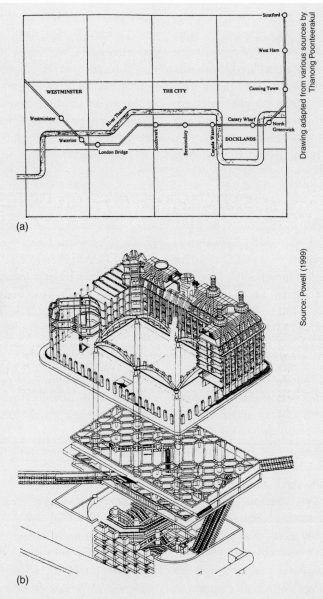

Drawing adapted from various sources by Thanong Poonteerakul

Source: Powell (1999)

Figure 10.15 The Jubilee Line extension. (a) The route and (b) the intersection of lines at Westminster station.

The decision to have a diversity of designers follows a precedent set in London during the 1930s and, more recently, in a diverse set of places – Genoa, Singapore and Rotterdam. The designs are 'hard-edged' and primarily related to global aesthetic trends rather than local traditions. The designs of the stations were first publicly exhibited in 1992 and were well received by design professionals, the press and the lay-public alike.

From an urban design point of view what has been important are the stations, their

Source: Wordsearch and the Royal Academy of Art (2001); courtesy of Foster and Partners, Architects

(a)

(b)

Figure 10.16 Canary Wharf Station. (a) A longitudinal section through the Canary Wharf station and (b) a view of the underground concourse.

links to and their catalytic effect on their surroundings. The stations are varied in nature not just because of their aesthetics but the way they relate to the ground level, to other modes of transportation and the way their surroundings have been handled. The lessons from Singapore and Hong Kong were well learnt. The largest of the stations is at Canary Wharf. It is 314 metres (1030 feet) in length (see Figure 10.16). Built through a cut-and-cover approach, it has a 'cathedral-like' internal space. The station plugs into the Canary Wharf development with the Canary Wharf towers being directly linked into it.

There are urban design projects at other stations such as Newham, North Greenwich and Southwark, and the second phase of development at Canary Wharf was due to get underway at the time of writing. These projects have, however, come largely as an afterthought and not in conjunction with the design of the line. The hope is that the developments at and around the stations by high-profile architects such as John McAslan, Chris Wilkerson, Norman Foster and Eva Jiricna will spur growth but be in tune with their surroundings. At West Ham, for instance, the paved square in front of the station is related to the residential scale of the area (see Figure 10.17).

The catalytic effect of the investment in the public realm is yet to be seen. The

337

Figure 10.17 The Square at West Ham station.

station at North Greenwich was located at a highly derelict location but it enabled the ill-fated Millennium Dome to be built and the festival to be held. Perhaps, Stratford has the greatest potential because of its connection to the new international station on the Channel tunnel and rail link. The multiplier effect of the investment in the line will depend on the state of the economy more than the state of the architecture. Time will tell. The line does bind parts of London long neglected into the whole. The urban and architectural image is very important in an era of the globalization of marketing. It establishes an air of up-to-dateness.

Major references

Pachini, Luca (2000). The Jubilee Line extension project. *Casabella* **64** (678): 64–83.

Powell, Kenneth (1999). *The Jubilee Line Extension*. London: Lawrence King Publishing.

Russell, James S. (2000). Engineering civility: transit stations. *Architectural Record* **188** (3): 129–33.

Wordsearch and the Royal Academy of Arts (2001). *New Connections, New Architecture, New Urban Environments and the London Jubilee Line Extension*. London: Royal Academy of the Arts.

Precinct Links: Binding Precincts into Units

The physical links binding precincts into coherent, identifiable units take many different forms. They are most commonly streets and pedestrian ways, but they can be greenways, bicycle paths, skyway links and underground passages. Underground pedestrian networks may seem to be a surprising way of linking elements together at the precinct level, but many cities have them.

Designing the Infrastructure to be Plugged Into

Designing the basic infrastructure – streets, a reticulated water supply system, sewers, electricity and communication systems – is very much the basis for urban development. It can lead development. La Défense in Paris could be included here as an example of a precinct with a multi-layered infrastructure layout into which new commercial buildings have been plugged. The same principle applies to most World's Fairs although in their case everything is done in a great hurry. The infrastructure is built and the individual exhibitors then plug their buildings into it. The example included here is Expo '92 in Seville.

Similarly, on a much vaster scale, suburban housing developments throughout the world consist of the infrastructure (roads, sewers, water and electric supply) being built by a property developer, public or private, and the plots sold off to individual owners to develop as they wish although many such developments are total urban designs (as is Raleigh Park described in Chapter 7) but others are all-of-a-piece urban designs in which the designs of individual houses are heavily controlled by design guidelines (e.g. as in Seaside, Florida, described in Chapter 8). In many developments the freedom of design allotted to individual owners is considerable.

Building, or purchasing, a house is the major investment decision of countless families and their design decisions are very much tempered by their perception of what can be sold easily if necessary. The house designs thus tend to be conservative and similar to what is being built elsewhere in the neighbourhood. In areas inhabited by the *nouveau riche* where individual display is an important aspect of status, there tends to be much greater idiosyncrasy in design. Unity, if achieved at all, is obtained through diversity. Standard suburban developments cater to the needs of the middle- and upper-income groups in a society (see Figure 10.18). Sites-and-services cater to low-income populations in third world countries.

In the sites-and-services approach to the creation of housing for the very poor, a new precinct is provided with roads and streetlights, sewers, and a reticulated water system. Each site is provided with connections to the sewerage system and a water tap. In some cases, where the clients have greater resources, the site may be supplied with a latrine and a multipurpose community room. The household-ers then build their houses themselves plugging them into the infrastructure

Courtesy of Metropolitan Area Planning Department, Wichita

(a)   (b)

Figure 10.18 The suburban environment. (a) Sedgwick County, Kansas and (b) Salt Lake City, Kolkata.

provided. The approach was pioneered in Africa and Latin America but has also been widely used in India. The example included here, Aranya Township in India, had much more thought than usual put into its design. In sites-and-services projects, the houses are literally built by the owners themselves although skilled craftspeople often assist. For wealthy people, in contrast, the division of labour is sharply defined. Contractors build their houses.

Middle income and wealthy people have the purchasing power to make the choices that fit their own needs, as they perceive them. Yet questions are being asked as to whether the market place is providing a sufficient diversity of neighbourhood types to give people a real choice. Most plug-in residential neighbourhood designs are highly conservative in nature and not responsive to the emerging demographic characteristics of the population or the needs of the people who are not actually doing the purchasing. For instance, the journey to school on foot independently by children is seldom a topic of consideration nor are the needs of the fragile elderly. The neighbourhood design types tend to be standard subdivisions. If they can be sold they are regarded as good.

The sites-and-services approach has had mixed successes. It works when the areas selected for development are close to jobs and it works when the projects are not heavily subsidized by the public sector. If a site is distant from jobs nobody wants to live there and if heavily subsidized the cash-strapped poor are likely to sell their plots at market rates to higher-income groups in order to obtain cash in hand.

Major references

Guy, Simon, Simon Marvin and Timothy Moss, eds. (2001). *Urban Infrastructure in Transition: Networks, Buildings, Plans*. London: Earthscan.

Turner, John F. C. (1976). *Housing by People: Towards Autonomy in Building Environments*. London: Marion Boyers.

CASE STUDY

Expo '92 Seville, Spain: a World's Fair (1976–92)

World's Fairs are temporary expositions where nations and organizations build pavilions whose architecture and contents celebrate themselves and their achievements. They draw large crowds and can act as catalysts for further development in the host city. The plan and infrastructure of the fair sites are important aspects of the overall design. They have to be easily plugged into by assorted pavilions designed by a variety of architects striving to outdo each other in attracting attention. The infrastructure also has to provide a pleasant (i.e. efficient, comfortable and interesting) circulation space for the pedestrians that throng the fairs on important days.

The 1992 World's Fair in Seville celebrated the 500th anniversary of the discovery by Europeans of the New World and its peoples. It was supposed to have paralleled a fair in Chicago but that city withdrew in 1987. The initial idea for a fair in Seville came from Felipe González, the socialist Prime Minister of Spain who hailed from Seville. King Juan Carlos picked up the idea in 1976. González saw it as an opportunity to do more for Seville than put it on the world map. He sought and obtained funding from the European Community (now European Union) programme for depressed areas for a new airport (designed by Rafael Moneo), a new railroad station (designed by Cruz/Ortiz) and a high-speed train (AVE) link to Madrid. (The introduction of the train reduced flights from Madrid by 90%.) He saw them to be necessary infrastructure elements to both run a successful World's Fair and as a catalyst for a more enduring impact on Seville. It would also consolidate Seville's position as capital of the Autonomous Andalusian region.

The site chosen in 1985 for the fair is an artificial island, Isla de la Cartuja, in the Guadalquivir River. The island falls between the river and an artificial flood control channel. Only a 425-acre (162-hectare) part of the island was used for the fair but the remainder was improved with vegetation. One of the problems facing the site designers was the difficulty of linking it to the historic core of Seville especially as obsolete rail tracks as well as the mainstream of the river intervened. Emilo Ambasz of New York and a consortium of Spanish engineers (Fernández Ordonez (brother of Spain's Foreign Relations Minister), Martinez Calzon, Junquera del Diestro and Perez Pita) were awarded first prize *ex aqueo* in an invited competition of 12 teams. It has been widely assumed that 'political considerations' weighed heavily in the decision to have joint-winners. The two teams were supposed to collaborate in producing a new design but that effort only lasted for 2 days.

The competition brief called for a theatre (to seat 2000), an auditorium (to seat 2200), a drama theatre (to seat 1500), an outdoor auditorium (to seat 10,000), an Olympic swimming pool (with seating for 5000), a planetarium and an arena for 25,000. As the programme changed no heed was paid to Ambaz's design. The problem that arose was due to the Fair's unanticipated success in attracting international exhibitors; the number increased from an expected 60 to 108.

Ambasz's scheme (see Figure 10.19) drew water from the river into three large

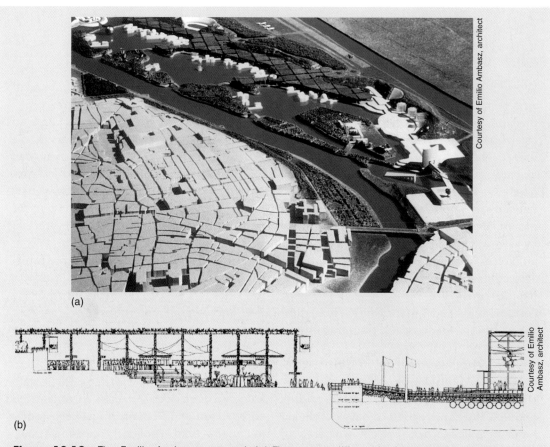

(a)

(b)

Courtesy of Emilio Ambasz, architect

Courtesy of Emilio Ambasz, architect

Figure 10.19 The Emilio Ambaz proposal. (a) The competition-winning proposal and (b) a cross section showing a barge plugged onto a wharf.

pools/lakes around which quays were located providing linkages into all the Park's infrastructure systems. He envisaged the exhibitors having their pavilions built on barges and moved along the river to plug-in to the site for the duration of the Fair. Once the fair was over the barges and their pavilions would 'sail' away and the park would remain. The other winning scheme was less dramatic. It kept the existing topography and proposed an ordered system of intersecting avenues in a grid form. The centrepiece – foreground element – was to be an 80-metre diameter moving model of the solar system.

Ambasz's design related a number of entrances on the Fair site to many points in the city via ferries – Venetian *vaporetti*. The Ordonez scheme was very much building oriented. It proposed bridges, buildings, monorails, roads and other artefacts that were financially rewarding to political leaders. Julio Cano Lasso, who was given the instruction to amalgamate ideas from the competition-winning schemes, assembled the implemented design (see Figure 10.20). The scheme was inward looking but linked to the city by a number of new bridges designed by such major figures as Santiago

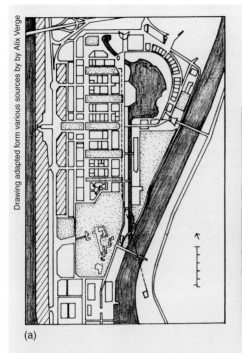

Figure 10.20 Expo '92, Seville. (a) The plan as developed and (b) general view of the fair.

Calatrava. The riverfront had a promenade along it but there was little to be viewed from it. The site was divided into three zones. The first was for Spanish regional pavilions. They created a dense cluster around a lake, the Lago de España. The second was for the international pavilions. They were located on the side of five parallel avenues (named after Edison, Newton, Curie, Einstein and Darwin) set at right angles to the main road, Camino de los Descubrimientos, connecting the Lago de España to the river. The third zone consisted of the permanent buildings. Here the fifteenth century Carthusian Monasterio Santa María de las Cuevas was restored especially for the Expo as a central exhibit. New buildings were added nearby: the Triana Tower (designed by Francisco Javier Sáenz de Oíza), the Pabellón de Descubrimientos (Pavilion of Discoveries

designed by Javier Feduchi and Eduardo Arroyo) and others including the Pabellón de Andalucía, the province in which Seville is located.

The site plan showed little ingenuity but functioned effectively. To deal with the summer heat 32,000 trees were planted to give shade and some visual unity to the scheme. The pavilions were simply plugged into the infrastructure provided. They were considerably more colourful than those at the previous World's Fair (in Osaka) and were built mainly out of natural stone and metal sheeting. Some had especially interesting features. The Kuwati Pavilion (designed by Santiago Calatrava) had a roof of wooden 'claws' that closed to keep out the midday sun. The other pavilions were also designed by architectural luminaries such as Tadao Ando (the Japanese Pavilion).

343

The question with World's Fairs is: 'What do you do with the site when the Fair is over?' Most of the World's Fairs are demolished after their run is over and the sites completely turned over for other uses. This observation is partially true of Seville too but it did also leave a lasting legacy. The permanent buildings remain but much of the site now serves new purposes. It was transformed into a complex of exhibition halls and museums, the Cartuga, a science park, and leisure areas. The Lago de España is now part of the Isla Mágica theme park that opened in 1997. The park recreates the travels of the sixteenth century Seville-based new world explorers but its major feature is The Jaguar, a rollercoaster that rushes along at 85 kilometres per hour (53 miles per hour)! The theme park is struggling financially. Who goes to Seville to visit a theme park? In summer?

Major references

Ambasz, Emilio, ed. (1998). Master plan for the Universal Exposition – Seville 1992: Seville, Spain. In *Emilio Ambasz: The Poetics of the Pragmatic: Architecture, Exhibit, Industrial Design*. New York: Rizzoli, 197–203.

Dixon, John M. (1992). World on a platter. *Progressive Architecture* **73** (7): 86–95.

Forgey, Benjamin (1992). Spanish Treasures (Expo '92, Seville). *Architecture* **81** (7): 72–9.

Novo, Francisco Garcia and Claudia Zavalete de Daute (2002). *Paisaje y urbanismo de la Expo '92*. Seville: Reditores.

CASE STUDY

Aranya Township, Indore, India: a sites-and-services scheme (1983–96)

Aranya (meaning forest) Township is a 7000-plot predominantly sites-and-services project located on an 86-hectare (212-acre) site on the fringe of Indore. The scheme was created for a projected population of about nine people per household making a total of 63,000 people. The developer was the Indore Development Authority (IDA) and the architect was Balkrishna V. Doshi and his Vastu Shilpa Foundation of Ahmedabad. The target population was mixed – 65% low-income people (the EWS, Economically Weaker Section) whose income was less than Rs 350 (1990$US30) per month and 35% higher income. The project thus had a social objective as well as providing shelter. The mix of people is more than on economic grounds. Hindus, Muslims, Sikhs, Buddhists, Jains and Christians live there.

The project was one in which plots were prepared and services provided by the IDA but the construction of houses was left to the owners of the plots. Five objectives dictated the design: (1) to ensure a fine living environment, (2) to create a sense of community, (3) to deal with the hot arid climate, (4) to create an efficient, cost-effective armature into which individual buildings could be plugged and (5) to provide for the way that life in low-income areas in India spills out onto the street and, in arid areas, onto the flat roofs of buildings.

344

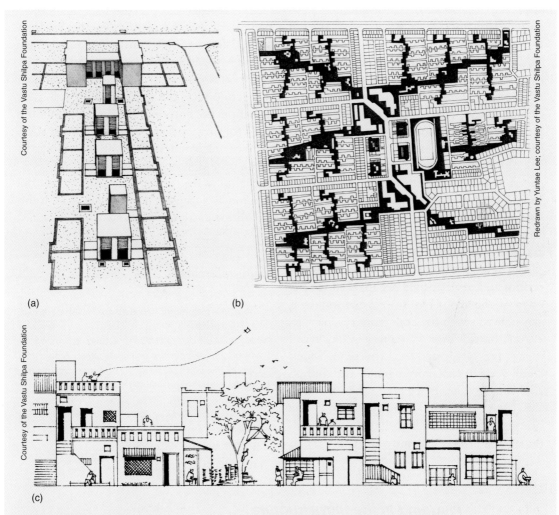

(a)

(b)

(c)

Figure 10.21 Aranya Township, Indore. (a) Typical building sites with service cores, (b) the site plan and (c) the type of development anticipated.

The infrastructure was laid out in a hierarchical manner with a central collecting point from where services branch to smaller collecting points to points on each block that serve a number of units. The location of the latrines was a problem. It is most economical to provide them in the front of buildings so that connections to mains are short, but the past research of the Vastu Shilpa Foundation at other sites-and-services projects had shown that this arrangement was much disliked by those who took up such plots. The latrines are thus at the back of the lots (see Figure 10.21a).

The site plan is innovative. Essentially a gridiron plan, it is arranged in a modified concentric pattern to create a mosaic of income-segregated sub-areas that build up into an integrated whole (see Figure 10.21b). The periphery of each sector is ringed with large plots entered directly from a road with the lower-income plots in the interior. The street pattern follows a hierarchy from larger roads to cul-de-sacs that form the smallest, and most heavily used, unit of communal space. The sale at a profit of the plots for the higher-income group subsidized services for the lower.

Community facilities are located at the centre of the plan and fingers of open space thread from there to the edges of the site. The core is arranged in a linear fashion and consists of four clusters of mixed commercial and retail uses. The large shops face the street and the small the courtyards. A school and athletic field are located on the edge of the core. The site layout makes it possible to reach the core from the periphery of the site in a 10-minute walk. Work places are integrated into the plan. Much small-scale retail, commercial and industrial activity takes place in the streets and in the houses. It was anticipated that the houses would be built to have a verandah facing the street, a room with the kitchen

behind it and the latrines in the back. A second floor could then be tacked on (see Figure 10.21c). The latrine–kitchen relationship is not ideal in Hindu households but economics, the desire to not walk past a latrine on entering the house, and the need for privacy dictate it. A demonstration project designed by Doshi was built to show potential residents the type of development that could take place. Is the scheme a success? It won the Aga Kahn award for design in 1995.

Major references

Bhatt, Vikram and Peter Scriver (1990). Aranya Township, Indore. In *After the Masters*. Ahmedabad: Mapin Publishing, 98–9.
Doshi, Balkrishna V. (1988). Aranya township. In *Mimar 28: Architecture in Development*. Singapore: Concept Media, 24–9. http://archnet.org/library/pubdownloader/pdf/4644/doc/dpt0587.pdf
Steele, James (1998). Aranya low-cost housing. In *The Complete Works of Balkrishna Doshi: Rethinking Modernism for the Developing World*. London: Thames and Hudson, 114–29.

Plugging In the Infrastructure

Links designed to bind existing parts of a precinct together are proposed for a number of reasons and take on several forms. The primary reasons are to enhance accessibility and to provide an amenity to pedestrians and/or bicyclists. In Charles Center, the skywalk system was designed to make the parts of the superblock easily accessible from each other, but also to both separate vehicular traffic from pedestrian on safety grounds and be a symbol of the unity in an area of diverse buildings.

The two case studies described here are very different in character. The infrastructure of the first is at the second floor level and is enclosed while that of the second is really below the street at basement level but open to the sky. The first was designed to segregate pedestrians and vehicular traffic and to provide a comfortable passage from building to building in the harsh Minnesota winter. The second was simply to make a city centre a more attractive place. Both have been catalysts for new development.

An alternative type not described here is the underground pedestrian network mentioned earlier in this chapter. That in Toronto connects 38 office buildings, 3 major hotels and 5 subway stations. It houses 1000 stores and restaurants. Montreal has its Golden Square Mile of protected walkways, reputedly the most extensive in the world. In Kansas City there is Tropolis, an underground business complex of 4 million square feet (371,600 square metres) with an employee population of 1300 people. It has wide, paved streets that are completely dry and 'brilliantly illuminated'. It is located in old mines. Sydney has extensive subterranean walkway in its city centre. They link the underground stations of its suburban railway system to basement shopping areas in adjacent blocks. The walkways themselves are lined with shops and lead to major destinations. They are well used.

Major references

Attoe, Wayne and Donn Logan (1989). *American Urban Architecture: Catalysts in the Design of Cities*. Berkeley and Los Angeles: University of California Press.

Young, Karen A. (1999). *Subterranean Commercial Development*. http://www.emich.edu/public/geo/557/book/d111.underground.html

CASE STUDY

The skywalk system, Minneapolis, Minnesota, USA (1959 to the present; planned completion 2015)

The Minneapolis skywalk system consists of pedestrian walkways that link the interiors of buildings in the office and retail core of the city at the second storey level (i.e. first floor level in countries using British English) (see Figure 10.22). These spaces consist of shopping galleries and hotel and commercial building lobbies. It is an indoor, climatically controlled network of links and places. It is not a unique example but it is the most extensive in the United States.

The idea to build such a system is credited to the president, Leslie Park, of a real estate company, Baker Properties. His goal was to have the city centre compete effectively with suburban shopping malls with their vast temperature-controlled internal spaces. Initially Park received little support from the city administration but in 1959, the Minneapolis City Planning Department commissioned him and an architect, Ed Baker, to develop a plan for such a system.

Park and Baker proposed a skyway scheme that would link buildings on Nicollet Mall, Minneapolis's main street. It would enable people to move from building to building without going outside. Escalators at the corners of each block at street level would provide easy access to the elevated walkways. To demonstrate the merit of the scheme, Park commissioned Baker to design Northstar Center, a mixed-use building. It was opened in 1959. The first link (1962) in what has become the skyway

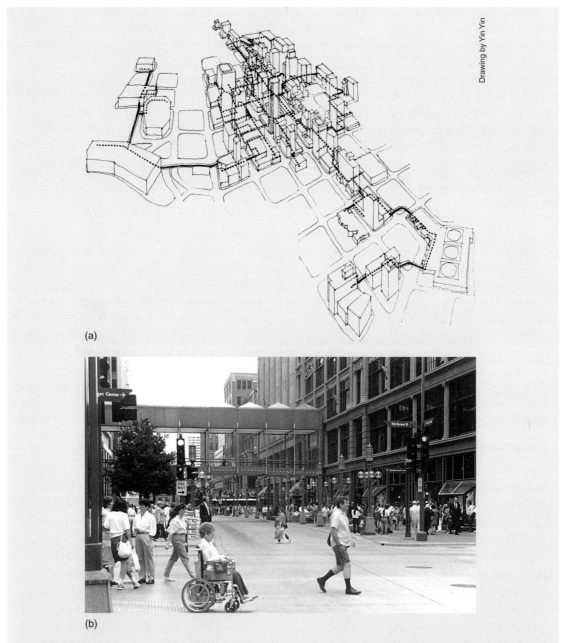

Drawing by Yin Yin

(a)

(b)

Figure 10.22 The skyway system, Minneapolis. (a) The skyway pattern and (b) Nicollet Mall.

system joined the Center to what was then the Northwestern National Bank. The construction boosted the value of second storey commercial space without reducing ground floor values. As the system grew, however, ground floor rentals were, indeed, affected.

Link after link followed. By 1990 there were 28 bridges connecting 27 contiguous blocks with the IDS Crystal Court as its primary hub. By 2002 there were 5 miles (8 kilometres) of skyways and tunnels, and 62 bridges (see Figure 10.22 for an example). They join 65 blocks linking 2000 stores, plus coffee shops and kiosks, 34 restaurants, 1500 apartment units, 4000 hotel rooms and 2 million square feet (190,000 square metres) of office space. In mid-2002, Minneapolis' city-planning department unveiled the final phase of the plan focusing on completing the remaining links by 2015. It also specified that the links (or alternatives) had to be operational while buildings were under construction or renovation.

The Skyway Advisory Service, part of the municipal government's Downtown Council, was formed in the late 1970s. While it is only an advisory service it has developed considerable political clout over the years. It is thus able to insist on particular types of links even though private corporations whose buildings are joined own the links. Building the links is not easy. To build across a street, owners first must obtain an encroachment permit and post a $500,000 bond to cover later removal costs if they become necessary. The cost of a link varies from about $550,000 to $6.3 million. The former is for a standard link between two buildings and the latter is the cost of the skyway and tunnel combination linking Minneapolis City Hall with the United States Court House, the Grain Exchange and the Jerry Haaf Memorial Ramp.

The design of the links must follow a number of guidelines and controls. The links must be at least 3.6 metres (12 feet) wide and no wider than 8.27 metres (27 feet), and be horizontal in appearance even if their passageway slopes. Street clearance must be 5.2 metres (17 feet) and they must have glass walls to make orientation easier for the users of the system. The trade-off is that heat gains and losses are high with such walls. The design guidelines for the exterior appearance are highly permissive so the look of the bridges varies considerably. They are supposed to be 'in harmony' with the buildings they link. Achieving 'harmony' is often difficult because the appearances of the buildings the links join are often very different. The links themselves cannot be used for retail purposes and the handing out of political literature is prohibited. They are truly just links. They do block certain vistas for the pedestrian in the street but they create new vistas for those on the links.

While the skywalk is in the ownership of many private hands, it is open to the public from 6.30 a.m. to 10 p.m. on weekdays and for shorter periods on weekend days. It is very well patronized especially during winter months when temperatures often plunge well below zero degrees celsius and even fahrenheit. The busiest link is between the IDS Block and the Baker Block. Twenty-three thousand people use it each day. They are primarily middle class and almost 60% of them are women.

Is the skyway a success? One hallmark of its success is the increase in the number of links over the years. They have been deemed to be desirable. It is certainly successful in terms of the comfort, ease and sense of security that it provides pedestrians. It is in terms of second floor retail activity. It has, however, taken much business off the street level. Closed shops attest to that. At the same time, the downtown area of the city has become more attractive to investors in terms of what it offers. It has enabled the city centre to compete with suburban sites for development although the cost of building bridges has deterred some organizations from locating in the city. Parking lots in fringe areas have had their patronage boosted and the usage of the city's bus system has increased because of the added convenience provided by the skyway links in moving around downtown. Some people worry about the way the system provides shops catering to the middle class and in doing so separates middle-class people and the poor thus creating a dual downtown society (Robertson, 1994).

Major references

Robertson, Kent A. (1993). Pedestrian strategies for downtown planners: skywalks versus pedestrian malls. *Journal of the American Institute of Planners* **59** (3): 361–71.

Robertson, Kent A. (1994). *Pedestrian Malls and Skywalks: Traffic Segregation Strategies in American Downtowns.* Aldershot: Avebury.

Skyway, Minneapolis. http://www.cala2.umn.edu/ skywayminneapolis/

CASE STUDY

Paseo del Rio, San Antonio, Texas, USA: a riverside walkway (1939–41, 1962 to the present and continuing)

The San Antonio River has its source 3 miles north of the city. In the downtown area it has paved walks along its banks. The design and implementation of these walkways, known as Paseo del Rio, or Riverwalk, is a pioneering example of a consciously designed riverfront park integrated with the buildings around it. In 1984 it received a Distinguished Achievement Award in the American Institute of Architects Honors Program. It is also an example of the effect that an individual with an idea can have on a city.

In the city centre the river runs at a level below the streets. In the 1920s work was done on stabilizing its banks. In 1929 it was proposed to pave it over as a flood prevention measure and to make it a sewer but this idea was not taken seriously. Robert Hugman, a local architect, aged 29, instead proposed the building of walkways along its banks. He was joined by groups such as the San Antonio

Real Estate Board, the San Antonio Advertising Club, and the local chapter of the Daughters of the American Revolution in lobbying business and civic leaders to develop the project. A number of people with property along the river agreed to pay $2.50 per foot of riverfrontage into a fund to finance riverfront improvements but the City Commissioners refused to move ahead with them. It was not until 1938, with support from the Works Projects Administration (WPA), that funds became available to implement the scheme. Upstream engineering projects had already been constructed to control the flow of water in the river. Once these projects were completed, the proposed improvements along the river could be implemented.

Hugman was appointed project architect and Robert Turk, the superintendent of construction. A pedestrian esplanade running for almost 2 miles (3 kilometres)

along the river and stretching for 21 city blocks was constructed with the funding available. It was budgeted to cost about 1940$US300,000. It, however, cost about $430,000 funded partially by a city bond issue of $75,000, a 1.5 cents per $1000 assessed value property tax on local owners and a WPA grant of $335,000. The development ultimately comprised 17,000 feet (about 5 kilometres) of walkways, 31 stairways leading down to the walkways from 21 bridges and 11,000 trees. Today, tall cypresses and dense foliage make for a tropical garden like atmosphere. To unify the project visually, Hugman used a local sand-coloured stone throughout. Figure 10.23 shows the state of the project in 1993.

Due to major cost overruns Hugman was dismissed as project architect and replaced by J. Fred Buenz in 1940, and the WPA project was completed. The result was very attractive. The onset of World War II further inhibited development. Lack of maintenance meant that by the 1960s, the river in downtown San Antonio had deteriorated and had an exaggerated reputation of being a hanging-out area for 'unsavoury types, vandals and derelicts'. Perceptions of its state sparked a series of redevelopment ideas. A San Antonio businessman, David Straus, started a campaign to boost the economic state of the downtown area and to restore the river and redevelop its surroundings. San Antonio's Tourist Attraction Committee proposed a redevelopment plan drawn up by MARCO Engineering but the plan was rejected as having too trite a character. In 1962 the San Antonio Riverwalk Commission was established and charged with developing a new master plan.

This plan, which received a design award from *Progressive Architecture*, was developed by a group led by Cyrus Wagner and sponsored by the American Institute of Architects. The improvements and redesign of the walkway acted as a catalyst for the building of hotels (eight in all), local shops and restaurants (Casa Rio was the first) along the river. It was also a selling point in San Antonio developing the 1968 HemisFair under the auspices of the Bureau of International Exhibitions and it was, in turn, a catalyst for the redevelopment of Riverwalk to which the fair was linked. The whole plan recognized the need for continuous upgrading and maintenance of the Riverwalk, something often neglected in urban designing.

The reclaiming of the river, as intended, reinvigorated San Antonio's central area. Riverwalk is now home to numerous cafés and restaurants. Some of the buildings that backed on to the river have been turned around to face it but the backs of others have simply been tidied up and act as a reminder of the former status of the river. Other buildings changed their uses (e.g. a college into a hotel). The plugged-in elements include the Hyatt Hotel, whose base and atrium acts as a link to the Alamo, the Convention Center, and River Center (a shopping complex). The Paseo del Alamo to Riverwalk, a link between Riverwalk and Alamo Plaza, is an extension designed by Boon Powell of Ford, Powell and Carson. The 17-foot (5-metre) height difference between the two is handled with a multi-level walkway and a series of descending plazas. A positive response to a user satisfaction study led to plans for the expansion of Riverwalk and a study by Skidmore Owings and Merrill was commissioned.

A third generation of development is now occurring. A team led by Ted Flato, David Lake, John Blood and Elizabeth Danze won a competition to design the International

Legend

1. Convention Center
2. Plaza Alamo
3. Villeta Assembly Hall
4. Hemisphere Park

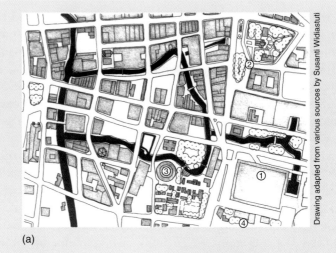

Drawing adapted from various sources by Susanti Widiastuti

(a)

Photograph by Jennifer Taylor

(b)

Figure 10.23 Riverwalk, San Antonio. (a) The plan and (b) a view from a bridge in 1993.

Center on the walk and another scheme, by architects Rick Archer, Tim Blonkvist and Madison Smith set out to link the historic Aztec Theater to Riverwalk. A plan by SWA for developing a 14-mile corridor along the river received a 2001 American Society of Landscape Architects Honor Award for Analysis and Planning. One design task is to make Riverwalk accessible to people in wheelchairs. Hugman did not foresee this necessity. In 2002 Ford, Powell and Carson, were once again, engaged to create further improvements (due for completion in 2010) along the river.

Today there are sightseeing cruises on the river and it is the site of the San Antonio Fiesta Parade of floats. Riverwalk is almost always filled with partygoers, children, tourists and locals. It is particularly 'crazy' during Fiesta. Riverwalk has proven to be a major asset to the city. Nine million people a year use it and it is estimated to contribute $800 million to San Antonio's $3 billion tourist industry each year. It was the location for the celebration of the San Antonio Spurs' victory when it won the United States basketball championships.

Keeping Riverwalk in good condition is expensive. It requires constant maintenance. The City's Department of Parks and Recreation has an annual budget of $4.25 million to maintain the walk. The department puts an extraordinary number of new plants into the ground each year. The effort yields results. The design has become a precedent for other cities to follow. Closed in rivers, abandoned rail tracks and a host of alleys can be turned into attractive assets for a city. Hugman deserves recognition for his foresight and persistence. Urban designers need both.

Major references

Black, Sinclair (1979). San Antonio's Linear Paradise. *American Institute of Architects Journal* **68** (9): 30–9.

Hammatt, Heather (2002). Going with the flow. *Landscape Architecture* **92** (1): 72–7.

Tyler, Ronnie C. (1996). San Antonio River. *The New Handbook of Texas*. Austin, TX: Texas State Historical Society.

Zunker, Vernon G. (1983). *A Dream Come True: Robert Hugman and San Antonio's River Walk*. Seguin, TX: The author.

Plugging In Components: Strategic Investments as Catalysts

National, state and city administrations often invest in specific buildings as catalysts to spur further development (see Chapter 6). In France, for instance, it was a national policy to invest in museums in the heart of many provincial towns to revitalize their cores by bringing in visitors. Los Angeles and Philadelphia are amongst other cities in the United States that have followed suit. Camden, New Jersey has an aquarium. Glasgow in Scotland has been revitalized through the arts. At least 90 U.S. cities are following the same tack with Arts Districts. In Glendale, California the investment was in parking garages to spur retail development. Many universities are plugging in 'magnet infrastructure' off campus to rejuvenate run-down neighbourhoods. The University of California, Riverside, for instance, has developed a Museum of Photography and a School of Visual Arts to attract young people downtown. In Chattanooga recently it has been two schools.

It is not the architecture of the buildings that is the attraction, but what the building's uses attract because of what they offer in terms of services to the area around them. The Guggenheim Museum in Bilbao may be an exception. It was, however, also part of a larger strategy. Museums attract visitors who spend money. Schools fall into a different category. They are parts of the infrastructure of everyday life. Good schools are essential in attracting middle-income families to live nearby. The catalytic effect is social, economic and physical. Middle-income families care for more than just surviving on a day-to-day basis: high-quality education for their children is highly prized.

Major references

Attoe, Wayne and Donn Logan (1989). *American Urban Architecture: Catalysts in the Design of Cities*. Berkeley and Los Angeles: University of California Press.
Vossman, Laura (2002). How many artists does it take to make a downtown? *Planning* **68** (6): 20–3.

A NOTE

Chattanooga, Tennessee, USA: schools as a catalyst for precinct revitalization (2000–2)

Many civic authorities and politicians in the cities of the United States (and elsewhere) now recognize the importance of the quality of the built environment in attracting private investment and middle-class residents. Chattanooga is a city that has relatively recently come to this realization (Naylor, 2003). Much is being invested in the capital web to encourage private investment. The whole riverfront is being rejuvenated. $US120 million will have been invested in its redevelopment by 2005 (the Tennessee Aquarium was completed in 1992). The streets and streetscape are being improved both in response to and as a catalyst for the upgrading of older buildings and the development of new residential units. Private financial resources are being put into public facilities both as philanthropic gestures and as a catalyst for the further creation of private investment opportunities. Using schools as a catalyst for urban upgrading may be unusual but it is not unique.

Public schools are usually built and abandoned in response to population demands represented by the number of school age children in a precinct, or district. As downtown residential populations dwindled in number and/or became restricted to single people and empty nesters, so schools were closed down. A number of U.S. cities, recognizing that good schools attract families to live in their districts, have recently taken a different approach. They have built schools in downtown areas to attract middle-class families back to the city as part of a public policy to create more diverse populations. In Chattanooga, Tennessee two elementary schools opened at the beginning of the 2002–3 academic year, 17 years after the last school had been closed.

The development of the schools is a product of aggressive policy formation, community support, civic leadership and philanthropy combining to achieve a social goal. The improvement of the quality of the physical environment was a vital component of the scheme. The urban design process began with a decision in 2000 by the Department of Education of Hamilton County (population 308,000 people) to create a K-5 magnet school downtown. The objective was to provide a local school for about 400 students who were being bused out of Chattanooga to suburban schools. Civic activists saw an opportunity for a more ambitious scheme.

The Planning and Design Studio in Chattanooga is officially an office of the joint Chattanooga–Hamilton County Regional Planning Agency which both funds and staffs it. The studio also receives funds from private philanthropic organizations. Karen Hundt, its head, perceived that one school would cater only for the existing poor in the city and that to attract more housing into the downtown area you needed an additional school, at least. The Department of Education did not have the financial resources to foot the $US8 million cost of a second school. A number of civic boosterism and philanthropic organizations came to the Board of Education's aid. The RiverCity Company, a non-profit organization committed to the revitalization of central Chattanooga raised $US4 million. Two local foundations, the Lyndhurst Foundation and the University of Tennessee at Chattanooga Foundation, provided an additional $4 million. The latter donation is typical of the concern that a large number of centrally located urban universities in the nation have for the settings around them. To attract good staff and good students the universities need to be located in pleasant settings with good community facilities. To further this end, the Board of Education opened the enrolment in the schools to both local children and the children of downtown workers, a procedure that immediately created a diversity of students.

The most important concern in site selection was cost. One school, the Herman H. Battle Academy for Teaching and Learning, was built on city-owned property while the other school is located on property dedicated to the city by the University of Tennessee. The Battle Academy is located in Southside, a 600-acre (240-hectare) brownfield site formerly a blighted industrial zone that, as part of the city's 1997 plan, was designated a revitalization district. In its plan the city hoped to increase the residential component of the area by about 200 units. Battle Academy has been built as a catalyst for attracting the additional residential population. Other incentives used to induce the middle income to live in the city are the creation of cultural facilities in the area (e.g. the Tennessee Aquarium).

The sites of both schools are small in comparison to the typical 13-acre (5.2-hectare) sites of suburban schools. Battle Academy is 3.3 acres (1.3 hectares) in size and the other school, Tommie F. Brown Academy of Classical Studies, is only 2.5 acres (barely 1 hectare), so the architects (TWA Architects, at Battle Academy and Derthick Henley at Brown Academy) had to design buildings taller than the norm. Even so, at Battle Academy recesses have to be staggered, but the playground, although tiny, also acts as a neighbourhood park after hours. Brown Academy is located adjacent to an abandoned railroad line that will be turned into a linear park and provide a playground for the school.

The city administration's policy is to encourage sustainable development. As a result the architects strove to reduce energy costs in both schools. The Battle Academy uses as much daylighting as possible, 'a roof garden for insulation and a water recycling system for filtering storm-water run-off to irrigate trees and other landscaping' (Kreyling, 2002: 33). Such designs are part of the, as yet, small involvement with

designing sustainable environments on the part of architects and urban designers.

Both schools provide field experiences for education students at the University of Tennessee and their pre-school programmes are attracting teachers who might otherwise be reluctant to teach in a downtown school. The long-run catalytic effect of the schools remains to be seen, but initial reports are optimistic and enthusiastic.

Major reference

Kreyling, Christine (2002). New Schools for downtown Chattanooga. *Planning* **68** (7): 32–3.

Commentary

In many ways, much of what has been discussed in this chapter involves city planning and project development practice. Some of the examples included (e.g. the schools for Chattanooga) are drawn from the literature aimed at professional city planners. An argument can be made for the inclusion of all these examples in Chapter 4 and certainly the Chattanooga schools in Chapter 6. All these case studies, however, show that the continuous development and maintenance of cities and urban design schemes are essential to their success. The world does not stand still.

Explicit in the projects included in this set of case studies are social and/or economic objectives but there is also a strong recognition of the importance of the physical environment in operationalizing social goals by providing the affordances for them to be met. Urban design thus becomes a major issue – a central concern – in much social and economic planning. Social objectives are often difficult to meet without consideration of the milieu in which behaviour takes place. This lesson is one that many social planners have yet to learn.

The goal of infrastructure projects is to have a catalytic effect on their surroundings – social and physical. As Attoe and Logan note, urban catalysts have a greater purpose than solving a functional problem (defining 'functional' more narrowly than in Chapter 1 here) or creating an investment, or providing an amenity:

A catalyst is an element that is shaped by a city and then, in turn, shapes its context. Its purpose is the incremental, continuous regeneration of urban fabrics. The important point is that the catalyst is not a single end product but an element that impels and guides subsequent development (Attoe and Logan, 1989: 45).

The case studies reinforce the observation that individual initiatives are crucial in perceiving opportunities for improvement in the built environment of cities. The studies also show that infrastructure covers a broad array of product types of which only a small sample has been addressed in this chapter. The studies show that the quality of design is crucial to the success of urban design endeavours. Quality is obtained through the coordinated action of diverse groups of people and individuals in a common cause. Design ideas come from precedents. Creative ones are inherent in the problems they address.

Lujiazui, Pudong, Shanghai in 2004

THE FUTURE OF URBAN DESIGN

PART 4

The labels given fields of human endeavour change as the issues perceived by society to be important change. Urban design is a label coined at a time, in the English-speaking world at least, when architecture and city planning were developing distinct and clearly separate identities. Whether or not the term 'urban design' will endure or soon be replaced by a more precise term or terms remains to be seen. The term will probably continue to be used loosely as it is now. Maybe it will be abandoned for the same reason – because it is imprecise. Parts 2 and 3 of this book have discussed the realm of urban design as perceived over the past 50 years through the description of 50-odd case studies. The range of concerns that these case studies display will remain and may well increase in breadth and depth in the future.

All the traditional design fields are undergoing change. City planning has broadened in its scope of concern in an attempt to be comprehensive in its outlook; landscape architecture has considerably extended its domain of interest from a horticulture base to include urban environments, while architecture has many practitioners who focus on different aspects of the built environment. If anything, architecture has contracted its scope of concern spinning off sub-fields as new environmental problems have arisen. Architecture and urban design were once seen as one endeavour everywhere. In some European countries they still are but as architects are being asked to address urban issues with greater thought, urban design may spin away to become an independent (although not exclusive) professional field.

There has been a shift in the intellectual processes involved in urban designing over the past 50 years. It is implicit in the case studies. Urban design began in an era when Modernist architectural ideas about the design of cities and their precincts held sway. Rationalist and Empiricist design paradigms vied for hegemony. Urban Design emerged as an identifiable professional field in response to the limitations of, particularly, architectural ideas about the nature of the future city as presented in the Athens Charter of Congrès International d'Architecture Moderne (CIAM) (see Sert and CIAM, 1944). The utility of Empiricist ideas, particularly as represented by the Garden City paradigm, was also strongly questioned (see J. Jacobs, 1961).

The world is a complex place. Whether or not it is growing increasingly complex and changing more rapidly than before, as we are wont to believe is open to conjecture. Maybe the observation that it is, is our contemporary conceit. The fundamental concerns of urban design have, however, been with us from the time that human settlements were first consciously designed. How do we deal with group interests in relationship to individual in urban development? How do we define the public interest?

While Modernist site designing ideas, if not architectural, still hold considerable sway in the minds of architects across the world, new paradigms have emerged. Most recently it has been the New Urbanist or Smart Growth movement that has been attracting the most international attention. As a basis for designing the future it possesses strong Empiricist tones as it draws heavily on past urban patterns that have worked well. The world, however, is changing.

It would be grossly unfair to claim that the Rationalists amongst urban designers were not centrally concerned with public interest issues, human life and human needs, or motivations. They were. Their concern was, however, based on their own perceptions of what the world should be. These perceptions were based on an analysis of what was wrong with the world rather than observations of what works and what does not. Our understanding of the functions of built form has been considerably broadened in recent years. The definition has been extended from the one that the Modernists used to one that recognizes the purposes served by the symbolic aesthetic qualities of the environment in terms of the self-images of the people who inhabit and use it. The case studies included here clearly show that.

Our understanding of how the world functions and what different patterns of built form afford people will undoubtedly deepen in the future. Maybe the world is no more complex than before but we are being asked to deal with the complexity rather than to develop a simplistic view of how the world works. Too often we redefine the problems of the world in a simpler, manageable way by eliminating many of the variables shown in Figure 1.6 from our domain of concern. We then design for that simpler world. It is the easiest thing to do. This approach can and has created further problems, many of them in terms of the functioning of the biogenic environment.

The greatest shift – in urban design thinking if not practice – during the 1990s has been carried through into the first decade of the twenty-first century. It may well be a major concern of the next generation of urban designers. It is the concern for the natural systems of specific terrestrial locations. The shift has resulted from a much greater understanding of the fragility of the planet Earth and its limited and depleting resources. An interest in the health of the planet by individual city planners goes back a long way (e.g. to Patrick Geddes in the first decades of the twentieth century), but it is only recently that it has become a major issue in discussions of urban design. The case studies included in this study of the field, or discipline, of urban design suggest that it is as yet seldom a major concern in practice. Chapter 11, Learning from the Case Studies: Current Issues in Urban Design takes the discussion of the foci of attention of our contemporary urban design efforts initiated in Chapter 1 a step forward. It focuses on the issues raised by the case studies and it outlines the issues that continue to be important as well as those that seem to be becoming so. With luck, two present concerns will disappear. Much urban and architectural design has to deal with antisocial behaviour and more recently with terrorism. In an equable world designing to reduce the opportunities for such activities will, one hopes, as Tony Garnier did in his design for the hypothetical Cité Industrielle (1917), not be necessary.

In this chapter, I also recapitulate the discussion of the scope of urban design in democratic, capitalist countries that permeates this book and the endless, but important, debate over individual and communal rights. Few developers and their architects favour any restriction on what they perceive to be their creative rights. Often they are fighting against antiquated or poorly considered building regulations and guidelines but often they simply want to get their own way in the face of community opposition. Those property developers who are strong proponents of urban design see it leading to urban environments of quality that reinforce their own investment decisions.

Debates over what is important and what is not will continue. Urban design projects of various types, scales and sizes will continue to be built. The conclusion is that the city is indeed and will continue be a collage of parts, some distinctive and others a mélange. So be it. What is important is that cities provide a rich set of behavioural opportunities and aesthetic displays that enrich the lives of all the people who constitute it. Urban design becomes particularly difficult in multi-cultural societies and in those where the interests of groups of the population fall outside the concern of market forces. Few of the case studies in this book have focused on the needs of the poor.

The final chapter of the book, Chapter 12, is a critical reflection on the ideas about the nature of urban design implicit in the typology proposed and the case studies. Urban design, thoughtfully carried out in response to diverse public interests, has much to offer the citizens of the world whatever name its activities go by. It has come a long way in the past 50 years in dealing with complex issues and diverse demands. As a result the questions now are: 'Is urban design becoming a profession and a discipline in its own right?' and 'If it is, should it be?' The argument in this book concludes by saying that the answers to these questions depend on the directions in which their members take the traditional design disciplines. I, personally, hope that urban design will continue to be a collaborative field of design rather than an independent discipline and profession.

11 Learning from the case studies: current and future issues in urban design

The urban designs, landscapes and buildings described in the case studies presented in this book have, with a few exceptions, been remarkably successful. The people who visit, use or live in them generally enjoy the results. They have been thoughtful responses to the concerns they address as their clients, property developers and designers have perceived the issues to be. None are whimsical, highly egotistical statements, although many have strongly opinionated designers behind them. A couple of them were misguided; in retrospect many have incurred opportunity costs – they could have been done better. They have all been carefully conceived and executed within the limitations of the resources, intellectual and financial, available at the time of their creation. Yet all have aspects that might be regarded, to put it gently, as poorly considered. Much can be learnt from them all.

The first lesson is that there is no single 'best practice' in urban design. All urban designs deal with a number of issues that are generic, or universal, in nature, but also concerns that are highly specific. Sorting out the complexities of a case and what is important and what is less so for whom is always difficult and arduous. The easiest way to deal with them is to assume that they do not exist – to ignore them and plough ahead. All the case studies presented here address some issues more thoroughly than others.

How well does the marketplace, as represented by property developers and their architects, respond to changes taking place in the world? It has certainly been slow in responding to changes in household types. Where it has responded it has been to the top end of the economic scale (e.g. the Canadian company Bosa Development Corporation in designing for the young affluent singles market in its developments in San Diego in the late 1990s and early 2000s; see Figure 11.1). By all reports, it has succeeded in meeting the needs of that highly mobile segment of the population very well. There are, however, many people whose needs are not being met by the marketplace and many issues that the marketplace is reluctant to address. Only two of the case studies included here – Pruitt-Igoe (see Chapter 7) and Aranya township (see Chapter 10), address the problems of the poor. The former is generally regarded as a failure in both public policy and architectural design terms while the latter is deemed to be successful. Both relied

Figure 11.1   New housing, Central San Diego in 2001.

on public funding. Would incentives and controls offered by governments encourage developers to address the problems of the poor?

Politicians have become reluctant to disturb the functioning of the property market. When urban design projects, whether total or all-of-a-piece, are carried out by private developers, the necessity to remain solvent makes them stick to what they know how to develop. Often they have to stick out their necks because the future is unknown. Sometimes those necks get chopped. Olympia and York, for instance, had considerable cash-flow problems in developing Canary Wharf in London. Nevertheless, property developers' goals are to maximize profit and minimize the potential of making a financial loss. Public sector developers are also concerned with a return, financial or social, on their investments. Many of the case studies covered in this book (e.g. Raleigh Park, Canary Wharf, Paternoster Square, etc.) have been private sector developer driven and the urban design qualities have been a direct response to perceptions of who the potential purchasers of real estate would be and what they value. Others, however, have stemmed from public sector initiatives (Gujarat State Fertilizer Corporation (GSFC) Township, Lujiazui, Euralille, etc.).

All of the cases covered here have involved some level of control over how the market operates in order to fulfil some public good. Raleigh Park had to acknowledge zoning and fire safety regulations and to design for flood control as demanded by public authorities (see Figure 11.2). The critics of any intervention in the development process beyond this level of dealing with public health and safety feel that in the long run, the marketplace will make individual property developers and their architects respond to the excesses of everybody doing 'their own thing'. The debate reflects the broader political debate between those who believe that markets work while incentives and controls do not and those who believe that the market does poorly in dealing with many public interest concerns. The growth in urban design has, strangely, been a result of both political attitudes! It has been a response to the substantive concerns of both economic conservatives and interventionists.

Substantive Issues

For urban designers substantive issues are those dealing with the patterns of the built environment and what they afford people. The marketplace has functioned reasonably well in dealing with the private realm. It has been less enthusiastic about dealing adequately with the public realm of cities. It is clear that in dealing with environmental issues and the state of the natural world that private sector property developers will not be taking the lead in devising new urban forms unless they perceive a profit to be made in doing so or they are forced to do so

Figure 11.2   New housing, Raleigh Park, Sydney in 2003.

through legislation. They will not deal with a greater range of concerns than they have to do in order to be profitable in the short run; long-term concerns will generally be neglected. Public sector developers are seldom better. What then are the urban design concerns that the case studies show? What have we missed?

There are many concerns. The key ones that have come up in the case studies, in no particular order, have to do with the range of variables to which attention is paid, how efficiently they are dealt with, the segregation and integration of activities and peoples, designing for a sense of place, and designing for a sustainable environment. Throughout any discussion on urban design the issue of changing worlds and changing values and how to consider them is a recurrent theme. So are the rights of individuals versus the rights of the community.

The Range of Variables (and People) of Concern

Urban designs differ in the range of variables considered in their creation. In much recent work in countries such as China (see Figure 7.1), Malaysia and South Korea (see Figure 11.3) access to sunlight in all habitable rooms is the determining criterion in defining the spacing of buildings. In the United States and Europe it was similarly so during the 1960s (e.g. Pruitt-Igoe; see Chapter 7). In these cases the functions of concern are those of the very basic of levels of human needs shown in Figure 1.6. They are indeed important. The issues that have emerged as now being of concern have been a response to the types of dull and, sadly, often dangerous environments of widely spaced buildings that weighting the single design criterion so heavily affords.

Figure 11.3   New housing, Seoul in 2000.

Each paradigm addresses some issues and not others. Brasília, La Défense and Pruitt-Igoe turned their backs on street-life; Battery Park City and Canary Wharf are street oriented. Clearly the two sets of designs are predicated on different assumptions about the nature and potential quality of streets. The concern in urban design in the western world is today increasingly focused on the quality of streets as seams for life and not simply as channels for vehicular movement. Access to sunlight remains fundamental to the quality of design in temperate and cold climates but the concern for sunshine needs to be tempered by the need to meet other requirements in order to provide people with fulfilling environments. Not every city has to be a Portland, Oregon, but much can be learnt from the richness of the urban design efforts in that city over the past 30 years, as expressed in the design of Pioneer Place (see Chapter 6).

The designs that receive attention in the architectural press and those favoured by architectural juries are bold in character. Bold designs are those in which geometric novelty and a single-minded focus on a few highly visible dimensions of design outweigh others. The history of recent architecture is littered with award-winning, highly publicized designs that have failed on many dimensions when they have been inhabited for a while. It is unfair to single out the much-maligned Pruitt-Igoe as an example as, indeed, has been done in this book, but it is one (see Chapter 7). Discrete, well-crafted, well-sited buildings and urban spaces may provide good living and working environments, but they attract neither the attention of politicians nor writers on architecture. They are not exotic enough.

Much recent design has focused on the imagery of the built environment. The aesthetic function of the environment as a statement of self-worth and for 'uplifting the spirit' is perceived to be important. Much recent landscaping of the squares and streets had focused on these issues with considerable, generally accepted success as in the design of La Place des Terreaux (see Chapter 5). Euralille and Lujiazui present different faces to the world. What should the focus of attention be? The case studies included here vary considerably in the problems and opportunities they address and in the importance paid to different variables.

Implicit in these observations is the question: 'For whom is one designing?' This question leads to many, many others. Who uses the public realm of cities? Who would use it more if it were designed in a different way? How does one deal with the often frowned on behaviours such as the hanging-out or skateboarding of teenagers? How does one make cities today as negotiable independently by 10-year-old boys and girls as many were 50 years ago? Does the physical design make any difference? The debate will continue but what is clear is that much urban design focuses on the values of the middle-aged elite. Should it? We need to consider the needs of the diverse sets of people who constitute a city – the young, the retirees, the able-bodied and the handicapped. Each project described in this book focuses, often by default, on particular groups of people. What is the model of people that we should have in mind?

Efficiency: Are Efficient Environments Efficient?

In urban design we seek efficient environments. How efficient should the layout of the public realm be? In terms of what? It is difficult to muster an argument for inefficiency on any dimension, but inefficiencies on one may result in benefits on another. In urban designing efficiency has often been seen in terms of ease of traffic movement, ease of access, ease of servicing and ease in phasing construction at a low cost. Such a view does not take into consideration the informal networks of communication that keep a functioning city or neighbourhood alive.

If one considers the range of design variables of concern in something like the way they are shown in Figure 1.6 then it is clear that any design is likely to be more efficient in meeting the demands on some dimensions than others. Streets designed for rapid high-volume traffic movement and with no kerb parking are inefficient and unpleasant for pedestrians. Efficient weather protection for pedestrians in Kyoto may not well display the aesthetic expression in the façades of buildings that it cuts across (see Figure 11.4). Much urban design involves a trade-off between effectiveness in meeting one design objective and another.

An efficient design today may not be so in the future. The design goal is thus to allow for change, to create urban designs that are robust, whose parts are easy to change. Short-term inefficiencies may prove to be long-run efficiencies. Elements of urban form, buildings in particular, should be able to be adapted or removed with relative ease. Row houses for instance, have proven to be easy to

Figure 11.4 Weather protection for pedestrians, Kyoto in 1992.

change, tenements more difficult and megastructures even more so. Factory buildings have been converted to many uses. The Ghirardelli Square and Clarke Quay are examples. Nowadays, many first generation suburban shopping malls (i.e. those built in the 1950s and 1960s) are being converted to a variety of other uses. They were efficient in serving their original purposes and they have proven to afford much in the way of conversions. Many will, however, be demolished. Bielefeld University (see Chapter 7) is operating very efficiently now in terms of movement patterns but how easy will it be to change without destroying its central idea. Urban designers need to recognize what efficiencies are necessary to support the way a city works and for whom they are necessary and for whom not. We need to think about how our work can be demolished!

The Segregation and Integration of Activities and People

Many of the generic ideas of the Modernists, when applied, have had disappointing results. Logical on paper, particularly at the beginning of the twentieth century in dealing with the industrial city, the segregation of uses tends to create dull environments. The dullness also arises from the simplicity of layouts and architectural forms heralded as part of the 'new machine age'. Pruitt-Igoe and Holford's Paternoster Square were reputedly dull physical environments. The response has been to advocate mixed-use environments.

The questions today and for the future are: 'What do we mean by mixed-uses?' 'How mixed should mixed-uses be?' And 'Are we talking about mixed-uses everywhere?' While areas of cities devoted to only one building type in terms of activities can be dull, the City or Canary Wharf in London and the Wall Street area of New York (see Figure 11.5), while deserted during the weekend, do hum during the working day. The argument against such single-use commercial areas is that they create inefficiencies in the use of transportation facilities. The argument against large single-use residential areas, whether they are single family detached homes or monolithic blocks of apartments, is that they provide poor educative environments for young children and adolescents have nothing to do. Teenagers are thus tempted to engage in antisocial behaviour for excitement. Yet few people want to live in constantly active places. Thus questions arise about what makes a good mix of experiences for children and how does one translate such a position into built form? What makes a lively business area? Maybe an efficient (and pleasant) business area is indeed one that empties after hours. There are other similar issues.

How integrated and segregated should the uses along streets be? The evidence from what are generally regarded as 'great streets' is that they should have a unity of uses and setback on both sides (see A. Jacobs, 1993). The rule of thumb is to make blocks (i.e. both sides of a street) have the same uses (e.g. single family detached homes or retail shop fronts). In doing so the potential for the development of 'face-block' communities is created provided the streets are not heavily trafficked. How use-segregated should individual buildings be? In Berlin 20% of commercial buildings should be residential to provide for the natural surveillance

Photograph by Susannah Lang

Figure 11.5   The Wall street area, New York in 2003.

of streets as hoped for in Pariser Platz (see Chapter 8). Answers to questions about the mix of uses depend on the objectives being sought in a project.

A number of politicians and designers are worried about the social stratification of society. Social-planning policies sought to make Pruitt-Igoe racially integrated. Singapore has a policy to make all residential areas house the different ethnic groups of the state in proportion to their representation in the total population. The goal is to avoid any area being stigmatized on racial grounds. How much should we strive to integrate or segregate people by ethnicity, culture or economic status? The answer is to let the market dictate people's choices. Will, however, the market provide choices? These questions are not urban design ones, but the affordances of different layouts and facilities can guide public policy decisions.

The effort to impose a behavioural norm through design and social legislation has been found to be wanting. The best way to avoid conflict seems to be to design for micro-segregation with macro-integration. What this means is that sub-areas should be designed with one population in mind while larger areas cater for the whole variety of people living within them. The layout of Aranya Township does that (see Chapter 10). Who should dictate such policies? In democratic societies people make choices for themselves. Urban patterns and building

369

types can be designed to afford the needs of different household types and ways of life but it cannot dictate them. People make choices for themselves, provided they have the means to do so. Thus it is the poor and powerless who have to make do with what is left. It is their needs that require special attention.

The Segregation of Vehicular and Pedestrian Traffic: the Nature of Streets

One of the goals of every development covered in the case studies here has been to house the comings and goings of people (on foot or in cars and other vehicles) in comfort and with efficiency and also, sometimes, with pleasure. Cars are an important part of everyday life. They are also sources of danger. How best to segregate or integrate pedestrian and vehicular traffic and how to deal with parking are recurring themes in urban design. Every case study included in this book has dealt with the concerns in one manner or another.

The major clash in urban design paradigms has been over the way streets are considered. Are they seams or edges? When is one form more appropriate than the other? As seams they join blocks together; as edges they divide districts. The superblock has been a generic urban design type keeping vehicular traffic on the periphery of districts and having the interior pedestrianized as in Brasília, Charles Center, Baltimore, La Défense in Paris, the GSFC Township in Vadodara and the State University of New York campus at Purchase and Paternoster Square.

Providing for pedestrian and vehicular traffic on separate planes vertically as in the skyway system in Minneapolis or pedestrian deck as in La Défense (see Chapters 10 and 8, respectively), or subterranean pedestrian passages has many advantages. It creates a safer world. If enclosed, pedestrian routes such as the skyway system in Minneapolis are also made more comfortable by protecting people from the vagaries of the weather (and air pollution). At the same time there is a sense that the richness of life is reduced. Does it matter? The segregated systems are often highly popular and cater to our desire for safety and comfort (see Figure 11.6). The skyway system at Charles Center in Baltimore, however, sees low usage. The 'uncomfortable' bustle of streets is more popular. How comfortable and safe should we strive to make the world? This question is answered in every design but it is seldom openly discussed. The 'woonerf' is a residential street type in which cars, pedestrians and playing children use the same space, often simultaneously. Each expects the others to be there. Cul-de-sacs function in much the same manner in many places. They are now regarded as 'old fashioned' by many architects even though they work well on many behavioural dimensions.

A Sense of Place

Every place has a 'sense of place'. It is not always that desired by critics; lay-people often grieve for the lost identity of places with which they are familiar

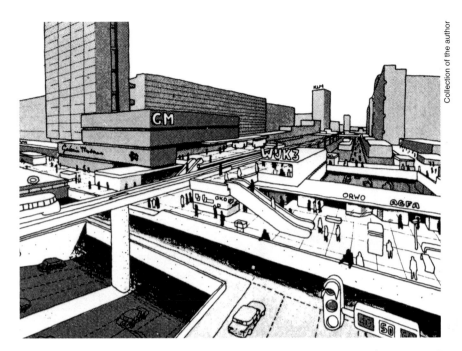

Collection of the author

Figure 11.6   An illustrative diagram of the vertical segregation of movement systems.

after changes have been made. It is not simply the result of a 'shock of the new'. It is a deep-seated feeling that what is being built is out of place. It affords no sense of 'being ours' to people. Much of what is proposed and/or built today, like the Cadillac-Fairview proposal for Portland (described in Chapter 6) pays little attention to its context, built or natural. Much architecture today sets out to shock. As Prime Minister Jawaharlal Nehru said about Le Corbusier's work in Chandigarh, it does make us sit up and think (see Chapter 7 and Lang *et al.*, 1997). Presumably, he thought it was in the Indian public's interest to do deal with change. Certainly the Chandigarh capital complex has a unique identity. The patterns of Le Corbusier's buildings have been picked up by architects and lay-people in the city to form a 'Chandigarh architecture'.

The term 'sense of place' deals with two concerns; one is sociological and the other psychological. The first has to do with the sense of one's location, or one's society's location, within a larger social unit, and the second with a sense of belonging to a region and a regional culture. In urban designing, the first has to do with the imagery of built forms and the meanings they communicate – their associational value, and the second with the ecological and cultural soundness of built forms with reference to local terrestrial and cultural conditions (Norberg Schulz, 1980). The sense of loss that many people feel has to do with changes on both dimensions. We seek better worlds. Property developers often lead the way.

Figure 11.7 The architecture of Lujiazui, Shanghai in 2004.

Some property developers work locally. The Rose Corporation does little work outside New York City. Bangkok Land, Henderson Land and New World Development all tend to focus on specific cities. They feel comfortable in dealing with familiar economic and political conditions. Sony, Daimler Benz and DB (Deutsche Bank) Real Estate are amongst the major property developers who work internationally. Whether locally or internationally based, property developers seldom care about local character nor do their clients. They are dealing with a global economy and frequently the values of the noveau riche. The noveau riche wish to gain respect by having what they perceive to be high-status environments in which to live and work or simply to show off to outsiders. They desire a new image for themselves. The built environments they seek exemplify their search however illogical it may be on other grounds (Olds, 2001). They want to break away from 'the shackles of the past'.

International developers and their architects, aided by municipal governments, have been successful in creating large, mostly all-of-a-piece urban designs that are clearly part of the global business scene. Their architecture takes one of

Photograph by George Turnbull

Figure 11.8　False Creek, Vancouver in 2004.

two forms. Buildings are either constructed of extensive amounts of glass, steel and expensive polished stones (even if slippery when underfoot), or they incorporate classical architectural elements of columns and pediments in a variety of ways. Some buildings are a mixture of the two. Others strive to be *glocal* – international with local referents in siting or in appearance (Lim, 2004). Much such architecture is extremely well executed. It pays little heed, however, to local climatic conditions or ways of life or architectural traditions in the way buildings meet the streets and create places. The architecture does, nevertheless, help in creating a sense of pride, of progress in the minds of many local people. It gets away from what are perceived to be parochial attitudes. This was the goal of many of the schemes discussed in this book. Breaking from traditions has been part of almost all architectural ideologies of the cognoscenti since the beginning of the twentieth century. People accommodate to many but not all changes. Much-loved areas of New York were once seen as outlandish but much new architecture fails to do more than shock.

Several hundred large-scale urban design projects are being built in the Asia-Pacific area alone. Lujiazui is not unique (see Figure 11.7). False Creek (see Figure 11.8) and Concord Pacific Plaza in Vancouver, Canada are a pair; Rinkai Funu-Toishin (Rainbow Town) Tokyo is another (Marshall, 2003). Canary Wharf in London is moving towards completion. Berlin is now seeing a number of mega-projects that are transforming the city. The Potsdamer Platz development (see Chapter 8) is an example. On a large or small scale many recent urban design projects respond to the global market and the aesthetics it demands.

Potsdamer Platz shows that global architectural imagery and the internalization of public space can be integrated with some local urban design precedents.

Urban and architectural designs such as Seaside, Florida and Battery Park City in New York (both described in Chapter 8) are examples of reactions to the seeking of a global imagery in urban design. They have local precedents on which to draw. Many people see them as dull and old fashioned but they are outsiders. Architectural theory has responded with the concept of critical regionalism (Frampton, 1983). It is imprecisely defined but it is an ideology that is against vernacularism, sentimentalism and the picturesque. It supports the position that architecture and, presumably landscape architecture and urban design, should be responsive to cultural and societal values but it is weak in addressing exactly what this position means in terms of design guidelines. Perhaps designing for a healthy biogenic, sustainable environment peculiar to specific climatic niches will steer architects and urban designers in the direction that they will have to go in defining a sense of place. Such a goal has both social and physical design dimensions and both urban spatial and building design implications.

A Healthy Biogenic Environment and Sustainable Development

All urban design projects change the nature of the terrestrial environment in which they are located. In terms of the health of the planet many of these changes have been detrimental. Cities suffer from high levels of pollution, many rivers are filthy, and irreplaceable energy resources are being depleted. Designing for a healthy natural environment and a built world healthy for people are two sides of the same coin. Dealing with the polluting effects of human wastes, automobiles and industries is already a major topic of discussion for city planners and public policy-makers. Progress has been made in addressing them. Other environmental issues are deemed to be less important.

In building new precincts of cities, private and public projects have been imposed on many sensitive landscapes. All of the case studies included here have hardened the surface of the earth, even those such as the Potsdamer Platz district of Berlin that have roof gardens (see Figure 8.49). Some developments, such as Battery Park City, have required much landfilling. Singapore continues to reclaim land from the sea to expand the state's dimensions. The Netherlands has stopped. Parts of Jakarta and Shanghai built on reclaimed land sink into the earth centimetre-by-centimetre each year.

There is increasing pressure for attitudes towards the natural world to change and for people to be husbanders rather than consumers of the land. More specifically for urban designers, there is a need to be discerning about the actions we advocate and a need to be more diligent in applying the principles for creating sustainable cities – those in which the embodied energy consumed in building and in running and maintaining designs are, at least low, if not replaceable.

Designing with climate in mind rather than in opposition is a necessary component of the effort to reduce energy costs. Much is understood about the differences in designing for tropical, temperate and cold climate cities, but the application of the principles (except in extreme climatic conditions) has to compete for attention with aesthetic concerns and the price of land as populations swell. In tropical areas, for instance, buildings should be set apart to allow breezes to waft through them, but economic forces push land values up and denser environments result. In hot arid climates such environments are necessary but cars take up considerable space.

There are some tentative examples of urban designs that address these concerns. Amongst the case studies, Potsdamer Platz recycles water and Battery Park City has attempted to respond to a number of concerns. For better examples one has to look farther afield. Davis in California has neighbourhoods in which ecological design has played a major part (see Figure 11.9a). The Olympic Village (Newington) for the Sydney 2000 Games shows what can be done in a typical suburban development although it is at a higher density than most (see

(a)
(b)
(c)
(d)

Figure 11.9 Images of sustainable environments. (a) Village Homes, Davis, California in 1993, (b) Newington, Sydney in 2005, (c) a green Sydney and (d) Ken Yeang's proposed towers for a tropical city.

375

Figure 11.9b). The design of the Sydney Olympic Games site as a whole was a valiant attempt at creating a 'green' environment. There are now ideas about the whole of Sydney (see Figure 11.9c).

The efforts to reduce energy costs in the Potsdamer Platz development has shown that much can be achieved in dense urban environments. Ken Yeang (2002) is exploring issues of urban design in tropical cities (see Figure 11.9d) and scholars at the University of Waterloo in Canada are amongst those looking at Arctic cities. There has been much interest in vernacular architecture and how it accommodates and is adapted to the climate of different locales. Equally important will be harnessing the powers of nature to heal the environment. Discovering the principles of how to use built environment patterns to channel breezes to flush the pollutants from cities, of how to use vegetation to cool tropical cities and reduce heat-island effects, and of how to recycle materials and wastes will all engage urban designers in the future. The engagement may well result in generic forms of cities that neither the Modernists nor the New Urbanists have considered. They will require cultural changes everywhere.

There are more explorations of ideas than action. Designing for environmental sustainability is not a concern that the marketplace is compelled to address. There are few immediate financial rewards in doing so. The issues will have to become public policy concerns translated into design controls and guidelines before they are seriously addressed by any of the professions in project design. Access to sunlight and daylight will remain important but concerns with how to obtain water and how to recycle waste water require more attention than is being given to them at the moment. Times are, nevertheless, changing. Cities such as Tokyo, Los Angeles, Singapore and Berlin are already creating legislation to encourage designers at both the urban and building level to design 'with nature in mind'. The knowledge of how to do so is becoming available even though the science is still weak.

Water Supply and Waste Disposal

The residents and/or users of all the developments described in this book, directly and indirectly, consume much water and generate much waste. If the entire world consumed as much water per capita as in the United States, there would now be a major supply crisis. The United States and Singapore are amongst the nations that import water. How do we deal with the design of cities so that less water is needed? Few designers seem to be considering the issue directly. All the case studies presented in this book deal with water supply and waste disposal in conventional ways.

There is some concern for how we use trees and other vegetation in landscaping cities in terms of their consumption of water (and the effect of their perspiration on local climates). The broader issues of water consumption have, however, yet to be addressed. No generic urban form or design solutions aimed at reducing water consumption as yet exist. When water becomes critically in short supply as a result of drought or political threats to cut it off, restrictions on its use for washing cars and watering lawns are put in place. When the drought is over consumption returns to normal. Are there other potential solutions?

At the other end of the cycle of acquisition, processing and consumption is expulsion. 'What should we do with our wastes?' 'Do we continue to use water to flush them into rivers and the sea?' 'Or do we try to incinerate them all?' And on a very different topic, 'How do we deal with the disposal of our dead?' Cemeteries are important places to many people but land is in short supply. In places such as Hong Kong traditional ways have had to give way to new, often creating considerable heartache. Hindus cremate their dead and scatter the ashes. Is this a worldwide solution? Adopting it would involve many cultural changes.

The same questions about consumption and disposal can be extended to the use of all natural resources. Do we have to wait until societies really feel the pinch – until the marketplace perceives that there is a crisis before we do anything? Do we design cities and their precincts to be easily recyclable? How do we deal with change? Did the Archigram group have the right idea?

Changing Technologies and Urban Form

Major changes in the geography of cities have resulted from changes in transportation modes aided by other technological developments, such as refrigeration, that changed living patterns. Changes in manufacturing technology over the course of the twentieth century resulted in a major change in urban land use patterns. The elevator allowed tall buildings. Air conditioning made Singapore and Las Vegas as we know them possible. The set of case studies included in this book show that the increase in the size of ships and the development of containerization resulted in opportunities for major new urban design projects in abandoned dock areas of cities. (Battery Park City, Darling Harbour, Canary Wharf, and the waterfronts of Singapore and Kuching are examples).

What will be the next major technological change that will affect ways of life of people? There has been an extraordinary amount of speculation on how developments in information technology will change patterns of daily life. For 30 years now we have been saying that they will radically change cities and urban forms but very little has yet changed in the patterns of the environment. 'The anticipated changes have yet to materialize' (Anthony Townsend, cited in Peralta, 2002). Radical changes may come when the power of the new technologies are fully exploited (Mitchell, 1999, 2003). Will they have the impact of the automobile on cities? We know that the increase in e-mail usage is correlated with the increase in face-to-face meetings. Is there a causal link?

Will changes in the way we drive cars, or even their very nature, change life? Will new developments in the way we handle wastes – say, through some sort of pneumatic system as already being experimented with in some cities – necessitate changes in the layouts of cities and their precincts? The evidence is not available to answer such questions. What we do know from past experience is that some

Figure 11.10 Two early twentieth century speculations on the twenty-first century city. (a) A 1911 image and (b) a 1928 image.

technological changes will come in surprising forms. If we design to allow for change, will that suffice? Or will present patterns of building and demolishing suffice? Will arcologies, as Paolo Soleri suggested, be the future generic urban design model for cities and their precincts? Science fiction writers seem to think so. We do know that past predictions of what our present world would be like have been way off the mark (see Mansfield, 1990, for examples; see also Figure 11.10).

The answer generally given to questions about the robustness of urban designs is that if the design has a strong idea behind it, it will survive changes in political attitudes and fiscal crises. The plan finally adopted, for example, for the Universidad Central de Venezuela in Caracas did not have the power, the boldness, behind it of the original proposal (Figures 7.27a and b). As a result it has afforded so many departures from it for the original design idea to be lost. Strong ideas do not have to be bombastic but they do have to have a powerful driving logic behind them. Battery Park City's design ultimately did (see Figure 11.11). Perhaps it is this lack of a mind-capturing logic that is lacking in the World Trade Center site design. There is no strong central idea to the scheme; it is a fragmented scheme and will most likely be implemented as such.

Figure 11.11 Battery Park City seen from across the Hudson in 2004.

The Impact of Vandalism, Crime and Terrorism

Vandalism and crime in general have a major impact on city life especially for the vulnerable in society. The vandalism of playgrounds, street furniture and other elements of the public realm has long been a problem and has resulted in the impoverishment of the environment in many societies (Ward, 1973). Graffiti has many defenders but hardly raises the self-image of the citizens of a city except for those who create it. Fear of crime has resulted in children having fewer opportunities for independent behaviour. Consider the impact of social and behavioural problems at Pruitt-Igoe or in many large British or French housing estates on everyday life.

The failings, real and imagined, of developments such as Pruitt-Igoe led Oscar Newman to formulate the concept of 'defensible space' (Newman, 1974). He argued that in housing precincts where there are clear demarcations of territories allocated to specific groups of people, eyes on the street and positive symbolic aesthetics that enhanced residents' self-image people take responsibility over the areas in which they live. The opportunities for criminal behaviour are thereby reduced. Often, however, in the design of prestigious building such as the Guggenheim Museum in Bilbao, other issues are perceived to be more important and defensible space patterns are neglected. The focus is on the building as a sculpture set in its own territory.

Reducing motivations to commit criminal behaviour is not an architectural or urban design problem but physical design responses – barbed or razor wire on walls, roller shutters blanking out shopwindows at night – reduce the attractiveness of the urban environment. We have learnt to live with television surveillance of many parts of the public realm but playgrounds, bus shelters and street furniture continue to be destroyed. Graffiti besmirches many walls. These acts are all annoyances and a threat to public safety. The threat of terrorism is, however, frightening.

There has been a growing concern, particularly in the United States with designing to reduce the impact of terrorism. The images of the destruction of the World Trade Center towers are so indelibly imprinted on people's minds, that

379

designing to mitigate the impacts, particularly of vehicles loaded with explosives being driven into buildings, is regarded as a fundamental aspect of public space design in the early twenty-first century. The consequence is that barriers, either overtly or as elements such as concrete flower boxes, are increasingly shaping significant public spaces. The objective is to prevent access by vehicles to the front doors and ground floor windows of buildings.

It would be a pity if buildings become designed as fortresses with blank façades on the ground floor. The result would be that the environment for pedestrians would be dull and would discourage people from walking along the streets. One can add murals and reliefs to make blank façades less boring as required in Bellevue, Washington, but such devices are hardly a substitute for the perception of activities. People enjoy vicarious participation in the lives of other people in the city. We need to free up the public realm for everybody to enjoy. Fears of crime and terrorism discourage us from doing so.

Procedural Issues

The urban designing process is complex. The way it should be carried out is open to debate. There are different ways of getting involved, of deciding on/designing the issues to address, different ways of designing solutions and different ways of evaluating, choosing and implementing them. There have been and are two major intellectual traditions in designing: the Empiricist and the Rationalist. The former involves learning from experience – from precedents – and the latter is based on logical design based on a set of idealistic propositions. Despite this generalization, many Empiricist urban designs have been highly idealistic and Rationalist ones have drawn from precedents as well, although that is often not admitted. Many designs are, however, products of a purely pragmatic design process.

The Nature of the Design Process

Models of design were introduced in Chapter 2. The process is full of ups and downs, backtracking and leaping ahead as, particularly, the all-of-a-piece urban designs included here show. Urban design process deals with 'wicked' issues – those that cannot be grasped with total comprehensive understanding. Problems and opportunities can never be perceived with total clarity; we can never identify all the issues of importance in a particular situation let alone deal with them. What the future holds for us is unknown although we can make sensible predictions about the future if we have sound empirical knowledge. This knowledge is, however, based on the present. The role of the urban designer is to provide ideas, bring attention to pitfalls and provide advice about the future.

The major initial decision from the designer's viewpoint in any design process is whether to get involved or not. Many decisions will already have been made before a designer is sought; a preliminary brief will, for instance, have been designed (see Figure 2.6). The decision to get involved will depend on how much the designer needs the work, and how much confidence he or she has in being able to do the job and how interested he or she is in doing it. Albert Mayer withdrew from designing Chandigarh because of a lack of interest in the scheme after the death of his colleague Mathew Nowicki. Le Corbusier was the replacement.

From the perception of a problem the process moves on to one of establishing goals and specific objectives, the design of a development programme based on the objectives, the exploration of potential solutions and the creation of implementation techniques. These techniques differ if one is dealing with a total, all-of-a-piece design or a piece-by-piece design. In the first case as in Brasilia the question is: 'How will *we* get the design built?' In the latter two cases it is: 'How will we get *them* to get it built?' What incentives, controls and guidelines are necessary to put in place to achieve desired results?

The way the exploration of potential solutions takes place depends on one's philosophical stance. Rationalists would argue that it should be based on pure reasoning, while Empiricists would be looking at precedents as the basis for identifying the issues and generating a design. In either case all the stakeholders will be making predictions about the outcomes of any proposals. Urban designing requires the continuous making of assumptions about the future – predictions about how a design will work if implemented, predictions about the nature of the future context in which the design has to work, predictions about the resources available, predictions about who is important and who not. Who is it that makes decisions?

Consider the design changes made in the evolution of Paternoster Square or Battery Park City! The process is value laden every step of the way based on images of personal and public interests. The concern here is not with all the issues raised by the experiences, implicit and explicit, in the case studies presented here, but rather with a subset of issues central to them. The first issue has to do with the role of the urban designer, the second with the role of information and how it is obtained and used, the third with the nature of creativity, and the last with how we think about the future. They all involve recurrent questions.

Who Leads?

While good timing and good luck play a part, the case studies show that strong leadership is an essential contributor to a project's success. First of all, somebody has to see an opportunity to do something. Many of what have turned out to be urban design projects have resulted from the initiative of a single person with a strong idea. In Boston, an architect, Benjamin Thompson, recognized the redevelopment possibilities of the Faneuil Hall-Quincy Market area (see Figure 11.12). He was later involved in the Ghirardelli Square renovation. It was a journalist, William Schofield, who led the effort to create the Freedom Trail in Boston. Robert Hugman, an architect, saw the potentialities of the San Antonio River. These people were private individuals who had a 'vision of what might be' but the major drivers of urban development in capitalist countries are private corporations.

Photograph by Deepti Nijhawan

Figure 11.12   Quincy Market, Boston in 1993.

Powerful, high-ego individuals with visions of their own often lead urban design efforts. Paul Reichmann of Olympia and York disregarded the advice of his most trusted lieutenants in the pursuit of his own dream for Canary Wharf. In the case of Glendale it was a couple of public officials who possessed a vision of what that suburban downtown could be; in Singapore it was originally consultants who produced ideas but then the civil service took over.

Citizens groups have been powerful advocates for specific types of urban development. Politicians clearly play an important role. Consider the role of President Kubitschek in pushing Brasilia ahead, Nelson Rockefeller at Battery Park City and, particularly, in the development of the State University of New York, Mayor Lindsay and the work of the Urban Design Group in New York, the presidents of France in the development of La Défense and the Parc de la Villette in Paris, Zhu Rongji in Lujiazui, Pierre Mauroy in Lille and Margaret Thatcher in the promotion of Canary Wharf. Politicians were dabbling in the development of the Barbican in London every step of the way. Particularly important have been groups in the business sector in pushing for downtown renewal projects. Such groups strove hard for the San Antonio River to be revitalized and for various the Lower Manhattan schemes. They, like residential neighbourhood organizations, have also led the way in fighting to prevent urban design projects that they perceive not to be in their own interests.

The public sector has had the primary responsibility in much urban design. It has traditionally been the initiator of infrastructure development, either in shaping urban development or catching up with it. Players in the public sector have hired consultants to produce conceptual plans for precincts of cities and they have been the developer of record for many urban designs. Housing authorities have been responsible for mass housing schemes everywhere in the world. The Battery Park City Authority was a creature of the public sector as was the Senior Consultants Committee in the initiation of the Lujiazui development in Shanghai.

In the immediate future we shall no doubt see much more cooperation between public and private sectors in both initiating and carrying through urban development schemes. Almost all of the all-of-a-piece urban designs described here have been cooperative ventures. The public policy concerns and dreams about what the future should hold will continue to be important. Incentives and design controls will play a large part in urban design projects in strongly market oriented, capitalist economies. It is, however, those people who really care about cities and the quality of life that urban environments can afford who should lead. Will they? In order to do so they will have to be able to present to their worlds images of futures that capture the imagination. These people will be strong individuals; they may come from the public or the private sectors. They will not be able to do things on their own. Urban design is a collaborative art.

The Nature of Public Consultation

Asking questions about the role of urban designers simultaneously raises the question, 'What is the role of the public in urban designing?'. The level of consultation in developing urban designs that the public expects varies from society to society and within a society from project type to project type. Sometimes there is no consultation. Did President Ceausescu consult the people of Bucharest before moving ahead with the building of the Avenue of Victory of Socialism (see Chapter 7)? Hardly! In some instances, proposed schemes are simply put on display for public comment and feedback. Few of the case studies here went beyond this level of consultation. Politicians' views have implicitly acted as surrogates for public opinion. The degree of attention to the public's responses varies. At the other end of the scale designs emerge through a full participatory design effort, often in sessions 2 or 3 days long in publicly conducted charettes. During charettes designers and stakeholders in a project work intensively to generate preliminary designs. These designs are then developed professionally in full design and engineering detail.

While many important ideas that have changed cities have come from well-informed and observant lay-people, it is often difficult to get the general public involved in thinking about what a project should be until a design is shown to them. It is, nevertheless, important to get them involved if they are to claim designs as their own and for such designs to be well cared for after implementation. If seen as the work of outsiders being imposed on them, the reaction can be hostile. The degree of vandalism of the public realm in projects around the world that have been built without consultation attests to this observation. Part of the problem with the Cadillac-Fairview proposal for what later became Pioneer Place in Portland was that it was seen as a foreign imposition (see Chapter 6).

The lay-public often cannot comprehend the consequences of designing in one manner rather than another. Often any environmental change is seen as negative. In many suburban communities, for instance, the fear of high-rise buildings is so embedded in ways of thinking that sensible discussion of the advantages and disadvantages of taller buildings, residential or commercial, seems impossible. In the development of the Denver Technological Center, pressure from the residents of surrounding areas resulted in a major constraint on the height of buildings. The result is the buildings are all of the same height and flat-topped (see Figure 8.66). While a sense of unity is achieved, it is hardly a visually exciting precinct.

How does one get the public involved and, more importantly in specific projects, how does one get all the stakeholders to actively engage in discussions before crises occur? Much of the public furor over the building of Darling Harbour arose because Sydneysiders did not grasp what the scheme would be like when completed (see Chapter 8). The media – newspapers and television – have been important in bringing visions of what places can be like to popular attention. They were constantly involved in Curitiba and in the design of Battery Park City and now the proposals for the World Trade Center site in New York. They have also been important in moulding people's attitudes. What the lay-public sees as desirable in illustrations is what they seek and, in turn, the press feeds images back to them of what they want to see. Advertisers dictate much. It is difficult to break into this cycle but urban designers have a role as educators. A detailed knowledge of case studies can be used in this educational process.

The Nature of Creativity

The design professions bestow great esteem on what they perceive to be 'creative' designers. Such designers are those who produce works that are geometrically, structurally or spatially a departure from the norm in response to what they see as problems needing to be addressed. The question is: 'What freedom of action should individual designers have in creating the public realm of cities?' Those observers who regard urban design as a fine art would argue for little or no outside interference into what an individual designer/artist does. The population simply has to live with the consequences in the name of Art. The 'art defence' – that some object or environment is an expressive act of an individual and thus a work of art – has been used to justify many design decisions, from pieces of sculpture to squares to streets, that are detrimental to the enjoyment of the city. Sometimes this has been a purposeful design objective. Making people feel uncomfortable, physically or psychologically, is, however, difficult to justify. Purposefully making poorly functioning places even worse with buildings or public art seems antisocial.

This discussion comes back to that on the rights of individuals and definitions of what is in the public interest with which this book began. The architectural position, if there is a unified point of view, is generally that one has to tolerate bad designs in the name of freedom of action on the part of all architects and their clients. In addition, seeing bad designs enables one to appreciate the good even more. Opinions differ on whether this argument is a strong one or not. In urban design, the quality of individual works – sculptures or building as sculptures – often does not affect the way cities are experienced provided the spaces created on the ground floor of a city, suburb or building complex function well in a multi-dimensional manner.

The problem arises when property developers and their architects focus on highly individualistic designs as objects in space in the name of art and in the furthering of their own careers. Fiscal conservatives argue that in the long run such competition results in a better world. The case studies fail to support this view. Indeed the whole basis for the existence of urban design is in ensuring that the basic requirements for making good public realms are fulfilled. What is regarded as good is always open to debate but there is now much empirically based theory and many examples, and even detailed case studies that provide the basis for sensible discussions about what should and should not be designed.

True creativity involves not the making of innovative building and urban forms but rather the designing of a problem in a new and more appropriate way and recognizing that specific patterns respond well to the problem. Maybe being able to evaluate designs well is the most important ability to possess in creative problem solving. Maybe it is the ability to see the affordances of innovative patterns.

Dealing with the Future

Dealing with the future is at the heart of urban designing. For public policy-makers and designers the question is: 'What kinds of futures do we seek?' Or is it simply 'What designs can be sold?' The procedural question is a more encompassing one than designing robust environments. How does one deal with potential changes in the future political environment while a job is in progress? Political change often brings projects that are long in gestation to a grinding halt or a change in direction. Battery Park City in New York and the Jubilee Line in London are examples of projects whose progress stopped and started due to changes in governments after elections and at Paternoster due to changes in property ownership.

The same concerns arise in dealing with the future state of the economy of a city or country. The questions in design are: 'Will sufficient funds be available to carry out a project?' and, perhaps, as importantly, 'Will the funds be there to maintain the project once it has been built?' Such concerns are seldom explicitly considered and seldom explained in the case studies of projects. Perhaps we are all optimists and believe that things will all work out well in the end. The world, however, is replete with forlorn public squares and parks, full of non-functioning, decaying, sometimes vandalized fountains.

Values change. Areas of the city become obsolete and others are gentrified. A general rule of thumb, implicit in much urban design, has been not to look forward into the future for more than one generation. Looking further ahead with any degree of accuracy is questionable. The saving grace for urban designers is that despite piecemeal changes taking place all around us, many patterns of behaviour tomorrow will be the same as today. Yet the world is not static. Changes in modes of transportation and communication shaped the present physical geography of cities. The basic physical structure of streets and open spaces inherited by cities at the precinct level adapted well to change over the whole course of the twentieth century. At the beginning of the twentieth century, who could have predicted the technological changes that occurred during it, particularly those of its first five decades, that have changed our lives so much? The automobile has enabled the development of far-flung suburbs but necessitated links that afford high-speed driving between them. Yet the street pattern in the very core of much-loved cities is essentially that of the nineteenth century and often earlier.

Who Pays?

The fortunes of urban design projects as they were implemented fluctuate with world economic conditions. A number of projects described here – Canary Wharf in particular – were boosted by the business booms of the early 1980s and late 1990s and battered by the economic recessions of the late 1980s and early 1990s. La Défense was similarly hit by economic ups and downs and the development of Lujiazui has stuttered with blips in the Chinese economy. The case studies show that deep pockets are extraordinarily helpful in getting projects built. The question is: 'Whose pockets?' One might presume that it is the public who should pay for the building or rebuilding of the public realm of cities. It is the 'public realm' after all. In the long run the public does pay for it either through taxes or through the increase in prices of goods and products when private sector players pay for the public realm upfront. It is more a question of who pays at the outset that is important.

One of the major questions that crops up, particularly in the design of infrastructure systems, is whether it is the users of a scheme or those who benefit from it who should pay for it. Presumably all the tourists who visit Paris, including those who never visit La Défense benefit from the centre's existence. Without it, central Paris might have become just another busy international city. Automobile drivers benefit from the development of public transit systems. They take traffic off roads. How does one tax the beneficiaries of an urban design project for what they gain from it?

The case studies described in this book show a variety of approaches to funding projects. In some cases developers have had to pay for some of the cost of the public or quasi-public infrastructure (as in the skyway system of Minneapolis). In other cases individual developers have to pay for the infrastructure piece-by-piece in order to get an all-of-a-piece design functioning. The incomes of Business Improvement Districts (BIDs) are derived from taxing owners whose properties fall into the district (see Chapter 9). The right of the public to have private enterprises pay for public goods required by society, but not a consequence of private profit-seeking endeavours, is more of an issue. Yet even here one can argue that for private organizations to flourish, public needs require attention. Still the question of who pays is a central one to what can and cannot be accomplished through urban design. In almost all the case studies presented here, public–private partnerships have played a role (see also, Fosler and Berger, 1982; Frieden, 1990; Frieden and Sagalyn, 1991).

The Degree of Control

Last but not least we come to the basic issue in urban design. It is one of long-standing. It concerns the rights of individuals to do what maximizes their own interests in competition with the rights of other individuals and the community as a whole. How much should governments intervene in the way the market shapes cities and their precincts? During the years covered by this book, the answer has varied. It has differed considerably from society to society and within the same society over time. It would seem that the public interest concerns rise to the forefront when cities appear to be in trouble or when opportunities for making cities better places are missed as the result of private greed or political indecision.

The design of buildings, the way they meet the street, their configuration and even some details were heavily constrained in some of the examples described here. The goal was to achieve precincts with a unified character through a unity in architecture and landscape. This goal is clear in all the total urban designs schemes mentioned. They, from Brasília to the Avenue of the Victory of Socialism to Kresge College, were seen to be and, in a sense, are single architectural designs. In city and large precinct design is this a good idea?

A sense of unity with some diversity has been achieved in all-of-a-piece schemes such as Seaside, Battery Park City, Pariser Platz and Paternoster Square. Many have foreground and background buildings by decree (e.g. La Défense, Canary Wharf and Battery Park City). At La Défense with a lengthy history of development behind it, the individual buildings reflect the design ideas/fashions prevalent in the decade in which the buildings were built with the whole project being held together by its landscape. The level of design control fluctuated and some architectural diversity has been achieved. Much, however, is sterile. Canary Wharf, on the other hand, has seen a heavier set of controls in place and as a result has ended up with a more unified set of buildings despite their individual nature. Yet it is less sterile than La Défense. Unity is, apparently, now not something sought in the World Trade Center development. The landscape will be crucial in holding that scheme together if it is to be perceived as a single project.

The debate of when to seek unity (or diversity, or chaos) in an urban design will continue. How controlled the design process should be, will continue to be argued. Few people are opposed to the use of zoning and building codes to ensure the meeting of public health and safety needs – the fundamental human needs identified in Figure 1.6. Will developers and their architects design sustainable environments, for instance, without being forced to be do so by design controls? Will they give a hoot about the context, geographical or cultural, of their proposals without having to work within design guidelines? A sense of place is also a basic human need. The degree to which the qualities of the built environment contribute to meeting it is unknown, but it is not insignificant. Should the design of the environment be left to multi-national companies whose idea of a sense of place is one that promotes themselves? At present, the answers emerge as a result of how the design process is conducted. It is a by-product of other decisions and not one addressed head on.

What is clear from the case studies is that the precision with which design objectives are stated, the guidelines are operationally defined and the review process is transparent, the greater the likelihood that the implemented design will meet the goals set for it (see Table 8.2). The goals that are set will always be political; the knowledge we have from the case studies and on ongoing person-environment research enable us to design the means to achieve ends with some confidence.

Commentary

The knowledge of case studies is important. While every situation faced by an urban designer is unique, many generic problems are addressed. The typology presented here demonstrates commonalities both in product and process types. Architects and other design professionals rely heavily on precedents, much more heavily than they do on abstract theoretical constructs of how the world functions. Every now and then a new paradigm is unveiled. The most recent in urban design is that of the New Urbanism, or Smart Growth, with its transect design paradigm (Ellis, 2002). The fundamental issues in urban design, however, remain remarkably the same. How we address them will differ over time and will depend on what we learn from experience, our own and from that of others.

The issues raised in this chapter are recurring ones. They have engaged the attention of city planners and urban designers, in particular amongst design professionals, over the span of time covered in this book. They will do so in the future. New concerns will certainly arise. Some will have stamina; others will be ephemeral. The consideration of what the nature of the public interest is, the way of defining it and designing based on that definition, will remain central to the work of urban designers in democratic countries.

Design professionals have many roles. One is certainly the public role of bringing the attention of both politicians and the lay-public to the opportunities for improving the built environment of cities. It is an activist role. There are architects and landscape architects vitally concerned with the future state of our planet who are strong advocates for designing 'with nature in mind'. There are those who are concerned with problems of particular population groups, particularly those whose voices are seldom heard in thinking about designs. They enrich the debate about what should be done about the public realm of cities. Ultimately, however, urban design is an *act of will* on the part of developers, public and private, and what a society encourages and allows them to do. Political fortunes and what the market dictates or allows will guide their actions. Urban design will continue to support and intervene in the operation of both the 'capital web' of investment decisions and the 'invisible web' of legal decisions that shape urban development. The design professions have much to offer in designing and redesigning cities and their precincts provided they understand the ways in which both these webs function. And provided they learn from past experience.

12

Afterthoughts: Urban design – field or discipline and profession?

Although it is difficult to reconstruct with precision the urban design history of the past 50 years, those who first used the term 'urban design' were concerned with large-scale multi-building architectural projects. These projects were necessitated in Europe by the devastation of World War II and in the United States by the changes taking places in cities as a result of new technologies, increased wealth, and changing ways of life and social values. Decolonization in Asia and much of Africa sparked new town and housing projects. Urban design was thought of as architecture particularly in Europe. Little distinction was made between city planning and architecture. The problem was that many politicians and architects alike saw the nature of cities and city life within an intellectual framework far removed from everyday life. Well-intentioned though much architectural thinking may have been, many of the projects simply did not work out well when built and inhabited and so were heavily criticized. In response the fields of architecture and city planning went in different directions.

The mainstream of architectural thought sought solace from the criticism of scholars, practitioners and critics such as Jane Jacobs (1961), Marshall Kaplan (1973), Peter Blake (1977) and Brent Brolin (1976) in the development of post-modern theories of aesthetics. City planners, particularly those in academia, turned their attention to the social and economic problems of cities that they considered more important. Luckily, a cadre of architects and planners and, on any extensive scale only much more recently, landscape architects, retained an interest in the qualities of the physical environment of cities. They focused their attention on how design can enhance or diminish the opportunities for people to achieve the positive aspects of what they are motivated to achieve.

This book has been about the efforts of these design professionals and many lay-people to improve the quality of cities in more than a piecemeal manner. True, some such efforts for and with people, young and old, rich and poor, and of different cultural backgrounds have achieved very little in providing the affordances that would help them fulfil their aspirations. At the same time, other such efforts have been highly successful particularly when they have dealt with life as lived. Many social policy and planning efforts have also been highly successful but others have been abject failures. Throughout these ups and downs, well-executed urban designs continued to make important contributions to people's quality of life. They give people enjoyment and a sense of pride and will do so in the future (Dreier *et al.*, 2001). The proviso is that urban design needs to be based more on an empirical rather than a purely rationalist foundation. Rationalist thinking will, however, make us consider future possibilities that are departures from failing traditions.

So What Then is Urban Design?

The case studies included in this volume show the breadth of urban design work. The field is concerned with specific design products varying in type from new towns, to precincts of cities, to elements of city infrastructure. The size of urban design endeavours has varied considerably over the past 50 years. Brasília is a national capital, Pariser Platz is a square, and Trudeslund consists of a group of houses. It is always concerned with the three- and preferably the four-dimensional world. Procedurally, urban design is concerned with four types of projects: total, all-of-a-piece, piece-by-piece and plug-in urban design. Substantively and procedurally urban design is thus concerned primarily with design policies and designing at the project level in order to intentionally shape the city.

Urban design concerns and activities clearly overlap those of other fields. It should do so. It does and should overlap city-planning endeavours concerned with broad policies about the distribution of activities in space and the linkages between them. Urban design products are produced under that umbrella and create it. Similarly, urban design does and should overlap civil engineering in ensuring the buildability of large-scale elements of infrastructure. It does and should overlap landscape architecture in its concern for the detailing of the space between buildings and in designing for sustainable futures. It does and should overlap architecture in its concerns for how buildings front and make, behaviourally and symbolically, the public realm.

The city is a collage of overlapping precincts, places and linkages (Rowe and Koetter, 1978). How should these elements be designed and organized? Should they be clearly differentiated or merged? These questions deal with broad policy concerns. The position taken here is that it is through political channels that communal decisions should be made, and it is the responsibility of politicians to set directions as representatives of those who elected them. Design professionals have to possess the competence to inform both politicians and the public about future possibilities, to challenge political assumptions, and to follow ideas through. They need stamina and considerable tenacity of purpose if they are to succeed.

A coherent city is not simply a haphazard collage. It is one of distinct and varied paths, districts, landmarks, edges and nodes. Kevin Lynch identified these elements as giving legibility to cities (Lynch, 1960). His research has held up well under considerable scrutiny since it was conducted 40 years ago. Edges are not as important as he thought they are; nodes are probably more important. Clear edges do give clarity to the boundaries of districts, or precincts. The projects in many of the case studies included here are bounded islands of development. Being also integrated into their surroundings would probably be a good idea. Battery Park City clearly has edges to it making it a unit, but on the landward side it is also clearly linked to the Lower Manhattan by streets patterns and view corridors. Urban design is particularly concerned with, in Lynch's terms, districts and paths. Good districts will almost certainly contain nodes and landmarks. They may be well defined with edges but it is the core area that matters most.

Urban design is thus project based, dealing with the public realm of human settlements and the buildings or landscape elements that define it. Specific projects take a number of forms depending on the type of process they involve, the type of product they are and the intellectual paradigm within which they are designed. The range of concern of urban designers is clearly broad and the project types varied, in terms of both procedures and products, as the case studies show. The questions are: 'If it can be defined in terms of its areas of concern, is there a body of knowledge that is unique to doing urban design well – in putting together projects?' and thus 'Is it a discipline in its own right or simply a field of professional design work?'

Urban Design, A Discipline?

The hallmark of a discipline is a body of unique literature, journals and its own processes of socializing new members into its ranks – into its norms of behaviour. The question then arises: 'How large does a unique body of knowledge and how exclusive do its norms of behaviour have to be for a sphere of activity to be regarded as an independent, if not exclusively so, discipline?' What evidence do we have?

Most of the items listed in the 'References and further reading' fall within the domain of a variety of existing disciplines. The list also includes part of an increasing number of books devoted to urban design. There are now a number of intellectually challenging journals, relatively young, devoted to urban design. Some have 'urban design' in their names, but the leading North American journal on urban design is called *Planning* because it also includes material on social and economic concerns, land-use planning as well as urban design! Europe has many journals dealing with 'urbanism' that cover urban design concerns. At the same time the number of journals devoted to urban design is considerably outnumbered by journals in the traditional design fields that include articles on urban design projects. True, many of these journals cover projects superficially and purely from their own professional viewpoint but they do bring attention to urban design projects being developed around the world.

The next question is: 'How are professionals inculcated with the norms of professional action and behaviour?' There are a few institutes and professional societies devoted to urban design but anybody can join them. The Urban Design Group in the United Kingdom is a loosely knit coterie of people with a common interest. It has regular meetings, organizes lectures and has its own journal. There is an Institute for Urban Design in the United States based and functioning mainly in New York, and similar loose groups of like-minded professionals around the world. The Congress for the New Urbanism is a powerful professional and lobbying group in the United States but with a worldwide membership and following. It has a manifesto, holds conferences and advocates 'smart growth'. It promotes its aspirations and values to professionals, public officials and lay-people. No legal bodies comparable to boards of architecture, however, control admission to a 'profession' of urban design.

'Urban designer' is not a protected title in the way 'architect' is (although in many places this legal protection is under review as other groups claim expertise in designing buildings). Most professional design societies have sections devoted to urban design, in much the same way that psychological societies have a section devoted to the study of environmental psychology. Urban design is professional work. It will be individual professionals and the educational institutions that guide the development of the field and, perhaps, the discipline of urban design.

Almost all, if not all, substantial urban design education is offered beyond undergraduate level. Until recently most such urban design programs required training in architecture for admission. This demand has changed as the skills required of urban designers have become more clearly defined. The prevailing belief amongst designers is still, however, that no special training or knowledge beyond that offered within the traditional design fields is necessary to be able to create good urban designs. The position is that if one is a well-trained city planner, a landscape architect or architect one can carry out urban design activities without any additional knowledge – that if one can design a building well, one can design a spoon or a city well (Vignelli Associates, 1990). It is a dubious claim.

Many observers (e.g. Schurch, 1999) see urban design as lying at the intersect of the interests of the three main professions concerned with the layout of the environment – architecture, landscape architecture and city planning, to which I have added civil engineering as shown in Figure 12.1a. This position reinforces that taken here. From the observations I have made above, however, my inference is that urban design while overlapping these fields has developed its own area of expertise. Its relationship to the traditional design fields now looks more like in Figure 12.1b. It has become what it should never have become – a discipline in its own right. In doing so, however, it allows the other three fields to pursue their own interests without worrying about the complex issues of urban development and urban quality beyond their traditional concerns.

Rightly or wrongly, urban design is increasingly taking on the form of a discipline. Like many other disciplines, such as those under the umbrellas of medicine or the social sciences, it is occurring where its interests intersect those of traditional fields. It draws on and helps to create urban geography, engineering, environmental psychology, climatology and the management sciences. No single person can encompass all this knowledge and bring it to bear on decision-making

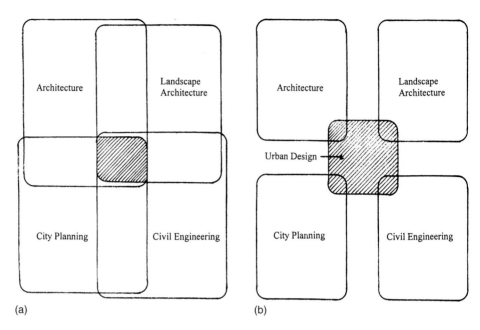

Figure 12.1 The traditional view (a) and the present state, (b) of the field of urban design in relation to the other design fields.

and designing. In whatever way urban design may or may not develop as a discipline, in action it will remain a collaborative task.

It will draw on the expertise of the three traditional design fields but it differs from them in that it has become more development oriented, more socially oriented and more conscious of the politically volatile nature of decision-making at the urban level. Professionals with a committed interest in urban design are, because no one else is doing it, slowly developing their own empirical knowledge base, their own organizations and their own journals. This book has focused on their professional efforts and has sought to outline, for the moment at least, the scope of concern of those who have made a commitment to urban design as one vehicle for improving city life as it evolves.

Conclusion

Urban design encompasses much. The objective of this book has been to display and understand its range of activities through the provision of a typology for classifying design projects. It has also presented a number of descriptive case studies that illuminate the typology. Case studies are probably the easiest way to display the work subsumed under the rubric 'urban design'. They have been categorized here by the process by which they have been carried out and by the type of product they are. Classification by type of product has been the tradition in architecture, but classifying by process gets closer to the essence of the nature of urban designing. Either way, the goal has been to show the scope of concern of urban designers.

The nature of its cities is an indicator of the state of a culture. Cultures are in a state of constant flux, sometimes slowly as in the second half of the twentieth century in the Western world and sometimes rapidly as in the first half. The economically developing world is rapidly undergoing the major upheavals, social, political and physical, that the so-called first world experienced more slowly earlier. Technological changes accompanied by a rise in the economic state of a society inevitably raise questions of what its people want to be and what kinds of environments, social and physical, they want to inhabit. Urban design activities will continue and will be buffeted by changes in the political attitudes that shape the future.

Urban designing will always require *acts of will* on the part of individual design professionals and lay-people, citizens, and politicians. In taking the field forward much can be learnt from the successes and limitations of the processes and products of the last half-century. There are now many fine examples of policies that have led to fine urban designs. There are many fine projects around the world. My own hope is that urban design will continue as a collaborative professional activity – a collaboration between public and private sectors of the economy, a collaboration between politicians, design professions and citizens, and between research and practice. If it is really to serve people well in the long run it must be based on an increasingly sophisticated body of knowledge about how cities function and the relationship between environment and human behaviour. It must be based on a much greater understanding of how the built and natural worlds interact than we now possess. More rigorous case studies than those presented here would steepen all designers' learning curve and would highlight what makes urban design an important and a unique professional activity.

Bellevue, Washington in 1989

References and further reading

Abel, Chris (2000). *Architecture and Identity: Responses to Cultural and Technological Change* (second edition). Oxford: Architectural Press.

Adjmi, Morris, ed. (1991). *Aldo Rossi: Architecture, 1981–1991*. New York: Princeton University Press.

A great place to live (2001). *The Guardian*. Friday, 7 September. *http://www.guardian.co.uk/ g2.story/0,3604,548152,00.html*

Ahmedabad Municipal Corporation (*circa* 2000). *The Heritage Walk in Ahmedabad*. Ahmedabad: Danapith.

Alexander, Christopher, Sara Ishikawa and Murray Silverstein (1977). *A Pattern Language: Towns, Buildings, Construction*. New York: Oxford University Press.

Alexander, Christopher, Hajo Neis, Artemis Anninou and Ingrid King (1987). *A New Theory of Urban Design*. New York: Oxford University Press.

Alexander Cooper Associates (1979). *Battery Park City: Draft Summary Report and 1979 Master Plan*. New York: The authors. *http://www.batteryparkcity.org/guidelines.html*

Ambasz, Emilio, ed. (1998). *Emilio Ambasz: The Poetics of the Pragmatic: Architecture, Exhibit, Industrial and Graphic Design*. New York: Rizzoli.

Anderson, Larz T. (2000). *Planning the Built Environment*. Chicago, IL and Washington, DC: Planners Press.

Arcidi, Philip (1991). Paolo Soleri's Arcology: updating the prognosis. *Progressive Architecture* **72** (3): 76–9.

Arnell, Peter and Ted Bickford (1985). *Aldo Rossi: Buildings and Projects*. New York: Rizzoli International.

Arnold, Henry F. (1993). *Trees in Urban Design* (second edition). New York: Van Nostrand Reinhold.

Attoe, Wayne (1988a). *Transit, Land Use, and Urban Form*. Austin, TX: Center for the Study of Urban Architecture.

Attoe, Wayne (1988b). Historic preservation. In Anthony J. Catanese and James C. Snyder, eds., *Urban Planning*. New York: McGraw-Hill, 344–56.

Attoe, Wayne and Donn Logan (1989). *American Urban Architecture: Catalysts in the Design of Cities*. Berkeley and Los Angeles: University of California Press.

Awards (2002). *Architecture Australia* **92** (November–December): 50–73.

Aynsley, Richard M. (1989). The politics of pedestrian level urban wind control. *Building and Environment* **24** (4): 292–5.

Bacon, Edmund (1969). Urban process: planning with and for the community. *Architectural Record* **145** (5): 113–28.

Bacon, Edmund (1974). *Design of Cities* (revised edition). New York: Viking.

Bahga, Sarbjit, Surinder Bahga and Yashinder Bahga (1993). *Modern Architecture in India. Post-Independence Perspective*. New Delhi: Galgotia.

Balfour, Alan (1978). *Rockefeller Center: Architecture as Theater*. New York: McGraw-Hill.

Balfour, Alan (1999). Octagon: the persistence of the ideal. In James Corner, ed., *Recovering Landscape: Essays in Contemporary Landscape Architecture*. New York: Princeton University Press, 87–100.

Balfour, Alan and Zheng Shiling (2002). *World Cities: Shanghai*. Chichester: Wiley-Academic.

Baljon, Lodewijk (1995). *Designing Parks*. Amsterdam: Architectura and Natura Press.

Baltimore Urban Renewal and Housing Agency (1959). *Charles Center Urban Renewal Plan*. Baltimore: The Agency.

Banerjee, Tridib, Todd Bressi, Philp Enquist and John Rahaim (2002). Is urban design on the right track? *Places* **15** (1): 81–4.

Banham, Reyner (1976). *Megastructure: Urban Structures of the Recent Past*. New York: Harper and Row.

Barnes, W. Anderson (1986). Ghiradelli Square: keeping a first first. *Urban Land* **45** (May): 6–10.

Barnett, Jonathan (1974). *Urban Design as Public Policy*. New York: Architectural Record.

Barnett, Jonathan (1982). *An Introduction to Urban Design*. New York: Harper and Row.

Barnett, Jonathan (1987). In the public interest: design guidelines. *Architectural Record* (August): 114–25.

Barnett, Jonathan (2003). *Redesigning Cities: Principles, Practice, Implementation*. Chicago: American Planning Association.

Bedarida, Marc (1995). Lione: la politica degli spazi publica. *Casabella* **59** (629): 8–23.

Benevolo, Leonardo (1967). *The Origins of Modern Town Planning*. London: Routledge & Kegan Paul.

Benevolo, Leonardo (1980). *The History of the City* [translated by Geoffrey Culverwill]. Cambridge, MA: MIT Press.

Benjamin, Andrew (1988). Deconstruction and art/the art of deconstruction. In Christopher Norris and Andrew Benjamin, eds., *What is Deconstruction?* New York: St. Martin's Press. 33–56.

Bentley, Ian (1999). *Urban Transformations: Power, People and Urban Design*. London: Routledge.

Bhatt, Vikram and Peter Scriver (1990). *After the Masters*. Ahmedabad: Mapin Publishing.

Biddulph, Mike (2003). Towards successful home zones in the UK. *Journal of Urban Design* **8** (3): 217–41.

Bilbao Ria (2000). Whole issue.

Billingham, John and Richard Cole (2002). *The Good Place Guide: Urban Design in Britain and Ireland*. London: T. Batsford.

Bingham-Hall, Patrick (1999). *Olympic Architecture: Building Sydney 2000*. Sydney: Watermark Press.

Birr, A. Kendall (1994). *A Tradition of Excellence. The Sesquicentennial History of the State University of New York at Albany*. Virginia Beach, VA: Donning.

Black, Sinclair (1979). San Antonio's Linear Paradise. *American Institute of Architects Journal* **68** (9): 30–9.

Blake, Peter (1977). *Form Follows Fiasco: Why Modern Architecture Hasn't Worked*. Boston: Little Brown.

Blakely, Edward J. and Mary G. Snyder (1997). *Fortress America: Gated Communities in the United States*. Washington, DC: Brookings Institution Press.

Bloomer, Kent and Charles W. Moore (1977). *Body, Memory and Architecture*. New Haven: Yale University Press.

Boles, Daralice D. (1986). SITE selected for Pershing Square. *Progressive Architecture* **67** (10): 36.

Brambilla, Roberto and Gianni Longo (1977). *For Pedestrians Only: Planning and Management of Traffic Free Zones*. New York: Whitney Library of Design.

Breen, Ann and Dick Rigby (1994). *Waterfronts: Cities Reclaim Their Edge*. New York: McGraw-Hill.

Breen, Ann and Dick Rigby (1996). *The New Waterfront: a World Wide Success Story*. London: Thames and Hudson.

Broadbent, Geoffrey (1990). *Emerging Concepts of Urban Space Design*. London: Van Nostrand Reinhold (International).

Brolin, Brent (1976). *The Failure of Modern Architecture*. New York: Van Nostrand Reinhold.

Broto, Carles (2000). *New Urban Design*. Barcelona: Arian Mostaedi.

Brownlee, David (1989). *Building the City Beautiful: The Benjamin Franklin Parkway and the Museum of Art*. Philadelphia: Philadelphia Museum of Art.

Bucci, Frederico, ed. (1998). *Company Towns*. New York: Princeton University Press.

Buchanan, Peter (1989). Paternoster pressure. *The Architectural Review* **185** (1107): 76–80.

Buder, Stanley (1990). *Visionaries and Planners: The Garden City Movement and the Modern Community*. Oxford: Oxford University Press.

Building Types Study 832 (2004). *Architectural Record* (April): 113–58.

Bunster-Ossa, Ignacio (2001). Landscape urbanism. *Urban Land* **60** (7): 36–47.

Calthorpe, Peter (1993). *The Next American Metropolis: Ecology, Community, and the American Dream*. New York: Princeton University Press.

Cantacuzino, Sherban (1973). The Barbican development, City of London. *Architectural Review* **154** (918): 66–90.

Capital Cities (1983). *Ekistics* **50** (299). Special issue.

Carmona, Matthew, Tim Heath, Taner Oc and Steve Tiesdell (2003). *Public Places, Urban Spaces: The Dimensions of Urban Design*. Oxford: Architectural Press.

Caro, Robert (1974). *The Power Broker: Robert Moses and the Fall of New York*. New York: Knopf.

Cavalcanti, Maria de Betânia Ochôa (1992). Totalitarian states and their influence on city form. *Journal of Architectural and Planning Research* **9** (4): 275–86.

Cavalcanti, Maria de Betânia Ochôa (1997). Urban reconstruction and autocratic regimes: Ceausescu's Bucharest in Historic Perspective. *Planning Perspectives* **12**: 71–109.

Cerver, Francisco A. (1997). *City Squares and Plazas*. New York: Hearst Books International.

Chen, Yuan (2000). The course of SZD planning and design. *World Architecture 2000 Supplement*: 5–9.

Chew, T. C. and C. K. Chua (1998). Development of Singapore's Rapid Transit System. *Japan Railway and Transport Review* **18**: 26–30.

Conybeare, Morrison and Partners (1990). *Kuching Riverfront Masterplan*. Sydney: The authors.

Cook, Peter, Warren Chalk, Dennis Crompton, David Green, Ron Herron and Mike Webb (1991). *Archigram*. Boston: Birkhäuser.

Cooke, Alistair (2000). *Memories of the Great & the Good*. London: Pavilion.

Cooper Marcus, Clare (1986). Design guidelines: a bridge between research and decision making. In William H. Ittelson, Masaaki Asai and Mary Ker, eds., *Cross Cultural Research in Environment and Behavior*. Tucson: University of Arizona, 56–83.

Cooper Marcus, Clare and Carolyn Francis (1990). *People Places: Design Guidelines for Urban Open Space*. New York: Van Nostrand Reinhold.

Cowan, Robert (2003). *Urban Design Guidance: Urban Design Frameworks, Development Briefs and Master Plans*. London: Thomas Telford Ltd.

Cox Group (2002). *Shanghai Waterfront Master Plan, China*. www.cox.com.au/projects/masterplanning_urban_design/index.html

Craighead, Paula, ed. (1991). *The Hidden Design Dimension in Land Use Planning Ordinances*. Portland, Maine: New England Studies Program, University of Southern Maine.

Craig-Smith, Stephen J. and Michael Fagence, eds. (1995). *Recreation and Tourism as Catalysts for Urban Waterfront Development: An International Survey*. Westport, CN: Praeger.

Crane, David (1960). The city symbolic. *Journal of the American Institute of Planners* **26** (November): 285–6.

Crawford, Margaret (1995). *Building the Workingman's Paradise: The Design of American Company Towns*. London: Verso.

Crooks, Cheryl (1985). Glendale's surprising rebirth. *Los Angeles* (July): unpaginated reprint.

Crooks, Mitchell, Peacock, Stewart (1971). Report. *The Urban Renewal and Development Project, Singapore*. Prepared for the United Nations Development Program Special Fund. Sydney: The authors.

Curtis, William J. R. (1988). *Balkrishna Doshi: An Architect for India*. New York: Rizzoli International.

Cuthbert, Alexander (2001). Going global: reflexivity and contextualism in urban design education. *Journal of Urban Design* **6** (3): 297–316.

Cuthbert, Alexander, ed. (2003). *Critical Readings on Urban Design*. Oxford: Blackwell Publishing.

Darling Harbour Authority (1985). *Darling Harbour: Draft Development Plan and Strategy, Planning Report*. Sydney: The authors.

Darley, Gillian (1978). *Villages of Vision*. London: Palladin.

Davis, Robert (1989). Seaside, Florida, U.S.A. *GA Houses* **27**: 90–123.

Davey, Peter (1998). Potsdamer Platz: development in Berlin. *Architectural Review* **205** (1223): 31–4.

De Graveline, Frederique (2002). *La Défense: Les Villes et leurs Projects: Projects Urbain en France*. Paris: Editions du Moniteur.

Del Rio, Vicente (1990). *Introdução ao Desenho Urbano no Processo de Planejamento*. São Paulo: Pini Editora.

Del Rio, Vicente (1992). Urban design and conflicting city images. *Cities* (November): 270–9.

Del Rio, Vicente and Haroldo Gallo (2000). The legacy of modernism in Brazil: paradigm turned reality or unfinished project? *Docomomo Journal* **23** (August): 23–7.

Department of Public Works and Services and the Council of the City of Sydney (1997). *George Street and Railway Square Redevelopment: Statement of Environmental Effects*. Sydney: The authors.

Dixon, John Morris (1992). World on a Platter. *Progressive Architecture* **73** (7): 86–95.

Dixon, John Morris (1999). *Urban Spaces*. New York: Visual Reference Library.

Dober, Richard P. (1992). *Campus Planning*. New York: John Wiley.

DoE (Department of Environment) (1997). *General Policy and Principles*. London: The authors.

Doshi, Balkrishna V. (1982). *Housing*. Ahmedabad: Stein, Doshi, Bhalla.

Doshi, Balkrishna V. (1989). Aranya township. *Mimar: Architecture in Development*. Singapore: Concept Media, 24–9.

Dovey, Kim (2004). *Fluid City: Transforming Melbourne's Urban Waterfront*. Sydney: UNSW Press.

Dreier, Peter, John Mollenkopf and Todd Swanstrom (2001). *Place Matters: Metropolitics for the Twenty-first Century*. Lawrence: University of Kansas Press.

Duany, Andres and Elizabeth Plater-Zyberk with Jeff Speck (2000). *Suburban Nation: The Rise of Sprawl and the Decline of the American Dream*. New York: North Point Press.

Ecola, Lisia (2004). Tales of a transit junkie. *Planning* **70** (9): 34–6.

Editorial (1951). Slum surgery in St. Louis: a new apartment type. *Architectural Forum* **94** (April): 128–36.

Edwards, Brian (1992). *London Docklands: Urban Design in an Era of Deregulation*. London: Butterworth Architecture.

Ellin, Nan (1999). *Postmodern Urbanism* (revised edition). New York: Princeton University Press.

Ellis, Cliff (2002). The New Urbanism: critiques and rebuttals. *Journal of Urban Design* **7** (3): 261–92.

EPAD (2002). *La Défense*. Paris: EPAD.

Epstein, David (1973). *Brasilia, Plan and Reality: A Study of Planned and Spontaneous Developments*. Berkeley and Los Angeles: University of California Press.

Eriksen, Richard (2001). Some sights to make eyes weep. *Paris Kiosque* **8** (4): 605. *http://www.paris.org/Kiosque/apr01/605slum.html*

Evenson, Norma (1973). *Two Brazilian Capitals: Architecture and Urbanism in Rio de Janeiro and Brasília*. New Haven: Yale University Press.

Fitzgerald, Charlotte (2004). Pedestrian-only malls not always the answer. *The Courier Mail*, 17 April. *http://www.planetizen.com/news/item.php?id=1287&rf=e*

Floyd, Nubra (1987). Kresge College. *Progressive Architecture* **68** (February): 76–9.

Forgery, Benjamin (1992). Spanish treasures (Expo92 Seville). *Architecture* **81** (7): 72–9.

Forgery, Benjamin (2004). World Trade Center plans rising above the squabbles. *Washington Post*, Sunday, 18 April, No. 1.

Fosler, R. Scott and Renee A. Berger, eds. (1982). *Public–Private Partnerships in American Cities: Seven Case Studies*. Lexington, MA: Lexington Books.

Frampton, Kenneth (1982). Towards a critical regionalism: six points for an architecture of resistance. In Hal Foster, ed., *The Anti-Aesthetic: Essays on Postmodern Culture*. Port Townsend, WA: Bay Press, 16–30.

Francis, Alan (1991). Private nights in the City Centre. *Town and Country Planning* **60** (10): 302–3.

Francis, Mark (2001). A case study method for landscape architecture. *Landscape Journal* **20** (1): 15–28.

Franck, Karen A. and Sherry Ahrentzen, eds. (1989). *New Households, New Housing*. New York: Van Nostrand Reinhold.

Franck, Karen A. and Linda H. Schneekloth, eds. (1994). *Ordering Space: Types in Architecture and Urban Design*. New York: Van Nostrand Reinhold.

Frascati, Guido (1989). Paradigm lost: exploring possibilities in environmental design research and practice. In Graeme Hardie, Robin Moore and Henry Sanoff, eds., *Changing Paradigms: Edra20/1989*. EDRA, 62–7.

Freedom Trail Foundation, The (2003). *www.thefreedomtrail.org*

Freeman, Allen (1986). 'Fine Tuning' a landmark of adaptive use. *Architecture* **75** (November): 66–71.

Freiman, Ziva (1990). Controversy: Paternoster Square. *Progressive Architecture* **71** (3): 115–6.

Frieden, Bernard J. (1990). Public-private development: dealmaking in the public interest. *Center* **6**: 26–35.

Frieden, Bernard J. and Lynne B. Sagalyn (1991). *Downtown Inc: How America Rebuilds Cities*. Cambridge, MA: MIT Press.

Garnier, Tony (1917). Une Cité Industrielle: etude por la construction de villes. Paris: Auguste Vincente. Reprinted (1990), New York: Rizzoli.

Garvin, Alexander (1995). *The American City: What Works. What Doesn't*. New York: McGraw-Hill.

Garreau, Joel (1991). *Edge Cities: Life on the New Frontier*. New York: John Wiley.

Gehl, Jan (1987). *Life Between Buildings: Using Public Space*. New York: Van Nostrand Reinhold.

Gehl, Jan and Lars Gemzøe (2003). *New City Space* [translated by Karen Steenhard]. Copenhagen: Danish Architectural Press.

Gehry, Frank O. (2002). Building at the Pariser Platz – remarks on the new Berlin. *Casabella* **66** (704): 4–11, 100–2.

Glancey, Jonathan (2003). It's a jumble out there. *The Guardian*, 3 November. http://www.guardian.co.uk/arts/critic/features/0.1076585.html

Glendale Redevelopment Agency (1986). *Urban Design Information*. Glendale: The authors.

Goldberger, Paul (1992). *The Architecture of Purchase College*. Purchase, NY: Neuberger Museum of Art.

Goldberger, Paul (2000). *The Architecture of Rem Koolhaas*. Los Angeles: Jensen and Walker.

Goldberger, Paul (2003). *Up form Ground Zero: Politics, Architecture and the Rebuilding of New York*. New York: Random House.

Goldfinger, Erno (1942). The elements of enclosed space. *Architectural Review* **91** (541): 5–8.

Golich, Vicki (2000). *Workbook on Case Teaching for Mount Holyoke College Case Method Project Faculty Development Workshop*. Mount Holyoke, MA: Harriet L. and Paul Weissman Center for Leadership and the Liberal Arts.

Gordon, David L. A. (1997). *Battery Park City: Politics and Planning on the New York Waterfront*. London: Routledge and Gordon & Breach.

Gosling, David with Maria Christina Gosling (2003). *The Evolution of American Urban Design: A Chronological Anthology*. Chichester: Wiley Academic.

Gosling, David and Barry Maitland (1976). *Design and Planning of Retail Systems*. London: The Architectural Press.

Gosling, David and Barry Maitland (1984). *Concepts of Urban Design*. New York: St. Martin's Press.

Gottschalk, Shimon S. (1975). *Communities and Alternatives: An Exploration of the Limits of Planning*. Cambridge, MA: Schenkman.

Grava, Sigurd (2003). *Urban Transportation Systems: Choices for Communities*. New York: McGraw-Hill.

Gruen, Victor (1964). *The Heart of our Cities – the Urban Crisis: Diagnosis and Cure*. New York: Simon & Shuster.

Guy, Simon, Simon Marvin and Timothy Moss, eds. (2001). *Urban Infrastructure in Transition: Networks, Buildings, Plans*. London: Earthscan.

Hammatt, Heather (2002). Going with the flow. *Landscape Architecture* **92** (1): 72–7.

Harvey, David (2003). Social justice, postmodernism and the city. In Alexander Cuthbert, ed., *Critical Readings on Urban Design*. Oxford: Blackwells, 59–63.

Hawken, Paul, Amory B. Lovins and L. Hunter Lovins (1999). Weaving the web of solutions: the Curitiba example. In *Natural Capitalism: The Next Industrial Revolution*. London: Earthscan, 288–308.

Hayden, Dolores (1984). *Redesigning the American Dream: The Future of Housing, Work and Family Life*. New York: Norton.

Hayden, Dolores (1995). *The Power of Place: Urban Landscapes as Public History*. Cambridge, MA: MIT Press.

Hedman, Richard with Andrew Jaszewski (1984). *Fundamentals of Urban Design*. Washington, DC and Chicago, IL: Planners Press.

Held, Virginia (1970). *The Public Interest and Individual Interests*. New York: Basic Books.

Heng Chye Kiang (2000). The night zone storyline; Boat Quay, Clarke Quay and Robertson Quay. *Traditional Buildings and Settlements Review* **XIX** (Spring): 41–9.

Heng Chye Kiang (2001). Singapore River: a case for a river of life. *Singapore Architect* **211** (September): 190–5.

Hester, Randolph (1975). *Neighborhood Space*. Stroudsburg, PA: Dowden, Hutchinson and Ross.

Hilbersheimer, Ludwig (1940). *The New City*. Chicago: Paul Theobold.

Hinkle, Ricardo (1999). Panning Pershing (the flaws and shortcomings of the Pershing Square project). *Landscape Architecture* **89** (6): 9.

Hinshaw, Mark L. (1983). The private sector builds a public space, Sixth Street pedestrian corridor, Bellevue. *Urban Design Review* **6** (4): 6–7.

Hinshaw, Mark L. (1994). Transforming suburbia: the case of Bellevue, Washington. In Brenda Case Scheer and Wolfgang Preiser, eds., *Design Review: Challenging Urban Aesthetic Control*. New York: Chapman and Hall, 111–18.

Holston, James (1989). *The Modernist City: An Anthropological Critique of Brasilia*. Chicago: University of Chicago Press.

Hopenfeld, Morton (1961). The role of design in city planning. *American Institute of Architects Journal* **35** (5): 40–4.

Houston Jr, Lawrence O. (1990). From street to mall and back again. *Planning* **56** (6): 4–10.

Houston Jr, Lawrence O. (1997). *BIDs: Business Improvement Districts*. Washington, DC: Urban Land Institute.

Houston Jr, Lawrence O. (2004). Capitalist tool. *Planning* **70** (1): 26–9.

Hoyle, Brian, David Pinder and M. Sohail Husain (1994). *Revitalising the Waterfront: International Dimensions of Dockland Redevelopment*. Chichester: John Wiley and Sons.

Inam, Aseem (2002). Meaningful urban design: teleological/catalytic/relevant. *Journal of Urban Design* **7** (1): 35–58.

Irazábal, Clara (in progress). The politics of development and urban design in Curitiba. In Vicente del Rio and William Siembieda, eds., *Beyond Brasilia: Contemporary Urban Design in Brazil*.

Izumi, Kiyo (1968). Some psycho-social considerations of environmental design (mimeographed).

Jacobs, Allan (1993). *Great Streets*. Cambridge, MA: MIT Press.

Jacobs, Jane (1961). *The Death and Life of Great American Cities*. New York: Random House.

Jacobs, Steven and Barclay G. Jones (1962). Urban Design through conservation. Unpublished manuscript, University of California at Berkeley.

James-Chakraborty, Kathleen (2000). *German Architecture for a Mass Audience*. London: Routledge.

Jencks, Charles (1993). *Unité d'Habitation*. London: Phaedon Press.

Johnson, Chris (2003). *Greening Sydney: Landscaping the Urban Fabric*. Sydney: Government Architect Publications.

Johnson, J. Eugene (1962). What remains of man? Aldo Rossi's Modena cemetery. *Journal of the Society of Architectural Historians* **1**: 38–54.

Jordan, David P. (1995). *Transforming Paris: The Life and Labors of Baron Haussmann*. New York: Free Press.

Kanda, Shun and Masami Kobayashi (1991). *Boston by Design: A City in Development: 1960 to 1990*. Tokyo: Process Architecture.

Kaplan, Marshall (1973). *Urban Planning in the 1960s: A Design for Irrelevancy*. Cambridge, MA: MIT Press.

Katz, Peter (1994). *The New Urbanism: Toward an Architecture of Community*. New York: McGraw-Hill.

Kayden, Jerold S. (2000). *Privately Owned Public Space: The New York City Experience*. New York: John Wiley.

Kleihues, Josef Paul (1987). *Internationale Bauausstellung Berlin 1987: Projecektübersicht*. Berlin: IBA.

Knack, Ruth (2003). Up close at the World Trade Center. *Planning* **69** (4): 11–13.

Koolhaas, Rem (1978). *Delirious New York: A Retroactive Manifesto for Manhattan*. London: Thames and Hudson.

Koolhaas, Rem (1998). *OMA/Remkoolhaas, 1987–1998*. Madrid: El Croquis Editorial.

Kozloff, Howard (2001). Sydney's Darling Harbour. *Urban Land* **60** (11–12): 82–6.

Kresge College. *http://www.greatbuildings.com/buildings/kresge_college.html*

Kreyling, Christine (2002). New schools for Chattanooga. *Planning* **68** (7): 32–3.

Krier, Rob (1988). *Architectural Composition* [translated by Romana Schneider and Gabrielle Vorreiter]. New York: Rizzoli.

Krier, Rob (1990). Typological elements of the concept of urban space. In Andreas Papadakis and Harriet Watson, eds., *The New Classicism: Omnibus Volume*. New York: Rizzoli, 213–19.

Kurokawa, Kisho (2000). Urban design of the public space system along the central axis. *World Architecture Supplement 2000*: 29–36.

Ladd, Brian (1997). *The Ghosts of Berlin: Confronting German History in the Urban Landscape*. London: University of Chicago Press.

Lai, Richard Tseng-yu (1988). *Law in Urban Design and Planning: The Invisible Web*. New York: Van Nostrand Reinhold.

Lang, Jon (1987). *Creating Architectural Theory: The Role of the Behavioral Sciences in Environmental Design*. New York: Van Nostrand Reinhold.

Lang, Jon (1994). *Urban Design: The American Experience*. New York: Van Nostrand Reinhold.

Lang, Jon (2000). The 'new' functionalism and architectural theory. In Keith Diaz Moore, ed., *Culture, Meaning Architecture: Critical Reflections on the Work of Amos Rapoport*. Aldershot: Ashgate, 77–99.

Lang, Jon (2002). *A Concise History of Modern Architecture in India*. Delhi: Permanent Black.

Lang, Jon, Madhavi Desai and Miki Desai (1997). *Architecture and Independence: The Search for Identity – India, 1880 to 1980*. New Delhi: Oxford University Press.

Larrañaga, Enrique (undated). The University City and the architectural thought in Venezuela. In *Obras de Arte de la Universitaria de Caracas/Works of Art of the University City of Caracas*. Caracas: Universidad Central de Venezuela, 45–62.

Lasar, Terry Jill (1989). *Carrots and Sticks. New Zoning Downtown*. Washington, DC: Urban Land Institute.

Leal, Ildefonso (1991). *Historia de la Universidad Central de Venezuela*. Caracas: Ediciones del Rectorado, Universidad Central de Venezuela.

Le Corbusier (1934). *La Ville Radieuse* (The Radiant City) [translated by E. Etchells and Eleanor Levieux]. Reprinted (1967), New York: Orion Press.

Le Corbusier (1953). *L'Unité d'Habitation de Marseilles (The Marseilles Block)*. [translated by Geoffrey Sainsbury]. London: Harvill.

Le Corbusier (1960). *My Work* [translated from French by James Palmer]. London: Architectural Press.

Lehman, Nicholas (2000). No man's town: the good times are killing off America's local elites. *The New Yorker* (June 5): 42–9.

Leonard, Stephen J. and Thomas J. Noel (1990). *Denver: Mining Camp to Metropolis*. Niwot: University of Denver Press.

Levy, Paul R. (2001). Downtown: competitive for a new century. In Jonathan Barnett, ed., *Planning for a New Century: The Regional Agenda*. Washington, DC: Island Press, 135–76.

Lewis, Nigel C. (1977). A procedural framework attempting to express the relationship of human factors to the physical design process. Unpublished student paper, University of Pennsylvania.

Lewis, Sylvia (1996). Mr. Precedent. *Planning* **62** (8): 10–15.

Lewyn, Michael (2003). Zoning without zoning. *http://www.planetizen.com/oped/item.php?id=112*

Liang, Low Boon, ed. (2002). *Proceedings of the Great Asian Streets Symposium*. Singapore: Centre for Advanced Studies in Architecture, National University of Singapore.

Libeskind, Daniel (2004). *Breaking Ground*. London: John Murray.

Lim, William S. W. (2004). *Have you been Shanghaied? Culture and Urbanism in Glocalized Shanghai*. Singapore: Asian Urban Lab.

Llewelyn-Davies (2000). *Urban Design Compendium*. London: English Partnership and the Housing Corporation.

Lochhead, Helen (1999). Sydney Afresh. *Architecture Australia* **88** (September–October): 68–75.

Loukaitou-Suderis, Anastasia and Tridib Banerjee (1998). *Urban Design Downtown: Poetics and Politics of Form*. Los Angeles and Berkeley, CA: University of California Press.

Low, Setha M. (2003). *Behind the Gates: Life, Security and the Pursuit of Happiness in Fortress America*. London: Routledge.

Lowe, Garrard D. (1996). Urban lessons from Paris. *Urbanities* **6** (1): 1–6.

Lubell, Sam (2004). Daniel Libeskind: is his plan still around? *Architectural Record* (April): 34.

Lubell, Sam, *et al.* (2004). Libeskind's World Trade Center guidelines raise doubts. *Architectural Record* (June): 47.

Lucero, Laura and Jeffrey Soule (2002). The Supreme Court validates moratoriums in a path breaking decision. *Planning* **68** (6): 4–7.

Lynch, Kevin (1961). *The Image of the City*. Cambridge, MA: MIT Press

Lynch, Kevin (1976). *Managing the Sense of a Region*. Cambridge, MA: MIT Press.

Madanipour, Ali (1996). *Design of Urban Space: An Inquiry into a Socio-Spatial Process*. Chichester: John Wiley.

Madanipour, Ali (2001). How relevant is 'planning by neighbourhoods' today? *Town Planning Review* **72** (2): 171–91.

Madanipour, Ali (2003). *Public and Private Spaces of the City*. London: Routledge.

Mansfield, Howard (1990). *Cosmopolis: Yesterday's Cities of the Future*. New Brunswick, NJ: Rutgers University Center for Urban Policy Research.

Marmot, Alexi (1982). The Legacy of Le Corbusier. *Built Environment* **7** (2): 82–95.

Marshall, Alex (2001). Seaside turns twenty. *Metropolis* (June): 68–72.

Marshall, Richard (2001). *Waterfronts in Post-Industrial Cities*. London: Spon Press.

Marshall, Richard (2003). *Emerging Urbanity: Global Projects in the Asia Pacific Rim*. London: Spon Press.

Mas, Elías (2002). The Ensanche of Bilbao. In *Euskal Hiria*. Victoria-Gasteiz: Central Publishing Services of the Basque Government, 134–41.

Maslow, Abraham (1987). *Motivation and Personality* (third edition revised by Robert Fraeger, James Fadiman, Cynthia McReynolds and Ruth Cox). New York: Harper & Row.

Mazumdar, Sanjoy (2000). Autocratic control and urban design: the case of Tehran, Iran. *Journal of Urban Design* **5** (3): 317–38.

McCamant, Kathryn and Charles Durett (1988). *Cohousing: A Contemporary Approach to Housing Ourselves*. Berkeley, CA: Habitat Press/Ten Speed Press.

McCarren, Barbara (1999). And in this corner (designing the landscape for the Pershing Square project). *Landscape Architecture* **89** (6): 9+.

Mello, Terezna Carvalho de and Paulo Henrique Battaglin Machado (1999). Do Desenvolvimento Urbano à Sustentabilidade. From Urban Development to Sustainability. Curitiba: IPPUC.

Melnick, Scott (1987). The urbanization of the suburbs. *Building Design Construction* **28** (3): 70–7.

Meyer, Han (1999). *City and Port: Urban Planning as a Cultural Venture in London, Barcelona and New York*. Utrecht: International Books.

Miao, Pu (2003). Deserted streets in a jammed town. The gated community in Chinese cities and its solution. *Journal of Urban Design* **8** (1): 45–66.

Michelson, William (1968). Most people don't want what architects want. *Transactions* **5** (8): 37–43.

Miles, Don C. and Mark L. Hinshaw (1987). Bellevue's new approach to pedestrian planning and design. In Anne Vernez Moudon, ed., *Public Streets for Public Use*. New York: Van Nostrand Reinhold, 221–31.

Millspaugh, Martin (1964). *Baltimore's Charles Center. A Case Study in Downtown Development*. Washington, DC: The Urban Land Institute.

Mitchell, William J. (1999). *E-topia: 'Urban life, Jim, but not as we Know It'*. Cambridge. MA: MIT Press.

Mitchell, William J. (2003). *Constructing Complexity • Nano Scale • Architectural Scale • Urban Scale*. Sydney: Faculty of Architecture, University of Sydney.

Minton, Anna (2002). *Building Balanced Communities*. London: Royal Institute of Chartered Architects.

Mirvac/Westfield (1997). Raleigh Park. A report submitted for the Urban Development Institute of Australia. Sydney: The authors.

Moholy-Nagy, D. M. A. Sybille P. (1964). *Carlos Raúl Villaneuva and the Architecture of Venezuela*. London: Tiranti.

Mohney, David (1991). *Seaside: Making an American Town*. New York: Princeton University Press.

Montgomery, Roger (1966). Comment on 'House-as-haven in the lower class'. *Journal of the American Institute of Planners* **32** (1): 23–31.

Montgomery, Roger (1985). Pruitt-Igoe: policy failure or social symptom? In Barry Checkoway and Carl V. Patton, eds., *The Metropolitan Midwest: Policy, Problems and Prospects for Change*. Urbana, IL: University of Illinois Press, 229–43.

Moudon, Anne Vernez, ed. (1987). *Public Streets for Public Use*. New York: Van Nostrand Reinhold.

Moudon, Anne Vernez and Wayne Attoe (1995). *Urban Design: Reshaping Our Cities*. Seattle, WA: Urban Design Program, University of Washington.

Moughtin, Cliff (1992). *Urban Design: Street and Square*. London: Butterworth Architecture.

Nakamura, Toshio, ed. (1982). *Aldo Rossi*. Tokyo: A & U Publishing Co.

New Barbican (1954). *Architects' Journal* **120**: 456–66.

Newman, Oscar (1974). *Defensible Space: Crime Prevention through Urban Design*. New York: MacMillan.

Nilson, Sten Ake (1973). *The New Capitals of India, Pakistan and Bangladesh*. London: Curzon Press.

Norberg Schulz, Christian (1980). *Genius Loci: Towards a Phenomenology of Architecture*. New York: Rizzoli.

Novo, Francisco Garcia and Claudia Zavalete de Daute (2002). *Paisaje y urbanismo de la EXPO92*. Seville: Reditores.

Ogden, Philip, ed. (1992). *Update: London Docklands: The Challenge of Development*. Cambridge, MA: Cambridge University Press.

Olds, Kris (1997). Globalizing Shanghai: 'Global Intelligence Corps' and the Building of Pudong. *Cities* **14** (2): 109–23.

Olds, Kris (2001). *Globalization and Urban Change: Capital, Culture and Pacific Rim Mega-Projects*. Oxford: Oxford University Press.

Orwell, George (1961). Politics and the English language. In *Collected Essays*. London: Secker and Warburg, 353–67.

Pachini, Luca (2000). The Jubilee Line extension project. *Casabella* **64** (678): 64–83.

Papadakis, Andreas C., ed. (1992). *Paternoster Square and the Classical Tradition*. London: Academy Editions.

Paseo de Alamo (1985). *Center* **1**: 85–7.

Paternoster Square. *http://www.paternosterlondon.co.uk*

Pegler, Martin (1998). *Streetscapes*. New York: Retail Reporting Corporation.

Peralta, Christian (2002). The shape of digital things to come. *Planning* **68** (9): 20–1.

Perry, Martin, Lily Kong and Brenda Yoh (1997). *Singapore: A Development City State*. New York: John Wiley and Sons.

Petcu, Constantin (1999). Totalitarian Bucharest 1980–9, semio-clinical files. In Neil Leach, ed., *Architecture and Revolution: Contemporary Perspectives on Central and Eastern Europe*. London and New York: Routledge, 177–88.

Pevsner, Nikolaus (1976). *A History of Building Types*. London: Thomas and Hudson.

Postrel, Virginia (2003). *The Substance of Style: How the Rise of Aesthetic Style is Remaking Commerce, Culture and Consciousness*. New York: HarperCollins.

Powell, Ken (2000). *City Transformed: Urban Architecture at the Beginning of the 21st Century*. London: Laurence King Publishing.

Powell, Kenneth (1999). *The Jubilee Line Extension*. London: Laurence King Publishing.

Project Sunrise Pty. Limited and Sunrise High Technologies and Design Pty. Ltd. (1983). *Urban and Landscape Design Report*. Sydney: The authors.

Punter, John (1999). *Design Guidelines in American Cities: A Review of Design Policies and Guidance in Five West Coast Cities*. Liverpool: Liverpool University Press.

Punter, John (2003). From design advice to peer review: the role of the Urban Design Panel in Vancouver. *Journal of Urban Design* **8** (2): 113–35.

Punter, John and Matthew Carmona (1997). *The Design Dimension of City Planning: Theory, Content, and Best Practice for Design Policies*. London: E & FN Spon.

Rainer, George (1990). *Understanding Infrastructure: A Guide for Architecture and Planners*. New York: John Wiley.

Rapoport, Amos (1993). On the nature of capital cities and their physical expression. In John H. Taylor, Jean G. Lengelle and Caroline Andrew, eds., *Capital Cities: International Perspectives*. Ottawa: Carlton University Press, 32–67.

Rauchstrasse, Berlin, Masterplan 1980–5, selected buildings. *www.krierkohl.de/projects/rauchstrasse.html*

Regional Plan Association (1927). *Regional Survey of New York and its Environs*. New York: Russell Sage Foundation.

Richards, Brian (2001). *Future Transport in Cities*. London: Spon Press.

Richards, James M. (1962). *An Introduction to Modern Architecture*. Harmonsworth: Penguin Books.

Robertson, Kent A. (1993). Pedestrian strategies for downtown planners: skywalks versus pedestrian malls. *Journal of the American Institute of Planners* **59** (3): 361–71.

Robertson, Kent A. (1994). *Pedestrian Malls and Skywalks: Traffic Segregation Strategies in American Cities*. Aldershot: Avebury.

Robinette, Margaret A. (1976). *Outdoor Sculpture: Object and Environment*. New York: Whitney Library of Design.

Rossi, Roberto (2000). Time Square and Potsdamer Platz. *The Drama Review* **42** (1): 43–8.

Rowe, Colin (1983). Program versus paradigm. *Cornell Journal of Architecture* **2**: 8–19.

Rowe, Colin and Fred Koetter (1978). *Collage City*. Cambridge, MA: MIT Press.

Rowe, Peter (1993). *Modernity and Housing*. Cambridge: MIT Press.

Rubenstein, Harvey M. (1992). *Pedestrian Malls, Streetscapes, and Urban Spaces*. New York: John Wiley.

Ruchelman, Leonard (1977). *The World Trade Center*. Syracuse, NY: Syracuse University Press.

Rudofsky, Bernard (1969). *Streets for People*. New York: Doubleday.

Runcorn Development Corporation (1967). *Runcorn New Town*. Nottingham: Midlands Engineering Co. Ltd.

Russell, Francis P. (1994). Battery Park City: an American dream of urbanism. In Brenda Case Scheer and Wolfgang Preiser, eds., *Design Review: Challenging Urban Aesthetic Control*. New York: Chapman and Hall, 197–209.

Russell, James S. (2000). Engineering civility: transit stations. *Architectural Record* **188** (3): 129–33.

San Francisco, City of, Department of City Planning (1985). *The San Francisco Downtown Plan: Final Report*. San Francisco: The author.

Sara Resorts, BhD (2000). *A Tribute to the People: Kuching Waterfront*. *http:/www/sedctourism.com/waterfront*

Scheer, Brenda and Wolfgang Preiser, eds. (1994). *Design Review: Challenging Urban Design Aesthetic Control*. New York: Chapman and Hall.

Scheer, Thornston, Josef Paul Kleihues and Paul Kahlfeld with Andrea Bärnreuther, eds. (2000). *City of Architecture of the City: Berlin 1900–2000*. Berlin: Nicolai.

Schneekloth, Lynda and Karen A. Franck (1994). Type: prison or promise? In Karen A. Franck and Lynda Schneekloth, eds., *Ordering Space: Types in Architecture and Design*. New York: Van Nostrand Reinhold, 15–38.

Schneider, Bernhard (1998). Invented history: Praiser Platz and the Brandenberg Gate. *AA Files* (Autumn): 12–16.

Schurch, Thomas W. (1999). Reconsidering urban design: thoughts about its definition and status as a field or profession. *Journal of Urban Design* **4** (1): 5–28.

Segal, Arlene (1999). Turning the tide: Guggenheim, Bilbao. *Planning: Architecture and Planning Review for Southern Africa* **163** (May–June): 4–9.

Sert, José Luis and CIAM (1944). *Can Our Cities Survive? An ABC of Urban Problems, Their Analysis, Their Solutions*. Cambridge, MA: MIT Press.

Sharp, Dennis (1991). *Twentieth Century Architecture: A Visual History*. London: Lund Humphries.

Sherer, Dean C. (2004). Arcosante: yesterday's vision of tomorrow revisited. *Calplanner* (March–April): 1, 5, 14.

Shirvani, Hamid (1985). *The Urban Design Process*. New York: Van Nostrand Reinhold.

Simmonds, Roger and Gary Hack, eds. (2000). *Global City Regions: Their Emerging Power*. London and New York: Phaedon.

Skyway, Minneapolis. *http://www.cala2.umn.edu/skywayminneapolis/*

SMRT Corporation Ltd. (2004). *Moving with Our Customers*. www.smrt.com.sg/smrt/index.htm

Soleri, Paolo (1969). *The City in the Image of Man*. Cambridge, MA: MIT Press.

Soemardi, Ahmad Riad (in progress). Urban design, power relations and the public interest. Unpublished doctoral dissertation. Sydney: University of New South Wales.

Southworth, Michael and Eran Ben Joseph (1997). *Streets and the Shaping of Towns and Cities*. New York: McGraw-Hill.

Spaans, Marjolein (2004). The implementation of urban regeneration projects in Europe: global ambitions, local matters. *Journal of Urban Design* **9** (3): 335–49.

Spirn, Ann Whiston (1984). *The Granite Garden*. New York: Basic Books.

Staff of New Urban News (2001). *New Urbanism: Comprehensive Report & Practice Guide*. Ithaca, NY: New Urban Publications, Inc.

Stamp, Gavin (1988). Romania's New Delhi. *Architectural Review* **184** (10): 4–6.

Stamps, Arthur E. (1994). Validating contextual urban design principles. In Neary S. J., Symes M. S. and Brown F. E., eds., *The Urban Experience: A People-Environment Perspective*. London: E & FN Spon, 141–53.

Steele, James (1998). *The Complete Architecture of Balkrishna Doshi: Rethinking Modernism for the Developing World*. London: Thames and Hudson.

Stein, Clarence (1955). Unpublished notes on urban design, University of Pennsylvania (mimeographed).

Stein, Clarence (1957). *Toward New Towns for America*. New York: Reinhold.

Stratis, William (2004). *World Trade Center Competition*. Corte Madera, CA: Ginko.

Symes, Martin (1994). Typological thinking in architectural practice. In Karen A. Franck and Lynda Schneekloth, eds., *Ordering Space: Types in Architecture and Design*. New York: Van Nostrand Reinhold, 15–38.

Tenant, Annie (2004). Sex and the city. Community and design. *Australian Planner* **41** (3): 36–7.

The town of Seaside (1985). *Center* **1**: 110–17.

Thomas, Derek (2002). *Architecture and the Urban Environment: A Vision for the New Age*. New York: Elsevier Science.

Thomas, Ray and Peter Cresswell (1973). *The New Town Idea*. Milton Keynes: The Open University.

Tiesdall, Steven A., Taner Oc and Tim Heath (1996). *Revitalizing Historic Urban Quarters*. Boston: Butterworth-Architecture.

Timmons, Heather (2003). Canary Wharf head plans bid. *International Herald Tribune*, Friday, 14 November: 14.

Torres, Felix (1987). *Paris La Défense: Métropole Européene des Affaires*. Paris: Editions de Moniteur.

Towndrow, Jennifer (1991). Darling Harbour. In *Philip Cox: Portrait of an Australian Architect*. Ringwood, Victoria: Viking, 254–64.

Trott, Gerhard (1985). *Universitat Bielefeld*. Bielefeld: Kramer-Druck.

Tschumi, Bernard (1987). *Cinégramme Folie: le Parc de la Villette*. Princeton, NJ: Princeton University Press.

Turner, John F. C. (1976). *Housing by People: Towards Autonomy in Building Environments*. London: Marion Boyers.

Turner, Paul V. (1984). *Campus: An American Planning Tradition*. Cambridge, MA: MIT Press.

Turner, Tom (1996). *City as Landscape: A Postmodern View of Planning*. London: E & FN Spon.

Tyler, Ronnie C. (1996). San Antonio River. *The New Handbook of Texas*. Austin, TX: Texas State Historical Association.

Universität Bielefeld (2004). *http://www.uni-bielefeld.de*

Urban Design (2004). *Architectural Record* (April): 168–70.

Urban Projects Unit, NSW Department of Public Works (1993). *George Street Urban Design and Transport Study – a Draft for Discussion with the Sydney City Council*. Sydney: The authors.

Uthman, Faud A. (1972). Charles Center, Baltimore: a case study of architectural controls through mandatory design review with an examination of architectural controls within the urban renewal process and through regulation. Unpublished doctoral dissertation. Philadelphia: University of Pennsylvania.

Vidarte, Juan Ignacio (2002). The Bilbao Guggenheim Museum. In *Euskal Hiraria*. Victoria-Gasteiz: Ceneral Publishing Services of the Basque Government, 153–8.

Vignelli Associates (1990). Design Vignelli. University of New South Wales, College of Fine Arts. Announcement of lecture series.

Villanueva, Paulina (2000). *Carlos Raúl Villaneuva/Paulina Villanueva/Macía Pintó*. New York: Princeton Architectural Press.

Vossman, Laura (2002). How many artists does it take to make a downtown? *Planning* **68** (6): 20–5.

Vuchic, Vukan (1999). *Transportation for Livable Cities*. New Brunswick, NJ: Center for Urban Policy Research, Rutgers University.

Wallace, David (1964). *The Planning Process. Baltimore's Charles Center – A Case Study of Downtown Renewal*. Urban Land Institute Bulletin 31: Washington, DC: Urban Land Institute.

Wallace, David (2004). *Urban Planning/My Way*. Chicago, IL: American Planning Association.

Wang, An-de, ed. (2000). *Shanghai Lujiazui Central Area Urban Design*. Shanghai: Architecture and Engineering Press.

Ward, Colin, ed. (1973). *Vandalism*. London: Architectural Press.

Wasserman, Jim (2004). Growth experts push new zoning to spark aesthetic renaissance. *San Diego Union Tribune*, 22 February. *http://www.signonsandiego.com/news.state/2004-0222-1144-ca-reinventinggrowth.htm*

Watson, Ilene (2001). An Introduction to Design Guidelines. *http:www.plannersweb.com/wfiles/w157.html*

Webber, Peter, ed. (1988). *The Design of Sydney: Three Decades of Change in the City Centre*. Sydney: Law Book.

Weston, Richard (2001). The end of the affair. *RIBA Journal* **108** (4): 13–16.

White, Morton and Lucia White (1964). *The Intellectual versus the City from Thomas Jefferson to Frank Lloyd Wright*. New York: New American Library.

Whyte, William H. (1980). *The Social Life of Small Urban Spaces*. New York and Washington, DC: The Conservation Foundation.

Williams, Katie, Elizabeth Burton and Mike Jenks, eds. (2000). *Achieving Sustainable Urban Form*. London: E & FN Spon.

Wordsearch and the Royal Academy of Arts (2002). *New Connections, New Architecture, New Urban Environments and the London Jubilee Line Extension*. London: The Royal Academy of Arts.

Worthington, Carl A. (1984). The Denver Technological Center: evolution of a pedestrian oriented community. *Ekistics* **52** (306): 260–6.

Yeang, Ken (2002). *Reinventing the Skyscraper: A Vertical Theory of Urban Design*. Chichester: Wiley-Academic.

Yin Robert, K. (2002). *Applications of Case Study Research*. Thousand Oaks, CA: Sage Publications.

Young, Barry (1988). Darling Harbour: a new city precinct. In Peter Webber G., ed., *The Design of Sydney: Three Decades of Change in the City Centre*. Sydney: The Law Book Company, 190–213.

Young, Karen (1999). *Subterranean Commercial Development*. *http://www./emich.edu/public/geo/557/book/d111.underground.html*

Zotti, ed. (1988). Un-malling a downtown [Oak Park, Illinois]. *Inland Architect* **32** (4): 14, 18.

Zunker, Vernon (1983). *A Dream Come True: Robert Hugman and San Antonio's River Walk*. Seguin, TX: The author.

Quincy Market/Faneuil Hall precinct, Boston in 1993

Index